LIBERTARIAN

VOLUME 10, ISSUE 1 (2018)

A JOURNAL OF PHILOSOPHY, POLITICS, AND ECONOMICS
libertarianpapers.org

Executive Editor | Stephan Kinsella (Houston, Texas)

Editor | Matthew McCaffrey (University of Manchester)

Editorial Board

Walter Block
Loyola University New Orleans

Paul Cantor
University of Virginia

Gerard Casey
University College Dublin

Gary Chartier
La Sierra University

Anthony Gregory
Independent Institute

Robert Higgs
Independent Institute

Hans-Hermann Hoppe
Property and Freedom Society

Jesús Huerta de Soto
Universidad Rey Juan Carlos, Madrid

Jörg Guido Hülsmann
University of Angers, France

Jason Jewell
Faulkner University

Roderick T. Long
Auburn University

Allen Mendenhall
Faulkner University

Roberta Modugno
University of Roma TRE

Jan Narveson
University of Waterloo

Hiroyuki Okon
Kokugakuin University, Tokyo

Sheldon Richman
Future of Freedom Foundation

Butler D. Shaffer
Southwestern Law School

Josef Šíma
Prague University of Economics

Edward Stringham
Trinity College

Frank van Dun
University of Ghent

Jakub Wiśniewski
Ludwig von Mises Institute Poland

Thomas E. Woods
Ludwig von Mises Institute

Ed Younkins
Wheeling Jesuit University

Aims and Scope

Libertarian Papers is a peer-reviewed journal of libertarian scholarship established in 2009. Its purpose is to advance scholarly research in disciplines of particular interest to the libertarian community, broadly conceived. The journal is interdisciplinary in scope, publishing original research from a wide variety of fields, especially philosophy, politics, and economics, but also legal theory, history, literary criticism, and social or cultural analysis. Its broader mission is to continue the tradition established by publications such as the *Journal of Libertarian Studies*.

Colophon

The cover image for this volume is Canaletto's *View of the Entrance to the Arsenal*.

Table of Contents

Libertarian Papers, Volume 10, Issue 1 (2018)

1. "Speculation and the English Common Law Courts, 1697-1845"
   by Jackson Tait.. 1

2. "Forcing Nozick Beyond the Minimal State: The Lockean Proviso and Compensatory Welfare"
   by Adam Blincoe.. 19

3. "Would-Be Farmer John and the Welfare State: A Response to Blincoe"
   by Jan Narveson... 49

4. "Quality Check: A Contextual Analysis of the Lockean Proviso"
   by J.K. Numao.. 61

5. "The Lockean Proviso and the Value of Liberty: A Reply to Narveson"
   by Adam Blincoe.. 83

6. "A Summary of the Philosophy of Spencer Heath"
   by Spencer Heath MacCallum and Alvin Lowi............................... 95

7. "Reconciling Competing Systems of Property Rights Through Adverse Possession"
   by M. Garrett Roth... 113

8. "Book Review: *The Economics of Law, Order, and Action: The Logic of Public Goods*"
   by Gerard Casey.. 127

Speculation and the English Common Law Courts, 1697-1845

Jackson Tait[*]

> In the same manner all laws against gaming never hinder it… yet all the great sums that are lost are punctually paid. Persons who game must keep their credit, else no body will deal with them. It is quite the same in stockjobbing. They who do not keep their credit will soon be turned out, and in the language of Change Alley be called a lame duck.[1]

IN 1766, ADAM SMITH keenly observed how essentially unenforceable regulatory legislation was in the chaotic eighteenth-century stock market. Yet according to economist Edward Stringham, the market continued to function under an informal self-regulatory system, a "self-policing club."[2] In the early eighteenth century, stock brokering was a relatively new occupation and in the process of professionalization. The earliest indication of individuals who

---

[*]Jackson Tait is a PhD candidate in history at Queen's University, Kingston. The author wishes to thank Doug Hay, the Western Legal Histories seminar at York University, and two anonymous reviewers from this journal for their comments at various stages of this article.

CITATION INFORMATION FOR THIS ARTICLE:
Jackson Tait. 2018. "Speculation and the English Common Law Courts, 1697-1845." *Libertarian Papers*. 10 (1): 1-17. ONLINE AT: libertarianpapers.org. THIS ARTICLE IS subject to a Creative Commons Attribution 3.0 License (creativecommons.org/licenses).

[1] Adam Smith, *Lectures on Jurisprudence*, edited by R. L. Meek, D. D. Raphael, and P. G. Stein (Oxford: Calarendon Press, [1766] 1978), 538.

[2] Edward Stringham, "The Emergence of the London Stock Exchange as a Self-Policing Club," *Journal of Private Enterprise* 17, no. 2 (Spring 2002): 1.

bought and sold securities on behalf of others for a fee is in John Houghton's biweekly newsletter, *A Collection for Improvement of Husbandry and Trade*, which published the first stock prices of the London market in the early 1690s. In June 1695, broker John Castaing advertised to buy and sell "all Blank and Benefit Tickets; and all other Stocks and Shares."[3] There was no clear delineation between active traders and stockbrokers at this time, and both were seen to promote speculative trading and investment strategies commonly believed to undermine the economy. Stockjobbers thus became the target of accusations of conspiracy and fraud. In 1696, shortly before the first regulatory statute was passed, the Commissioners of Trade reported that the "pernicious Art of Stock-jobbing" had "wholly perverted the End and Design of (manufacturing) Companies and Corporations" for "private Profit."[4]

Seven key regulatory acts were passed into law from 1697 to 1737 that set out regulations limiting the number of brokers, setting licensing fees, restricting time bargains, capping broker's fees, and establishing standards for record keeping.[5] Evidence suggests that virtually none of these laws were adhered to or seriously enforced. An apparent gap existed between the legislation and judicial enforcement of regulations. In the few cases brought before the English common law courts from 1697 to 1845, the courts predominantly avoided enforcing stock market regulations and upheld private contracts between individuals.

The 'lame duck' system based on reputation and good credit was, as Adam Smith suggested, very effective. However, occasionally a dispute that could not be resolved ended up in the courts. The relatively consistent refusal to enforce regulatory legislation in cases involving broker licensing, speculation, and transfer of securities suggests that the justices were not acting as state representatives, but as members of the informal London stock exchange. In this manner, justices, who were often 'active in the stocks' themselves, demonstrated that they were acting as an integral part of the private self-regulating stock exchange 'club.' Further, the legal decisions that upheld private contracts involving transfer of securities have important implications for our understanding of the development of judicial interpretation of commercial contract law in the eighteenth century.

---

[3] John Houghton, *A Collection for Improvement of Husbandry and Trade*, June 28, 1695.

[4] *House of Commons Journal* 11 (November 25, 1696).

[5] The ten regulatory bills that failed to pass in this time period indicate the vigorous contemporary debate surrounding stockjobbing. See: Julian Hoppit, *Failed Legislation, 1660–1800* (London: Hambleton Press, 1997), 581.

In 1977, Williamson Evers observed the "internal inconsistencies" in the contemporary interpretation of contract law stemming from the "conflicting" influences of "expectation" and "natural rights" schools of interpretation.[6] The expectation school of interpretation, originating in medieval common law and the concept of *assumpsit*, views contracts as protecting expectations or promises. This approach is further characterized by a case-by-case *ad hoc* decision-making process. Interpretation based on expectation was used throughout the feudal period and into the eighteenth century. In contrast, the natural-rights school, emerging in the latter part of the eighteenth century, interprets contracts as direct instruments for the protection of ownership and exchange of property. This interpretative approach, also known as freedom of contract, is more formal and standardized, and focuses on the literal terms of the agreement. Scholars have often made a hard delineation between expectation and natural-rights schools of interpretation, associating them with particular economic policies. Although there is certainly conflict between the two schools, evidence suggests the relationship between judicial interpretation and economic policy was much more fluid. Those who follow Patrick Atiyah and his influential *Rise and Fall of Freedom of Contract* exclusively associate feudal law with price and wage regulations and judicial paternalism, and freedom of contract with laissez-faire capitalism. Atiyah's argument is based on his interpretation of the development of the perception of the private contract in English law. In English law before 1770, according to Atiyah, the terms of a private contract between individuals were considered secondary to "community" values of "fairness," "just price," and "just wage." In fact, Atiyah claims that a contractual promise in the eighteenth century was "neither a necessary nor sufficient condition for the existence of a legal duty."[7] Atiyah discounts the importance of the private contract in the eighteenth century, associating the executory contract with the laissez-faire economic policies of the nineteenth century. Atiyah further dismisses commercial contracts, claiming that contracts involving "speculative risk" in the eighteenth century were interpreted inconsistently, with "no way of predicting" the outcome of a case:

---

[6] Evers argues in favor of a "title-transfer model" as an "appropriate law of contracts for a free society." Murray Rothbard similarly argues for title transfer as the "proper... basis" of a "libertarian, natural-rights... property-rights theory." See Williamson M. Evers, "Toward a Reformulation of the Law of Contracts," *Journal of Libertarian Studies* 1, no. 1 (1977): 3, 10; and Murray N. Rothbard, *The Ethics of Liberty* (New York: New York University Press, [1982] 1998), 147.

[7] P. S. Atiyah, *Rise and Fall of Freedom of Contract* (Oxford: Oxford University Press, [1961] 1979), 146–47, 167–69, 176.

one day the court would uphold a commercial contract, and the next day it would overturn a similar contract.[8] Atiyah predominantly draws his conclusions with respect to eighteenth-century English law from examples of equity cases before the Court of Chancery. However, equity cases fell outside the bounds of the regular common law and typically concerned trusts, estates, land, debt, and guardianship. Cases heard in the courts of equity usually dealt with circumstances of hardship, where a judgment of mercy was sought. Bankruptcies were frequent examples of circumstances that could lead one to a court of equity. Equity judgments represent too specific circumstances from which to draw general conclusions regarding the law of contract, and are inapplicable to a more regularly disputed contract where one of the parties is not experiencing extreme hardship.

This article will demonstrate that for contracts involving transfer of securities on the stock market, the judiciary tended to uphold private contracts between individuals and free market exchange throughout the eighteenth century, regardless of interpretive approach. The decisions of the judiciary in the English common law courts before 1770 in cases involving transfer of securities indicate a more complex history of commercial contract law than has been asserted by Atiyah and others.[9] As Atiyah observes, freedom of contract was a developing theory, particularly in the latter part of the century, and many commercial-contract cases were certainly not decided from a modern freedom-of-contract perspective. However, the older common law expectation model was not antithetical to free market exchange or protection of private property. In three key cases that will be discussed in this article, the courts and judiciary, under the rules of traditional common law, supported an unrestricted transfer of securities by disregarding regulatory statutes and upholding private contracts between individual traders. These cases, although few, indicate the existence of a private stock market, one of the many historical and evolving markets pre-existing those of the nineteenth century that frequently operated outside the bounds of feudal regulation. The four nineteenth-century cases that will be examined show that English courts, from a modern natural-rights perspective, continued to uphold independent contracts and consequently continued to support the private regulatory

---

[8] Atiyah, *Rise and Fall*, 176, 194.

[9] See also James Gordley, *The Philosophical Origins of Modern Contract Doctrine* (Oxford: Clarendon Press, 1991); and A.W. B. Simpson, *A History of the Common Law of Contract: The Rise of the Action of Assumpsit* (Oxford: Clarendon Press, 1975).

system that had evolved out of the many voluntary exchanges of 'Change Alley.[10]

Historiography

The historiography of the regulation and enforcement of stockjobbing has not previously considered the possible influence of the self-regulating aspect of the stock exchange on judicial decisions. Henry Keyser examined judicial interpretation of breach-of-contract cases in his 1850 study *The Law Relating to Transactions on the Stock Exchange*.[11] C. F. Smith looked at the legislative history of the regulation of stockbrokers in his 1929 article in the *American Economic Review*.[12] Stuart Banner considered how the eighteenth-century judiciary adapted older rules of property and markets to the new stock market in his comprehensive history *Anglo-American Securities Regulation*.[13]

Opponents of stockjobbing, or active stock trading, frequently pointed to the lawlessness of the new industry, claiming that brokers operated outside of proper authority with their "extravagant and unaccountable" methods.[14] The ways of the stockjobber were a "new mistery"[15] having "diverse arts and strategems."[16] Opponents argued that speculation was not a method of investing but a clever fraud used by brokers and jobbers to control price fluctuations for private gain and to swindle money from the unwary. Indeed, conspiracies and fraud did exist in the chaotic atmosphere of the fledgling stock market. Swindles were an integral part of the early stock market, from deliberately spread rumors intended to raise or lower stock prices—such as lost East India Company ships, imminent Spanish invasion, or the death of

---

[10] The seven key cases discussed in this article would not have come before a court of equity, as they directly concerned federal statutes.

[11] Henry Keyser, *The Law Relating to Transactions on the Stock Exchange* (London: L. H. Butterworth, 1850).

[12] C. F. Smith, "The Early History of the London Stock Exchange," *American Economic Review* 19, no. 2 (1929): 202–16.

[13] Stuart Banner, *Anglo-American Securities Regulation: Cultural and Political Roots, 1690–1860* (Cambridge: Cambridge University Press, 1998).

[14] *A Proposal for Putting Some Stop to the Extravagant Humour of Stock-jobbing* (London: 1697).

[15] Daniel Defoe, *The Villainy of Stock-Jobbers Detected* (London: 1701), 4.

[16] *A Proposal*.

Queen Anne—to entirely fraudulent joint-stock companies, such as the unchartered North Sea venture promoted by Francis Caywood in 1722.[17]

Daniel Defoe describes a typical attempt at price manipulation in his 1703 pamphlet *The Villainy of Stock-Jobbers Detected*:

> If Sir F--- had had a mind to buy, the first thing he did was to commission his brokers to look sour, shake their heads, suggest bad news from India… till perhaps the stock would fall 6, 7, 8, 10 per cent, sometimes more. Then the cunning jobber had another set of men employed on purpose to buy, but with privacy and caution, all the stock they could lay their hands on.[18]

Those who advocated state regulation of the new broker occupation articulated a variety of reasons for the necessity of control, including conspiracy to raise and lower stock prices, fraud, increasing the national debt, "engrossing" cash, and generally destroying the economy. However, the underlying reason was really a fear of that which they did not understand: speculation. Following the South Sea Bubble of 1720, critics of stock speculation and trading considered South Sea Company stock to have had "imaginary" value at its highest price of nine hundred pounds:

> At the height of the South-Sea stock, lands, as well as every thing else, were raised to an extravagant price; yet, as that proceeded from the general delusion which all men lay under, as to the imaginary value of South-Sea stock, and a supposed vast increase of their riches, which very soon appeared chimerical and groundless.[19]

R. H. Mottram defines "speculation" in his 1929 classic, *History of Financial Speculation*, as "dealing in fluctuating values." Mottram notes there is no evidence for use of the word in this modern sense until at least 1850.[20] In 1755, Dr. Johnson defined "speculation" as "examination by the eye," suggesting that the concept of "dealing in fluctuating values" was not yet fully articulated.[21] 'Stockjobbing' is the closest eighteenth-century word to the

---

[17] Richard Dale, *The First Crash: Lessons from the South Sea Bubble* (Princeton: Princeton University Press, 2004), 18; *Rex v. Caywood* (1722) 1 Strange 472, 93 ER 641.

[18] Defoe, *Villainy*, 1703, cited in Smith, "Early History," 212.

[19] John Castaing, *Course of the Exchange, and other things*, July 12, 1720; *Kien v. Stukeley* (1722) I Brown 191, 1 ER 506.

[20] R. H. Mottram, *A History of Financial Speculation* (London: Chatto and Windus, 1929), 3, 41. For a modern theory of the positive aspects of speculation as a stabilizing influence in the currency market, see Milton Friedman, "The Case for Flexible Exchange Rates," in *Essays in Positive Economics* (Chicago: University of Chicago Press, 1953), 175–77.

[21] Cited in Mottram, *History*, 2.

modern concept of 'speculation' as defined by Mottram. The newly forming concept of modern speculation in the eighteenth century accounts for the varied and contradictory definitions of a stockjobber, who was sometimes a legitimate broker, investor, or trader, and sometimes a gambling, swindling knave. Dr. Johnson, for example, defines stockjobber as "a low wretch who gets money by buying and selling shares in the funds."[22] The stock trader speculates in Mottram's sense, while earlier, eighteenth-century legislators defined stockjobbing more narrowly and in line with Dr. Johnson's definition.

City of London Broker Regulation

The first of the seven statutes that attempted to regulate speculation was the 1696 *Act to restrain the Number and ill Practice of Brokers and Stock jobbers*. The Broker's Act was the first legislative attempt to differentiate a stockbroker from a jobber and from the respectable commodities broker, where in practice there was often no distinction. According to the statute, anyone selling cattle, corn, or coal was not to be "esteemed a Broker." The act instituted licensing requirements for the City of London and Westminster, which limited the number of official stockbrokers to one hundred. The brokers were to take an oath before the lord mayor of the City of London to perform their duties "without fraud or collusion."[23] They were issued a silver medal bearing their names and the king's coat of arms. Stockbrokers' names and addresses were to be recorded and publicly displayed at the Royal Exchange and at London Guildhall. They were not to trade on their own accounts. Their fees were capped at ten shillings *per centum*. They were to keep a registry book in which they were to enter all contracts within three days. The time between the contract date and the transfer date of the stock was limited to a three-day period.

This requirement to register contracts was a deliberate attack on speculation, which effectively limited time bargains to seventy-two hours, making them almost worthless. Time bargains were credit transactions whereby an investor contracted to buy or sell shares at a future date and price. A length of time longer than three days was necessary to make the contract financially viable by giving enough time for the market to fall or rise. It was not necessary to own the actual shares to engage in a sell transaction. This was the speculative trading practice that came under the most criticism,

---

[22] Samuel Johnson, *A Dictionary of the English Language* (London: J. F. and C. Rivington, [1755] 1785).
[23] 8&9 William III c.32.

and it was associated with reckless gambling. According to an early-nineteenth-century critic of time bargains, "Gamblers of all denominations in the Stock Exchange" buy and sell "fictitious property to the amount of millions."[24]

The intention of the legislators, not merely to regulate a new industry, but specifically to curb speculation is apparent throughout the text of the act. The preamble to the Broker's Act states:

> Whereas divers Brokers and Stock Jobbers, or pretended Brokers, have lately set up and carried on most unjust Practices and Designs, in selling and discounting of Tallies, Bank Stock, Bank Bills, Shares and Interest in Joint Stocks, and other Matters and Things, and have, and do, unlawfully combined and confederated themselves together, to raise or fall from time to time the Value of such... as may be most convenient for their own private Interest and Advantage.[25]

The emphasis on speculator control of price fluctuation is a commonly repeated theme in the eighteenth-century stockjobbing debate. Defoe argued in 1701 that the new "Mistery or Machine of Trade" was responsible for fluctuations in East India Company stock:

> The Old East India Stock by the arts of these unaccountable People, has within 10 years or thereabouts, without any material difference in the intrinsick value, been sold from 300l. per Cent. to 37l. per Cent. from thence with fluxes and refluxes, as frequent as the Tides, it has been up at 150l. per Cent. again... nor can any Reasons for the rise and fall of it be shown, but the Politick management of the Stock-Jobbing Brokers.[26]

In his complaint, Defoe gives an excellent example of a healthy and regularly traded stock. This pervasive anxiety about price fluctuation reveals a fundamental misunderstanding regarding the regular ebb and flow of supply and demand in which high and low price thresholds are expected. As historian W. R. Scott has observed, regarding price instability in the early eighteenth-century, "It is remarkable that the quotations display so little of the see-saw movement due to market manipulation, but on the contrary

---

[24] A Gentleman of the Exchange, *The Cause of the Rise and Fall of the Public Funds Explained* (London: C. Chapple, 1814), 29.

[25] 8&9 William III c.32.

[26] Defoe, *Villainy*, 1701.

follow well defined lines of movement."[27] The considerable and consistent emphasis on price fluctuation reveals a pervasive trepidation about possibly exaggerated market volatility, which legislators associated with economic instability.[28]

If some members of Parliament thought speculation undermined the economy, the City of London may have thought otherwise. The city's reluctance to strictly enforce the penalty provisions in broker legislation ensured de facto support for speculation and the new trading industry as well as continued revenue for the city. Under a new statute, 6 Anne c.16, the city retained control over regulation of brokers through licensing and levying an annual fee of forty shillings. The city frequently prosecuted unlicensed brokers at the Court of Aldermen to enforce payment of the annual fee in order to raise revenue, but significantly did not enforce the hefty penalties of five hundred pounds that would have put most out of business.[29] The majority of brokers ignored the law, and it was estimated in 1761 that two-thirds of brokers remained unlicensed.[30]

This reluctance to enforce the strict terms of the statute reveals the widening gap between legislators and the courts. In 1767, the City Chamberlain, a lower court and traditional office responsible for revenue collection, prosecuted brokers referred to as T---J and J---S for "buying and selling government securities for their friends" without a license.[31] Both defendants were tried and acquitted by special jury. These cases were featured in *The Annual Register* as a victory for the average investor and public credit, suggesting a popular support for stock trading and investing. *The Annual Register* sympathized with the jury, concluding that,

> it is now settled, that every person is at liberty to employ his friend to buy or sell government securities, without being obliged to be at the expence of employing a broker; which will be a great

---

[27] W. R. Scott, *The Constitution and Finance of English, Scottish and Irish Joint-Stock Companies to 1720*, vol. I (Cambridge: Cambridge University Press, 1912), 358–59.

[28] Anne Murphy has argued that business failure in the 1690s was not connected to stock speculation but due to the considerable exposure to risk that new businesses faced. See Anne L. Murphy, *The Origins of English Financial Markets: Investment and Speculation before the South Sea Bubble* (Cambridge: Cambridge University Press, 2009), 71.

[29] E. V. Morgan and W. A. Thomas, *The Stock Exchange: Its History and Functions* (London: Elek Books, 1962), 64–65.

[30] Thomas Mortimer, cited in Morgan and Thomas, *Stock Exchange*, 65.

[31] *The Annual Register* 10 (December 1767): 68; Morgan and Thomas, *Stock Exchange*, 65; C. F. Smith, "Early History," 214–15.

inducement for people to lay out their money in the funds, and consequently a great addition to public credit.[32]

Time-Bargain Cases

The following three time-bargain cases were heard before the Court of King's Bench. King's Bench originally heard cases considered to be a "breach of the peace" and a threat to the rights, *jura regalia*, of the Crown.[33] It is significant that by the 1830s, cases involving the stockjobbing acts were more frequently heard at the Court of Common Pleas, a court that heard disputes between subjects that did not involve the Crown. This shift in court location suggests the declining relevancy of the stockjobbing statutes to private contractual disputes between traders. Stock-transfer contracts were clearly interpreted from a freedom-of-contract perspective by the 1840s.

In *Smith v. Westall* (1697), one of the first cases prosecuted under the Broker's Act, Chief Justice John Holt unwittingly created the foundational precedent that allowed the legal continuance of time bargains.[34] In this decision, the conservative chief justice strictly upheld the new regulatory legislation and did not protect the damaged party in a broken time-bargain contract. Holt was known for being insensitive to accused parties, having a high degree of respect for parliamentary legislation, and applying the law strictly. Significantly, he did not think the bench should innovate in the areas of commerce and trade, as witness his rulings in *Clerke v. Martin* (1702) and *Buller v. Crips* (1703), where he refused to equate promissory notes with bills of exchange. His decisions reflect his view that bankers and creditors were threatening the established protective debt laws with their new innovations and that legal acceptance of the new bills of exchange should come from parliament and not from the courts.[35]

It is therefore not surprising that Holt declared the time bargain in *Smith v. Westall* as illegal under the terms of the Broker's Act. The events of the case are as follows: Smith, the plaintiff, and Westall, the defendant, made a time bargain in February, predating the May 1 start date of the statute. Smith was to transfer bank stock to Westall upon the latter's request. According to the contract, Westall had until May 10 to request transfer of the

---

[32] *The Annual Register*, 68.

[33] T. W. Williams, *A Compendious and Comprehensive Law Dictionary Elucidating the Terms and General Principles of Law and Equity* (London: Gale and Fenner, 1816).

[34] *Smith v. Westall* (1697) 1 Ld. Raym. 316, 91 ER 1106.

[35] Paul D. Halliday, "Holt, Sir John (1642–1710)," in *Oxford Dictionary of National Biography* (Oxford: Oxford University Press, 2004, online edn., Oct. 2009).

shares. Westall did not request the shares, because he wanted out of the bargain. Smith prosecuted Westall, and Westall pleaded the statute as his defense, arguing that he should be released from the contract as time bargains were illegal under the terms of the Broker's Act. Defendants in time-bargain cases commonly misused the statutes in this manner to avoid performance of a contract. Holt, however, decided in favor of the defendant Westall, as the latter had not requested the shares before May 1. According to Holt, the contract fell under the terms of the statute in this case and was therefore void. It is evident from Holt's judicial history that he did not support speculative contracts. This is further suggested by Holt's 1703 exacting decision in *Callonel v. Briggs*, where he declared that "if the plaintiff do not set forth in his declaration that he was at the South Sea House… on the day agreed, at such a time, and staid 'till the last hour of the day to transfer his stock, he cannot maintain his action."[36]

It is thus ironic that *Smith v. Westall* became the foundational precedent for the legal allowance of time bargains. In *Mitchell v. Broughton* (1701),[37] Holt's ruling in *Smith v. Westall* was employed to create a loophole that would allow time bargains to continue legally. Similar to *Smith v. Westall*, *Mitchell v. Broughton* concerned a broken time bargain. Broughton, the defendant refused to transfer shares to Mitchell, the plaintiff. Broughton pleaded the Broker's Act in order to be released from the contract. Mitchell had requested the transfer of the shares in writing within the three days allowed by the act. The court decided in favor of Mitchell and upheld the time bargain. This ruling created a precedent that if shares were formally requested within the three days allowed by the statute and the transfer occurred at a later date, then the bargain would be legal.

The creative interpretation of *Smith v. Westall* in *Mitchell v. Broughton* exemplifies how the common law ad hoc decision-making process was applied to support unregulated market exchange. In upholding Mitchell and Broughton's time bargain, the court aimed to give justice in the case of a broken promise. The court record of the case in fact begins with a description of the "special promise to transfer stock," indicating that the court viewed the contract between Mitchell and Broughton from the older perspective of promise and expectation.

The 1804 decision in *Heckscher v. Gregory* deviated from the general trend to support private stock-transfer contracts. In this case, a private contract was dismissed in favor of the statute. Under the 1734 statute 7

---

[36] *Callonel v. Briggs* (1703) Holt, K. B. 664, 90 ER 1267.
[37] *Mitchell v. Broughton* (1701) 1 Ld. Raym. 674, 91 ER 1349.

George II c. 8, known as Barnard's Act, which outright banned time bargains, a seller could sue for damages in the case of a broken contract after he had resold the same shares to someone else. The seller was then eligible to claim the price difference between the first and second contract in damages. The statute attempted to prevent speculative contracts by legislating the physical transfer of securities. In this dispute, Heckscher had a contract to sell stock to Gregory at a specific price. Gregory refused to accept and pay for the stock after the market price suddenly dropped by thirteen pounds. Heckscher then contracted to sell the stock to another party. This contract had not yet been executed at the time Heckscher began legal action against Gregory. The court record notes that this second contract was considered "not completed" and "only a contract for sale." Counsel for Heckscher argued that actual transfer of the shares was "not necessary to support the action." The court disregarded the pending contract and interpreted the statute strictly: as the stock had not been transferred by the commencement of the lawsuit, Heckscher's claim fell outside the bounds of the rule. Justice Le Blanc referred to time bargains as "gambling transactions" and dismissed Heckscher's claim, noting that the case "would turn out to be one of those transactions that the legislature meant to prevent."[38]

Nineteenth-Century Cases

In *Rex v. Dodd* (1808), Lord Chief Justice Ellenborough avoided enforcing the Bubble Act of 1720. *Rex v. Dodd* (1808) was the second case to be prosecuted based on the Bubble Act.[39] The statute made it illegal to sell or transfer shares in unchartered joint-stock companies, and was repealed in 1825 after over a century of neglect.[40] Ellenborough argued that the court should not interfere in the obviously illegal activities of the two unchartered companies in *Rex v. Dodd*, due to the eighty-seven-year gap since the most recent prosecution of the act, and because the case involved an aware investor and not a vulnerable shareholder. An individual posing as an investor to entrap the instigators of two joint-stock schemes initiated the action. The justice declared that since the case was "brought forward by a party who does not profess to have been himself deluded… the statute having been passed principally for the protection of unwary persons from delusions of this kind; the Court think, in the exercise of their discretion, that

---

[38] *Heckscher v. Gregory* (1804) 4 East 608, 102 ER 964.
[39] *Rex v. Dodd* (1808) 9 East 516, 103 ER 670; 6 George I c. 18 (1720).
[40] Banner, *Anglo-American*, 76, 78, 79.

they should not now enforce the statute."[41] *Rex v. Dodd* particularly highlights the general wariness of the courts to interfere in the regulation of the stock market.

In 1836, the Court of Common Pleas held strictly to the text of Barnard's Act in ruling that the statute did not apply to transactions on foreign securities. In *Wells v. Porter*, a broker, Wells, sued his client, Porter, for nonpayment for work done on the client's behalf to buy and sell time bargains on Spanish and Portuguese public stocks. Porter argued that the contract between himself and Wells should be considered void under the terms of the statute. The court disagreed and judged in favor of Wells. The justices concurred that the statute did not apply in this case and that it should not "extend" to include foreign stocks. The court upheld the contract between the two parties, asserting that the plaintiff should be able to recover damages.[42] *Wells v. Porter* is significant in that the court supported both speculative contracts on foreign stocks and freedom of contract. This decision indicates a clear shift in judicial interpretation from an expectation perspective to a modern natural-rights-based perspective by the 1830s for cases involving transfer of stock.

In *Mortimer v. M'Callan* (1840), the judiciary continued to avoid enforcing legislation passed against speculative contracts, and took a modern perspective in deciding to uphold the specific terms of the contract between the two traders. Mortimer brought an action against M'Callan for nonpayment of transferred shares. M'Callan pleaded Barnard's Act in order to be released from a contract he had made with Mortimer. Counsel for M'Callan argued that the contract was "null and void" because at the time the parties entered into the contract, Mortimer did not own the shares he intended to sell. Mortimer's counsel asserted that the act only applied when the physical transfer of shares had not taken place and therefore did not apply in this case, as stock had already been transferred to M'Callan. The court agreed and decided for the plaintiff in enforcing payment of the broken contract.[43]

Justice Cresswell upheld the terms of a stock-transfer contract in *Humphrey v. Lucas* (1845). In this case, the defendant, Lucas, refused to transfer the agreed-upon shares to Humphrey, the plaintiff. Lucas claimed that the plaintiff was not permitted to sue, given a rule of the Liverpool Stock

---

[41] *Rex v. Dodd* (1808).

[42] *Wells v. Porter* (1836) 2 Bing. (N.C.) 722, 132 ER 278. See also *Oakley v. Rigby* (1836) 2 Bing. (N.C.) 732, 132 ER 282.

[43] *Mortimer v. M'Callan* (1840) 7 M. & W. 20, 151 ER 662.

Exchange. Because Humphrey's broker did not disclose the name of his principal at the time of the contract, the rules of the exchange stated that Humphrey's broker was then solely and legally responsible for the contract. However, the court found in favor of Humphrey, dismissing the rule of the Liverpool Exchange. Justice Cresswell stated that the law on the matter was "clear... [A]n agent duly authorized may make a contract in his own name... [T]he principal may afterwards sue upon it." Significantly, Cresswell made his judgment solely on the basis of freedom of contract: "The only question on this record... is whether the plaintiff made a contract with the defendant or not. I think he did." [44]

Conclusion

It is clear that in the general lack of enforcement of legislation regarding speculation, a breach existed between legislators and the judiciary. Legislators were suspicious of stockjobbing practices and passed statutes accordingly. With few exceptions, the courts did not enforce the legislation when they had the opportunity to do so. This apparent support for the stock market is highly suggestive of a shared interest in investment, trading, and speculation among the judiciary. Lord Ellenborough invested 74 percent of his entire fortune in government stocks. Lord Mansfield was known to be a shrewd investor in stocks, government securities, and land. Mansfield gradually built his net worth of more than £500,000 not through inheritance but through wise investment strategies. Sir John Nicholl owned £91,000 in consolidated annuities and was a known stock speculator.[45] Justices such as these, who were both stockjobbers and judicial officers, were in a prime position to act on behalf of fellow investors, as members of the self-regulating stock club.

In the evolving system of self-policing within the stock-brokering and stockjobbing community, brokers who trespassed the rules of the private club were punished by expulsion and public embarrassment. Particularly those with poor credit were expelled from the coffeehouses and other places of exchange. The names and addresses of the 'lame ducks' were written on a public blackboard.[46] The blackboard system was still in use in London in

---

[44] *Humphrey v. Lucas* (1845) 2 Car. & K. 152, 175 ER 64.

[45] James Oldham, "Murray, William, First Earl of Mansfield (1705–1793)," in *Oxford Dictionary of National Biography* (Oxford: Oxford University Press, 2004, online edn., Oct. 2008); Daniel Duman, *The Judicial Bench in England, 1727–1875: The Reshaping of a Professional Elite* (London: Royal Historical Society, 1982), 135, 143, 137–38.

[46] Stringham, "Emergence," 6; Morgan and Thomas, *Stock Exchange*, 61.

1814 after trading had moved from the informal coffeehouse venue to the formal stock exchange building. A critic of the "self-constituted and congregated" power of the London Stock Exchange described the practice thus: "All is conducted upon honour; but if a man get into difficulties which he thinks he cannot recover from, he makes a dash (a high risk speculation;) if he be lucky, he takes the profit, if not, he leaves the house and gets stuck upon the Black Board, which is kept for the purpose."[47]

Barnard's Act was finally repealed in 1860, according to Banner largely due to "over a century" of "ineffectiveness."[48] Contemporary literature indicates that illegal speculation continued regularly in open defiance of the legislation and that a great many investors and brokers made their living in speculative time bargains. In 1850, lawyer Henry Keyser observed, "A numerous and highly-respectable body of men earn their livelihood by the daily and hourly violation of the clauses of the statute" (Barnard's Act).[49] The cumulative reluctance to enforce legislation regarding speculation, for well over a century, suggests that the judiciary supported the self-determining legal system of the emerging London Stock Exchange, playing an important role in buffering the nascent industry from any kind of real governmental interference.

References

Primary Sources:

The Annual Register or a View of the History, Politicks, and Literature for the Year 1767. Vol 10. London: J. Dodsley, 1767.

Castaing, John. *Course of the Exchange, and other things.* London, 1720.

Defoe, Daniel. *The Villainy of Stock-Jobbers Detected, and the Causes of the Late Run upon the Bank and Bankers Discovered and Considered.* London: 1701.

A Gentleman of the Exchange. *The Cause of the Rise and Fall of the Public Funds Explained; with Observations on the Mischievous Tendency of Time Bargains, and the Absolute Necessity of Abolishing the Present Stock-Exchange, and Establishing an Open Public Market.* London: C. Chapple, 1814.

Great Britain. *House of Commons Journal* 11 (1696).

---

[47] A Gentleman of the Exchange, *Cause of the Rise and Fall*, 34–35.
[48] Banner, *Anglo-American*, 107.
[49] Keyser, *Law Relating*, 152.

Houghton, John. *A Collection for Improvement of Husbandry and Trade.* London, 1695.

Johnson, Samuel. *A Dictionary of the English Language.* London: J. F. and C. Rivington, [1755] 1785.

Keyser, Henry. *The Law Relating to Transactions on the Stock Exchange.* London: L. H. Butterworth, 1850.

A Proposal for Putting Some Stop to the Extravagant Humour of Stockjobbing. London: 1697.

Smith, Adam. *Lectures on Jurisprudence.* Edited by R. L. Meek, D. D. Raphael, and P.G. Stein. Oxford: Clarendon Press, [1776] 1978.

Cases:

Callonel v. Briggs (1703) Holt, K.B. 664, 90 ER 1267

Heckscher v. Gregory (1804) 4 East 608, 102 ER 964

Humphrey v. Lucas (1845) 2 Car. & K. 152, 175 ER 64

Kien v. Stukeley (1722) I Brown 191, 1 ER 506

Mitchell v. Broughton (1701) 1 Ld. Raym. 674, 91 ER 1349

Mortimer v. M'Callan (1840) 7 M. & W. 20, 151 ER 662

Oakley v. Rigby (1836) 2 Bing. (N.C.) 732, 132 ER 282

Smith v. Westall (1697) 1 Ld. Raym. 316, 91 ER 1106

Rex v. Caywood (1722) 1 Strange 472; 93 ER 641

Rex v. Dodd, (1808) 9 East 516, 103 ER 670

Wells v. Porter (1836) 2 Bing. (N.C.) 722, 132 ER 278

Secondary Sources:

Atiyah, P. S. *Rise and Fall of Freedom of Contract.* Oxford: Oxford University Press, [1961] 1979.

Banner, Stuart. *Anglo-American Securities Regulation: Cultural and Political Roots, 1690–1860.* Cambridge: Cambridge University Press, 1998.

Dale, Richard. *The First Crash: Lessons from the South Sea Bubble.* Princeton: Princeton University Press, 2004.

Duman, Daniel. *The Judicial Bench in England, 1727–1875: The Reshaping of a Professional Elite.* London: Royal Historical Society, 1982.

Evers, Williamson M. "Toward a Reformulation of the Law of Contracts." *Journal of Libertarian Studies* 1, no. 1 (1977): 3–13.

Friedman, Milton. "The Case for Flexible Exchange Rates." In *Essays in Positive Economics.* Chicago: University of Chicago Press, 1953: 157–203.

Gordley, James. *The Philosophical Origins of Modern Contract Doctrine.* Oxford: Clarendon Press, 1991.

Hoppit, Julian. *Failed Legislation, 1660–1800.* London: Hambleton Press, 1997.

Murphy, Anne L. *The Origins of English Financial Markets: Investment and Speculation before the South Sea Bubble.* Cambridge: Cambridge University Press, 2009.

Morgan, E. V., and W.A. Thomas. *The Stock Exchange: Its History and Functions.* London: Elek Books, 1962.

Mottram, R. H. *A History of Financial Speculation.* London: Chatto & Windus, 1929.

Rothbard, Murray N. *The Ethics of Liberty.* New York: New York University Press, [1982] 1998.

Scott, W. R. *The Constitution and Finance of English, Scottish and Irish Joint-Stock Companies to 1720.* Cambridge: Cambridge University Press, 1910.

Simpson, A. W. B. *A History of the Common Law of Contract: The Rise of the Action of Assumpsit.* Oxford: Clarendon Press, 1975.

Smith, C. F. "The Early History of the London Stock Exchange." *American Economic Review* 19, no. 2 (1929): 202–16.

Stringham, Edward. "The Emergence of the London Stock Exchange as a Self-Policing Club." *Journal of Private Enterprise* 17, no. 2 (Spring 2002): 1–19.

Williams, T.W. *A Compendium and Comprehensive Law Dictionary Elucidating the Terms and General Principles of Law and Equity.* London: Gale and Fenner, 1816.

Forcing Nozick Beyond the Minimal State: The Lockean Proviso and Compensatory Welfare

Adam Blincoe[*]

I. Introduction: Taxation, Compensation, and Forcing Nozick beyond the Minimal State

In *Anarchy, State and Utopia*, Robert Nozick notes that a vice of patterned principles of distributive justice is that they "necessitate *re*distributive activities."[1] He argues that even a modest amount of free exchange will almost certainly upset a pattern of wealth distribution. Consequently, any state that seeks to maintain a particular pattern of wealth distribution will need to periodically carry out a redistribution of wealth, often in the form of taxation on earnings, which for Nozick is "on par with forced labor."[2] This unfree labor is abhorrent to Nozick's libertarian sensibilities; it runs counter to a strong claim of self-ownership and an

---

[*]Adam Blincoe is Honors Faculty Scholar at Longwood University. He thanks John Simmons for extensive comments and discussion concerning early drafts of this essay, Jan Narveson for comments he gave on an earlier version of the paper presented at the Eastern APA, and two anonymous reviewers for their comments.

CITATION INFORMATION FOR THIS ARTICLE:
Adam Blincoe. 2018. "Forcing Nozick Beyond the Minimal State: The Lockean Proviso and Compensatory Welfare." *Libertarian Papers*. 10 (1): 19-48. ONLINE AT: libertarianpapers.org. THIS ARTICLE IS subject to a Creative Commons Attribution 3.0 License (creativecommons.org/licenses).

[1] Robert Nozick, *Anarchy State and Utopia* (Basic Books, 1974), p. 168. See pp. 160–74 for his full account.

[2] ASU, p. 169 (see also the related footnote further clarifying this claim).

emphasis on individual rights.[3] Yet, it seems not all taxation is beyond the pale for Nozick.

In part 1 of *Anarchy, State and Utopia* (ASU), Nozick argues for the legitimacy of a minimal state. The activity of this state consists largely (perhaps solely?) in protecting its citizens from harm and executing punitive justice when harms are committed against its citizens. In the course of his argument supporting the minimal state, Nozick appears to accept a limited amount of taxation (and apparent redistribution) as legitimate.[4] One might ask though, what makes taxation in support of the minimal state legitimate and taxation in support of patterned conceptions of distributive justice illegitimate? For Nozick, the difference lies in the fact that the former serves a compensatory purpose and the latter does not. That is, the minimal state can tax its clients to compensate nonclients within its territories who have been deprived of the benefits of privately enforced justice.[5] This is an expression of the principle of compensation Nozick develops in chapter 4 of ASU, namely, that those disadvantaged by a prohibition on certain risky activities are to be compensated for their disadvantages.[6]

In this essay, I will be concerned with another sort of compensation and how it forces Nozick's position to (d)evolve beyond the acceptance of a merely minimal state (and its merely minimal taxation). The principle of compensation already at work in Nozick's minimal state is important because it sets a precedent that at least *some* taxation is legitimate, and therefore not on par with forced labor. In what follows, I will argue that Nozick's entitlement theory, and his treatment of the Lockean proviso in particular, forces him into a dilemma involving the compensation of people with rather low welfare prospects. Either (a) Nozick must admit that taxation for the purpose of guaranteeing a compensatory level of welfare (and not merely for protection from harm) is legitimate or (b) he must admit that his entitlement theory

---

[3] For Nozick and many libertarians, a strong claim of ownership over one's labor (and the products of one's labor) is simply an extension of a strong claim of self-ownership; see J. H. Bogart, "Provisos and State of Nature Theories," *Ethics* Vol. 95, No. 4 (Jul. 1985), p. 832. For a statement of this theme in Nozick, see ASU pp. 167–74.

[4] See especially pp. 110–15 in ASU. In what follows, I assume that the compensation paid to nonclients, funded by client fees, is akin to taxation. Nozick implies this by admitting that such compensation is at least *apparently* redistributive.

[5] Nozick, ASU, pp. 110–15 (see especially p. 114).

[6] Ibid, p. 87. This is as close to a definitive statement as Nozick gives of the principle he develops over the latter portion of chapter 4. See pp. 78–87 for Nozick's justification of this principle.

cannot satisfy the Lockean proviso. Thus if Nozick wants to maintain the Lockean principles of his entitlement theory, he will be forced further left within the libertarian camp.[7]

To develop this dilemma, I will first briefly outline Nozick's entitlement theory. Then I will consider Nozick's treatment of the Lockean proviso and identify some problems regarding generations subsequent to an original resource acquisition. Ultimately, I will argue that Nozick's particular formulation and interpretation of the Lockean proviso will support compensation for those who lack the opportunity to appropriate certain resources now. Thus, Nozick's entitlement theory will have to significantly revise (or drop) some of its Lockean principles or expand to guarantee a compensatory level of welfare. This is a significant result since most alternative provisos employed by libertarians are as strict as Nozick's or stricter.[8] Hence, if Nozick's proviso leads to a welfare state, it is likely most other alternatives will as well.

II. Nozick's Entitlement Theory: Historical, Not Patterned

Nozick's entitlement theory (henceforth ET) addresses the topic traditionally known as distributive justice, though Nozick prefers to talk about justice in "holdings" rather than a distribution of wealth and resources.[9] Nozick's entitlement theory outlines three activities to consider to properly determine justice in holdings: (1) original acquisition (how something originally comes to be held), (2) transfer of holdings, and (3) the rectification of past injustices. Nozick succinctly summarizes entitlement theory with respect to the first two areas as follows:

> If the world were wholly just, the following inductive definition would exhaustively cover the subject of justice in holdings.

---

[7] Here all I mean by "further left" is a position that puts greater emphasis on equality of wealth distribution (but does not necessarily seek to achieve absolute equality).

[8] Werner, "Self-Ownership and Non-Culpable Proviso Violations," *Politics, Philosophy & Economics* Vol. 14, no.1, (2015), p. 71.

[9] ASU, pp. 149–50. This is because Nozick thinks the term "distribution" can imply (incorrectly) that there was some sort of central or original act of distribution performed by an authoritative distributing party. If one approaches the question like this, then it is a natural question to ask whether the distribution was carried out well, and if not, whether we should engage in redistributing the world's resources and wealth. Nozick prefers the more neutral term of "holdings," which refers to the same sorts of material resources and wealth that are involved in issues of distributive justice.

1. A person who acquires a holding in accordance with the principles of justice in acquisition is entitled to that holding.

2. A person who acquires a holding in accordance with the principle of justice in transfer, from someone else entitled to the holding, is entitled to the holding.

3. No one is entitled to a holding except by (repeated) applications of 1 and 2.[10]

Because some (many) people have come by their holdings in ways inconsistent with principles 1 and 2, Nozick recognizes the need for a complete entitlement theory to include some principles governing the rectification of past injustices.[11] In summary, according to ET, "a distribution is just if everyone is entitled to the holdings they possess under the distribution."[12]

It is clear from this description of ET that what matters is the historical process and not the distributive pattern that is the end result of this process. Theoretically, any sort of distribution of holdings may be just as long as it results only from just acquisition and transfer. Nozick distinguishes this sort of theory from patterned conceptions of distributive justice that strive to achieve (at least approximately) and maintain a certain pattern of wealth distribution. On such theories, a distribution of wealth could be unjust despite having a completely just history of original acquisition and transfer.

Nozick thinks a state seeking to maintain some end-result pattern, rather than merely a just process, will need to engage in a frequent redistribution of holdings that were come by in a perfectly just manner.[13] Put differently, if the state allows consensual transfers of holdings, the process that results in a particular distribution may be perfectly just, but in virtue of its tendency to upset the desired pattern, its results will have to be frequently voided. For Nozick, this sort of state intrusion into what citizens wish to do with their holdings violates ownership rights. Nozick thinks his historical ET avoids this intrusive and frequent redistribution. However, a closer look at

---

[10] ASU, p. 151.

[11] Ibid, p. 152. Nozick is largely silent on just what these principles of rectification might look like on ET.

[12] Ibid, p. 151.

[13] It is clear in ASU that the justice of holdings transfers is governed largely by consent.

Nozick's theory of justice in acquisition shows he cannot entirely avoid this sort of redistributive activity.[14]

III. Justice in Acquisition: Nozick's Version of the Lockean Proviso

The consequences of ET come into focus when we add a bit more detail to its principles governing transfer and original acquisition of holdings. From Nozick's brief discussions of transfer of holdings, it appears that justice in this activity is largely (perhaps solely) a product of consent.[15] If all parties involved agree to a transfer or exchange of holdings, assuming no extenuating circumstances of coercion or deceit are involved, the transfer will be just. This means that if the original acquisition of the holdings (from the mass of unappropriated worldly resources) is just, then an unbroken line of consensual transfers should (for the most part)[16] guarantee all future holdings to be just. In this way, ET's principles of transfer are justice preserving.[17] Explaining how something can come to be justly held in the first place involves Nozick in more complex considerations.

To elucidate justice in acquisition, Nozick employs a version of the Lockean proviso (henceforth LP). Locke's proviso states that in order to be

---

[14] In one sense, Nozick might be able to respond to my eventual argument that he can still avoid this sort of redistribution. This is because eventually I will argue that while ET will have to involve a more pervasive and intrusive redistributive activity to support a substantial social-welfare minimum, this redistribution remains a compensatory activity in light of non-extant opportunities to acquire certain resources. However, it still remains that this sort of redistribution, even though compensatory in nature, is one Nozick seeks to avoid because of its sheer pervasiveness and intrusiveness. It is also important to note that the compensatory taxation Nozick admits as legitimate is imagined to be fairly minimal.

[15] See especially ASU, pp. 150–53 and 157–58. Unfortunately, like several important principles operative in Nozick's ASU, we do not get an explicit and definitive statement of the principles of justice in transfer. Despite this, it is clear that consent is what is doing the work in ensuring the justice of transfers. This of course coheres well with Nozick's libertarian principles involving ownership of self and labor, and his stress on the inviolability of the individual in general. For more on how ET expresses Nozick's belief in the inviolability of individuals and the illegitimacy of using them (without consent) as resources for others, see Bogart, *Lockean Provisos and State of Nature Theories*, pp. 831–33 and Sarkar, *Lockean Provisos*, p. 48.

[16] Nozick recognizes a few exceptions that might arise in extreme cases. These possibilities will be discussed below.

[17] Nozick, ASU, p. 151.

just, an acquisition of some resource from nature must leave "as much and as good" for others to acquire for themselves.[18] Nozick thinks the general force of this proviso is that an acquisition may not worsen the situation of others. If an acquisition does not worsen the situation of others, then it is just and yields permanent property rights.[19] More will need to be said about how an acquisition might make another worse off. Initially, Nozick brings up what I will refer to as the zip-back argument, which leads him to amend the LP. The argument is as follows:

> It is often said that this proviso once held but now no longer does. But there appears to be an argument for the conclusion that if the proviso no longer holds, then it cannot ever have held so as to yield permanent and inheritable property rights. Consider the first person Z for whom there is not enough and as good left to appropriate. The last person Y to appropriate left Z without his previous liberty to act on an object, and so worsened Z's situation. So Y's appropriation is not allowed under Locke's proviso. Therefore the next to last person X to appropriate left Y in a worse position, for X's act ended permissible appropriation. Therefore X's appropriation wasn't permissible. And so on back to the first person A to appropriate a permanent property right."[20]

Nozick answers this argument by specifying what it means to worsen an individual's situation for the purposes of the LP in conditions of scarcity.[21] With this specification, he softens the requirement imposed by the LP on acquisition and thereby protects most sorts of acquisition from falling prey to the zip-back argument.[22] Focusing on welfare instead of actual appropriation makes the proviso much easier to satisfy,[23] especially in light of what Nozick allows as compensation for those no longer able to appropriate. Helga Varden gives an excellent summary of how Nozick recasts the LP into a weaker version. She writes:

---

[18] Locke, *Two Treatises of Government*, section 27 (cited in Nozick, ASU, p. 175).

[19] Nozick, ASU, pp. 175–76.

[20] Nozick, ASU, p. 176.

[21] Liberty Fitz-Claridge, "Wilt Chamberlain Revisited: Interpretative, Practical, and Theoretical Problems for Fried's Left-Lockeanism," *Libertarian Papers*, Vol. 7, No. 1 (2015), p. 62.

[22] Nozick, ASU, pp. 176–80.

[23] That is, the proviso on this reading is much easier to satisfy than some other plausible alternative renderings. See Werner, "Self-Ownership and Non-Culpable Proviso Violations," pp. 69–70.

[Nozick] suggests that a person may appropriate under conditions of scarcity given that he "compensates" newcomers who, as a result of the appropriation, face conditions under which original appropriation is no longer possible [ASU, 178]. Compensation, Nozick maintains, can consist in either access to use the landowners' land or access to use or acquire some of the social product that landowners have produced upon their land. And since the capitalist system produces a large social product and newcomers have access to this social product through markets, it reconciles the landowners' original appropriation of all the land with the newcomers' right to acquire a fair share of material resources. Softening the proviso is seen as maintaining its core idea that the property appropriation must not leave others in a worsened condition."[24]

With this weakening of the LP,[25] Nozick introduces a new requirement of compensation into his ET. An appropriation does not have to leave more of the same resource for others to appropriate, as long as those who originally acquire the resource compensate those who cannot acquire it for themselves later.[26] It seems then that an originally just acquisition, followed by a seamless series of justice-preserving transfers, is not sufficient to guarantee the justice of a particular distribution of holdings, at least not without compensation. Below I will highlight two particular situations in which this is the case: a person unable to appropriate a vital resource in a context of extreme scarcity, and the more common case of the poor individual in conditions of moderate scarcity. Nozick recognizes the need to compensate both sorts of people. However, I will argue that in the latter case, Nozick greatly underestimates the magnitude of compensation required to justify the appropriations in question.[27] The case of the poor individual will force Nozick to admit much more substantial levels of compensation and push his ET beyond the minimal state.[28]

---

[24] Varden, *The Lockean "Enough-and-as-Good" Proviso: An Internal Critique*, pp. 426–27.

[25] Although it is debatable whether Nozick's version of LP is in line with Locke's own intentions, I will continue to refer to Nozick's version of Locke's proviso as the Lockean Proviso or LP.

[26] Below we will discuss in greater detail the types of compensation Nozick allows.

[27] As we will see below, this way of stating things is not entirely accurate, since it is really the system as a whole, and the current distribution of holdings, that will not be justifiable without compensation (according to the LP).

[28] By "developed" here I only mean to refer to a system of private property that has existed for some time so as to yield many of its characteristic benefits and scarcities. I will have more to say on this topic below.

IV. Nozick's Proviso and Cases of Catastrophe or Extreme Scarcity of a Vital Resource

Nozick thinks a theory of appropriation incorporating his weakened LP will be well suited to handle extreme situations in which "someone appropriates the total supply of something necessary for life."[29] He also acknowledges that the LP will add certain constraints to the principles of just transfer in these situations.[30] Thus, in certain extreme circumstances, Nozick admits, just transfers will not necessarily preserve an unfettered property right to holdings gained by a legitimate original appropriation: "Each owner's title to his holding includes the historical shadow of the Lockean proviso on appropriation."[31] Nozick maintains that if owning a certain resource makes others fall below a baseline of welfare, then there will be constraints on what one can do with one's property, and these constraints flow from the LP's requirement not to make others worse off by an act of appropriation.[32] Preston Werner has noted that this means that what is supposed to be Nozick's principle of justice in transfer actually "applies to all ownership post-appropriation [i.e., original appropriation], regardless of whether it has been transferred amongst owners or not."[33] This is important for my argument below because it sets a precedent: in principle, Nozick's theory allows for a distribution of holdings to become unjust even though it has been subject to a seamless chain of just transfers. Two examples given by Nozick illustrate this point well: the first involves a desert dweller who appropriates the only water source in a given area, and the second involves a castaway who washes up on a privately owned island.[34]

In the case of the desert water source, the person's original appropriation is just. However, if severely dehydrated travelers come upon his water source, the owner cannot justifiably deny them water just because he owns it. Nor can he charge them exorbitant rates for use of the water. Such actions on the part of the owner would mean that his original appropriation of the water hole greatly worsened the situation of the travelers. Had he not appropriated the water hole, the travelers would have

---

[29] ASU, pp. 178–79.

[30] Ibid, p. 179.

[31] Ibid, p. 180.

[32] Nozick does not settle on an answer to the question of how to calculate an appropriate baseline. The exact level of the baseline is not important here. For his brief considerations on this baseline calculation, see ASU, pp. 177–78.

[33] "Self-Ownership and Non-Culpable Proviso Violations," p. 81n7.

[34] I add a bit of my own detail to these examples to better illustrate my points.

drunk their fill for free; now they may be impoverished or die as a result of the original appropriation. Similarly, the woman who comes to hold an island in a just manner still cannot justifiably reject a desperate castaway as a trespasser. Had she not appropriated the island, the castaway might have used its resources for survival. Certainly, such an appropriation in conjunction with an ordinarily legitimate no-trespassing rule worsens the castaway's situation.

These two examples highlight an important feature of ET: in some extreme cases, otherwise justly obtained holdings can be justly constrained. If a castaway will die if you enforce a strict no-trespassing rule on your island, then your property right is constrained in this case. The welfare of others, in certain circumstances, sets a limit on how one can use one's justly obtained holdings (at least these sorts of natural holdings). It is also important to note that these examples show that the LP does not only govern original acquisition; it also governs current holdings. In one sense, the injustice of refusing water to the desert traveler cannot plausibly be traced to the original appropriation of the watering hole. The person who carried out this original act may have had no idea that this resource would one day be necessary for another person's survival. Perhaps the original appropriation was even carried out at a time when many such holes existed in the area but subsequently all water sources but this one dried up.[35]

V. Extant Challenges to Nozick's LP

Before presenting my own dilemma for Nozick's LP, I will briefly consider two other challenges in the literature. Though I think these concerns may present a problem for Nozick's ET, I will argue they present much less of a problem than my own objection.

First, in his 2015 paper "Self-Ownership and Non-Culpable Proviso Violations," Preston Werner seizes on the sort of extreme scenarios I introduced above to argue that Nozick's LP will end up demanding, under certain special conditions, the donation of organs. Werner develops a scenario involving two people, A and B, on an island. Each knows they will both contract a deadly kidney disease by the age of thirty. A and B also know that on this island a special plant, *Curea*, grows. They know that if taken prior to age thirty, *Curea* will keep the gene that causes the kidney disease latent (and harmless) for life (but if one does not consume the plant, only a kidney

---

[35] This point will be especially important below when we consider the more common case of the poor person in conditions of relative scarcity.

transplant will save one's life).[36] Werner asks us to imagine that A appropriates half of the island's *Curea* and consumes all of it (much more than is needed to prevent the disease). A leaves the other half of the *Curea* untouched for B to appropriate before the age of thirty. However, after A has consumed half of the *Curea*, but before B consumes any, a tsunami destroys the half of the *Curea* that A had left untouched.[37] Werner argues that in this scenario, "B *has a claim* to (at least) one of A's kidneys."[38] This is because, though the appropriation was perfectly just at the time, after the tsunami, B is made much worse off than she would have been had A not appropriated half of the island's *Curea*. A must compensate B, and the only compensation that will bring B close to the level of welfare she would have had if A had not appropriated the *Curea* is the transplant of a kidney.

Second, Eric Mack presents some problematic implications for Nozick's proviso when it is faced with particular scenarios of resource acquisition. He asks us to consider Adam, who gains legitimate ownership over an island and then labors extensively to prevent the island from disappearing into the sea by building retaining walls and planting protective plants. This appropriation of an originally unowned island has made it possible for unfortunate castaways to access what would have otherwise been an inaccessible or nonexistent island.[39] One such scenario Mack calls "Unrequited Love," and it goes as follows:

> Adam, the proprietor of the island, allows the able-bodied Zelda ashore but then refuses to reciprocate Zelda's budding romantic passion for him—a fate which Zelda experiences as worse than death. ("Far better had he never allowed me to come under his cruel sway").[40]

In this case, Adam's appropriation and work to preserve the island has made Zelda worse off, since without it the island would never have existed and she would have died rather than be struck with this agonizing (worse than death) unrequited love. Hence, Nozick's LP maintains (quite

---

[36] "Self-Ownership and Non-Culpable Proviso Violations," p. 71.

[37] Ibid., p. 72.

[38] Ibid., p. 72.

[39] Eric Mack, "The Self-Ownership Proviso: A New and Improved Lockean Proviso," *Social Philosophy and Policy*, Vol. 12, No. 1 (1995), p. 193.

[40] Ibid., p. 194.

counterintuitively) that Adam owes Zelda some compensation.[41] Another counterintuitive case Mack calls "Paternalist Caging." It goes as follows:

> Adam, the proprietor of the island, refuses to allow Zelda to come ashore. However, Zelda inadvertently enters an offshore cage which Adam has constructed to catch (large) sea mammals. Rather than releasing her, Adam proceeds to furnish her with far more life-sustaining and satisfying conditions than she would have enjoyed had she been allowed ashore and otherwise been treated justly by Adam. (Had she not entered the cage, he would not have been able to effectively bestow his paternalist largesse.)[42]

Again, Nozick's proviso, when applied to this case, seems to produce starkly counterintuitive results. Since Adam has compensated Zelda with improved welfare, his continued caging of her is apparently not unjust.[43]

These challenges posed by Werner and Mack are unique in that they do not (like many other objectors) merely argue that Nozick's LP is too permissive and therefore not morally plausible. Instead, they argue that Nozick's LP leads to starkly counterintuitive results as it is. What should we say about these challenges? Werner claims that under certain circumstances, Nozick's LP requires compensation that includes organ donation. A defender of Nozick's might employ a reasonable constraint on the form compensation can take (perhaps one involving a strong claim to bodily integrity or self-ownership). A strong claim to self-ownership is after all among the intuitive starting points of almost any libertarian theory. With respect to Mack's cases, it is not clear that Nozick's LP is committed to such counterintuitive results. In particular, a defender of Nozick's might try to avoid the force of "Unrequited Love" by putting limits on what sort of welfare (or sources of welfare) should be considered for purposes of compensation; perhaps not just any idiosyncratic desire merits compensation.[44] Moreover, the force of the paternalist case could be blunted by considering the real welfare value (subjective though it is) of being free to do as one pleases and live as master

---

[41] Mack states Nozick's LP is a "welfare proviso… according to which any noninvasive action is acceptable if and only if it yields as much welfare for its recipient as would have been enjoyed by her in the pre-property state" (p. 212). Mack goes on to explicitly claim that Nozick's proviso would vindicate Adam in paternalist cases (like "Paternalist Caging" below) and also endorse Zelda's complaint against Adam in cases like "Unrequited Love."

[42] Ibid., p. 194.

[43] Mack recognizes this explicitly with respect to this and other paternalist cases on p. 212.

[44] I address this further below in my objections section.

of one's own life, not caged in relative luxury.[45] That is, we react against this case so strongly because we do not really believe that the caged person, lacking autonomy, can be better off.

Despite my doubts as to the merits of these objections, a defender of Nozick's should address such worries. However, the challenge that these sorts of problems pose is fairly limited. This is because Werner's and Mack's challenges depend on examples that are incredibly idiosyncratic. If these objections do hold, it is clear that they will hold only under very special (and rare) circumstances. These sorts of challenges merit a response, but they do not show that Nozick's ET leads to anything like a welfare state. In the following section, I will develop a much more troubling challenge to Nozick's ET. It is more troubling than Werner's and Mack's concerns because it rests on a much less idiosyncratic sort of case: the parties to be compensated are numerous. Hence, the compensation called for in my challenge will be extensive. This, I argue, means Nozick's ET, as it stands, leads to a redistributive welfare state.

VI. The Case of the Poor in Conditions of Moderate Scarcity

In a contemporary capitalist system, the case of the poor in conditions of moderate scarcity is common and therefore potentially more problematic for Nozick's theory. In such a system, certain resources, such as land, have become too scarce to be affordable by large swaths of the population. If ET deems that this large group must be compensated for their inability to appropriate resources, then Nozick will have to move beyond the minimal state to one that guarantees some compensatory level of welfare. This move would involve the state in activities beyond protective services and punitive justice, such as taxation of those able to appropriate (or who already have appropriated) for the purpose of funding a compensatory redistribution of wealth. This is precisely the sort of intrusive redistribution for welfare purposes that Nozick wishes to avoid. Such a state would no longer be minimal. Yet, Nozick himself seems to acknowledge the need to compensate this significant group of people who are currently unable to appropriate resources for themselves.[46]

---

[45] I will return to this issue in my own critique of Nozick below.

[46] Nozick himself does not identify this group as poor. However, this term seems appropriate. In conditions of moderate scarcity, where land is available at a price, it is the poor (and perhaps some lower middle class?) who cannot afford to appropriate land via purchase. Henceforth, I will refer to those people who are unable to appropriate various resources in a developed system of private property as the poor.

Nozick avoids moving beyond the minimal state by highlighting the substantial social benefits of a developed system of private property. He acknowledges the need to compensate the poor in such systems. However, according to his weaker version of the LP, this compensation need not come in the form of an opportunity to appropriate some particular (or any) resource. The compensation may also take the form of presenting an opportunity to use the resource in question, or an opportunity to use or appropriate social goods flowing from others' appropriation of the resource.[47] According to Nozick, in developed private property systems, this compensation has already been paid in excess. This is because the benefits of a developed system that allows permanent private property are available to the poor, and available to a degree that more than makes up for their own inability to appropriate resources for themselves.

This claim has some plausibility given the substantial benefits private property systems have made, and continue to make, possible. Nozick lists some of the relevant considerations as follows:

> social considerations favoring private property: it increases the social product by putting means of production in the hands of those who can use them most efficiently (profitably); experimentation is encouraged, because with separate persons controlling resources, there is no one person or small group whom someone with a new idea must convince to try it out; private property enables people to decide on the pattern and types of risks they wish to bear, leading to specialized types of risk bearing; private property protects future persons by leading some to hold back resources from current consumption for future markets; it provides alternate sources of employment for unpopular persons who don't have to convince any one person or small group to hire them, and so on.[48]

---

[47] Nozick, ASU, pp. 176–78.

[48] Ibid, p. 177. Paeans to the great variety and extent of the benefits of a system of private property, or unfettered capitalism, are common in the libertarian literature. For other examples, see David Schmidtz, *Elements of Justice* (Cambridge: Cambridge University Press, 2006), 56; and Eric Mack, "The Self-Ownership Proviso: A New and Improved Lockean Proviso," *Social Philosophy and Policy*, Vol. 12, No. 1 (Winter 1995), pp. 212–16. For a particularly strong statement of the benefits of private property systems, see also Jan Narveson's "Property Rights: Original Acquisition and Lockean Provisos," *Public Affairs Quarterly* Vol. 13, No. 3 (Jul. 1999), pp. 216, 220–23. Especially relevant is Narveson's passage on pp. 222–23, where he writes, "Thus the original intent of the Lockean proviso is met, in spades, by the on-going process of human production stimulated by individuals' interests, protected by property rights. What is 'left' for others

Features such as these have led to a proliferation of modern conveniences and innovations that have made life longer and more comfortable. Benefits as diverse as the vaccination for smallpox, indoor plumbing, biscuits in a can, Twitter, and minimalls have ostensibly arisen because of the efficiency, innovation, and culture of risk taking that private property makes possible. In light of access to these benefits, Nozick thinks the modern-day poor person has been more than compensated. The poor have not been made worse off by these appropriations of property, because without them they would lack many modern advances. In other words, it is the by-products of the system itself, as a whole, that compensate the poor for their inability to appropriate resources. They are better off with the system and its benefits than they would be with the opportunity to appropriate but without the benefits of the system.[49] It is at this point that I will challenge Nozick's position. In brief, I think a large group of people are worse off in such a system.

To frame my argument, it is helpful to highlight how Nozick responds to a similar challenge leveled by Fourier. Nozick writes:

> Fourier held that since the process of civilization had deprived the members of society of certain liberties (to gather, pasture, engage in the chase), a socially guaranteed minimum provision for persons was justified as compensation for the loss… But this puts the point too strongly. This compensation would be due those persons, if any, for whom the process of civilization was a *net loss*, for whom the benefits of civilization did not counterbalance being deprived of these particular liberties.[50]

My contention is that compensation is due to certain poor persons in a developed system of private property because the progression of this sort of civilization has been a net loss for these people. The benefits of this system

---

is, overwhelmingly, the opportunity to avail themselves of the production of their fellows. As society becomes more complex in its differentiation of products and skills, we are increasingly dependent on propensities to exchange on the part of their fellows, who meanwhile become reliable producers and exchangers. Thus what's left for others is not merely 'as good,' but much better from the start, and as time goes on incomparably better."

[49] It is for this reason that Nozick thinks the LP will rarely come into play, and so will not merit any sort of pervasive redistributive activity on the part of the state. He goes as far as to suggest that the contexts meriting constraint on otherwise just holdings may very well be coextensive with catastrophe situations. See ASU, pp. 181–182.

[50] Nozick, ASU, p. 178n.

do not counterbalance such people's lost opportunity to appropriate. Thus a sizable portion of the poor remain uncompensated.[51]

VII. Farmer John on the Frontier vs. Waiter John in the Trailer Park

Jan Narveson contends that "in the United states today, far more people are employed serving food in restaurants than on the farms that produce the food in the first place; waiters and waitresses, cooks and cashiers—all are better off than they could ever have been on any primitive farm."[52] These words come in the midst of Narveson making a point similar to Nozick's—namely, that the benefits of a developed system of private property make it so nearly all (or perhaps all) will be better off. I think both Narveson and Nozick are wrong about this, and Narveson's suggested comparison is as good as any to show why. Let us consider, then, the cases of the primitive farmer and the modern waiter.

To carry out this comparison we will consider an individual, John, who finds himself on the lower rungs of the socioeconomic ladder. John has an intense desire to execute the modest life plan of farming his own land. We will consider John in two conditions, one in which he is able to execute his life plan and become a primitive farmer and another in which he is unable to appropriate the necessary land and so must settle for a job as a waiter. The geographic locations of both cases will be the same. The time period (and thus the relative development of the system of private property) will be the main difference.

(a) Farmer John on the Frontier: The Colony of Virginia in the 1740s

First, let us consider John growing up in the colony of Virginia in the 1740s. He is born into a family working its way out of indentured servitude. As a result, he grows up poor. As soon as he is old enough to hold a hoe, he goes to work farming someone else's land alongside his father. From an early age, John develops an intense desire to gain mastery over his life by farming

---

[51] Helga Varden raises a more basic worry about this sort of compensation. She thinks it violates the essentially bilateral nature of the sort of justification or compensation that the LP requires. She thinks the benefits of a system at large cannot compensate those unable to appropriate. Each appropriator must guarantee compensation of those made worse off. For Varden's account of this difficulty, see "The Lockean 'Enough-and-as-Good' Proviso: An Internal Critique," pp. 427–28. I will pass over this difficulty here, but it does appear to be an issue any Lockean theory of appropriation will have to address.

[52] "Property Rights: Original Acquisition and Lockean Provisos," p. 223.

his own land. It soon becomes clear he will never be able to afford land in the colony (he can never seem to earn the excess funds to buy it). For this reason, he decides to move to the frontier and claim some land of his own. He and his wife move to what is now the state of Kentucky.

John takes only what his mule can carry. The trip, even in late spring, is risky. In the first season, John and his wife only have time to set up a temporary shelter to make it through the winter. Life is precarious for that first year. But in following seasons, John and his wife are able to clear and farm a modest plot, and build a modest cabin. Within a few years, John's now-growing family has a fairly stable food supply consisting of crops and trapped animals. By most measures, even compared to his contemporary society, he is not materially well off. Frontier life is primitive, and even his impoverished parents, back in the colony, have a few more amenities than John does. However, for John, this loss in material comfort is easily outweighed by the achievement of his utmost desire: John is his own master and lives off his own plot of land. The ability to pursue his cherished life plan is a great boon to John's level of welfare. Moreover, he does not experience his work as drudgery imposed on him by another. He engages in all of his efforts as his own boss, working directly for the good of his family and the achievement of his cherished dreams.

(b) Waiter John in the Trailer Park: The State of Virginia in the 1990s

Now consider John in an analogous situation in the 1990s. He is born into a family mired in a cycle of poverty in a semi-rural area of Virginia. His mother and father are immigrants and have not been able to obtain jobs that pay more than minimum wage. They work hard, sometimes at multiple jobs, but finances are tight. As soon as John is old enough, he works jobs after school to help out. Eventually John drops out of high school to help support his family by working full time as a waiter in the local Shoney's restaurant. Throughout this time, John develops an intense desire to gain mastery over his life. He develops a life plan of one day supporting his own family by farming his own land. It soon becomes clear he will not be able to afford even a modest plot of land, let alone a pristine Kentuckian plot ripe for farming, trapping, and hunting. Unlike John of the 1740s, this John has no option to move west and acquire some such unclaimed land on the frontier. So John settles for a life as a waiter, a form of labor he experiences as menial drudgery, unconnected with his deepest desires. He gets married and moves into a modest trailer he and his wife pay for by working overtime. He is able to raise a family, but his backyard garden is a far cry from the farm of his dreams. His work load does not even allow him the time or energy to properly tend to his small kitchen garden.

(c) Is Farmer John Worse Off than Waiter John?

It is my contention that farmer John is significantly *better* off than waiter John. A Nozickian argument would no doubt point to all of the modern amenities and innovations available to waiter John and not available to farmer John. Farmer John grew up in a much less developed system of private property, which means many of its benefits have yet to be realized. Waiter John's trailer has indoor plumbing, electricity, and food refrigeration. Food bills are often hard to pay, but he does not have to worry about catching or growing his food. His children attend the local public elementary school and receive periodic vaccinations. Waiter John also has a color television with five channels, a secondhand spring mattress, and a fridge full of Busch Lite. Farmer John's cabin life lacks these modern wonders. Does this not clearly show that a modern waiter is better off than a frontier farmer? I think not.

The reason Nozick and Narveson are wrong on this point is because they weight (non-natural) material wealth too heavily when determining a person's welfare.[53] If we focus on material wealth and comfort, it is at least plausible that waiter John is better off than farmer John. The modern trailer occupant may appear more materially wealthy than the average cabin dweller on the North American colonial frontier.[54] Once we consider other factors, such as subjective life satisfaction, it becomes clear that for some Johns, frontier farming is a significantly better life overall. Being able to pursue and ultimately achieve one's life plan of self-mastery is enough to outweigh much in the way of material wealth and comfort. Even in the mere pursuit of his own farm, farmer John is already realizing a level of self-governance and autonomy that is off-limits to waiter John. Waiter John cannot plausibly pursue, much less attain, his life plan. This cannot be easily made up for. I contend that vaccinations, electric heat, and drive-throughs at McDonald's

---

[53] I use the qualifier "non-natural" here because I think libertarians such as Narveson and Nozick often greatly undervalue undeveloped nature. They focus (quite appropriately) on all the great things that can be done with nature once it is developed, but they often ignore all that is lost through development (such as the enjoyment of pristine natural beauty) and the bad things added (such as massive amounts of pollution and traffic).

[54] I say "arguably" here because I think Nozick, Narveson, and other libertarians often underestimate the purely material value of pristine natural resources in their (somewhat) justified lauding of appropriated/developed resources. A pristine plot lacks valuable infrastructure, but it also lacks pollution; it may be subject to predators absent from developed territories, but it still has plenty of animals to hunt and trap (and to seek to leave to hunt and trap on others' land).

are just not enough to overcome this loss. The condition of waiter John is worsened by the system of private property as a whole (at least at this late stage of its development).[55]

VIII. Nozick's Dilemma: Move beyond the Minimal State or Violate the Lockean Proviso

Many people in the contemporary United States (or a society like it) are in a situation analogous to waiter John, and in a less developed system of private property, many would have the opportunity to become a farmer John. If this is the case, then many poor people are worse off than they would be in a situation with much less appropriation. And if this is the case, then Nozick is wrong about how often the LP is likely to come into play. Indeed, the LP will apply to so many people in a society of private property similar to the present United States that Nozick's ET will be forced to endorse a state that goes well beyond the minimal activities of protection and punitive justice. The Nozickian state will need to guarantee a compensatory level of welfare.

This guarantee of welfare will be required in order to compensate those (many) people who are worse off in light of how far the system of private property has developed and how much they value autonomy or self-mastery. Material wealth and comforts, at the right level, could perhaps compensate for lost opportunities to appropriate land. However, the more appropriate compensation might be to make it possible, for those who desire it, to purchase land to farm (or make some other opportunity possible short of appropriation).[56] Whatever form the compensation takes, it will cost the state some money, which means the state will need to institute a redistributive tax scheme. Thus, as Nozick has developed it, ET will require a more than minimal state in many possible (and actual) systems of private property (for example, those akin to the United States'). He would have to drop the LP requirement in order to avoid this outcome. Assuming my argument can withstand objections, it looks as if Nozick will need to either abandon the LP or endorse some sort of redistributive welfare state.[57]

---

[55] Below I will make the case that this applies to earlier stages of development as well.

[56] If more people opt for this situation than the available land can support, then other comparable opportunities or increased material wealth would need to be offered.

[57] For an alternative case for how Nozick's ET might justify some sort of welfare state, see M. Davis, 1987, "Nozick's Argument for the Legitimacy of the Welfare State," *Ethics* 97 (3), pp. 576–94. Davis's account of this is distinct from my own and ultimately

IX. Objections and Replies

If my argument succeeds, Nozick is forced into a dilemma. However, there are some objections a Nozickian is likely to level against my argument. In concluding this essay, I will answer three of the most obvious (and substantial) objections to my case.

a. We Can't Satisfy Every Crazy Idiosyncratic Life Plan

Someone might challenge my inclusion of a life plan as irrelevant in determining who is and is not owed compensation. There are all sorts of odd life plans, and yet it would seem absurd to require the state to compensate each one. Imagine that instead of farming, a person wished to live in a state without cars, for no other reason than the satisfaction of knowing that cars were not within the borders of his home state. Such states existed at an earlier stage in the private property system of the United States. Given an ardent desire for this life, such a person may be worse off now than he would have been in the United States of 1828. Should we then hold the government hostage to every idiosyncratic desire that can no longer be achieved as a result of the advanced stage of the private property system?[58] I do not think so.

In brief, I think it is perfectly legitimate for the government to refrain from compensating people with idiosyncratic desires. The life plan I focus on in my examples directly involves land appropriation. Furthermore, in the context of the life plan of someone like farmer John, the land appropriation serves the purpose of allowing him greater autonomy. In Mack's terms, access to resources such as land allows people to exercise their "world interactive" powers/capacities, which is what it means to exercise one's autonomy. That is, one cannot exercise autonomy in the world if a sufficient amount of that world is not available for interaction.[59] Providing access to important resources such as land makes such autonomy possible. No longer must farmer John work for others; he lives off his own efforts on his own property. Thus, this life plan not only appeals to resource appropriation (which is rightly constrained by the LP), but it also appeals to a Lockean libertarian value of individual liberty (which the LP is meant to preserve). Ultimately, what is problematic about a poor person not being able to

---

fails for reasons ably pointed out by Joachim Wundisch in his 2014 article "A Free-Rider Perspective on Property Rights," *Libertarian Papers* 6 (2): 145–61.

[58] This is the same problem Mack raises in his unrequited-love case presented above. See his "The Self-Ownership Proviso: A New and Improved Lockean Proviso," p. 194.

[59] Ibid, pp. 186–88.

appropriate land is his dependence upon others for the use of resources[60] and how that dependence can dramatically decrease one's autonomy (via a much narrower purview for one's world-interactive powers). Not being subject to such dependence (and autonomy constraint) is a great good that calls for compensation if lost. These sorts of setbacks are relevant for the LP and should therefore be compensated in any theory incorporating this principle. More idiosyncratic setbacks have little discernible connection to the LP or the foundational intuitions of any plausible libertarian theory; hence, they can be legitimately ignored.

If these considerations do not convince the objector, then it might be enough just to point out that the state can only address relatively pervasive welfare concerns. A state cannot practicably respond with compensation to the idiosyncratic desires of specific groups or particular people. The sort of case I present, concerning John, applies to whole classes of people.[61] The desire to live off one's own land is a common one; however, it is easy to imagine that many people mired in the cycle of poverty would opt for the life of farmer John even if they did not have a lifelong dream to farm.[62] Thus, those whose condition will be worsened by not having this opportunity of appropriation (namely much of the poor in a well-developed system of private property similar to the United States') will be many. This is a pervasive welfare concern that the state governed by the LP can and should address.

---

[60] For more on this theme, see Varden, "The Lockean 'Enough-and-as-Good' Proviso: An Internal Critique."

[61] Some might question the pervasiveness of a strong desire to farm one's own land. Some might question such a desire as an overly romanticized picture of how "poor country folks" think. Such objectors would do well to remember that there are whole communities in the contemporary United States who still view farming as the most desirable sort of life. There are whole rural communities organized around who gets what land and what they will do with it. And there are whole communities that would happily forgo much modern convenience to preserve a relatively simple farming lifestyle. This desire to live off one's own land is neither rare nor strange. Perhaps it could be characterized as a natural expression of the human desire for, and pursuit of, independence and self-governance.

[62] This is especially likely to be true if such people were raised in a less developed environment where farming was a more common lifestyle.

b. Is Frontier Farmer John the Proper Baseline for Comparison?

A more serious objection to my argument involves my baseline for comparison. A defender of Nozick might say I stacked the deck in my favor by choosing to compare farmer John with the modern poor. Though living at a much more primitive time, a person in 1740s Virginia would already be experiencing the benefits of a private property system. John does not travel over the Appalachians naked and empty-handed. He brings with him warm clothes, an ax, a domesticated mule, and some food stores made possible by the private property system. Even if John did walk naked into the woods, he still would have benefited from the skills he learned by growing up in society. The more proper baseline for comparison (so the objection would go) is the existence of a truly primitive hunter-gatherer.

I have three responses to this objection, at least one of which should satisfy the objector. First, one could claim precisely the opposite: that I stacked the deck in Nozick's favor. I did not compare farmer John to someone existing in a pure Nozickian minimal state (with its dearth of state-run social programs). Waiter John lives in 1990s Virginia and has the benefit (among others) of subsidized vaccinations at the local free clinic, free road use, and free education for his children.[63] Indeed, many of the modern material marvels that Nozick touts, and that weigh heavily in his calculus of compensation for what the poor are unable to appropriate, would in fact be out of reach for someone like waiter John. Hence, I could make my focal comparison above much more favorable for my argument.

Second, I could argue that I have in fact already chosen the proper baseline for comparison. Nozick originally states that the system of private property itself more than compensates those who are unable to appropriate at some later stage. But if compensation is requisite, it is not the original appropriation that comes into question. Nor is it the system as a whole at all times that comes into question. Rather, what comes into question is the system as a whole at some stage (or stages) in its development, namely the stage(s) at which it is no longer possible to appropriate some resource. This is already evident in Nozick's treatment of the catastrophe examples above. Such examples show that in Nozick's ET, the LP does not apply merely to original appropriations; it also comes into play to constrain holdings long after such appropriations. In the case of well-advanced systems of private property (such as the United States in the 1990s) the distribution of holdings, and not some original appropriation, is constrained by the LP. Thus, it is

---

[63] Of course, if John pays taxes then road use and education are not really free. I am assuming he is poor enough that his tax rate is rather modest.

perfectly appropriate to compare waiter John to farmer John rather than to a hunter-gatherer who has not benefited at all from a private property system. Private property *simpliciter* is not the problem; the relative degree of development of a private property system is.

Third, I might respond to the objection by accepting this new, proper baseline. Consider the Native American tribes of 500 CE in North America. In general, I could contend that the lifestyle of a hunter-gatherer in a small band society might yield a higher welfare than that of waiter John, with all of his modern amenities but mired in poverty. Many libertarians dismiss this possibility almost out of hand, perhaps thinking this conclusion could only result in a wildly romantic (and inaccurate) view of hunter-gatherer life (one that glosses over the many gruesome hardships suffered by such societies). Fortunately, we do not have to depend on armchair judgments of what life was like for hunter-gatherers. The best data we have indicate that, while certainly grim in certain respects, the life of the average hunter-gatherer was significantly better than that of a person like waiter John.

Recently, a book has been published that addresses this very question: are poor people in developed capitalist systems of private property better off than the average hunter-gatherer? *Prehistoric Myths in Modern Political Philosophy* is co-authored by a philosopher (Karl Wilderquist) and an anthropologist (Grant McCall). Wilderquist and McCall were troubled by how often the quality of life of hunter-gatherers factored into the arguments of political philosophers and how few data such quality-of-life judgements were based on. It turns out that when one actually engages with the available data, significant numbers of people today appear worse off than the average hunter-gatherer. While the modern rich and middle class (in a place such as the United States) are better off than almost any hunter-gatherer, the poor are considerably worse off. Wilderquist and McCall draw on our best data for what the life of these ancient peoples was like and on anthropological data gathered from the few hunter-gatherer societies remaining today.[64] I do not have the space to cover all of their findings in detail. Here I will simply highlight some of the most important ways a hunter-gatherer existence outstrips the lives of many modern poor persons such as our waiter John.[65] Wilderquist and McCall key on four broad measures of the quality of life.

---

[64] Wilderquist and McCall, *Prehistoric Myths in Modern Political Philosophy*, Edinburgh University Press, 2017.

[65] To read about the data and their analysis of it in depth, see especially chapter 10.

(1) Social and cultural satisfaction

As a general rule, prehistoric peoples were extremely social.[66] Although ancient hunter-gatherers did not have the satisfaction of creating and consuming things such as symphonies and novels, "ethnographic and historical accounts report that all indigenous communities have rich cultural lives with art, music, dance, storytelling, and so on. People in band societies have many opportunities for social interaction in a community that often makes them feel like an integral part."[67] Furthermore, the social/cultural opportunities of more advanced societies are often off-limits to the poor[68] (think of the price of symphony or play tickets, or the sort of education that would allow one to enjoy a complex novel). Also, the poor in advanced capitalist societies often need to work far too much to have the time or energy to enjoy such activities. Moreover, "ethnographers report a distinct lack of a discontented minority in band societies. Suicide rates are low... The commonplace misery of discontented people in state society [today] seems to have no equivalent in band society... accounts of nomadic foragers attests to their being surprisingly content."[69] Though many poor people in modern industrial societies are socially isolated and discontented, hunter-gatherer societies do not produce such groups of people.[70]

(2) Material well-being

Material well-being is usually the primary focus in accounts that depict hunter-gatherer life unfavorably. Modern capitalist economies produce such a wide variety of goods with such great efficiency that it seems obvious even the worst off live better than the average hunter-gatherer. However, as Wilderquist and McCall point out, "the problem with this view stems both from the over-identification of material income with material wellbeing (Kenny 2006) and from the fallacy of composition... [Such productivity] makes it *possible* for everyone to consume far more and work far less, but it does not ensure that everyone *actually does* consume more and work less."[71]

In the area of leisure, the average hunter-gatherer is not only doing better than the modern poor person, but also significantly better than the

---

[66] Wilderquist and McCall, p. 178.
[67] Ibid., p. 178.
[68] Ibid., p. 178–79.
[69] Ibid., p. 179.
[70] Ibid., p. 179–80.
[71] Ibid., p. 180.

modern middle class.[72] One rather pessimistic study of a particularly hard-working hunter-gatherer group (the Ache) put their weekly work at about forty-nine hours (nine hours over the standard US workweek). However, this figure included many activities involved in running a household that the typical US worker does in their "leisure" time. When we correct for this, it turns out the average middle-class person works (including nonmarket work and childcare) about fifty-five hours per week. That is six hours more than a fairly hardworking hunter-gatherer group.[73] Some hunter-gatherers work far less (as few as nineteen hours a week).[74] Moreover, the hours hunter-gatherers did work must have felt much freer. They had a task, and it was largely up to them how to complete it. Hunter-gatherers were essentially their own bosses.[75] This is true of very few moderns, especially the poor.

When it comes to meeting the basic needs of all group members, hunter-gatherer societies outdo even places as wealthy as the modern United States. Hunter-gatherer societies have a strong safety net and fairly equal distribution of goods. If there is food among the group, no one goes hungry.[76] Although modern capitalist economies have much more wealth to dispose of, it is uneven in its distribution. Hence, extreme poverty continues even in places as wealthy as the United States, where 3.55 million children live in households making less than two dollars a day and 14.5 percent of all households experience food insecurity. As of 2013, some 640,000 Americans were homeless.[77] And homeless Americans face difficulties that do not exist in hunter-gatherer societies such as having to eat out of the garbage or "having no legal place to eat, sleep, or urinate… not to mention a place to hunt, gather, fish, or farm."[78] Moreover, challenges such as these lead to levels of stress nonexistent among hunter-gatherers, who are generally content and confident that their environment will provide all they need.[79]

(3) Health and longevity

But don't hunter-gatherers die young and live a life bereft of all the health-inducing wonders to which even a modern of modest means has

---

[72] Ibid., p. 184.
[73] Ibid., pp. 185–86.
[74] Ibid., p. 185.
[75] Ibid., p. 187.
[76] Ibid., p. 187.
[77] Ibid., p. 190.
[78] Ibid., p. 190.
[79] Ibid., pp. 189–91.

access? Not exactly. The average life expectancy of a hunter-gatherer is significantly less than the average life expectancy of someone in a modern industrialized society. However, a life expectancy of thirty-five does not mean people expect to get old and die at the age of thirty-five. Rather, old age for a hunter-gatherer might be somewhere in their seventies, but the average is brought so low because of high infant and child mortality.[80] Once she survived childhood, a hunter-gatherer could expect to live a reasonably long life.

It is true that hunter-gatherers lack the benefits of modern medicine, but they are in turn healthier than citizens of industrialized societies in several significant ways.[81] Hunter-gatherers "are largely immune to the chronic degenerative diseases which produce the greater part of all mortality in affluent nations."[82] Ailments such as obesity, heart disease, diabetes, and stroke fall into this category. A superior diet and low exposure to toxins is thought to account for the extremely low incidence of cancer among hunter-gatherers. Just "one forager woman in 800 develops breast cancer, while in the United States it is more like one in eight."[83] So, along with the cures and treatments of many diseases, modern capitalist society has delivered many other deadly conditions that did not afflict our hunter-gatherer ancestors at all.[84]

(4) Freedom

When it comes to negative freedom (freedom from constraint), hunter-gatherers clearly have the upper hand over poor persons in capitalist societies. Hunter-gatherers are essentially their own bosses. They decide how, when, and to what extent they will hunt and gather. If one dislikes how their band is doing things, one is free to pick up and move elsewhere, essentially starting a new band society. This would seem to be the height of freedom from constraint. This option is not available to the poor in modern societies, where there is often no unowned periphery to which one can move. Moreover, the

---

[80] Ibid., pp. 193–94.
[81] Ibid., p. 195.
[82] Ibid., p. 195.
[83] S. B. Eaton and S. Eaton (1999), "Hunter-Gatherers and Human Health," in R. B. Lee and R. Daly (eds.), *The Cambridge Encyclopedia of Hunters and Gatherers*. Cambridge: Cambridge University Press, pp. 449–56.
[84] Ibid., p. 195.

modern-day homeless often lack a place to sleep, have sex, or even urinate legally.[85]

But one might argue that modern capitalist societies provide a host of opportunities unavailable to hunter-gatherers, and in this sense a modern person is much more free (i.e., free to take advantage of a myriad of opportunities available in a market economy). Wilderquist and McCall contend that the average modern person does have a greater freedom of opportunity but poor people do not.[86] For example, modern capitalist societies present great educational opportunities; however, few of the poor can take full advantage of such opportunities. Moreover, the greater proliferation of education has created a condition wherein those who lack higher education lack knowledge and skills necessary to flourish in their society. Many new job "opportunities" are created, but are in practice not really open to those unable to gain a certain sort of education. In hunter-gatherer societies, every person has the opportunity to learn all the skills they need to thrive in society.[87]

I have only surveyed a few highlights from the extensive research Wilderquist and McCall draw on concerning hunter-gatherer well-being compared to modern persons in capitalist societies. It is clear, however, even from this brief treatment, that this is not an unfavorable comparison for my argument against Nozick. In fact, one should note that the inequality that results in such an unfavorable comparison of the modern poor with hunter-gatherers would likely be *worse* under a Nozickian state, with its dearth of social programs and absence of social safety net. Hence, choosing the baseline of ancient hunter-gatherers does not weaken my case; it strengthens it.

c. Might Nozick Be Focusing on Opportunity for Welfare, Rather than Actual Welfare?

One final objection to my argument seizes on just what Nozick means when he considers whether someone is made worse or better off. So far I have proceeded on the assumption that Nozick is considering something like the welfare of the person in question, all things considered. However, when Nozick is describing the application of the LP he may only be focused on the narrower aspect of opportunity for well-being. Perhaps Nozick (or a

---

[85] Ibid., p. 202.
[86] Ibid., p. 199.
[87] Ibid., p. 200.

Nozickian) could argue that while the actual welfare of the poor is worse, the opportunity for welfare is nevertheless increased. It is in this way that those unable to appropriate certain resources are better off.

I have two related responses to this objection. First, the way the term "opportunity" would function in such an argument is problematic. In one sense, it is quite plausible to say that increased opportunity for well-being, if high enough, might serve as sufficient compensation for lost opportunities to appropriate in an advanced system of private property. For example, the lazy person, in the right conditions of climate and food availability, may have been able to achieve some moderate level of well-being with little work (simply gathering resources from the abundant commons). The fact that such a person can no longer achieve the same level of well-being while remaining lazy is now compensated by increased opportunities to participate and prosper in a market economy. One might plausibly argue that the state is not required to compensate such a person any further than to allow her the opportunity to work for a living (i.e., achieve a moderate level of welfare by giving up being lazy). Such an answer may do for people who refuse to take advantage of increased opportunities for welfare, but it will not suffice in our focal case of waiter John. Waiter John is not lazy or otherwise unwilling to take advantage of opportunities for improved welfare; he is making a great effort to attain his dream of farming his own land. I contend that waiter John and many like him ardently attempt to better the situation of themselves and their families but this attempt is largely unsuccessful.

At this point the Nozickian might respond that this is unfortunate but beside the point. The LP requires compensation in terms of increased opportunity for welfare; it need not guarantee actual success. However, there remains the problem of determining just what counts as increased opportunity. For example, unlike farmer John, waiter John has the benefit of the additional "opportunity" to play the lottery. If he won, he would certainly have the means to achieve his dream of farming his own land. The problem of course is that the lottery does not represent an increased opportunity for welfare in the right way. It is a new opportunity to better one's well-being, and it can do so to a much greater degree than most avenues open to farmer John; yet, it is rarely a successful venture.

The developed system of private property in which waiter John lives provides many new opportunities for bettering one's lot. An implication of what I have argued in this paper is that these avenues are not often successful for people like waiter John. If this is the case, then it is misleading to say the modern-day market economy compensates people like John via increased opportunities to promote one's own welfare. If these "opportunities," when pursued, are rarely successful for whole swaths of people (because of the disadvantages associated with the cycle of poverty), then it is not clear in what sense they are genuine opportunities.[88]

My second response to this objection builds on the first: focusing on this sort of "opportunity" rather than actually achieved welfare is an implausible rendering of the motivation for the LP and its force as a moral principle (at least as it is employed by Nozick within the framework of ET).[89] Why would opportunities be relevant at all, or worth preserving, if (when taken advantage of) they did not often lead to increased welfare? An opportunity has little value if it is unlikely to be successful. Thus, if we assume that such "opportunities" are what the LP seeks to preserve for those who are unable to appropriate a resource, then ET becomes morally implausible. This is similar to a point Mack makes concerning autonomy and access to the world's resources. One may be free to exercise one's world-interactive powers (that is, free from any direct constraint on their use) and yet may still be constrained indirectly by being deprived of access to resources in the world with which one could autonomously interact.[90] It is not enough that someone is merely unconstrained in the world. They also need to have access to resources with which to interact. Hence, one can be

---

[88] Undoubtedly, modern market economies do provide increased genuine opportunities for some (perhaps many) poor people. For example, we could consider Anne the waitress, who wants to start her own business. She does not yet have a family to support and is fortunate enough to save some money and qualify for a small-business loan. The existence of people like Anne does not overcome my argument against Nozick. For Nozick to avoid being committed to a more extensive state, it has to be the case that relatively few people are like waiter John. On the contrary, I contend that many people in current private property systems are relevantly similar to him. And as with waiter John, the seemingly increased opportunities for welfare are for the most part not panning out.

[89] This parenthetical remark is added because there might be other renderings of the LP that are plausible if employed outside Nozick's ET framework. For example, one might think Locke originally meant the LP to secure the opportunity to utilize (if one wished) one's fair share of the earth's resources. This sort of rendering, however plausible within Lockean theory, will not help Nozick, for two reasons. First, he tries to argue that people need not be given the ability to appropriate land or any other resource (as long as they are compensated), and this rendering would seem to imply that all need to be given the opportunity to appropriate. Second, Nozick already identifies what he believes to be a substantial problem for such a theory in the form of the "zip-back" argument. Hence, within ET, if the LP is to work and remain morally plausible, it will need to reference actual welfare or at least opportunities that have a significant possibility of success.

[90] "The Self-Ownership Proviso: A New and Improved Lockean Proviso," pp. 186–92.

deprived of autonomy of action by being cut off from the world's resources in a sufficiently extreme manner. Likewise, one's autonomy can be curtailed by being deprived of any opportunities for flourishing in the world that are at all likely to pan out. Lack of genuinely viable opportunities is just another way the exercise of one's world-interactive powers can be constrained.

Hence, the lack of opportunity to appropriate needs to be compensated, not merely because compensating opportunities represents an avenue to increased welfare, but because these opportunities are often successful. If land, when appropriated and farmed, often yielded only weeds, then there would be less need to compensate for the loss of opportunity to appropriate. It is only because this opportunity often leads to increased welfare (i.e., the land is fruitful if worked in a responsible manner) that the loss of this opportunity demands compensation. It is for this reason, and with this motivation, that it is plausible to situate the LP as a moral principle within Nozick's ET.

Nozick interprets Locke as seeking to preserve the ability of others to appropriate a resource because a lack of this ability is likely to make them worse off. Nozick's amendment of the LP in light of the zip-back argument is only plausible if his concepts of "worse off" and "better off" are linked to actual welfare. He need not guarantee that every poor person actually achieves a certain level of welfare, but he does need to compensate such people with sufficiently promising opportunities. It has been my contention that developed systems of private property, similar to the system operative in the United States, fail to provide such opportunities for a substantial portion of the population.

X. Conclusion: Redistributive Taxes Are Compensatory, Not Akin to Forced Labor

Nozick himself builds the framework that forces the dilemma advanced above. He sets the precedent of compensatory taxation early in ASU in arguing for the minimal state. He allows the LP to constrain current holdings in the case of catastrophe, and he admits that, in principle, those unable to appropriate in current well-developed systems of private property should be compensated. Where I disagree with Nozick (and Narveson), and where Nozick is ultimately mistaken, is in just how beneficial an advanced system of private property is for the poor. Once we consider more than just material wealth and convenience, and take into account subjective life satisfaction, it is clear that many poor people are worse off in a more developed system of private property. And this conclusion is not just the product of some romanticized vision of the grandeur of the wilderness or the simple pleasures of farming.[91] The really weighty welfare good made possible by living off one's own land is the increased autonomy, the ability to be one's own master and self-govern to a greater degree. This is a welfare good that is hard to outweigh. For this reason, if Nozick wishes to maintain the Lockean credentials of his hypothetical state, it will have to go beyond minimal activities and minimal taxation and implement some compensatory level of welfare and more extensive redistributive taxation. Contrary to what Nozick thought, such taxation is not on par with forced labor, and this is because it is compensatory. Thus, followed to its (un)natural conclusion, Nozick's Lockean libertarian entitlement theory leads to the development of a welfare state.

---

[91] Although these are perhaps more substantial considerations than some academics realize.

Would-Be Farmer John and the Welfare State: A Response to Blincoe

Jan Narveson[*]

Adam Blincoe aims to show that libertarianism, at least in Robert Nozick's version, is faced with a dilemma: "Either (a) Nozick must admit that taxation for the purpose of guaranteeing a compensatory level of welfare (and not merely for protection from harm) is legitimate or (b) he must admit that his entitlement theory cannot satisfy the Lockean proviso."[1] So what is Nozick's version—and in any case, what is the *correct* version—of this famous proviso? (I assume Blincoe is not just making scholarly points about Nozick, but rather about his fundamental idea, libertarianism.) Locke famously says that someone's acquisition is just "since there was still enough, and as good, left for others; and more than the yet unprovided could use. So that in effect, there was never the less left for others because of his enclosure for himself. For he that leaves as much as another can make use of, does as good as take nothing at all" (*2nd Treatise of Civil Government*, §33). Almost all modern commentators have drawn from an earlier passage: "For this Labour being the unquestionable Property of the Labourer, no Man but he can have a right to what that is once joined to, at least where there is enough, and as good left in common for others" (§27). Both passages leave open a crucial question:

---

[*] Jan Narveson is professor emeritus of philosophy at the University of Waterloo.
Citation Information for this Article:
Jan Narveson. 2018. "Would-Be Farmer John and the Welfare State: A Response to Blincoe." *Libertarian Papers*. 10 (1): 49-60. Online at: libertarianpapers.org. This article is subject to a Creative Commons Attribution 3.0 License (creativecommons.org/licenses).

[1] Adam Blincoe, "Forcing Nozick beyond the Minimal State: The Lockean Proviso and Compensatory Welfare," *Libertarian Papers*, vol. 10, no. 1, 2018, pp. 19-48. Unattributed page references are to that paper.

what if there is not enough and as good for others? Locke speaks here of land in particular, so another question is whether there is any special priority to that particular resource. Many, including Blincoe, seem to think there is.

Speaking from the vantage point of the twenty-first century, "too little" would seem to be an obvious possibility too, assuming a certain general agricultural technology. But too little for what, exactly? People went into the American wilderness in the seventeenth to nineteenth centuries to make a living and, especially, to grow an adequate food supply for themselves and their families. At the time, "enough and as good" was quite a bit and pretty good indeed: prime farmland in central North America, top-class material for the agriculture of the time. But as agricultural technology improved, the required amount diminished. It was down to around one large living room's worth in about 1970, and at the present day, if what is in question is the ability to raise enough to live on, then that quantity is actually zero: we no longer need *any* land to grow ample food stocks on, as the upper floors of large buildings suffice provided you are happy with a vegetarian diet.[2] Nozick's tack on this is to generalize:

> A process normally giving rise to a permanent bequeathable property right in a previously unowned thing will not do so if the position of others no longer at liberty to use the thing is thereby worsened… it does not include the worsening due to more limited opportunities to appropriate… Someone whose appropriation otherwise would violate the proviso still may appropriate provided he compensates the others so that their situation is not thereby worsened.[3]

Has he generalized correctly? If being able to go down to the corner store and satisfy your daily caloric requirements for a very modest outlay counts, then present-day technology, especially in agriculture, solves the problem neatly for all but the absolutely indigent. A serious question arises of just what constitutes worsening when we talk of being "thereby worsened." As we will see, everything, for Blincoe's argument, depends on this. A first shot at it is easy: if your action deprives someone of something he legitimately owned, then you violate the intended proviso. But legitimate ownership traces back, via whatever exchanges intervened, ultimately to initial appropriation, which is what the proviso is intended to apply to.

---

[2] This is no longer sci-fi-level conjecture. See Ian Fraser, "The Vertical Farm: Growing Crops in the City, without Soil or Natural Light," *New Yorker*, January 9, 2017, available at: https://www.newyorker.com/magazine/2017/01/09.

[3] Robert Nozick, *Anarchy, State and Utopia* (Oxford: Blackwell, 1974), p. 178.

Here, Locke (and almost everybody) obscures the situation by asserting that, after all, God "gave the World in common to all Mankind" (§32). I will table the logically prior question of how Locke or anybody knows what God had in mind. Is he sure He did not give it to the Jews, for instance, rather than all mankind? I will confine myself to the question of just what He *did* thereby "give" us. Suppose procreation proceeds apace and the population outruns the available food supply. Then what? It would seem that *any* appropriation—including Farmer John's—sufficient to feed an individual will "thereby worsen" the situations of others in that case.

Again, we can run into complexities that we need not address here, especially because we can simply point out that the production of capitalist society is such that it is easy for all to avail themselves of sufficient food and much, much else. Nozick might then be understood to be implying that anyone who genuinely did not have enough calories—the "basic wherewithal" of life—and was unable to acquire the now wholly owned land with which he might have been able to provide it for himself would be owed a social minimum of some sort. While I think (and will argue below) that is wrong as well, I can agree that, as Blincoe observes, "focusing on welfare instead of actual appropriation makes the proviso much easier to satisfy" (Blincoe, p. 24). Blincoe notes too that Nozick thinks his formulation takes care of the appropriation of, say, the only water hole in a desert area or of an island on which an unfortunate castaway washes up. What does the fortunate acquirer of the water hole or the island owe to the thirsty traveler or the castaway? Nozick seems to say it is enough to keep the latter two alive. And in so doing, he appears to imply that we will need more than just liberty. That is, we must not only refrain from doing violence to these folks, but also allow them some water or whatever else even if they did nothing to acquire it themselves from the resources still available after others' appropriations.

I have previously insisted that the Lockean proviso prohibits "only (and all) worsening *in respect of previously acquired possessions.*"[4] (I unfortunately left out the qualification that the possessions in question must themselves have been legitimately acquired by libertarian criteria—that is, without robbing or otherwise invading somebody else. I will assume this qualification is met.) Now, our own bodies are "acquired" at birth. Thereafter we have parents and others who may provide sustenance or whatever at will, and later on, when we have some capability, we are entitled to whatever we find or make that

---

[4] Jan Narveson, "Property Rights: Original Acquisition and Lockean Provisos," *Public Affairs Quarterly*, vol. 13, no. 3, 1999, pp. 205–27, and in my *Respecting Persons in Theory and Practice* (Lanham: Rowman and Littlefield), ch. 8, pp. 111–30.

was not already found or made by others, along with whatever we acquire by free exchange or gift (e.g., from loving parents). This understanding makes it clear that the traveler in the desert, or the castaway, does not have the basic libertarian right to provision by owners of now-needed resources, which is presumably what Blincoe is talking about.

There are all sorts of good reasons why we nevertheless should in general be ready to help such unfortunates, but that does not amount to recognition of basic rights. Of course, conventions with considerable force are usually in place. Having traveled in Algeria, for example, I can attest that motorists there will always stop if they spot a stranded traveler, and it is certainly a norm of the desert that one do so. (This is prior to the age of jihadism, to be sure. What travelers would do nowadays, I do not know. But in just about everyone's normal experience, the observation is reiterated in innumerable contexts: flood victims taken in by neighbors, you and I tossing a dollar or two into the hat of the beggar, so many of us sending off a hundred or two hundred a year to agencies devoted to helping remote indigents, and so on.) The point is that the all-too-ready inference that libertarianism requires a system of coercively supplied support for the indigent can and should be resisted. It does not follow from any version of the proviso that is compatible with the principle of liberty from which Locke and Nozick intended to derive it.

Enter Farmer John

But now a new question looms. Blincoe turns to

> the more common case of the poor individual in conditions of moderate scarcity. Nozick recognizes the need to compensate both sorts of people. However, I will argue that in the latter case, Nozick greatly underestimates the magnitude of compensation required to justify the appropriations in question. The case of the poor individual will force Nozick to admit much more substantial levels of compensation and push his ET [entitlement theory] beyond the minimal state. (p. 25; footnotes omitted)

There are two ways to counter this argument. One is that people nowadays, despite often being unable to acquire land, are better off because of the manifold goods they can now acquire instead. Indeed they are; but the claim will be plausible only if we suppose that what is at issue is certain fairly typical values that just about everyone has, specifically regarding supplies of food, water, clothing, and shelter. We do not normally extend this to more exotic desires.

But what if those are not the relevant values in a given case? Blincoe now imagines "an individual, John, who finds himself on the lower rungs of the socioeconomic ladder. John has an intense desire to execute the modest life plan of farming his own land" (p. 33). Given his circumstances, John is currently a waiter, doing all right but not nearly well enough to save enough capital to realize his real life ambition, which is to live as he could have done in America in 1740, where after much sweat and toil, "John is his own master and lives off his own plot of land. The ability to pursue his cherished life plan is a great boon to John's level of welfare." So, as things are now, "Waiter John cannot plausibly pursue, much less attain, his life plan."

The situation is as follows, then:

> Waiter John also has a color television with five channels, a secondhand spring mattress, and a fridge full of Busch Lite. Farmer John's cabin life lacks these modern wonders. Does this not clearly show that a modern waiter is better off than a frontier farmer? I think not...
>
> The reason Nozick and Narveson are wrong on this point is because they weight (non-natural) material wealth too heavily when determining a person's welfare. (p. 35)

Blincoe thinks John, who had his heart set on being an independent farmer, which he could have been if those nasty capitalists had not moved in first and devoted the desired land to more efficient farming (profitable exchange in turn leading to manufacturing and such), is in fact worse off, given his desires, than he would have been in the eighteenth century. Now, alas, there is no land left that Waiter John can afford to buy.

The case for Nozickian compensation to such as John apparently runs as follows: Before others' acts of appropriation, there was plenty for all. After them, there is not, even though no one steals anything from anybody. This leaves many worse off than in the pre-appropriation condition. So compensation is due them.

The case as it stands is very shaky, of course. That John's heart is set on having land is irrelevant: Libertarianism does not promise that we will realize our dreams, whatever they may be. What it promises is only freedom, and that John has, along with everyone else (I am assuming). Everyone's exercise of that freedom led to a situation in which John cannot get what he wants. It often does, for all of us. Could John actually have what he wants now? Sure, if all sorts of things had been different, as Blincoe's depiction of the 1740s version of Farmer John exemplifies. But our question is whether we (the rest of us, I guess) owe him a plot and some primitive tools as a result of our previous actions, and the answer to that, I shall argue, is no. What we owed him and everybody else is, as Locke's "law of nature" makes perfectly clear, not to worsen his situation as it was. He never did have that farm, and it is not the eighteenth century anymore, so the fact that an earlier predecessor might have been in a position to have one is not to the point. Nobody has at present deprived him of it.

Have we deprived him of the *opportunity* to acquire a farm? No. The available land is now all owned by people, none of whom, evidently, are ready to give it to John to help him realize his dream or sell it to him at a price he would be able and willing to pay. But one might point out that if he did have either the money or the borrowing power to pursue that wish, there is always land for sale, typically within the capability of persons of normal means to buy if they are really ready to sweat it, as eighteenth-century John obviously was. But suppose Waiter John really is incapable, however persistently he tries, to manage that. Then one is tempted to say: so it goes. I have always wanted a 747, but, alas, it is far beyond my means, and nobody seems to want to supply me with one for free. Tough, but it is nobody's fault.

What the acquisition of available land does is to prevent anyone from simply acquiring that particular bit of land by stumbling upon it and setting up shop. But mankind never had an obligation to save some land for the Johns of this world (nor did Locke's God!), and it never will. Mankind does not have an obligation to save up for everybody who wants to live out his 1740s daydreams. A world in which most people did so is unlikely to have existed, to be sure, and is certainly not available any longer. But that fact is not such as to convict us of depriving John of something to which he is entitled by libertarian criteria.

Who, we should ask, does John think he is? Back in the days when all people were hunter-gatherers, the Johns among them would not have been able to conceive of becoming pioneer farmers. Were they deprived of farmland? One presumes not. Twenty centuries later, as it happens, a would-be Farmer John can not only conceive of but actually realize such a dream. But then, two centuries later still, becoming an inefficient gentleman farmer or a Thoreauvian independent is, we will assume, too expensive for John. What makes it too expensive is its inefficiency, the progress of everyone else (progress as seen by all those others), and our own particular inabilities combined with bad luck (as would-be farmer John sees it: bad luck at having been born two centuries too late).

Still, we can all have whatever we want (in the way of nonlethal goods and services), up to the limit of what we can afford. But does anyone owe us a higher income? Why? Thieves do, if we have been robbed, and no doubt assorted governments might, owing to their muddled policies and the ill-conceived visions on which they waste our money. But Johns are not owed the realization of an eighteenth-century dream financed by taxes imposed by people who sympathize with the Johns but paid by people most of whom do not sympathize with them—at least, not to the point of being ready to give them enough money. (Maybe they should try crowdfunding.)

As I say, the Lockean proviso appears to have been intended by Locke to be about land in particular. But in that form, it is untenable, as contemporary commentators all realize. With seven billion of us, there simply is no way to "leave enough, and as good, for others" if land is the unit of value. (Of course, we all, plutocrats and marginal farmers alike, do leave enough and as good for whoever can afford it, if they are interested.) But are we left with, if not enough land, then something else that is "as good"? If the measure of value is the dreams of individuals, then we very likely are not. But it is inconceivable that Locke meant that. If the measure of the relevant value is provided by the market though—as of course it should be—then the comparison is between what John can acquire with his twenty-first-century waiter's income and what he could acquire with what would be the economic value of his eighteenth-century pioneer's income. Then the modest wage wins by a huge margin. With his current level of income, John can realize many dreams that he would not have had in the eighteenth century as well as some that he would (such as watching programs on his nice color TV). Which is better? That is for John to decide. But we do not have to cater to his preferences by fulfilling them. All we owe him is that we not intervene in his life to prevent him from even trying, provided the restriction that he respect others' rights. Success is not part of the bargain. Liberty is.

We must remember that no one is in a position to compensate a would-be eighteenth-century John for becoming only a twenty-first century waiter instead. The waiter John has not been deprived of anything, for he never had what Blincoe alleges he was deprived of: the opportunity, without cost, to pull up stakes, go forth into a wilderness, and put it under the plow (or whatever his fancied farming life would be like). It is possible that some of his remote ancestors were deprived of such opportunities. Perhaps they ran afoul of a press gang, or a criminal gang, or whatever. But the parents of modern John were not so deprived, and presumably did what they could for young John without having acquired anything at the expense of anyone else in the process. How could the relevant baseline be anything else, if it is only the right to liberty that is in question?

Of course, Locke is wrong anyway, at least on one account of his claims. Acquirers owe it to all that they not acquire what is already someone else's. That is the substance of Locke's law of nature. But they do not owe to everyone else not yet arrived on the scene the opportunity to acquire the same sort of thing their predecessors may have acquired before them, including land. Suppose it is true, as Blincoe states in a footnote, that the desire for land is neither rare nor strange. That does not mean it is satisfiable, or that we owe everyone the satisfaction of this non-rare desire. Is Blincoe suggesting that modern efficient farms in Iowa, with production worth several million dollars a year, be broken up and returned as plots to the contemporary poor, for them to work on with eighteenth-century technology? Or that those big, hugely productive, and highly profitable farms should be broken up, involuntarily, à la Stalin and Mao, thus violating the very sort of freedom Blincoe believes the pioneers had? (Suppose would-be farmer John has his dream realized. Will he be happy to have his modest plot broken up to accommodate even poorer immigrants with similar dreams?)

The State-of-Nature Baseline

Talk of legitimate acquisition requires, in the end, a baseline: what is our point of departure in assessing the worsening and bettering of situations? The law of nature has it that we owe it to all to not worsen their situations (insofar as they are themselves innocent of violations of the law of nature). What is our basic situation, as humans? Just what do we have the duty not only to refrain from depriving people of—bringing them below that level—but in fact to provide if it is lacking? In material terms, contrary to what so many (including Blincoe) seem to think, there is none.

Blincoe states:

> But if compensation is requisite, it is not the original appropriation that comes into question. Nor is it the system as a whole at all times that comes into question. Rather, what comes into question is the system as a whole at some stage (or stages) in its development, namely the stage(s) at which it is no longer possible to appropriate some resource. (p. 39)

Of course, it is no longer possible to appropriate any exhausted resource. No mere normative principle can, King Canute-like, control the amount of stuff in the world. But if we respect the Lockean law of nature, we also cannot take it from someone who happened to get to it first and who is therefore now the legitimate owner. What we owe each other, what we are to refrain from worsening others in respect of, and so, what we "started out with," is not any particular amount of any particular sort of stuff (land, food, or whatever) but rather freedom (i.e., nonviolence), the very thing we lack in the hypothetical state of nature that contractarian theory hopes to save us from. And we all can extend that good to all, to the richest and the poorest, without any consequent deprivation, and we can do so at any time.

Meanwhile, anyone, rich or poor, can deprive anyone else of liberty, or at least reduce his supply of it, given enough spleen, ill will, and energy. Indeed, it is the intent of Locke's law of nature to forbid precisely that: it bids us that we not deprive anyone of his (or her) health, life, liberty, or property, all of which deprivations are ways of attacking him (or her). But so long as we refrain from depriving anyone of those things, we are home free as far as fundamental Lockean justice is concerned, and doing so does not leave people with a farm as their fair share. And if someone has very little health, liberty, or property, then that is very sad, and it will be very easy for us not to deprive him of the little that he has (you cannot take from somebody what he does not have), but we do not violate the Lockean law by not taking steps to improve his situation.

Consider the important case of someone who *has* been deprived of something to which he has a just claim—but deprived by someone else. For example, if A has enslaved B, does C owe it to B to free him, even if he can? What do we, who did not do that depriving, owe him as compensation? Basically, nothing. It would, of course, be lovely, or possibly heroic, if C did some such thing. But C did not put B in that state, and so has no basic duty to get him out. Many Dutch non-Jews took steps to prevent numerous Jews from falling into the hands of the Nazis, at great risk to their own lives. They are heroes. They were not compensating those Jewish people (unless we assume prior complicity, which we in general cannot). They were going beyond the requirements of sheer duty, and we owe them our admiration, but not our payrolls or our lives, for it.

Freedom leaves us, instead, with the right to seize whatever opportunities we can find that are compatible with their being voluntarily offered and taken. The sky is the upper limit, and of course the gutter the lower. But in neither case need the individual in question have been invaded and despoiled by anyone.

That is a far cry from contemporary conceptions of social minima and the like, of course. The point is that there is no way to justify those minima, in general, on the basis of restitution for former wrongs, if liberty is our guide. (Whether we can justify such things on the basis of some kind of contemporary social contract, specific to the circumstances of our time, is another question. My point is only that so far as the fundamental agreement with our fellows is concerned, the minima simply are not included.)

Contemporary Life, Hunter-Gatherers, and What "We" Owe

Blincoe appeals to the recent work of Karl Widerquist and Grant McCall[5] in support of the expanded claim that the contemporary poor are actually worse off, by and large, than the hunter-gatherer societies of many millennia past (and some at present, as in New Guinea and the Amazon). These comparisons are, of course, dodgy. It is not only that in all likelihood, most hunter-gatherers would jump at the chance to join the ranks of today's "poor" such as Waiter John, who, as Blincoe says, manages to have "a color television with five channels, a secondhand spring mattress, and a fridge full of Busch Lite" (p. 35). Some evidence is perhaps provided by the fact that they apparently have taken that chance in comparable situations. For examples, see Jared Diamond's account of his return to Port Moresby, New Guinea, sixty years after first contacts with the natives: "New Guinea highlanders in 1931 were scantily clothed in grass skirts, net bags over their shoulders, and headdresses of bird feathers, but in 2006 they wore the standard international garb of shirts, trousers, skirt, shorts, and baseball caps… [In the interval, they] had learned to write, use computers, and fly airplanes."[6]

What matters, however, is whether the alternatives are relevant. As depicted by many anthropologists, hunter-gatherer communities were anarchic. Modern societies are anything but. Still, it is just possible for people in contemporary states such as the United States to create social units of comparable types. It is even legal, and some people do it, though they cannot quite escape the long hand of government by doing so. And it is not popular, for whatever that is worth. Does the compensation Blincoe calls for include dismantling the government? He does not seem to recognize that possibility. Instead, he takes it that governments could assess the relevant variables in the good life and then compensate the unhappy would-be farmers so as to make their lives more like those of hunter-gatherers as depicted by Widerquist and McCall (and their many sources). (We might note that to do this, one requisite step would seem to be to kill off around 90 percent of the American population, since that is the only way that everyone could be a Farmer John. It would also reduce them to something like the agro-technological level of their eighteenth-century forebears, which I suppose is part of the Farmer John dream, since otherwise the corner store beckons as a more sensible and much less stressful alternative.) Otherwise, Blincoe will likely have to make

---

[5] Karl Widerquist and Grant McCall, *Prehistoric Myths in Modern Political Philosophy* (Edinburgh: Edinburgh University Press, 2017).

[6] Jared Diamond, *The World until Yesterday* (New York: Viking, 2012).

do with the sort of efforts the American welfare state currently does make. What he says is:

> This guarantee of welfare will be required in order to compensate those (many) people who are worse off in light of how far the system of private property has developed and how much they value autonomy or self-mastery. Material wealth and comforts, at the right level, could perhaps compensate for lost opportunities to appropriate land. However, the more appropriate compensation might be to make it possible, for those who desire it, to purchase land to farm (or make some other opportunity possible short of appropriation). Whatever form the compensation takes, it will cost the state some money, which means the state will need to institute a redistributive tax scheme. (p. 36)

In this passage, Blincoe seems unaware—like so many "liberal" writers of today—of the extent to which America already has instituted a redistributive tax scheme. The results make America's much-lamented income inequality look quite a bit different from what most people, evidently including Widerquist and McCall, seem to think, as pointed out recently by Robert Samuelson.[7] And as to costing "some money," does Blincoe think welfare states are cheap? The American government's budget is currently devoted, to the tune of a couple of trillion dollars, to health, retirement, and other welfare expenditures, in addition to comparably huge amounts from state and local governments. Whether it is actually due to these state activities that American poor people are as well off as they are[8] (in these conventional terms) is extremely difficult to say since we do not know how they would fare if things were as vastly different as the absence of government welfare expenditures would make them. That is subject matter for further investigation, going well beyond the terms relevant to the present discussion.

The advantage of liberty in this regard is that instead of having a central coercive agency decide what is good for people, they get to proceed on their own values, apart from the restriction that they be nonviolent ones. Whether the result will be that people live like ancient hunter-gatherers or modern

---

[7] Robert Samuelson, "The Messy Truth about Income Inequality," *Washington Post*, March 22, 2018, available at: https://www.washingtonpost.com/opinions/the-messy-truth-about-income-inequality/2018/03/22/4504af5a-2de0-11e8-8ad6-fbc50284fce8_story.html?utm_term=.e196e26102f8.

[8] For one among many quick summaries of the situation, see Robert Rector, "Poverty and the Social Welfare State in the United States and Other Nations," *Heritage Foundation*, September 16 2015, available at: https://www.heritage.org/welfare/report/poverty-and-the-social-welfare-state-the-united-states-and-other-nations.

Waiter Johns is indeterminate. To be sure, we often will not succeed in achieving our goals, especially if our desires are as exotic as would-be farmer John's. Still, we can well ask: is there any compensating for that?

Blincoe concludes with the claim that compensatory taxes are not forced labor. But what he proposes to compensate people for is something we do not owe them. And all taxes, as such, would seem to be forced labor on the face of it, for Nozick's obvious reason: they compel us to part with money we have legitimately earned and had no choice about paying. We should not seize upon over-hasty formulations by Nozick as the ultimate analysis of what liberty is all about.

Quality Check: A Contextual Analysis of the Lockean Proviso

J.K. Numao[*]

Introduction

IN CHAPTER FIVE of the *Second Treatise* (1689),[1] "Of Property," Locke makes an attempt to justify the individual's right to appropriate natural resources from the common stock in the state of nature subject to what has come to be known as the "sufficiency limitation/proviso," "enough-and-as-good proviso," or "Lockean/Locke's proviso"[2]—namely, a proviso requiring "enough, and as good" be left in common for others after one's appropriation (Locke 1988, II.27, 33).[3] Locke's proviso has generated much debate among scholars, especially in libertarian circles, particularly about how

---

[*] J.K. Numao is assistant professor of foreign languages and liberal arts at Keio University, Japan. He would like to thank Dr. Takuya Furuta for his comments on an earlier draft, and also two anonymous reviewers for their invaluable comments and suggestions.

CITATION INFORMATION FOR THIS ARTICLE:

J.K. Numao. 2018. "Quality Check: A Contextual Analysis of the Lockean Proviso." *Libertarian Papers*. 10 (1): 61-82. ONLINE AT: libertarianpapers.org. THIS ARTICLE IS subject to a Creative Commons Attribution 3.0 License (creativecommons.org/licenses).

[1] References to Locke's *First Treatise* and *Second Treatise* (Locke 1988) are by treatise number (I or II) and paragraph number.

[2] I will be using these terms interchangeably hereafter.

[3] Some commentators have raised questions about the role of this clause as a proviso. See, e.g., Waldron (1979) and Schmidtz (1990). Jeremy Waldron argues that the proviso is best understood not as a proviso but as a sufficiency condition, while David Schmidtz claims it is best seen as an imperative requiring appropriation.

best to interpret it and which reading can be best defended from a normative standpoint. This article aims to contribute to the former, exegetical question of how best to understand Locke's proviso through a contextual analysis of his often neglected writings. In the process, it will also defend the reading from two criticisms, one that it is untenable and the other that it is potentially imperialistic. In doing so, it also offers an outlook that blends certain aspects of left- and centrist libertarianism, broadening the options for the normative discussion. The article will end with a brief reflection on the implications of the reading defended for how libertarians might understand and approach Locke's proviso.

It is necessary briefly to clarify what is meant by "how best to interpret" the proviso, not least because more than one sense is suggested in the literature. What I wish to do is to approach what Locke himself could have meant by the proviso—that is, to try to understand Locke on his own terms. This should be distinguished from a Locke-inspired approach that tries to show what Locke would or should have said if he had had our "superior vantage-point" (Otsuka 2003, 1–2; cf. Mack 1995), or from the normative approach that seeks to identify the most "plausible," the "right," or the "correct" interpretation from a normative standpoint (Narveson 1999, 205, 208; Wendt 2018, 169). The normative question will not be the focus of this article.

The reading I identify as Locke's is one that shares the language and structure of left-libertarians' analysis while making a weaker demand than the left (in fact, more like that of centrist and right-libertarians), and in actual content coming closer to the centrists. As many commentators have noted, there is both a quantitative ("enough") and qualitative ("as good") component in the proviso (e.g., Tomasi 1998, 450). In this article, I will be concerned only with the qualitative aspect. Regarding the qualitative component, left-libertarians have suggested that Locke was defending a strict egalitarian proviso, one that demands people be left with both a "quantitatively and qualitatively similar bundle of natural objects" (Steiner 1977, 45). Right-libertarians reject this reading and accuse the left of attributing to Locke an untenable and even preposterous doctrine, and instead interpret Locke as requiring less stringently that only as good a resource as existed before the appropriation took place must be left for others (Mack 2013; see also Mack 1995; 2002).[4] Falling in between are

---

[4] Indeed, some left-libertarians also concur that this is the "best interpretation" of the proviso. See Vallentyne (2013).

centrist libertarians, who argue that the proviso requires sufficient resources be left for an independent living (Simmons 1992, 292–98).

In this article, I will argue that the existing literature has overlooked how Locke actually talks about quality in chapter 5. Indeed, most analyses tend not to be based on a systematic treatment of how Locke employs the idea of quality and qualitative equality in the chapter. While most analyses naturally tend to focus on the text of the proviso itself, or, at most, on the proviso considered within the context of the chapter, I will take as my starting point Locke's commentaries on wine in his journal entries and *Observations upon the Growth and Culture of Vines and Olives* (1680) together with his remarks on land in his writings about interest rates. What will emerge from my analysis is that Locke's proviso was structurally formulated in the left's mold, and coherently so (contra the right-libertarian criticisms), showing that Locke thought it would be easily met, thanks to his optimism informed by the particular circumstances of the seventeenth century and, more importantly, by the specific way he believed qualitative equality could be achieved, which rendered inequalities in certain other aspects irrelevant.

Locke's Proviso and the Problem of Indeterminacy

In this section, I will briefly sketch the interpretation of Locke's proviso I will be defending and show how it shares a common structure with that of left-libertarians' analysis. I then introduce the concerns and criticisms made by other libertarians and non-libertarians (and indeed by some left-libertarians) that such a reading is impractical in logistical (as opposed to normative) terms. In response, I will show that Locke had the intellectual resources to be mindful of such a problem, thereby exonerating him from any potential charge of inadvertence, and in turn, paving the way for an investigation into how the proviso is immune to the above criticisms.

I maintain that the "as good" requirement in Locke's proviso should be understood as mandating a qualitatively equal resource be left for others after one's appropriation. I do not enter into the question of whether this requires an equal quality of the same resource or whether it could be any resource that could be deemed of equal quality. Also, as indicated above, I do not discuss the quantitative part of the proviso in any detail. As I understand it, Locke seems to require only that enough and not an equal amount must be left.

The reading of Locke's proviso I defend is along the lines of what Hillel Steiner has called the "exact similarity requirement": "It imposes an egalitarian structure on individuals' appropriative entitlements, prescribing to each quantitatively and qualitatively similar bundle of natural objects" (Steiner 1977, 45). It also bears similarity to Michael Otsuka's "egalitarian proviso," which requires that one leave an "equally advantageous share of unowned worldly resources" (Otsuka 2003, 24), a formulation, Otsuka notes, that has the advantage of not confining him to such a resource-based specification of the resource to be left as Steiner's formulation does (Otsuka 2003, 47n).

I defend this reading at this point simply on the basis that it is the most straightforward reading, and, later in the article, on the basis of, or rather bolstered by, the fact that it is explainable and defensible in Locke's own terms. Indeed, when Jan Narveson, a right-libertarian, introduces five different interpretations of the proviso, noting the third of these as the "qualitative equivalence" reading—the egalitarian one we have been looking at—he writes that this is "the most obvious reading," or "natural reading," or the "most popular and natural understanding of Locke's proviso" (Narveson 1999, 210–11).[5] Yet, while it may be the most natural reading, it faces strong opposition from right-libertarians and others.

The objection to this literal interpretation stems less from a linguistic concern about whether the clause can in fact be read thus than from a logistical concern that if it is interpreted in the egalitarian mold, the proviso would have to be seen as requiring the impossible, and Locke, who propounded it, would have to have been incredibly confused. Thus, in his assessment of the egalitarian reading of the proviso, Narveson remarks that it is "hopeless" and a "complete cropper." If just as good a resource need be left for B after A's acquisition, there is a "horrendous problem" of "specifying the relevant kind to the satisfaction of all possible comers." Supposing B is entitled to "an equally fertile area of land," we must ask: "Is the land down the road 'as good'? Even if its soil is identical, perhaps the sun doesn't shine as well on it, or the shade trees along its borders are less numerous, or it's farther from town" (Narveson 1999, 210–11). Likewise, A. John Simmons, a centrist libertarian, observes that the idea of enough and as good was not an "especially clear notion." He writes, "Neither the quantitative nor the qualitative aspects of the requirement wears its meaning on its face. And however these are read, the practical difficulties of calculation in determining when enough and as good has been left are bound to be enormous, if not insuperable" (Simmons 1992, 295). If there is no way of determining what can count as "as good," then the worry is that initial acquisition is impossible, and the precept of law of nature requiring us to preserve ourselves and others cannot be met—we must starve to death (e.g., Waldron 1979, 325; Locke 1988, II.6). Thus the egalitarian reading is faced

---

[5] It should be noted that Narveson himself is not interested in arriving at the "definitive interpretation of Locke" in his article (Narveson 1999, 205).

with the crucial problem of indeterminacy with respect to qualitative equality of resources.

The problem of indeterminacy might give us reason to prefer the right-libertarian or centrist libertarian's interpretation of the proviso, which makes the less stringent demand (in an egalitarian sense) of not harming others by one's acquisition or ensuring that sufficient resources are left for an independent living (Kelly 2007, 76; Mack 1995; 2002; Simmons 1992). However, what I propose to do is to try to show that while in the end Locke's proviso does settle somewhere close to the centrist's sufficiency requirement, we need not deny that Locke was calling for some kind of qualitative equality. In other words, while Locke's proviso required qualitative equality in the resources to be left, what that stipulated was only that qualitatively sufficient resources with respect to survival and reasonable comfort be guaranteed.

Before moving on to the task of showing how this reading of Locke's proviso is immune to the problem of indeterminacy, I will attempt to flesh out how Locke in fact talked about quality and qualitative equality in his writing. While what emerges from this survey might seem obvious and redundant to some readers, I nonetheless maintain it is important to lay it out, partly because it demonstrates what ideas were available to Locke, and so it can help us to see what views we can reasonably attribute to him, but also because it may defend him from the potential charge that he lacked foresight in not being able to see that there could be a plurality of ways in which the quality of a certain resource can be understood (Lloyd Thomas 1995, 110). What becomes apparent through this survey is that Locke could have been mindful of most of the typical criticisms leveled at the egalitarian reading, thus suggesting that if his proviso indeed shared the language and structure of the left-libertarians' (as I argue), the content of such a proviso would need to be different from a demand for exact qualitative equality in all aspects.

Despite the fact that there has been much discussion about Locke's proviso, as I see it there has not been much discussion about how Locke actually talks about quality in chapter 5 and how those assumptions figured in his argument there. Wherever one stands concerning Locke's proviso, it seems the interpretations or appraisals are based solely on a textual analysis of the proviso itself and its variants in the chapter, a limited number of other passages in the chapter, or the proviso considered within the overall discussion of the chapter. I wish to add another dimension to the debate by making use of resources outside the *Second Treatise* and thereby cast a different light on the proviso. Thus, wherever one finds oneself in the debate, there is something to gain from the analysis below—or so I hope. Focusing on land,

I will show that Locke understood both geological and geographical differences in the quality of land that seem equal at first sight.

The first thing I demonstrate is that Locke was aware that land could be the same in quantity (i.e., equal size) but of different quality. Moreover, I am talking about land that might very well be supposed to be of equal quality. To this end, I want to turn to *Observations upon the Growth and Culture of Vines and Olives*. Between 1675 and 1679, Locke spent time in France, and, among other things, learned and made observations about viticulture and wine making. His observations are recorded in his journals, and thereafter made their way to *Observations*, which he sent to his patron the Earl of Shaftesbury, to be received by the latter in February 1680. In his journal, Locke records how the appearance of land could be deceptive, causing misleading perceptions of its quality: At Pouly, "the wine is excellent good, & the soyle where the vineards are, full of litle stones soe as one would think it a very barren soyle" (Locke 1953, 248). Moreover, commenting on the difference in quality of soil in vineyards of the same region, he writes in *Observations*: "[T]here is such a particularity in the soil, that at Mr. Pontac's, near Bourdeaux, the merchants assured me that the wine growing in the very next vineyards, where there was only a ditch between, and the soil, to appearance, perfectly the same, was by no means so good. The same also they observe about Montpelier, where two vineyards, bounding one upon another, constantly produce the one good and the other bad wine" (Locke 1823, 329–30).

Locke also takes note of the relationship between sunlight and the quality of the vineyard: "They plant their vineyards both in plains and on hills, with indifferency; but say that on hills, especially opening to the east or south, the wine is best" (Locke 1823, 329). His tone is stronger in the diary: "[T]he vineard must have an opening towards east or South, or else noe good is to be expected" (Locke 1953, 51). What these passages show is that Locke had the notion of *terroir*—that is, the idea that idiosyncrasies of a region's climate and soil quality affect the quality of wine (Unwin 1998, 128). It shows that for Locke, while a piece of land could be in the same region and have the appearance of the same quality, the soil quality for wine making could be different; and even if the soil quality were the same, the openness of the land to sunlight could also influence the quality of the wine, and hence, the quality of the land for wine making. Thus Locke understood the geological differences in land quality. From this, we can also say that should he be confronted with the question of what would count as equally fertile land (cf. Narveson's questions above), he would be fully aware of how it could lead to the problem of indeterminacy.

We can also see that Locke held these views from the 1660s to the 1690s; that is, we may suppose that Locke was writing the *Second Treatise* with such knowledge around the late 1670s and early 1680s. In his early memorandum on interest (1668) and subsequent work *Some Considerations of the Consequences of the Lowering of Interest* (1692), Locke makes the following observation about land both in the earlier and later writings: "Land in its soyle being different, as some fertill, some Barren, and the products of it very various both in their sorts and value too according as their quantity and vent varies" (Locke 1991, 180); or "Land in its Soil being different, as some fertile, some barren; and the Products of it very various, both in their Sorts, goodness and vent" and so "is not capable of any fixed estimate by its quantity" (Locke 1991, 246). While this observation about the difference in land quality due to the soil quality is more general than his observations about vineyards, it still shows that he would have been mindful that the quality of land of equal size could be different from what it might seem at first sight.

A closer examination of the *Second Treatise* itself also reveals that Locke understood a geographical sense of land quality contrary to what is sometimes supposed (cf. Lloyd Thomas 1995, 110).[6] By this, I mean the worth of a piece of land depends on its distance from the epicenter of something desirable—say, economic activity. Locke writes: "For I ask, What would a Man value Ten Thousand, or an Hundred Thousand Acres of excellent *Land*, ready cultivated, and well stocked too with Cattle, in the middle of the in-land Parts of *America*, where he had no hopes of Commerce with other Parts of the World, to draw *Money* to him by the Sale of the Product?" (Locke 1988, II.48).

To be sure, this point is made in regard to a separate point about how the invention of money would motivate and enable people to enlarge their possessions. However, at the same time, it shows that a land rich in a geological sense would not have the same attractiveness, and hence worth, as a piece of land with an equal or lesser quality in a geological sense but with access to money economy. Locke seems to be suggesting that the former would be of less use than the latter and that while we might suppose for

---

[6] D.A. Lloyd Thomas seems to suggest that Locke did not recognize this: "Even if the plain extends on and on, and consists of uniformly fertile land (and no one else was there to begin with), land is not as good if it is far from existing settlement. Locke seems to be thinking very literally of the material resources necessary for survival, and not to be considering such things as the disadvantages of being in a remote place. However even from the point of view of physical survival it is usually better to be near the help of settled civilized society."

some other individual the latter might be of more worth (e.g., someone who wants to live a simple, self-sufficient life free from the consumerism of the big city), the point remains: the geographical location of a piece of land could affect its quality, and Locke was aware of that.

So by turning our eyes to Locke's writings on vineyards and interest rates, and also by a closer examination of chapter 5 itself, we can see that Locke was aware of differences in land quality in both a geological and geographical sense both before and after the writing of the *Second Treatise*. Therefore, it seems plausible to assume that if Locke had meant by the enough-and-as-good proviso that an appropriator needed to leave as good a piece of land, being mindful of the differences in land quality in these aspects he would have also been mindful of the difficulty of doing so. The question for us then is this: if Locke's proviso is to be understood in the literal sense of demanding qualitative equality, yet Locke himself is conscious of the problem of indeterminacy, how did he think the proviso was achievable?

Absences and Assumptions in Chapter 5 to Locke's Idea of Qualitative Equality

Once we appreciate that Locke could have been mindful of the impracticality of leaving a qualitatively equal piece of land, it helps us take note of some interesting and peculiar absences in chapter 5, which in turn helps us see more clearly what he might have been doing with the proviso, namely, conceptualizing qualitative equality in terms of sufficiency. There are two absences (a) I note. They are: (a1) an absence of talk about barrenness of land and (a2) an absence of talk about the differences in the natural resourcefulness of land having some kind of impact on the outcome. These absences then call attention to two assumptions (A) Locke made: first, (A1) the land remaining after acquisition is assumed to have a degree of fertility, and second, (A2) in terms of its resourcefulness, it is equal to others. Let me start by expanding on the first absence and assumption (a1 and A1).

As we saw above, in his writings on interest rates, Locke noted that some land may be fertile while other land lies barren. However, in chapter 5 of the *Second Treatise*, Locke curiously does not talk about land being barren (a1). He does talk about "wasteland," but that is not the same as it being barren. Wasteland, Locke defines, is "[l]and that is left wholly to Nature, that hath no improvement of Pasturage, Tillage, or Planting," and "is called, as indeed it is, *wast*; and we shall find the benefits of it amount to little more than nothing" (Locke 1988, II.42). In other words, it is uncultivated land. While the monetary value we reap from wasteland may not be much, this is not the same as saying such land cannot be productive with some kind of intervention. In fact, Locke's wasteland is potentially productive, and so a degree of fertility is supposed, whereas "barren" suggests a stronger, indeed, natural lack of this potentiality.[7] It is true that in Locke's time, Devonshire was known as a naturally barren land that was made productive thanks to the husbandry of the local farmers (Wood 1984, 60), but in Locke's example the county is described as an "equally *fertile* land" (Locke 1988, II.37, my emphasis), as the "uncultivated wast of America," which Locke later describes as a place "rich in Land" and whose inhabitants "Nature... furnished as liberally as any other people, with materials of Plenty, *i.e.* a fruitful Soil, apt to produce in abundance, what might serve for food, raiment, and delight" (Locke 1988, II.41).

The first of Locke's assumptions to register then is that he seems to assume a degree of fertility of land (A1). This might be explained by saying he was optimistic about the natural resourcefulness of land thanks especially to the discovery of the naturally blessed continent of America (Farr 2009), but it is also consistent with his belief in a God who provides for humankind (Locke 1988, I.41). Furthermore, this optimism seems also to relate to the faith he had in the power of labor. For a fuller story, however, we need to turn to the next absence and assumption (a2 and A2).

The second absence is that Locke seems not to accredit natural land quality for outcomes (a2) and so seems to neutralize the differences in the base or initial quality of land—that is, he makes such differences irrelevant to his discussion such that he can assume their initial land quality to be equal (A2). It is important to note that I am not using the term "quality of land" in Locke's sense of "value of land," which is computed by the income the land generates through the production of saleable commodities (Locke 1991, 180; Locke 1988, II.43). By quality of land, I am referring to the land's natural fertility or resourcefulness, its potential to yield quality products. So while land may be naturally fertile and so be of quality, its value may be very little without labor. The two, however, might also be related.

Returning to the point at hand, as in the passage cited above (Locke 1988, II.41), when comparing England and America, or more generally cultivated and uncultivated land, Locke sets these as "equally fertile land," "an acre of Land, of an equal richnesse" (Locke 1988, II.37), "an Acre of the

---

[7] *OED*, s.v. Barren: "Of Land: producing little or no vegetation; not fertile, sterile, unproductive, bare." Compare Locke 1991, 181: "Land produces naturally something new profitable and of value to man kinde, But mony is a Barren thing and produces nothing." Being barren, money does not, and cannot, generate anything new.

same Land" (Locke 1988, II.40), "an Acre of as good Land" (Locke 1988, II.43). Land in the New World, the land in the commons, is assumed to be of equal natural quality to land in England already appropriated. One may quickly object that Locke makes this assumption for an obvious reason: he is trying to establish the point that labor makes the difference in the value produced by land, all things being equal. To bring out the contrast between what he perceives as the state of affairs in England and America, Locke supposes the initial quality of land to be equal, with labor generating a great difference—that is, one hundred to one in terms of provisions (Locke 1988, II.37) or five pounds to than less a penny in terms of income (Locke 1988, II.43). Indeed, in *Some Observations*, he states: "The value of Land is raised, when its intrinsick worth is increased, *i.e.* when it is fitted to bring forth a greater quantity of any valuable Product. And thus the value of Land is raised only by good Husbandry" (Locke 1991, 357). Crucially though, in emphasizing the impact of labor, he effectively takes attention off the difference in initial natural quality of land and reduces its importance in the discussion, thereby creating the space to see different pieces of land as equal. In fact, his point seems precisely to be that the initial quality of land itself did not matter, and that it was the effect, and so value, of labor that we need to appreciate. He remarks: "The ground which produces the materials, is scarce to be reckoned in, as any, or at most, but a very small part of it [i.e., value]" (Locke 1988, II.42).

Significantly, however, this idea that the natural fertility of the land is negligible seems to contradict the ratio between labor and land quality in the observations he had made about wine making. Locke notes in *Observations*:

> Upon the skilful mixture of these several sorts of grapes, as well as on the propriety of the soil, depends, in a great measure, the goodness of their wine: though, as far as I could observe, it was not so far improved as it might; nor any other great care taken, but that there should be always a mixture of white grapes when they made their red wine, which will otherwise be too thick and deep-coloured. (Locke 1823, 334)

Likewise, in his journals, he makes the following two observations, emphasizing the difference natural land quality can make:

> The goodnesse of their wine to drink seems to depend on two causes, besides the pressing & ordering the fermentation. One is the soyle they plant in, *on which very much depends the goodnesse of the wine*; and this is a constant rule, seting a side all other qualities of the soyle, that the vineard must have an opening towards east or South, or else noe good is to be expected. The other is a mingling of good sorts of wine in their vineyards, for they seldome make red wine of red grapes alone; it will be too thick & deepe coloured except the

> Spiran which, they say, will make good wine by its self, but to make their red wine pleasant & delicate, they use to mingle a good quantity of white grapes with the red. (Locke 1953, 51, my emphasis)

And:

> But to make their wine, they generally plant of all these sorts togeather (except the Muscat) in their vineyards, & upon the skilful mixture of these, *next to* property of the soile, the goodnesse of their wine does much depend, but the soile is *so considerable* that two fields which only a ditch parts, doe one yield good wine & the other constantly bad" (Locke 1953, 52, my emphasis).

How can we make sense of this difference of emphasis? How can we explain the weight Locke puts on the natural quality of the land for wine making, but not for the case of husbandry in the *Second Treatise*? There are a number of possible explanations. One might simply be that Locke is not talking about natural quality of soil, but soil that has already been treated (or in other words, benefited from labor) in the case of the French vineyards, and not so in the *Second Treatise*. In fact, Locke notes that the locals "turn the ground" (Locke 1823, 331). However, even if this is the case, he also notes the "particularity in the soil," which, comparing vineyards only a ditch apart, is "to appearance, perfectly the same," but in terms of the final product, "by no means so good" (Locke 1823, 329). This also suggests he was thinking about the *natural* quality of the soil.

Another explanation might be that he came strongly to believe that labor—that is, good husbandry—could dramatically transform the quality of the soil, no matter how poor the quality was. While clearly optimistic about the effect of labor, there is reason to believe that Locke was not completely enchanted by its power, maintaining a critical perspective and being mindful of bogus inventions and technology. In *Observations*, he comments skeptically on a practice of making fruitful grapevines: "I have been told that a sheep's horn buried at the root of a vine will make it bear well even in barren ground. I have no great faith in it, but mention it, because it may so easily be tried" (Locke 1823, 331). Moreover, in the 1690s, Locke was consulted by a friend, John Cary, who was worried about being called a "projector," a pejorative term for those promising purported improvement schemes, for his tract on commerce (Locke 1979, 634).[8] So, while there was optimism about

---

[8] For an extensive study of projectors in early modern England, see Yamamoto (2018).

technological improvement during Locke's time, there was also skepticism about it. Locke, I believe, showed signs of both.

The most natural explanation, I believe, is that in the *Second Treatise*, while the (American) land was naturally rich and so could potentially yield plenty, Locke's point was that potentiality had of itself no value in monetary terms. Unless the potential is brought out by tilling the land, planting the grapevines, and harvesting the fruits, the land was of no value no matter how good its natural quality. This seems to be the key to understanding Locke's point. If, through our labor, we make a hogshead of wine from the land, the value we produce in that respect changes the value of the land from, say, one to one thousand. Now suppose also that thanks to the natural quality of the soil, we produce a very high quality wine, making the value of the land two thousand. It seems Locke's interest in the *Second Treatise* is with this first jump—from one (no wine) to one thousand (hogshead of average wine)— and not the jump from the average-grade wine to the high-grade wine.

At this point, I believe it helps to consider the difference in the subject matter, and, hence, the goal sought between the two writings, to understand why the jump from one to one thousand should be more of a concern for Locke in the *Second Treatise*. This is also the linking piece that bridges the discussion about absences and assumptions in chapter 5 and the discussion of how the idea of qualitative equality works in Locke's proviso. Locke's comments on the effects of soil quality in his *Observations* concern the quality of wine rather than whether it is a reasonably delightful beverage—that is, whether it is a valuable product compared to something like plain water (which is, of course, valuable, but not as valuable commercially speaking under the circumstances Locke is supposing).[9] In contrast, in the *Second Treatise*, the apparent faith in labor and disinterestedness in initial land quality (a2) (together with the assumption about a certain degree of fertility of land [A1]) seems to be a result of the goal of appropriation and labor being the less luxurious one of self-preservation and a reasonably comfortable life (Locke 1988, II.44). God had willed people to appropriate and labor to "improve it for the benefits of life," Locke writes, to take them out of their "penury" (Locke 1988, II.32). On Locke's calculation, that did not require too much in terms of the land left in a spatial sense (Locke 1988, II.33, 34,

---

[9] Although Locke takes note about the soil's effects on the quality of wine, he seems to have not been too concerned about the qualities of different French wines he was drinking. See Unwin 1998, 135.

36) and also, it seems, in a qualitative sense (Locke 1988, II.42),[10] although he does assume that land in America had all the natural blessings, "a fruitful Soil, apt to produce in abundance, what might serve for food, raiment, and delight" (Locke 1988, II.41).

We have seen Locke's disinterestedness in the initial quality of land (a2), but what of the supposition of the equality of the quality of land hinted above (A2)? Why would he believe the land in America and England to be of equal quality? Given the specific end of subsistence and convenience in the *Second Treatise*, Locke could suppose the land to be of equal quality to that end. Since the initial quality of land could be supposed good enough in the first times and in the present in America, and since it was labor that could be supposed to produce the greater part of the necessities and comforts of life in quantity and quality, though differences in land quality could exist, for the specified end they could be supposed equal. In other words, the metric of equality is relative to its end. Inequalities not related to the end could be ignored and only the relevant part measured. For subsistence and convenience, the land quality *was* equal.[11] And with the help of labor, one could equally secure these goals.

Again, one might immediately object that Locke does not talk about equality of land in this way, but rather in terms of equality of economic outcomes. In the *Second Treatise*, he writes: "An Acre of Land that bears here Twenty Bushels of Wheat, and another in *America*, which, with the same Husbandry, would do the like, are, without doubt, of the same natural, intrinsick Value" (Locke 1988, II.43). In this equation, an equal piece of land would therefore imply one that produces the same quantity of sellable products. It is interesting to note, however, that Locke stops here at saying that the equality of commodities in quantity produced (i.e., twenty bushels of wheat) seems to imply equality of land value.[12] Given that in his early writings on interest rates Locke assumed that the annual income derived from the land would determine its value, it would seem then he would also have to assume that the wheat from the two pieces of land in the example cited

---

[10] For that matter, it also did not seem to require too much effort. See Locke 1991, 493–95, "Labor."

[11] For discussions on how scales of equality are determined, see Evans 1981, 1393; McCloskey 1966, 54; Westen 1990, 30. This discussion might also have similarities with what John Rawls terms "range property." For a discussion, see Waldron 2002, 76–77.

[12] Cf. Locke (1991, 357): "The value of Land is raised, when its intrinsick worth is increased, *i.e.* when it is fitted to bring forth a greater *quantity* of any valuable Product. And thus the value of Land is raised only by good Husbandry" (my emphasis).

would be of the same market value to be able to say that the land is of equal value. However, he says nothing about the quality of the wheat produced, and so too about the potential differences in the (geological) quality of the land that yielded them. This is an interesting omission not least because he later says in *Some Considerations* that the products of land cannot yield "any fixed estimate by its quantity" (Locke 1991, 246). If the quality of wheat was different between two lands, then we might assume they would be of different value if sold in the same market, and thus would, by implication, make the two lands of different value. Nevertheless, if we suppose that the Lockean market's perspective of the wheat's use is informed by the measure of subsistence and comfort, then it could be the case that the wheat from the two lands may be of equal commercial value notwithstanding any qualitative differences between them, and so would in its turn make the value of the land producing them the same. Given that, the two lands can be supposed to be of equal value without being equal in quality as a matter of fact.[13] But if the two lands producing the same quantity of wheat are equal in value, then from that market's perspective, the wheat and hence the land can be supposed to be of equal quality too, given that the differences in the wheat have no effect on the market price. Thus, the idea of qualitative equality being relative to the purpose is not inconsistent with what Locke says about equal land value in the *Second Treatise*.

We are now in a place to see why Locke would have introduced the enough-and-as-good proviso's requirement of qualitative equality without such concern over its application and implementation as modern commentators have expressed. Given the emphasis he put on appropriation and labor aimed at improving the benefits of life, qualitative equality was required only for this end. Thus differences (inequalities) in land quality in geological and geographical aspects became unimportant. What mattered was whether there were sufficient resources in qualitative terms for our subsistence and convenience, and no more than we could use.[14] To meet this

---

[13] We can also say that while two pieces of land may be equally productive (yielding twenty bushels of wheat each year), if sold at different markets (which need not be far away but are under different circumstances), due to their geographical location, there may be a difference in income, hence, a difference in the value of the land. Thus, the land may be equally productive, but of different quality and value. Cf. Locke 1991, 496–500, "Venditio."

[14] How we see the relationship between what is enough and what we can make use of is an interesting but indeed intricate question. It is complicated because the relationship may be relative to the person. An incompetent person may only be able to make use of

A Contextual Analysis of the Lockean Proviso

limited requirement was also to meet the requirement of equality. Qualitative equality was not required on all fronts.

To conclude this section, then, we can suppose Locke to have put forward a proviso requiring qualitative equality without being troubled by the problem of indeterminacy (which he could have been mindful of) because the objective of appropriation was for the limited end of securing the natural resources for subsistence and the benefits of life, which one could improve by combining it with one's labor; and because it was for this specific end, and given too we could suppose the initial conditions of existing land to be reasonably good (A1) (i.e., it was not barren and so was workable), Locke could assume that differences in land quality did not matter that much and could suppose different pieces of land equal for that end (A2). Qualitative sufficiency for survival and comfort could be seen as guaranteeing qualitative equality.

An Inconvenient Implication of Qualitative Equality in the Proviso

So far, I have shown that Locke could be understood as offering a proviso requiring qualitative equality, while defending him from the problem of indeterminacy by showing the peculiar way in which he conceptualized it. In this final section, I want to point out one negative implication of a reading that does not take into account the specific purpose Locke had assigned to appropriation (in other words, that the proviso requires people to leave, say, "as good *simpliciter*" as opposed to "as good for the benefits of life"). My intention in bringing this up is to exonerate Locke (pre-emptively) from a criticism he had foreclosed, and also to reinforce the sense of qualitative equality he was putting forward, which was limited to a specific end.

Twice in chapter 5, Locke refers to the inland of America, each time to make a slightly different point. In the first case, in paragraph 36, Locke introduces the inland to make a point about how it was like the first ages—vacant—and to claim that while people could appropriate land there, they would only take little and would not be injuring other people. The other, in paragraph 48, as discussed earlier, is that people would not have the motivation to appropriate that much because they would not be able to trade with the outside world; they would keep to the "spoilage limitation"—that is, appropriating only what one could make use of before it spoils (Locke 1988, II.31). The latter reference, I noted, also shows that Locke recognized a

---

little, but it may be enough, while it may not be enough for another person who has greater physical needs.

geographical sense of land quality: being isolated from economic activity would lower the value of the land relative to other land of the same geological quality but closer to the epicenter of such activity.

Now, there is a question about who is appropriating land in the inlands. Because they do not cultivate the ground, the indigenous population, on Locke's description, do not seem to possess the inlands (Goldie 2016, 556; cf. Bishop 2006). If we suppose Locke is talking about English settlers, then we need to answer the following question: if the settler is entitled to a piece of land that is as good as others, who is the other we are comparing him or her to? If we suppose this settler is entitled to as good land as English people with access to commerce, this has important consequences. This would mean that to equalize the (geographical) quality of land, we would need to ensure that the inland is connected with the market. This, in other words, would justify English economic expansion into the inlands of America. Of course, this does not prevent indigenous peoples from owning land, but it would come at the cost of radically altering their (presumed) way of life, not to say losing their culture entirely.

If this was the consequence of the requirement of the proviso's qualitative equality, it is quite significant. Although the colonialist reading of Locke is nothing new, incrimination is traditionally reserved for the spoilage limitation (Arneil 1996, 143): because the indigenous population is wasting the land, the English settlers may appropriate it. On traditional accounts, the sufficiency limitation also has a role in ensuring no injury is done to the indigenous peoples by leaving enough for their subsistence. But it only plays a negative role. Only the spoilage limitation gives the justification for active colonization, whereas if an unspecified qualitative-equality reading is granted ("as good *simpliciter*"), it shows that there may be a duty to equalize the quality of land for inland English settlers, and this can be understood as doing work actively to justify English expansion. This would be the negative consequence of the qualitative-equality reading of the sufficiency limitation accepting at the same time the possibility of geographical quality of land.

However, we may reject this reading because Locke had foreclosed it by specifying where equality was required. It was not blank, unspecified equality of quality vis-à-vis others he was calling for. If it were equality on all fronts, then given that there were both inland and coastal settlers, equalizing the quality of land between them means the proviso may require coastal settlers with access to the market to provide equal access for inland settlers. However, Locke's proviso was rather a call for an equality of resources necessary for survival and the conveniences of life; in this case, while there would be a gap in the geographical quality of land between the coastal and inland settlers, the inland settlers would have enough and as good to subsist and enjoy a reasonably comfortable life, while they would also be able to leave as much to others settling inland because they would have neither the motivation nor the means to enlarge beyond a limited point. The qualitative-equality reading without a parameter would not only have to face the indeterminacy problem, but it would also create space for justifying colonialism. While we may not completely free Locke from the latter charge, at the very least we can say he did not do it through the sufficiency limitation. Thus Locke's proviso was assumed to be realizable and did not open a way to justifying expansion in the name of equality.

Concluding Remarks and Implications

When pondering why America should have been on Locke's mind at the time of composing the *Second Treatise*, David Armitage writes, "After all, wines, silks and oils are not prominent among the products alluded to in 'Of Property'" (Armitage 2013, 103). In a similar manner to something John Dunn once said about Jesus Christ and St. Paul in the *Two Treatises of Government*—that while they "may not appear in person in the text," "their presence can hardly be missed" (Dunn 1969, 99)—what I have tried to do in this article is to show that while wine did not appear markedly in chapter 5, assuming the knowledge Locke had acquired about wine making and land quality was available to him at the time of writing the *Second Treatise* can help us see how Locke intended the proviso to operate.

What my analysis shows is that Locke's proviso can be understood as sharing a common structure with left-libertarians' analysis without falling prey to the indeterminacy problem, although we need to pay close attention to how Locke conceptualized equality. As the left has claimed, Locke might be understood in the literal sense of demanding that enough and qualitatively equal a resource be left for others. However, as right-libertarians say, this is not to be taken as requiring equal quality in all conceivable aspects (Mack 2009, 63; 2013). The key question for Locke is this: equality of what *for what*? If we are entitled to equally good land for subsistence and comfort, this purpose informs whether equality of a certain kind (e.g., qualitative equality of resources) has been met.[15] Thus the demands on equality are relative to

---

[15] Cf. Varden (2012, 424). In her article, Helga Varden inquires: "Obviously, different pieces of land can provide enough resources to secure survival and conveniences, but in virtue of what can we demonstrate that they are 'as good'"? In response, we can note that the answer is in the question itself: in virtue of securing survival and convenience.

and shaped by the prescribed purpose. Conceptualizing equality as such, Locke can bypass the problem of indeterminacy.[16]

In closing, I sketch the implications of my exegetical analysis of Locke's proviso for libertarians. The first implication is that Locke cannot be pigeonholed in a left-right-center categorization. Locke displays traces of different strands of libertarian interpretations. The Lockean proviso I have depicted requires qualitative equality as the left has suggested, yet, because of the conditions under which it operates, the standard of equality is effectively broadened so that qualitative sufficiency can satisfy the qualitative-equality requirement, putting Locke in line with centrist and right-libertarians in terms of setting a lower bar than the left, and in terms of content closer to centrist libertarians. Yet he cannot be labeled as or claimed by any one of these groups. His proviso is in its own way unique and should be appreciated as such.

To see more clearly the space Locke occupies, let me briefly compare and contrast my rendering of the proviso with those of Eric Mack and A. John Simmons, representing the right and center respectively. Note I am doing this only to highlight the difference between them and not to show that one is superior to the other in a normative sense. There are a number of similarities between Locke's proviso as I present it and Mack's version, which he dubs the "self-ownership proviso" (Mack 1995; 2002). Both my version and Mack's are less stringent than the left's strict egalitarianism, in my interpretation requiring sufficiency vis-à-vis an individual's comfortable preservation and in Mack's requiring "a baseline of noninterference with that individual's employing his self-owned labor in pursuit of his comfortable preservation" (Mack 2013; see also Mack 1995). More specifically, the self-

---

[16] I do not intend to say that the subsistence and comfortable life scale is without its difficulties. As Lloyd Thomas noted (note 6 above), even if we suppose Locke was "thinking very literally of the material resources necessary for survival, and not to be considering such things as the disadvantages of being in a remote place," we may still say "from the point of view of physical survival it is usually better to be near the help of settled civilized society." In other words, geographical quality of land would have implications for our survival and comfort, and hence would have to enter our calculation of leaving as good for others. Other problems might include dealing with people with expensive tastes. However, all I am claiming is that Locke's perspective would significantly reduce the number of questions relative to a demand for qualitative equality without any relevant criteria. Also pace Lloyd Thomas, the point I am making is that Locke did have the resources to envision such problems, but simply did not see them as relevant from his perspective of what was necessary for survival and comfort.

ownership proviso "is satisfied if and only if the institution, development, and elaboration of private property yields an economic environment that is at least as receptive to that individual's deploying his talents, efforts, and time in pursuit of his comfortable preservation as the pre-property environment would have been" (Mack 2013; see also Mack 2009, 63). Moreover, like the Locke I have depicted, Mack maintains that it is "relatively easy for a socioeconomic system to satisfy the demands" of the proviso (Mack 2002, 245).

However, a point to note is that Mack's self-ownership proviso is concerned not so much with one's entitlement to property as with one's use of property, namely the concern that people may not harm others (i.e., disable their "world interactive powers," or "capacity to affect [their] extra-personal environment in accord with [their] purposes") by using their property while the property might rightfully belong to them (Mack 1995, 186–87). Thus, as Fabian Wendt points out, in a case in which an individual's economic opportunities are limited not as a result of another agent's use of property nor in a case where an individual's opportunities are open but the individual does not have sufficient resources, Mack's proviso seems to offer little in support (Wendt 2018, 179). In contrast, the Lockean proviso I have illustrated maintains that individuals are entitled to a qualitative equal—that is, sufficient resources for comfortable preservation.

Centrists like Simmons similarly argue that the proviso should guarantee individuals what is sufficient for an independent living: they must be guaranteed what is needed for their self-preservation and self-government (Simmons 1992, 292–98). However, while the centrist's sufficientarian proviso might call for sufficiency of resources, it may be open to the left's criticism of not taking seriously enough people's equal entitlement to resources (e.g., Vallentyne and van der Vossen 2014). This takes me to the second implication I wish to highlight.

My second point is that Locke's proviso as it stands invites us to appreciate that equality can be conceptualized in broader terms, which is defined by the end for which it is demanded. For Locke, the purpose and scale of equality was fixed by the idea of subsistence and convenience derived from the duties and rights prescribed to us by God. On this scale, exact qualitative equality of resources was not needed, but rather resources that were qualitatively sufficient for survival and comfort could meet the requirement of equality. However, the point I have tried to impress is that it is an account of equality.

The point of this article has not been to say that Locke was a left-libertarian egalitarian. For Locke, equality mattered, but not in all conceivable senses. He had his own way of identifying which aspects of it mattered, and devised a realistic way of guaranteeing a certain form of equality to individuals living in a unique world where no two things are exactly the same. Locke shows we can remain sensitive to equality yet at the same time adopt a realistic perspective ensuring that equality exists not for its own sake but for the goal of achieving a reasonable living for all, a living that can be made better or worse through human effort. What is interesting therefore is the way he blends the ideal of equality with a kind of realism. Thus, in contrast to centrists, Locke can exploit the rhetorical force of equality. Whether this blend between left- and centrist libertarianism does better from a normative standpoint than the unadulterated formulations, however, is a subject for another paper.

References

Armitage, David. 2013. "John Locke, Carolina and the *Two Treatises of Government*." In *Foundations of Modern International Thought*. Cambridge: Cambridge University Press.

Arneil, Barbara. 1996. *John Locke and America*. Oxford: Clarendon Press.

Bishop, John Douglas. 2006. "Locke's Theory of Original Appropriation and the Right of Settlement in Iroquois Territory." In *John Locke*, ed. Peter Anstey, 254–77. New York: Routledge.

Dunn, John. 1969. *The Political Thought of John Locke*. Cambridge: Cambridge University Press.

Evans, Bette Novit. 1981. "Equality, Ambiguity, and Public Choice." *Creighton Law Review* 14: 1385–1408

Farr, James. 2009. "Locke, "Some Americans", and the Discourse on "Carolina"." *Locke Studies* 9: 19–94.

Goldie, Mark. 2016. "Locke and America." In *A Companion to Locke*, ed. Matthew Stuart, 546–563. Chichester: Wiley Blackwell.

Kelly, Paul. 2007. *Locke's Second Treatise of Government*. London and New York: Continuum.

Lloyd Thomas, D.A. 1995. *Locke on Government*. London and New York: Routledge.

Locke, John. 1823. "Observations upon the Growth and Culture of Vines and Olives." In *The Works of John Locke*, vol.10. London: Thomas Tegg.

Locke, John. 1953. *Locke's Travels in France 1675–1679*, ed. John Lough. Cambridge: Cambridge University Press.

Locke, John. 1979. *The Correspondence of John Locke*, vol.5, ed. E.S. De Beer. Oxford: Clarendon Press.

Locke, John. 1988. *Two Treatises of Government*, ed. Peter Laslett. Cambridge: Cambridge University Press.

Locke, John. 1991. *Locke on Money*, 2 vols., ed. Patrick Hyde Kelly. Oxford: Clarendon Press.

Mack, Eric. 1995. "The Self-Ownership Proviso: A New and Improved Lockean Proviso." *Social Philosophy and Policy* 12 (1): 186–218.

Mack, Eric. 2002. "Self-Ownership, Marxism, and Egalitarianism" (Parts I and II). *Politics, Philosophy & Economics* 1: 75–108 and 237–76.

Mack, Eric. 2009. *John Locke*. New York and London: Bloomsbury.

Mack, Eric. 2013. "Locke on Property." "Liberty Matters" Online Discussion. Available at: http://oll.libertyfund.org/pages/john-locke-two-treatises-1689.

McCloskey, H.J. 1966. "Egalitarianism, Equality and Justice." *Australasian Journal of Philosophy* 44 (1): 50–69.

Narveson, Jan. 1999. "Property Rights: Original Acquisition and Lockean Provisos." *Public Affairs Quarterly* 13 (3): 205–27.

Otsuka, Michael. 2003. *Libertarianism without Inequality*. Oxford: Clarendon Press.

Schmidtz, David. 1990. "When is Original Appropriation Required?." *The Monist* 73 (4): 504–18.

Simmons, A. John. 1992. *The Lockean Theory of Rights*. Princeton: Princeton University Press.

Steiner, Hillel. 1977. "The Natural Right to the Means of Production." *Philosophical Quarterly* 27: 41–9.

Tomasi, John. 1998. "The Key to Locke's Proviso." *British Journal for the History of Philosophy* 6 (3): 447–54.

Unwin, Tim. 1998. "Locke's Interest in Wine." *Locke Newsletter* 29: 119–151.

Vallentyne, Peter. 2013. "Peter Vallentyne's Response to "Mack on Locke on Property"." "Liberty Matters" Online Discussion. Available at: http://oll.libertyfund.org/pages/john-locke-two-treatises-1689.

Vallentyne, Peter and van der Vossen, Bas. 2014. "Libertarianism." *Stanford Encyclopedia of Philosophy*. Available at: https://plato.stanford.edu/entries/libertarianism/.

Varden, Helga. 2012. "The Lockean "Enough-and-as-Good" Proviso: An Internal Critique." *Journal of Moral Philosophy* 9: 410–42.

Waldron, Jeremy. 1979. "Enough and as Good Left for Others." *Philosophical Quarterly* 29: 319–28.

Waldron, Jeremy. 2002. *God, Locke, and Equality*. Cambridge: Cambridge University Press.

Wendt, Fabian. 2018. "The Sufficiency Proviso." In *The Routledge Handbook of Libertarianism*, eds. Jason Brennan et al, 169–83. New York and London: Routledge.

Westen, Peter. 1990. *Speaking of Equality*. Princeton: Princeton University Press.

Wood, Neal. 1984. *John Locke and Agrarian Capitalism*. Berkeley: University of California Press.

Yamamoto, Koji. 2018. *Taming Capitalism before its Triumph*. Oxford: Oxford University Press.

The Lockean Proviso and the Value of Liberty: A Reply to Narveson

Adam Blincoe*

I. Introduction

"THE VALUE OF ANYTHING lies in what we can do with it."[1] Jan Narveson originally wrote those words while considering the value of natural resources in the context of developing a properly liberal reading of the Lockean proviso. It would seem Narveson is largely correct. Even if one does not restrict the value of things in the world to instrumental value, it is clear this is largely what it consists in. We value stuff because we can do stuff with it. It is usually the activities themselves (and our enjoyment of them) that we see as intrinsically valuable. This account of value is especially apt when applied to liberty itself. That is, we do not value liberty per se; rather, we value "what we can do with it." One could imagine a world in which the exercise of one's liberty was so restricted (i.e., a world in which we could do little with our liberty) that one might as well have no liberty at all; perhaps this is a world where one in fact lacks any liberty worthy of the name. Narveson favors a reading of the Lockean proviso derived from, and only constrained by, the more fundamental principle of liberty.[2] He thinks this

---

*Adam Blincoe is Honors Faculty Scholar at Longwood University.

CITATION INFORMATION FOR THIS ARTICLE:

Adam Blincoe. 2018. "The Lockean Proviso and the Value of Liberty: A Reply to Narveson." *Libertarian Papers*. 10 (1): 83-94. ONLINE AT: libertarianpapers.org. THIS ARTICLE IS subject to a Creative Commons Attribution 3.0 License (creativecommons.org/licenses).

[1] "Property Rights: Original Acquisition and Lockean Replies," *Public Affairs Quarterly* 13, no. 3 (July 1999): 221.

[2] See page 52 of "Would-Be Farmer John and the Welfare State," *Libertarian Papers* 10, no. 1 (2018): 49–60.

results in a liberal theory of property that avoids requiring compensation or a social-welfare minimum for the poor. I will argue that the principle of liberty itself leads to such requirements.

This is an extension of an argument begun in my essay "Forcing Nozick beyond the Minimal State: The Lockean Proviso and Compensatory Welfare."[3] Narveson recently wrote a forceful reply in this journal entitled "Would-Be Farmer John and the Welfare State: A Reply to Blincoe."[4] Despite our ultimate disagreement, there is plenty of initial agreement between myself and Narveson concerning Nozick's rendering of the Lockean proviso. The Lockean proviso constrains initial acquisition of resources; the key question is *how* it constrains this acquisition.[5] The proviso requires one to leave as much and as good for others.[6] Nozick takes this to mean that one's acquisition is just if it does not worsen another's plight, not with respect to the ability to appropriate resources, but rather with respect to personal welfare. Narveson agrees with me that, in focusing on welfare, Nozick (and ostensibly others) make the proviso much easier to satisfy.[7] This is because, apparently, those who cannot appropriate some resource can still benefit from the immense social capital produced from the use of those resources by others.[8] Narveson also seems to agree that this is the right reading of Nozick's treatment, and I take it he concedes some of my case against Nozick: namely, that this focus on welfare opens Nozick up to an objection (at least in principle). I advanced this objection in my original essay, in which I argue that, if one considers certain important subjective elements of welfare, it turns out there are many poor people today that are worse off, even given all the social goods to which they have access through markets. Here is where our disagreement begins.

---

[3] *Libertarian Papers*, 10, no. 1 (2018): 19–48.

[4] *Libertarian Papers* 10, no. 1 (2018): 49–60. I would here like to thank Professor Narveson for his thoughtful response.

[5] Initially the proviso is to constrain this acquisition from the state of nature, but Nozick shows through what has been termed the zip-back argument that this constraint extends to the present day. See *Anarchy, State, and Utopia* (Basic Books, 1974), 176. See also my own treatment of Nozick's zip-back argument in "Forcing Nozick beyond the Minimal State," p. 24.

[6] Locke, *Second Treatise of Government*, ch. 5, section 27.

[7] "Would-Be Farmer John and the Welfare State," p. 51.

[8] See footnote 48 in "Forcing Nozick beyond the Minimal State" for a list of liberal theorists who make this point.

First, Narveson thinks my argument fails because it is clear (to him) that the contemporary poor are not worse off (in any relevant way) than they would have been in a world without the system of private property and the original resource acquisition that leads to such a system. It is here that Narveson misses the strength of my case (because of my own somewhat misleading presentation) by focusing on the more superficial sort of worsening associated with not being able to appropriate land, rather than the deeper (and more relevant), liberty-restricting worsening. I am happy to have the opportunity to clarify this point below. This clarification will lead to the consideration of a deeper disagreement that is more central to the liberal project of justifying private property and the motivations for liberalism as a whole.

Narveson clearly disagrees with Nozick, Locke, and many others who assume (at least implicitly) a sort of joint ownership of the world prior to resource acquisition.[9] Narveson thinks this is the first and fatal error many (even libertarian) theorists make. It is this error that leads to the Lockean proviso's constraining later appropriation in ways that, at least in principle, might include compensation, social-welfare minimums, or both. Departing from what he deems an unfortunate trend stretching from Locke to Nozick and beyond, Narveson advocates a more pure liberalism that rejects this thesis of original joint ownership of the world's resources. Instead, Narveson favors a Lockean proviso constrained by, and derived from, nothing other than the principle of liberty itself. Narveson laments that most liberal theorists (including Locke) have failed to do this; so much the worse for their less pure forms of liberalism.[10] In his reply to my essay, Narveson writes,

> The point is that the all-to-ready inference that libertarianism requires a system of coercively supplied support for the indigent can and should be resisted. It does not follow from any version of the proviso that is compatible with the principle of liberty from which Locke and Nozick intended to derive it.[11]

Below I will argue that Narveson's own rendering of the Lockean proviso fails to be compatible with the principle of liberty whence he intends to derive it. If Narveson's proviso is compatible with the principle of liberty, it is only a rather anemic form of liberty that is preserved. Hence, Narveson's form of liberalism, with its austere Lockean proviso, falls short of a main goal of, and motivation for, liberalism: the preservation of personal liberty.

---

[9] "Property Rights," pp. 212–16.
[10] Ibid., p. 212–16. See also Narveson, "Would-Be Farmer John," p. 51.
[11] "Would-Be Farmer John," p. 52.

II. It is Not about the Land (Per Se): The Deep Reason Why Farmer John Is Better Off

Narveson thinks his rendering of the Lockean proviso is not subject to the possibility of required compensation for the poor who are now unable to appropriate resources from nature; but ostensibly Nozick's rendering *is* subject to such a requirement. Nozick himself clearly acknowledges this in *Anarchy, State, and Utopia*; he simply thinks this compensation has been paid many times over via the social capital produced through the system of private property itself, which is available to the poor through markets.[12] In my original essay, "Forcing Nozick beyond the Minimal State," I argue that this is not the case; to do so I lean heavily on a focal case involving a would-be 1990s farmer John. John cannot realize his farming dreams, because he is too poor to purchase land, and unlike a would-be farmer John in eighteenth-century North America, there is no unclaimed land to simply appropriate for this purpose. I take it Narveson concedes that Nozick's entitlement theory is in principle open to such a case, but holds that in practice my argument fails.[13] To make this case, Narveson leans heavily on the fact that I focus on the need for land resources and John's particular dream of farming. Narveson casts farming one's own land as a rather exotic desire for this day and age, perhaps on par with his desire to own a 747 jet.[14] He goes on to conjure up the rather bleak details of what would be involved in realizing such a dream for all potential John's, including the killing "off of around 90% of the American population, since that is the only way that everyone could be a Farmer John. It would also reduce them to something like the agro-technological level of their eighteenth-century forbears, which I suppose is part of the Farmer John dream, since otherwise the corner store beckons as a more sensible and much less stressful alternative."[15] Stated in this way, it does appear absurd; the state (or whoever) cannot have a responsibility to compensate latecomers to appropriation for just any old thing they happen to desire (but cannot now obtain).

---

[12] See especially pp. 174–82.

[13] I think Narveson concedes this implicitly, because he does not call this part of my case into question in his response. More explicitly, he does refer to Nozick's "over-hasty formulations" concerning the analysis of liberty (p. 60). I take it Narveson thinks Nozick and Locke depart from what a pure and consistent liberal position should be. Such a position (like Narveson's) would not be subject even in principle to cases like my would-be farmer John.

[14] "Would-Be Farmer John," p. 54.

[15] "Would-Be Farmer John," p. 58.

Besides the obvious point that the state need not compensate in kind,[16] and the fact that desire for one's own land is not all that exotic even today, there is a more central point: Narveson's focus on land (and primitive farming) misses the strength of my argument. Land is not important per se, it just happens to be the sort of resource that is especially useful for realizing the more central and pervasive goal of self-mastery.[17] Having land to farm and hunt allows one the liberty to live and raise a family without being subject to working for someone else. Land represents the opportunity to be one's own master instead of doing the bidding of another by engaging in the potential drudgery of wage labor.[18] Desire for land then is really just standing in for the more basic and pervasive desire for liberty. This is the deeper reason why the average primitive farmer on the frontier is better off than the average poor wage laborer of today. Being able to govern one's own life is a great welfare boon, the likes of which outweighs much in terms of material wealth.[19] Moreover, not only is self-mastery a common desire, it taps directly into the intuitions that make libertarianism so appealing. Humans seek (and will forgo much for) personal autonomy and the avoidance of being at the mercy of others. Of course, Narveson (and others) could accept most of this and still argue that the welfare good of self-mastery simply is not substantial enough to outweigh all of the social goods available today to the poor

---

[16] Some other sort of compensation could be given. But even if sufficient compensation were practically impossible, this would not detract from my argument. It would simply show that the state and system of private property it sanctions is unjustified according to certain liberal theories. So much the worse for the Lockean theory of acquisition that leads to this conclusion (or so much the worse for states).

[17] I address this point in my original essay, "Forcing Nozick beyond the Minimal State," pp. 46–47. Narveson seems to miss this, though in his defense I did bury it in an objection section towards the end of the essay.

[18] Of course, wage labor need not be drudgery; my contention is only that it often is.

[19] My engagement with the work of Widerquist and McCall in their excellent book (*Prehistoric Myths in Modern Political Philosophy*, Edinburgh University Press, 2017) is relevant here. In my original essay, I only briefly highlighted some of the relevant arguments and data from their book concerning hunter-gatherers and how their lives would have been better in many important respects than many of the contemporary poor (see pp. 39–44). Narveson dismisses this comparison rather quickly (see pp. 58–59), with arguments and data that Widerquist and McCall capably treat (and respond to) at length in their book. I do not have space to treat this fully here, but I would suggest that the work of Widerquist and McCall is not so easily dismissed. They produce relevant data (both from extant hunter-gatherers and past groups) that support compelling arguments. Narveson and political philosophers in general will actually have to engage in-depth with this challenge.

through the market. I think this sort of position is the result of undervaluing the welfare boon of self-mastery and overvaluing material wealth. Absent a more extensive treatment, on this point I will just have to agree to disagree with Narveson.

However, beyond this, Narveson will be quick to point out that people (even the very poor) are welcome to try to achieve self-mastery and work to escape a life of drudgery. No one is stopping them; they are at liberty to attempt their dreams. But I wonder whether here we should put "liberty" in scare quotes. We are now in a position to approach Narveson's more substantive case against my essay—namely, that my argument against Nozick is largely irrelevant to the (properly) liberal theorist. This is because Nozick (and Locke before him) departs from a pure and consistent liberalism. Such a liberalism does not focus on welfare results (or even opportunities), but only on the preservation of liberty. A pure liberalism is not even in principle vulnerable to compensation requirements. Any classically liberal proviso (Lockean or otherwise) must be secondary to the principle of liberty. To paraphrase Narveson: any principle governing resource acquisition should be consistent with and derived from the principle of liberty.[20] As long as the liberty of the poor is preserved, no compensation is called for because no properly liberal proviso is transgressed. Putting aside the issue of what liberalism should be, is Narveson right? Is his more austere rendering of the proviso effective at eliminating any requirement of compensation? I do not think so. To see why, we will need to consider just what liberty is. Any liberty worth preserving will result in a Lockean proviso that in principle admits of a compensation requirement.[21] If this is the case, then even Narveson's account of resource acquisition, with its austere proviso, will have to consider what sort of compensation is required in practice.

III. Narveson's Austere Proviso and the Value of Liberty

It is clear that Narveson thinks Nozick and Locke (among others) go astray in their treatment of the Lockean proviso. According to Narveson, any such proviso should be consistent with and derived from the more

---

[20] See, for example, Narveson's "Would-Be Farmer John," pp. 52, 57, and "Property Rights," pp. 214–18.

[21] By "compensation requirement" here I mean to highlight the sort of compensation that may be owed to poor people unable to appropriate resources such as land (and hence achieve a level of self-mastery) because of the late stage of the private property system. I am not referring to the sort of compensation everyone accepts as appropriate—that is, for things such as theft and assault.

fundamental principle of liberty. So how should a classical liberal read Locke's proviso concerning resource acquisition? In his essay on this topic, "Property Rights: Original Acquisition and Lockean Provisos," Narveson begins with Nozick's rendering of the proviso: "A process normally giving rise to a permanent bequeathable property right in a previously unowned thing will not do so if the position of others no longer at liberty to use the thing is thereby worsened."[22] Narveson then asks the key question, "Made worse how?"[23] In other words, what is the relevant sort of worsening for the liberal? Narveson considers five possibilities, settling on the most austere with respect to the potentially worse-off person.

For Narveson, the relevant sort of worsening only applies to someone's liberty. One's acquisition runs afoul of the (properly understood) Lockean proviso only if it restricts, or interferes with, the liberty of others. The Lockean proviso then just restates the principle of liberty in the context of resource acquisition. Several quotes from Narveson concerning resource appropriation make this clear. In his response to my original essay, he writes concerning John (who is unable to appropriate land) that "all we owe him is that we not intervene in his life to prevent him from even trying, provided the restriction that he respect others' rights. Success is not part of the bargain. Liberty is."[24] Further down, Narveson seems to equate freedom itself simply with freedom from the violence of others.[25] Narveson is explicit about what this nonviolence involves a few pages on, writing,

> Locke's law of nature… bids us that we not deprive anyone of his (or her) health, life, liberty, or property, all of which deprivations are ways of attacking him (or her). But so long as we refrain from depriving anyone of those things, we are home free as far as fundamental Lockean justice is concerned, and doing so does not leave people with a farm as their fair share. And if someone has very little health, liberty, or property, then that is very sad, and it will be very easy for us not to deprive him of the little that he has (you cannot take from somebody what he does not have), but we do not violate the Lockean law by not taking steps to improve his situation.[26]

Narveson thinks all the principle of liberty requires is that we not interfere with what others already possess as property, including themselves.

---

[22] *Anarchy, State, and Utopia*, p. 178, quoted in Narveson's "Property Rights," p. 207.
[23] "Property Rights," p. 207.
[24] "Would-Be Farmer John," p. 55.
[25] Ibid., p. 56.
[26] Ibid., p. 57.

Anything else is fair game; acquiring anything not already in the possession of the person in question will apparently not deprive them of their liberty in any relevant way. According to Narveson, the Lockean proviso (read in light of Locke's principle of liberty) requires nothing more than that. Hence, according to Narveson, little else besides outright theft or assault will fail to satisfy the proviso (properly understood). However, even if we grant that the Lockean proviso be read in light of the more fundamental principle of liberty, Narveson is still mistaken concerning the potential extent of its constraint. This is because Narveson is working with a rather anemic conception of liberty.

It actually is possible to deprive someone of their liberty without stealing their property or assaulting their person. To see how this could be, consider a few examples from Eric Mack.[27] Imagine a scenario in which a peaceful group of large men form a circle around a woman (Zelda) sleeping in the woods. None of the land is previously owned. No trespass occurs. But upon waking, Zelda finds she cannot escape the circle and the men accuse her of assault when she attempts to break through their peaceful circle. Consider another scenario, in which Zelda lives on an island with Adam. Adam encases all of the valuable, useful resources in his own justly obtained and constructed shells. Zelda cannot get at the resources without breaking the shells, whereby Adam can accuse her of destruction of his property.

In the first scenario, it appears Zelda has been deprived of liberty despite there being no assault on her person or theft of her property. But perhaps Narveson would be fine including such a case of imprisonment in his list of possible deprivations of liberty. The second case is more troubling for Narveson because it involves someone depriving another not just of resources, but of their liberty.[28] This is because, as Narveson said, "the value of anything lies in what we can do with it."[29] Mack's cases highlight that liberty requires space to act, and stuff in the world to act with and on; otherwise, liberty of action is no liberty at all. Mack himself focuses not on liberty but on self-ownership and its extension through the use of world-interactive powers; though, he ends up making the same point I wish to make concerning liberty. The use of one's liberty to act *is* the use of one's world-interactive powers (to use Mack's term), and this involves use of, and

---

[27] "The Self-Ownership Proviso: A New and Improved Lockean Proviso," *Social Philosophy and Policy*, 12 no. 1 (1995): 195–96.

[28] This is really just a minor extension of Mack's own argument in "The Self-Ownership Proviso."

[29] "Property Rights," p. 221.

interaction with, some bit of the world. One could construct many other cases (indeed Mack has several more) in which an Adam-like character denies a Zelda-like character her liberty while avoiding any assault or theft; he simply denies her interaction with the world such that she is effectively deprived of her liberty of action. If Narveson thinks a Lockean proviso may constrain acquisition when it deprives another of her liberty, then he must be open to some simple appropriations (involving neither theft nor assault) being so constrained.

Thus far, this is largely an in-principle point and is not too troubling for Narveson on its face. Narveson will surely want to argue that in practice such a concession (that some non-theft, non-assault appropriations may be constrained by the Lockean proviso) will make little to no difference.[30] Indeed, Mack is no friend of welfare compensation schemes himself; though he acknowledges that in principle some activities of mere appropriation may call for compensation, in practice the more pervasive and mundane appropriations will not. Mack cites a reason for this, with which Narveson surely agrees: the private property system as a whole, and the modern market order, are on the whole enabling of people's world-interactive powers, rather than disabling.[31] The modern market allows people to enter into complex economic relationships and introduces a vast array of diversity into how one might employ one's world-interactive powers. People are not offered merely as much and as good in opportunities to utilize their world-interactive powers (i.e. their liberty) but much more and much better.

But now I can run the same argument against Mack that I originally advanced against Nozick (and against Narveson above). Once we in principle allow that one can be deprived of liberty without theft or assault, we can ask whether one is deprived of liberty in practice. Narveson and Mack would say no. However, my case involving Farmer John and his inability to appropriate land suggests otherwise. Mack is right to point out that the modern market economy has created a vast swath of opportunities to exercise one's world-interactive powers; the sheer number of new ways to be *at liberty* in economic action dwarfs those that have been put out of reach of the contemporary poor (such as farming one's own land). However, we have to ask just what

---

[30] Indeed, Narveson seems to say this much in a note in which he acknowledges Mack's "Self-Ownership" approvingly. He justifies omitting a treatment of Mack's proviso because he thinks practically it would come to much the same as his own austere proviso in terms of compensation required. See endnote 2 in Narveson's "Property Rights."

[31] "The Self-Ownership Proviso," pp. 212–16.

sort of opportunities are available and whether they are not merely more refined forms of liberty deprivation. It is my contention that the live options left to many of the poor in contemporary market economies amount to work of mind-numbing drudgery under the close control of someone else. Many have no choice but to work at such jobs or be homeless (some lack even that choice).[32] In other words, for many people the private property system as a whole, including the markets open to their economic activity, have been on net disabling rather than enabling with respect to their world-interactive powers (i.e., they can no longer be masters of their own lives as they could if land was available to appropriate). Their autonomy is greatly limited by being stuck in a cycle of poverty and low-wage labor. What the system has enabled them to do is work long hours for low pay by serving fast food, cashiering at Walmart, digging ditches, telemarketing, and so on. This list is indeed longer for the contemporary poor person in an advanced market economy than it was for a pioneer farmer on the frontier; but offering someone a thousand new ways to be less at liberty is still offering them to be less at liberty.

As I see it, Narveson has three potential ways to respond to this argument, none of which seem promising. First, he could revise his reading of the Lockean proviso to something more like Nozick's rendering, which focuses on individual welfare as the relevant sort of worsening. I have already argued (in my original paper) why this will result in a requirement of compensation: the welfare boon of self-mastery simply outweighs the welfare gained for much of the contemporary poor through the market. Furthermore, Narveson has made it very clear such an option is a non-starter. Such a reading of the proviso is precisely how *not* to be a consistent liberal theorist. Second, Narveson could deny that people stuck in a cycle of poverty and low-wage labor are in fact deprived of their liberty by being denied self-mastery to any substantial degree. I cannot treat such a contention here at length and am happy to rest on the prima facie strength of my case given the plight of much of today's poor in contemporary market economies.[33] Third, Narveson could deny that the sort of liberty I am focusing on is at all relevant for the liberal theorist.

---

[32] And Widerquist and McCall highlight just how many liberties are off limits to the homeless in particular, who often have no legal place to urinate, have sex, sleep, etc. See *Prehistoric Myths in Modern Political Philosophy*, p. 190.

[33] Here I am thinking of an advanced economy akin to the one we have in the United States. My case becomes much stronger if we consider the poor person living in a shanty town in modern-day Mumbai or Rio de Janeiro. My case also becomes much stronger if I consider a fictional libertarian state that lacks the social-welfare programs already aimed at alleviating the effects of poverty.

I take it that this last sort of response is most likely. Narveson may acknowledge the plight of the poor, and acknowledge it to be a sad plight indeed, but maintain it is not one in which they have been deprived of liberty. They are at liberty to engage in the market economy such as it is and apply themselves as best they can. If the most likely result of this is a life of drudgery through wage labor, that is sad; but no one is depriving them of their liberty (in the relevant sense), so no properly liberal proviso is transgressed. But Mack's cases have already shown that one can be deprived of liberty through mere appropriation (without imprisonment, theft, or assault), so one can ask just what sort of appropriations leave others at liberty. And to see whether an advanced market economy (and all the appropriations that have led to it) still leaves others at liberty, we are driven to ask: just what is liberty (in the relevant sense)? We could define liberty in a rather minimal way, wherein as long as one has access to a market economy, one is at liberty to act. Never mind that the economic activity open to many is exhausting, mind-numbing drudgery in which one is under the close control of others for the majority of one's life. Or we could define liberty in a more substantial way that involves not a guarantee of, but at least a decent shot at, gaining and maintaining a level of self-mastery. Liberty is, after all, not valuable merely for giving one any old opportunity at self-mastery; rather, it is valuable when it can be used to pursue opportunities that have a reasonable chance of success. This is why the liberty to play the lottery is of such little value. It has been my contention that the live opportunities for many contemporary persons in market economies are ones that deny the sort of self-mastery that would be available in the absence of these economies and the appropriations that led to them.

If Narveson goes with the first, minimal definition of liberty, then he can indeed escape the strength of my argument. However, the result is a position that lacks much of what makes liberalism or libertarianism attractive in the first place. Classical liberalism is supposed to preserve personal liberty; this is a powerful motivation for liberal theory. But we value liberty because of what we can do with it. Being free to pursue plans that have little chance of success, or a life that is devoid of self-mastery, is not really to be *at liberty* in the relevant sense. The attraction of liberalism is that it secures the liberty of individuals to pursue (at least) modest life plans in such a way that there is a decent chance of success. Why care about liberty if in practice it amounts to the functional equivalent of servitude? A liberalism that secures only an anemic sense of liberty has ceased to be properly liberal. A more plausible liberalism would employ a more robust conception of liberty, and this in turn results in a more morally plausible Lockean proviso. Such a proviso would recognize that we have not left "as much and as good" for others if whole swaths of the population are "free" to be homeless, live a life of low-wage drudgery, or play the lottery in hopes of escaping this dilemma. Such a proviso would require some compensation to be given to those who, because of the level of development of our market economy, can no longer simply appropriate land and thereby gain self-mastery.

IV. Conclusion

In my original essay, I argued that the implications of Nozick's entitlement theory end in a welfare state that seeks to advance the welfare of its poorer citizens as a form of compensation for the lack of genuine opportunity for self-mastery. Narveson thinks he can avoid all of this by rendering the Lockean proviso in such a way that it neglects welfare altogether and only focuses on liberty. However, the same sort of argument can be advanced against even this austere proviso. In contemporary market economies, whole swaths of people are deprived of their liberty of action in the world to a significant degree. They have little hope of achieving self-mastery. Narveson can deny the empirical accuracy of this contention, or he can retreat to an anemic conception of liberty. I am satisfied that the former tack is prima facie implausible and the latter results in a liberalism that has abdicated that which made it distinctive and attractive. Narveson's liberalism does preserve liberty, but only a sort that one is substantially not at liberty to use. The value of something rests in what we can do with it. If Narveson's liberalism does little to preserve *substantive* liberty, then I can admit it is a consistent view, though I fail to see its value.

A Summary of the Philosophy of Spencer Heath

Spencer Heath MacCallum and Alvin Lowi[*]

Introduction

THIS PAPER SURVEYS the life and work of a neglected libertarian philosopher, Spencer Heath (1876–1963). Heath is little known today because he worked independently, published little, and, having no formal academic connections, lacked students to work with his ideas. Yet he is notable for developing a comprehensive and wholly nonpolitical philosophy of capitalism based on a view of evolving society, and for showing strong optimism for the future. Heath was especially concerned to outline an authentic natural science of society, one that would be capable of generating dependable technologies. This enabled him in 1936 to self-publish a monograph, *Politics versus Proprietorship*, in which he forecast the continuing evolution of society leading in the foreseeable future to the private production, guided by normal profit motivation, of all public services. This was the first statement of the proprietary-community principle.

Libertarians finding that a hostile or defiant attitude toward government drains their creative energies will be inspired by Heath's wholly constructive outlook. Others, seeking to reconcile traditional Judeo-Christian teachings with the rapidly changing conditions of the modern world, will likewise find

---

[*] Spencer Heath MacCallum, grandson and literary executor for Spencer Heath, is a social anthropologist living in Casas Grandes, Chihuahua, Mexico. Alvin Lowi, who knew and had many conversations with Heath in the last years of his life, is a thermodynamicist and professional engineer in private practice in Ranch Palos Verdes, California.

CITATION INFORMATION FOR THIS ARTICLE:
Spencer Heath MacCallum and Alvin Lowi. 2018. "A Summary of the Philosophy of Spencer Heath." *Libertarian Papers*. 10 (1): 95-111. ONLINE AT: libertarianpapers.org. THIS ARTICLE IS subject to a Creative Commons Attribution 3.0 License (creativecommons.org/licenses).

Heath's philosophy valuable. The thoughtful layperson may be intrigued by such diverse and seemingly strange questions as the following:

- How can Heath's *action* hypothesis make it possible to derive the speed of light, near-absolute-zero temperature, and atomic explosion instead of only postulating these?

- How is society distinguished functionally from mere population?

- Can the quality and the quantity of a population be distinguished numerically?

- How was the development of number concepts critical in the evolution of society?

- How can society qualify as a distinctively new life-form on the earth?

- Was the historical Jesus an intuitive poet with a vision of the future?

- Was it accidental or on purpose that Jesus, uniquely among the world's major religious figures, stated the golden rule in the positive form?

- Can it be shown by the *action* hypothesis that scientists and theologians are addressing the same reality?

- How is the emergence of society changing our psychology, specifically with respect to the emotions that move people to fight or flight on the one hand or to creation and discovery on the other?

- How is the cosmos unalterably set in the direction of progress?

Heath expressed his ideas much more in conversation than in his writing, and much of what he did write was lost. But on his death in 1963, a grandson and co-author of this paper, Spencer Heath MacCallum, collected his extant writings, notes, and correspondence, largely handwritten, and transcribed and numbered them, making up the Spencer Heath Archive. As computer and scanning technology developed, he began to digitize the archive, still a work in progress. When complete, it will be domiciled at the Universidad Francisco Marroquín, in Guatemala, where MacCallum has been a visiting professor.

The authors of this all-too-brief summary of Heath's philosophy have taken pains to present his ideas accurately and, so far as possible, in his own words as found in the archive and recalled from conversations. MacCallum worked closely with his grandfather for several years before his graduate studies in anthropology, and Lowi, who has a background in physics, also had extensive contact and conversation with Heath. Now in their late eighties, MacCallum and Lowi were incentivized to prepare this primer on Heath's philosophy for the benefit and inspiration of those who will come after.

Biographical Brief

After earlier successful careers as a professional engineer and a practicing patent attorney, Spencer Heath became widely known as a pioneer in early aviation. In 1907, with his law client Emile Berliner, he successfully demonstrated the helicopter principle—that rotary blades can lift the weight of an engine from the earth. Later he developed the first machine mass production of airplane propellers and supplied most of the propellers used by the Allies in the First World War.[1] After the war, he developed and

---

[1] Spencer Heath Archive, Item 2742, article abridged from the *Baltimore Sun*, August 12, 1922, under the headline, "SAYS PLANES WILL HAVE GENERAL USE: Spencer Heath Predicts Big Demand for Flying Craft":

> Baltimore has the largest and only exclusive manufacturing plant for the production of aeroplane propellers in the United States. During the late war the factory produced and supplied 75 percent of the propellers on flying machines used by the armies of the United States and allied governments, particularly for the war planes of England and Canada. England alone purchased some 10,000 of them.
>
> The concern in question is the American Propeller and Manufacturing Company. Its product is the "Paragon" propeller and the president, general manager and founder of the business is Spencer Heath, who not only designed and perfected the various types of propellers in use, but designed and manufactured the special machinery utilized in the manufacture of "Paragon" propellers.
>
> Recently, Mr. Heath devised a perfected gear propeller, the pitch of which can be changed at will. This enables aviators to instantly adjust their machines to all atmospheric conditions and to land and take off with greater safety. The device is also expected to assist in solving the question of aeroplanes landing on the decks of ships. On dirigibles it enables the engineer to reverse or go ahead as easily as a steamship entering her dock.
>
> In 1910 the first hydro-aeroplane ever raised by its own power was taken off the water by a "Paragon" propeller. This propeller is still flying. In the same year G. H. Curtiss, using a "Paragon" propeller, at Los Angeles won the great speed contest, defeating Radley in a Bleriot, Ely in a Curtiss, Parmelee in a Wright and Lathan in an Autonette. The first United States Army dirigible was driven by a "Paragon" propeller, and since that time tens of thousands of them have been in use in the United States Government.

demonstrated the first successful engine-powered and engine-controlled variable and reversible pitch propeller, a technology requisite for large-scale commercial aviation. His forecasting of general aviation that year, as opposed to aviation merely for sports or military applications, made news.[2]

In the summer of 1929, Heath sold all of his patents and technical facilities and two years later retired from business to devote himself fully to the study of his long-time interest, the philosophy of science. He set out to discover what the successful sciences, those that had given rise to dependable technologies, had in common that could help in the development of an authentic natural science of society. In his major work, *Citadel, Market and Altar*,[3] he outlined such a science.

Soon "Paragon" propellers were flying everywhere: on South American rivers driving boats, over the Andes, in Mexico for Carranza, in Alaska carrying the United States mail, in Canada on the first dreadnaughts, in the air fleets of China and Japan, on the military machines of Siam, with the Black Sea fleet in Russia, on training planes in England, with the Allies in France, with the United States Army and Navy at all their flying fields and in many other parts of the world. Even the first naval seaplane to cross the Atlantic Ocean, the NC4, was equipped with "Paragon" propellers. When the people learn more about aviation, Mr. Heath says, traveling by air will be as much a matter of course as by train or automobile.

---

[2] A detailed study of Heath's role in early aviation is in preparation by Evan Davies of the Institute of Historical Survey Foundation.

[3] Spencer Heath, *Citadel, Market and Altar* (Baltimore: Science of Society Foundation, 1957). Heath's other publications, available from Spencer H. MacCallum:

Heath's Parliamentary Table. Compiled by Spencer Heath. Washington, DC, 1906.

"Propeller Theories," *Journal of Franklin Institute*, 1912.

"Aeronautical Propellers," *Journal of the American Society of Naval Engineers*, 29 (3) (August 1917). Revised October 1917.

Articles on aeronautical engineering, various journals, 1912–1930.

Politics versus Proprietorship, self-published in mimeograph, 1936.

"Why Does Valuable Land Lie Idle?" *Appraisal Journal* 7 (3) (July 1939).

Progress and Poverty Reviewed and Its Fallacies Exposed (Baltimore: Science of Society Foundation, 1952).

"Solution for the Suez," privately circulated October 1956.

Citadel, Market and Altar (Baltimore: Science of Society Foundation, 1957).

"The Capitalist System," *Libertarian Papers* 7 (2015).

His examination of the fundamentals of physics suggested to Heath that the dimension known in its technical sense as *action* was a more fundamental quantity than the abstract concept *energy*, since action contains the element of time, or duration, making it a more realistic, observable quantity. It struck Heath that a reformulation (literally) of physics in terms of this more realistic property might lead to a new integration and simplification of the physical sciences. And indeed this hypothesis has been found to have merit in recognition of the universal principle of least action and Planck's discovery of the quantum of action as the foundation for quantum mechanics, operational calculus, and the theory of electromagnetic radiation emission.[4] The principle of least action is now seen to be the most fundamental principle in physics, displacing the energy-conservation principle, which can be derived from it, while the converse has never been accomplished. The *action* concept led Heath directly to his idea of reality being experienced in terms of events rather than as a stream, or continuum, of consciousness, and this concept became the basis of his all-encompassing philosophy.

Heath materially helped found the Henry George School of Social Science in New York City in 1932, and for several years lectured there on population theory and land economics. He had been attracted to the Georgist movement since the 1890s for its championing of free trade in all but land.[5] But now, examining private property in land from a functional standpoint as called for by his *socionomy* (the name he would later adopt for his scientific approach to society), he discovered that, far from being a pathology, the institution of private property in land is basic to social life. As it evolved and matured, Heath believed, it would make Henry George's Philosophy of Freedom, as it was called, self-consistent—that is, wholly nonpolitical and spontaneously self-enacting.[6] From his functional understanding of land ownership, he was able to forecast, as once he had forecast commercial aviation, the spontaneous emergence of a major industry for producing and

---

"Society, Its Process and Prospect," *Libertarian Papers* 8 (2016).

"What Is Distribution in the Market Process?" *Libertarian Papers* 9 (2017).

"Malthus's Doctrine in Historical Perspective," *Libertarian Papers* 9 (2017).

[4] See the Wikipedia article, "Principle of Least Action."

[5] Henry George, *Progress and Poverty* (Appleton, 1881).

[6] Spencer Heath, *Progress and Poverty Reviewed and Its Fallacies Exposed* (Baltimore: Science of Society Foundation, 1952). The intention of this polemic was to draw attention to the by-then largely neglected Land Question and ultimately to provoke constructive thought on the part of Georgists.

administering all public community services contractually, for profit, in the competitive free market. His 1936 monograph, *Politics versus Proprietorship*,[7] showed proprietorship to be the grand alternative to politics, and it was also the first statement of the proprietary-community principle.

Remarkably, Heath was not a social reformer. Rather, based on his wide reading, his experience in the market, his scientific and technical preparation and pursuit of authentic social science, and his keen observation of things around him, he was forecasting the direction in which he saw societal evolution moving.

In these same years, Heath perfected his unique view of the historical Jesus as an intuitive poet who anticipated a world without politics, a voluntaryist world in the perhaps distant future which is only now, two thousand years later, beginning to come about and which he called, poetically, the kingdom of God on earth. That was the vision. But he also had the method, the means, and the social technology to realize the kingdom. The method was the golden rule. It is significant that his rule is stated in the positive form because, when practiced, mutually and reciprocally, it is the sole ethic in capitalist, free-enterprise behavior. It is a command to engage in contracts: to go into business, doing for others in the manner we would have others do for us, which is to say, with regard for their wishes.[8] It is incorrect to say that this rule is found in most major religions. The positive formulation is unique in that it is a command to *do*, not refrain from doing. It alone is a command that can be practiced.[9]

These investigations preceding World War II formed three legs of a philosophy of creative capitalism which Heath set out in his *Citadel, Market and Altar*, self-published in 1957. The mid-twentieth century being a time of

---

[7] Reprint of *Politics versus Proprietorship*, privately published by Heath in mimeograph, 1936, is available free on request from Spencer MacCallum. For discussion of the social role of land ownership, see MacCallum, "Freedom's Ugly Duckling: A Fresh Take on Private Property in Land," *Libertarian Papers* 7 (2): 135–55.

[8] For evidence that the historical Jesus had a thorough grounding in contracts, see Libertarian Christian Institute, "Economics and the Parables of Jesus with Jeffrey Tucker," Podcast Episode 44, December 11, 2017.

[9] A book compiled by MacCallum from Heath's unpublished writings and correspondence, *Economics and the Spiritual Life of Free Men* (scheduled for publication in late 2018), fully develops this idea and its implications for the world now emerging.

ascendant statism, the book received only a limited circulation, mainly as a gift, but did inspire some significant responses.[10]

Summary of the Philosophy of Spencer Heath

The Scope of Heath's Inquiries

Spencer Heath seriously addressed three broad fields of inquiry and showed them to be interlocking: (1) the philosophy of natural science and the nature of knowing, (2) human social organization, and (3) the spiritual life. By *spiritual* he meant the aesthetic and creative—the non-necessitous part of life, the part that is pursued for its sake alone. Out of these three threads of

---

[10] The following are some of the responses to Heath regarding gift copies of his *Citadel, Market and Altar*: John J. Grebe, Director, Nuclear and Basic Research, Dow Chemical: "Your analysis gets closer to a measure of our performance as a society than anything I have come in contact with so far." Virgil Jordan, Chancellor, National Industrial Conference Board: "When I had the happy surprise of getting your book… I thought I would be able—as I have so often in my many years of book reviewing—to read it and write you about it much sooner than this. But I found it so stimulating, so fruitful of suggestion, so penetrating in its perception that I have not yet exhausted its content, and it will probably occupy my thoughts for the rest of the summer." William Ernest Hocking, Professor Emeritus of Philosophy, Harvard University: "For two months I have been enjoying your letter and your book, and a sense of fellowship… because we have come through experience, not pure speculation, on some of the same ingredients of any durable civilization for the future." Roscoe Pound, Dean Emeritus, Harvard Law School: "[The subject] is one in which I have a deep and abiding interest. Here is a book of the first importance… an outstanding contribution to a crucial problem of our times." O. Glenn Saxon, Professor of Economics, Yale University: "It is not only a highly stimulating and exciting presentation of the fundamental philosophy and principles of a free society, but shows the positive, constructive, and flexible features of these principles that are essential to the survival of any society in the revolutionary changes through which the entire world is now rushing to an early climax.." Charles C. Gillispie, Professor of History of Science, Princeton University: "Your book is so original in its approach and so unconventional in the scope of the subjects embraced that I find it extremely interesting." Rose Wilder Lane, libertarian author: "It is impossible to express my delight in your *Citadel, Market and Altar*. This is the book I have been wanting, waiting for, indeed weakly yelling in print for: an empirical, *scientific* approach to 'social science.' I am happier than larks ever were, now that it is written." F. A. Harper, economist and founder, Institute for Humane Studies: "a breakthrough of scientific reasoning into the realm of human relationships."

diverse character he wove a whole-cloth philosophy, a single, unified perspective on human life.

Science

To begin at the beginning, Heath found that a person's first consciousness is of *self* and *not-self*. For human beings live in two worlds, the subjective and the objective. Our subjective life is not limited to what we can experience of the objective world; in it we can entertain dreams and phantasmagoria without end. But the world outside of self, the objective world, is unyielding. We experience it incompletely and can speculate about it but never know it with certainty. Only so far as we learn about it, however, can we increase our likelihood of survival. As we learn how things work in the objective world, we are able to make predictions that enable us to live in it—to not get run over in the streets, for example. As we gain this knowledge of how things work, we build a congruence, a correspondence, between our inner and outer worlds; our mind takes on a measure of the rationale—the *mind*—of nature. The process by which we accomplish this, whether under controlled laboratory conditions or in the barn or on the street corner, is fundamentally the scientific method. To the extent that we attain this *at-one-ment* with the universal, we live rather than die, we achieve our aims, and we dream and objectify our dreams.[11]

This knowledge of the not-self is at first empirical, cut-and-try. But at some point in the human experience, we obtain knowledge of numbers and systematize our observations. Formal scientific method arises. Now the knowledge that was intuitive and empirical begins to be rational (literally concerned with *ratios* of the numbers of things). As we develop rationality in our minds congruent with that found in nature, we begin to advance our at-one-ment with the world of nature around us.

---

[11] Heath occasionally hyphenated words to emphasize their etymological origin and clarify their meaning in context. The word *atonement* is more commonly found in the Hebrew ritual for Yom Kippur, in which it has come to stand for repentance for misdeeds. But the etymology favors Heath's usage, which is contemplation of nature for the purpose of harmonizing one's relationship with it. His usage is actually more in keeping with the original Hebrew sentiment, which referred to the story of Jacob in the Old Testament, in which Jacob was known as Israel, the one who grapples with God, or nature (for some). Thus, the Children of Israel celebrate Yom Kippur as the day of at-one-ment with nature. Intimations of a scientific inclination are unmistakable.

Heath makes two generalizations about the not-self that are borne out by observation in each field in which we have developed successful science, i.e. that yields dependable technologies. First, so far as we can apprehend, all nature consists of happenings, or events, which have three quantifiable aspects. In Heath's terminology, these are *mass*, *motion*, and *time*, measurable in grams, centimeters, and seconds, or their derivatives.[12] Even with the aid of instruments, there are upper and lower limits to our ability to experience, and measure, events. Second, within the range of human experience, all events are composed of discrete lesser events. At each level of integration, events organize into larger events, which in their turn become units for still greater events. To illustrate, electrons and other subatomic particles organize into atoms, atoms into molecules, molecules into living cells, cells into complex organisms, and these into societies, or superorganisms. At every level, the combining units must become fully individuated before organization is possible, for their very diversity is the basis of their functional integration, which presupposes freedom of each to manifest its individual nature. To the extent that the integrity of any unit is compromised, it cannot enter into the making of a higher-order (i.e., more complex) individual. Hence, at each level the constituent units are appropriately called *in-dividuals*.

The test of successful science is that it support rational projection, hence giving rise to practical technologies. Technology, in turn, consists in purposefully altering the ratios of the mass, motion, and time aspects of events to effect desired changes. To illustrate the concept, hypothetically varying the composition of an event whose quantity is maintained constant can yield such qualitatively distinct manifestations as near-absolute-zero

---

[12] For the derivation of Heath's terms consistent with the customary units of physics, see Alvin Lowi, "An Elementary Concept of Action from a Physics Viewpoint" (unpublished paper). Lowi believes Heath was on the track of a wholly new integration of the physical sciences starting with a reformulation of physical theory in terms of energy-in-action, or *action*, which can be experienced, not of energy, which is an abstraction. This accomplishment would fulfill a promising but neglected line of inquiry hinted at in the work of Lagrange, Hamilton, Maupertius, Euler, and Helmholtz, among others, at the turn of the twentieth century and before. (See Max Planck, *Treatise on Thermodynamics*, translated by A. Ogg [London: Longmans, Green, 1903].) The effect would be not only to simplify the sciences but to strengthen theory by more firmly grounding it in observational experience, since the fundamental quantities would be more directly observable. As Lowi points out, "That 'action' is more fundamental to physical theory than energy... is no longer a controversial idea. We not only have the quantum theory; we also know that the energy conservation principle can be derived from the principle of least action but not the reverse" ("A Call for Action," *Science News* 139 [1], May 11, 1991).

temperature (least motion that can be experienced even with instruments), atomic explosion (greatest motion), and speed of light (least time).

Human Society

Applying these generalizations to human population, Heath found the means for differentiating the quality of a population from its quantity. By quantifying population as a human event measurable in quantity of action, he found in the durational component of the action a quantification of the viability of that population in terms of the longevity of its individual members, thereby successfully bridging the gulf in meaning from its quantitative (purely numerical) aspect to its qualitative (aesthetic worthiness, durability, reliability, beauty, value, etc.) aspect. Comparing two populations as events that are quantitatively alike when measured in life-years,[13] we find that the population manifesting the greater life span is the more viable of the two since more of its numbers live beyond the period of biological reproduction—replacement of its members—and into their productive and creative years. Though its numbers are fewer, by living beyond the period of procreative imperatives, the members have greatly expanded their opportunity to produce and create beyond their own biological needs. In contrast, a population suffering a short mean life span remains at a subsistence level, absorbed in day-to-day survival, regardless of the numbers involved or the territorial density of its communities, if any exist.

What accounts for the observed difference between two such populations? What is it that enables members of one to live longer on

---

[13] The unit of measurement for the energy manifested in a population is not merely the highly variant individual life of the mean. It is the *life-year* of that hypothetical mean, which makes the measurement actually a quantity of action, not energy: hence, the action manifested in a population. One average person (energy) living one year (duration) constitutes the action (energy times time) of a single life-year. Ten average persons living an average span of ten years represents the action of a hundred life-years. A million with an average span of twenty-five years is a total action manifestation of twenty-five million life-years for that generation. A half-million with a span of fifty life-years represents the same number of life-years. It is clear, then, that while the quantity of human life as an event can be measured in terms of action, the quality of that life cannot be so measured merely by enumeration alone. The quantity of action per generation may remain the same while great changes occur in the constituent numbers, viz. the above example in which for a given amount of action, the generational event can have a small population with a long life-span or a populous one with a short span. (See Spencer Heath, *Citadel, Market and Altar,* p.11. Baltimore: Science of Society Foundation, 1957.)

average? With respect to developing a social technology, can we learn something from a comparison of the two? Heath's answer is that the difference between the two populations lies in the degree of individuation, or integrity, of the individual units and how that affects the possibility of functional interrelations among them. Recall that organization at all of the various levels in nature arises from the spontaneous interaction of units that are entire and uncompromised *in-dividuals*, each freely and fully expressing its own nature. In which of our hypothetical populations—the populous or the enduring—are the individual members more freely operating and congenial? In which are they more compromised and collisional?

Where individuals, through cooperation, evolve forms of spontaneous order, we see the development of society. In Heath's concept, population alone is not sufficient to constitute society; behavior is the key. Wherever in a population we observe individuals freely engaging in reciprocal relations, there and to that extent only are we observing society. The first human societies were severely limited to small, face-to-face populations and heavily dependent upon systems of kinship terminology for assigning roles and ordering customary relations within the group. But with the discovery of mathematics, and with it the possibility of accountancy and an entire complex of contractual market institutions, the reciprocal relations can become impersonal, and, being impersonal, universal, potentially including all people. Without knowing that I exist, the coffee grower in Brazil provides my morning cup of coffee. Commerce being blind to race or ethnicity, the whole earth becomes a web of reciprocal services, freeing men and women to cultivate their personal lives within their circles of familiars.

With the maturation of society, we have the emergence of a distinctly new life-form on the earth, a biological organism marked by a function not shared by any other, namely the potential to interact creatively with its environment so as not to exhaust and despoil it but to make it progressively more capable of supporting its own kind of life, and not necessarily at the expense of any other.

Examining this emerging life-form, Heath recognized three functional aspects, symbolically expressed in the title of his volume *Citadel, Market and Altar*. The first was the defensive, or protective, function, affording that security of persons and property upon which all else rests. This he might have called the *integrity function*, since it has to do with maintaining the integrity of the constituent units: individuals. While this can require the use of defensive force, the major part of this function is provided by voluntary or customary observance of the distinctively social institution of *property*. The second function he recognized, symbolized as *Market*, was that of exchange, whereby people attend to one another's biological needs with benefit to each and sacrifice of none. It maintains the organism alive at any given level but is not, in and of itself, progressive. If Citadel and Market denote the immunity function and the metabolic function, respectively, then *Altar* symbolizes the psyche, for it includes all the non-necessitous activities people engage in for their own sake: the aesthetic and recreational arts, religion, philosophy, pure research in the sciences, and the like. If the Market maintains the society at a given level, the Altar, through its discoveries feeding back new technologies into the marketplace, advances society to new levels, ever enabling it to transcend itself. As the Citadel enables the Market with greater and greater efficiency to solve the problems of sustaining life, so the Market, by progressively freeing men and women from bondage to biological need and natural risk, grants them passage into the realm of the Altar—the realm of creative artistry, inspiration, and motivation to pursue higher goals.

In *Citadel, Market and Altar*, Heath outlined his rationale for a natural science of society and explored in some detail one proposed application of social technology, a means whereby he thought the marketplace, under normal profit motivation, could and ultimately would undertake to provide all public services, replacing the present tax-based and insolvent administration of our public communities. For the name of this new natural science of society, he suggested a little-used but already-existing word, *socionomy*, defined by *Webster's New International Dictionary* as "the theory or formulation of the organic laws exemplified in the organization and development of society."

The Spiritual Life

Heath observed that all action requires motivation. Intellectualizing alone, the mere idea of a contemplated act, does not suffice for this purpose. For the primitive person, enslaved to the vagaries of environmental circumstance, the need for motive power is satisfied to a major degree by the emotions of fight or flight—namely, rage and fear. But what energizes the social-ized person,[14] in whose situation the need to choose fight or flight no longer predominates? In a civilized situation, the emotions of rage or fear are largely counterproductive or irrelevant. What is the emotion that moves men and women to acts of creation and discovery? Heath found his answer to this question in the aesthetic response to beauty.

---

[14] By inserting a hyphen, Heath reclaims for free-market use a word that otherwise signifies an advocate of political (i.e., coercive) action of some kind. Following Franz Oppenheimer's distinction between the *economic* and the *political*—between society and its contrary, political government—a social-ist is someone practicing voluntary exchange.

While in agreement with the voluntaryist ideal of many of today's anarchists and libertarians, defiance of authority was conspicuously lacking in his philosophical position. No social reformer was he, no militant relying on anger or moral outrage. His ambition was to lay the foundation for an authentic natural science of society. In keeping with this goal, he strove to so inspire others with a sense of the still-hidden beauty in the evolving social order that, under aesthetic motivation, they would begin to make discoveries there like those in the established fields of the natural sciences.

For Heath, the office of religion, as of all the arts, was to lift individuals out of their mundane rounds and, through inspiration, assist them in discovering and utilizing their creative potential. In his view, aesthetic experience and religious experience were synonymous. It was entirely natural, therefore, that Heath should recognize in Judeo-Christian teachings important correspondences with the beauty he saw and, even more, intuited in the social field. In this tradition as in no other, and especially in the precepts of Jesus, he discovered a rich language of discourse for conveying the beauty he saw in evolving social relationships. By utilizing this language, he hoped to a significant degree to counteract the poor image that free-market capitalism has received at the hands of collectivists of all degrees over the past hundred years or more. In his interpretation of Judeo-Christian teachings, he was as sincere and devout as he was original.

Almost incidentally, in discussing Christianity, Heath noted a correspondence between the early church fathers' intuitions of the triune nature of the Ultimate Reality and the findings of modern science. Whereas the Christian theologian speaks of Substance, Power, and Eternity,[15] or, in more personal and immediate terms, of Father, Son, and Holy Spirit, the scientist speaks of gram, centimeter, and second and their derivatives to describe the mass, motion, and durational-time aspects of events. Both are treating of the same reality, the one in absolute terms, the other in relative, or finite, terms. One is dealing with conceptions only, the other with objective experience, which is necessarily finite since we are finite creatures. The one treats of the Infinite Whole, the other of its finite manifestations, or parts.

But Heath's most fundamental insight in the religious field had to do with the person and teachings of the historical Jesus, whom he saw as an intuitive poet who had a glimmering of the full potential of humanity that would be realized through the universal society, only now emerging two-

---

[15] Robert Flint, "Theism," in *Encyclopedia Britannica*, 9th edition, vol. XXIII, p. 240: "One substance in three persons, of which the first eternally generates the second, and the third eternally proceeds from the first and second."

thousand years later, which he called the kingdom of heaven on earth. Jesus saw that the key to this kingdom, cast in more explicit terms Moses's injunction to "love your neighbor as yourself," was to *do* for others in the same manner you would have them do toward you—which is to say, with full regard for their wishes in the matter. This positive rule is the formula for free enterprise and everything it entails, whereas the negative statement, merely to refrain from harming anyone, makes no history. Except for a limited application in stressful circumstances, it is sterile.

By pointing out that service is the objective side of love, and building on this simple insight, Heath accomplishes a major integration of market economics with Judeo-Christian religious doctrine. The reward for obeying the will of God—his command of the golden rule—is life and life abundant. And indeed, life expectancy has increased spectacularly in the last two-hundred years with the worldwide spread of commercial enterprise. Jesus made it abundantly plain that it is not just good intentions but doing the will of God that counts. Many businesspeople believe their intentions are selfish or even bad, but that mindset belongs to the past and has still to catch up with their behavior. So long as they are practicing business and not cheating—which is not business but its contrary—they are serving their fellows as they would be served and thus are fulfilling the will of God.

Precisely because service in the marketplace is impersonal, it can become universal, which makes it divine love. As our practice of divine love lifts us progressively out of bondage to necessity and into the realm of the creative arts pursued for their own sake alone, we come increasingly under aesthetic motivation, which in Heath's poetic terms is the inspiration of the Holy Spirit. In this heavenly kingdom, made heavenly by the practice of divine love, we increasingly enjoy that promised perfect freedom which is obedience to God's will. That freedom comes about through men progressively discovering the rationale underlying the processes of nature, which is to say the mind of God as manifested in the works of God, and thereby achieving at-one-ment with God.[16]

---

[16] This religious interpretation, which Heath developed in the 1930s or earlier, is entirely consonant with the biological and religious perspective developed by the biologist Edward McCrady. In evolutionary terms, McCrady, like Heath, describes the emerging human society as a superorganism, while in theological terms he describes it as the Mystical Body of Christ. As McCrady's guest, Heath spent the 1956 academic year in residence at the University of the South at Sewanee, auditing classes in advanced theology and developing further his understanding of the Christian doctrine of man. At the time, McCrady was completing his book, *Seen and Unseen: A Biologist Views the Universe.*

The Cosmic Polarity

The unifying concept of Spencer Heath's philosophy overall is his recognition that the cosmic process is unalterably set in the direction of progress. That is, the cosmos is continually reorganizing its constituent threefold events not randomly, but to maximize the third and qualitative aspect: durational time. Thus are events ever becoming more real in the Platonic or Pauline sense of those things being most real that most endure. The rationale underlying this is simple: those events that are better organized, in the sense of their constituents exhibiting more reciprocity in their relationships, will outlast those events whose parts are more collisional, resulting in a bias over time in favor of the former. Hence the earth is becoming greener, meaning more alive, every day, and the emergence of the human societal life-form, which is only just beginning, is the apex to date, so far as we know, of that process.

Spencer Heath did not name his philosophy, perhaps to avoid it seeming to be something complete and final. For he always considered his thinking to be a work in process and hoped it might inspire others to carry it further than he was able. But an earlier, unpublished paper by Heath, "The Ascendant Order in Nature: Toward a Philosophy of Knowledge," compiled, edited, and titled by Don Erik Franzen, combined with the fact that Heath had been greatly influenced by Emerson in his early years, suggested the name *ascendentalism*, a term not yet to be found in the dictionary. It is suggestive of Emerson's *transcendentalism*, but, unlike that term, which can suggest movement merely from one level to another, the new term implies movement indefinitely upward.

Epilogue

What is the relevance of Heath's philosophy for the world today, in which socialism so strongly appeals to the rising generation? Heath's own words provide some hints about the lasting value of his ideas:

> Socialism is simply the ultimate of government taxation and control. It has a false but definitive philosophy, and likewise, a false religion with glowing promises of utopian freedom under political change. Capitalism, until of late, has been relatively inarticulate. It practices the golden rule of each serving others as he would be served, yet has little conscious knowledge of the sound philosophy and vital religion that it constantly puts into practical effect six days of the week.

> Libertarian efforts seem to be addressed more to the necessity to escape than to the desire to attain, more to deploring what is evil than to glorifying what is good. The movement is handicapped for

want of emotional fire and enthusiasm as well as for want of a transcendent ideal. And economics, on the other hand, is almost drably utilitarian. It has no utopian dream, no ravishing goals.

Beyond the primarily materialistic aspect of economics, we need to comprehend the basic exchange technology of the social organization in its overall aspect as an evolving (or developing) high form of life. In the golden-rule relationship, and no other, its members rise from being pensioners pressing against a diminishing subsistence, into their spiritual nobility of building not mere subsistence and utility but ever more order and beauty in their world. As in the unborn child, the organs and parts of this high form of life, consisting of its specialized members and groups, are slowly taking form in the womb of time, all unseen and unrealized by the conscious minds of men. How can men be awakened with understanding, that it may sing in their hearts and minds and quickly speed the coming dawn?

Let us seek fuller understanding of our free-enterprise system as an ideology on the march toward a genuine utopian goal. Capitalism is not a finished product. Historically, free enterprise has only just begun—the beginning of a long-delayed fulfillment of the Palestinian vision of abundant life and length of days. When we catch the vision of what freedom has in store, then we will have our transcendent goal, a vision that will be realized because implemented by freedom and thus sanctioned in the divine.

Let us counter the socialist strategies with a positive dynamism, conscious of the divine organic process if not the final goal. For socialism appeals only to the animal instincts, whereas we have vast oceans of rational beauty and aesthetic appeal at our command.

A major objective of Heath's was to help birth an authentic natural science of society, meaning a science that could generate dependable social technology. Discovering what the existing successful sciences had in common, he published in *Citadel, Market and Altar* an initial outline of a wholly rational science of society, successfully bridging for the first time the gap between the quantitative and the qualitative.

Heath looked to others to fill in this outline. How were they to do this? As Heath stated in his will, it had been "a guiding motive, purpose and desire of my life to promote knowledge and understanding of the structure, functions and processes of the voluntary, non-political and mutually beneficial social organization in its correspondence with the harmonious structures and dominantly integrative processes of the material and physical world." He believed that in science, as in any other field, the psychological prerequisite for discovery is aesthetic motivation under the inspiration of beauty—pursuing for its own sake beauty dimly seen or intuited. He also believed that the most profound gift we can offer our fellow human beings, our most valued service, is inspiration. Consequently, it followed that his approach to the subject in speaking and writing should be in large part aesthetic, religious, and poetic.

Reconciling Competing Systems of Property Rights through Adverse Possession

M. Garrett Roth[*]

I. Introduction

THE LEGAL CONCEPT of adverse possession, in which title to property may change hands without compensation because a disseisor (i.e., would-be owner) holds the property as his own for a specified period (e.g., squatter's rights), has been a longstanding component of the common law. Though clearly utilitarian in its desirable ramifications for the usage of scarce resources (those using the land for productive purposes without complaint by prior claimants are thereby made owners of the land),[1] this convention might easily clash with a Lockean-libertarian scheme of property rights, in which unowned resources, once appropriated, customarily may never be reappropriated (except in the case of explicit abandonment), having been permanently taken out of the commons. In this paper, I shall attempt to reconcile the idea of adverse possession writ large with a strict Lockean-libertarian scheme of property rights. To do so, I shall appeal to the inherently temporal nature of appropriation of unowned land; if sufficient

---

[*]M. Garrett Roth is assistant professor of business at Gannon University. He wishes to thank John McNulty, Florenz Plassmann, William McAndrew, and two anonymous referees for helpful comments on previous drafts of this paper. The author also wishes to thank Walter Block for providing the impetus for the central idea of the article.

CITATION INFORMATION FOR THIS ARTICLE:

M. Garrett Roth. 2018. "Reconciling Competing Systems of Property Rights through Adverse Possession." *Libertarian Papers*. 10 (1): 113-126. ONLINE AT: libertarianpapers.org. THIS ARTICLE IS subject to a Creative Commons Attribution 3.0 License (creativecommons.org/licenses).

[1] See Posner (2007, 78–84) for a utilitarian defense of adverse possession without consideration of transaction costs.

labor mixing (or some variation thereof) is the means by which land is made private, a consistent treatment of property rights would also allow for the forfeit of neglected property because the improvements that created the property right have dissipated. Thus, by permitting adverse possession, property right creation and property right retention both appeal to the physical realities of the customary homesteading scenario.

The tension between adverse possession and a libertarian scheme of property rights has not gone without previous discussion. In his article "Adverse Possession and Perpetuities Law: Two Dents in the Libertarian Model of Property Rights," Robert Ellickson concludes that joint acceptance of adverse possession and unconditional perpetuities makes Richard Epstein an inconsistent libertarian. But in the article referenced by Ellickson, "Past and Future: The Temporal Dimension in the Law of Property," Epstein's logic on adverse possession, though somewhat convoluted, is that of a libertarian pragmatist. He argues that any alternative to a first-possession theory of property rights as a default rule is unworkable:

> Who needs it [adverse possession]? How much of a temporal priority is needed to offset substantial use? ... The demands for "substantial use" could only induce a proliferation of borderline cases that place ownership (and hence the right to use and dispose) in limbo until the question of substantial use is resolved. Delay has its costs. These [transaction] costs should be minimized to reserve the bulk of resources for the productive use of assets.[2]

However, Epstein subsequently accepts adverse possession because, in a world of transaction costs, "the costs of making that determination [as to the original owner] continue to mount over time."[3] Thus, Epstein's cost-based framework provides both an argument against alternatives to first possession (based on the costs of settling disputes over substantial use) and a counterargument in favor of adverse possession because of the eventual infeasibility of establishing the original appropriator.

In essence, Epstein identifies two types of enforcement costs and judges those arising from establishing the original appropriator to be more burdensome than those arising from establishing substantial use. However, his appeal to enforcement costs fails to settle the more fundamental philosophical conflict over the a priori permissibility of adverse possession within a libertarian system of property rights; the existence of a rule that limits transaction costs in property disputes does not imply that the rightful

---

[2] Epstein (1986, 672).

[3] Ibid. (p. 676).

owner of the property will be established, were such costs to be ignored. Thus his argument, though convincing (and consistent) on its own terms, is unhelpful at a more basic philosophical level.

Alternatively, one might justify adverse possession on the Humean-Hayekian grounds that a common law principle, having been adopted and employed for many centuries, should be embraced as part of a spontaneous order of property rights. As with Epstein's transaction-costs argument, an appeal to custom does not establish whether adverse possession is or is not a priori consistent with a Lockean-libertarian scheme of property rights.

The primary purpose of this article is therefore to reconcile original appropriation of resources with the "temporal dimension" Epstein discusses. Such revision does not rule out the common libertarian dictum of a perpetual claim on (previously unowned) property as illegitimate per se, but rather as one extreme on a spectrum of what I shall call "temporal attitudes" toward property rights.[4] In short, I argue that because the human improvements on unowned resources (which grant ownership) depreciate over time, a consistent labor theory of property rights must also consider a temporal dimension for retaining a property right over resources. Such temporal considerations are already inherent in homesteading theory with respect to the requisite speed of homesteading. Thus, the temporal dimension of possession is simply another continuum, or sorites, problem to be contextually resolved.[5]

Though a strict adherence to Locke's paradigm is not a justification for a philosophical proposition, the convenient byproduct of accepting a temporal dimension in property retention is a system of property rights more in keeping with Locke's original parameters than the perpetual retention position, which does not allow for adverse possession in any form. Specifically, Locke's disdain for unused "surplusage" and waste, as expressed in both treatises of government, suggests that some provision for appropriation of neglected property is a desirable feature of any property rights system rooted (either loosely or strictly) in a Lockean paradigm of natural rights.[6] Thus, insofar as conflicts between modern homesteading

---

[4] Proudhon's (1840) mutualism, in which users are necessarily owners, would lie at the other end of the spectrum of temporal attitudes.

[5] See Casey (2012) on the sorites problem inherent in the transition from possession to ownership of property.

[6] Radin (1986) admits of this possibility in her characterization of Locke ([1764] 2005) as a theory of property acquisition rather than retention. Roark (2012), in contrast,

theory and its origins in Locke exist, they are greatly diminished by accepting a temporal element in the retention of ownership. This convergence is, however, secondary; the argument is meant to pertain primarily to modern libertarian understandings of property rights as originating from Locke and is, therefore, not a re-evaluation of or direct appeal to Locke qua Locke. Likewise, I only attempt to resolve the much-discussed tension between the Lockean proviso (as a broader and thornier issue than his attitude toward simple wastage of resources) and extensive private property rights insofar as a legal system including adverse possession better embraces the proviso than a system that does not.[7]

My purpose is also not to offer a protracted defense of a Lockean-libertarian property rights system as in, for example, Nozick (1974) or Rothbard ([1982] 2003). Though Nozick (1974, 150) is deliberately ambiguous about the parameters of "justice in acquisition," [8] the topic of adverse possession is, nevertheless, particularly important for any historical theory of distributive justice, in which present distributions are evaluated based on their origins rather than a time-slice desideratum for present resource allocation.

Lastly, it is important to note that the typical parameters for the present application of adverse possession law are only a practical approximation of the theoretical principle described in the paper; in practice, a property right can be wholly re-established by the original owner via formal reassertion of that property right at any time during the period before adverse possession rules apply.[9] Thus, the argument presented does not endorse any particular version of adverse possession as currently in place, but rather relies on the concept as the most comparable, widely understood legal principle to which the philosophical tenet of a temporal element in homesteading can be

---

advocates applying a Lockean proviso in both the acquisition and use of previously unowned resources.

[7] Schmidtz (1990) argues that the Lockean proviso mandates appropriation of resources to avoid a "tragedy of the commons," whereas Sanders (1987) argues that the proviso is self-defeating and better ignored altogether.

[8] Though Nozick (1974) raises objections to the labor-mixing paradigm, including his well-known tomato-juice example, Miller (1989, 49) notes that Nozick seems to tacitly accept this criterion for just appropriation nonetheless.

[9] If, for example, the law specifies a twenty-year window to establish ownership via adverse possession, the current owner can reassert her property right by fiat after nineteen years and eleven months with no consideration for any (philosophical) claims of partial ownership via labor mixing, etc., by the would-be homesteader.

compared. Moreover, the common concept of squatter's rights only applies here insofar as the squatter has made substantial improvements upon the land such that a property right would be in order *were the land to have been unowned* at the squatter's initial habitation. Mere occupation of land is not to be conflated with the type of conscientious labor mixing that would both bestow and, more to the point of the paper, transfer rights of ownership.

II. Introducing a Temporal Dimension to Property Retention

Throughout this section, I employ the original criterion espoused by Locke ([1764] 2005) in establishing property rights—namely, the mixing of one's labor with previously unowned resources. However, the entropy-based argument in favor of adverse possession is equally valid whether one's criterion is labor mixing, adding a requisite degree of value (regardless of the labor component), or the more general idea of forging an objective link between owner and resource.[10] The labor-mixing paradigm is employed in particular because it is distinctly Lockean *and* typically libertarian as well as being more easily understood in concrete terms than, for example, the creation of an objective link.

Before proceeding with a summary and critique of the non-temporal approach to property rights retention, I begin by clarifying the difference between "abandoned" and "neglected" property. For my purposes, the important distinction is whether the rightful possessor of the property asserts any claim of ownership. If the former owner renounces his property rights through either word or deed (e.g., in the latter case, leaving a table lamp next to his garbage can on trash-collection day), the property can be considered abandoned and immediately becomes homesteadable. The owner of neglected property has, in contrast, ceased to mix his labor with his property but has not renounced his ownership.[11] Utilitarian objections to the homesteadability of abandoned property notwithstanding,[12] I fully accept its validity and focus instead on the subject of neglected property.

---

[10] Hoppe (1989, 23) endorses this criterion.

[11] Neglected property may also be seen as having been steadily diminishing in added value, thereby rendering it homesteadable. Alternatively, a situation in which one's objective link has not been reasserted through action during a specified period might qualify as neglected property. Thus my argument applies equally to rival conceptions of original appropriation.

[12] See Posner (2007, 36).

The customary labor theory of property rights can be distilled into the following two assertions: (i) an individual acquires ownership in land by mixing a sufficiently large quantity of labor (call this quantity L) with a sufficiently small quantity of land (call this quantity H); (ii) homesteaded land becomes the unqualified property of the homesteader into the infinite future.[13] Libertarian notions of property rights that accept assertion (i) overwhelmingly adopt assertion (ii) as a logical consequence.[14] Indeed, Rothbard ([1982] 2003, 64) explicitly allows for unqualified idleness in property once homesteaded. I shall argue, to the contrary, that assertion (ii) is only one extreme in the range of temporal attitudes toward homesteaded land. Whether or not deviations from this perpetual retention position are accepted as libertarian, I shall argue that a system of property rights that allows for transfer of title to neglected property through a similar means to original appropriation (the common law principle of adverse possession) is both logically consistent and more in line with Locke than the perpetual retention alternative.

To illustrate the temporal aspects of homesteading, consider the following scenario: a tract of wild (unowned) land is cleared, plowed, and sown by a homesteader. He mixes sufficient labor with the land to acquire a property right. After the homesteader dies, the field is neglected. Five hundred years later, the field has returned to a state indistinguishable from that of nature. Thus, through the application of labor, the homesteader has *temporarily* removed the field from the state of nature, because the means by which the property right was first established dissipate over time. Nonetheless, the perpetual retention position would grant exclusive control of the property to the heirs of the original homesteader. However, this infinitely protracted resource privilege is inconsistent because it grants *permanent* ownership of land despite the *temporary* means by which land is originally appropriated.

In some circumstances, land may indeed return to a state indistinguishable from that of nature. Such total deterioration of prior

---

[13] For a detailed exposition and justification of assertion (i), see Locke ([1764] 2005, Book II, Chapter V). The issue of whether private land deliberately kept wild for the purposes of hunting, recreation, etc., is homesteadable, while a worthwhile topic, is peripheral to my argument here. Though one could argue that fencing off and advertising land as private is sufficient for a property right, I will deliberately evade the question by assuming *some* value to L without being at all specific about that value.

[14] Though not typically classified as libertarian, the most notable exception is Proudhon's (1840) philosophy of mutualism, referenced previously.

homesteading efforts is not necessary, however, to render neglected land homesteadable. Note that even under a perpetual retention position, the original homesteader may or may not encounter truly virgin land (supposing any land can be presumed to have had no previous labor mixing employed whatsoever). Indeed, fresh homesteading could be undertaken on any piece of land whose original developer fell short of the requisite L units of labor needed to establish a property right. Thus, the residue of previous homesteading efforts should not rule out such land as not rehomesteadable. Rather, the requisite degree of neglect leaves residual improvement somewhere between L and total dissipation of all development to the property in question.[15]

Though agrarian examples most readily illustrate both the homesteading paradigm and my exposition of rehomesteadability, the philosophical principle easily translates into industrial property as well. If, for example, a vacant warehouse has not been maintained for a protracted period and the value of the property (with abandoned warehouse) is less than or equal to that of a comparable vacant lot, the market value of prior improvements has dissipated entirely and the land is rehomesteadable just as previously cultivated farmland would be. The argument would also readily apply to (non-abandoned) brownfields, where previous industrial pollution of a land parcel has essentially increased the quantity of labor needed to homestead the property well beyond that of any virgin commons.

The more fundamental objection may arise that once homesteaded, land cannot, by definition, become homesteadable. Apart from being tautological in its reasoning, drawing such sharp distinctions between homesteaded and non-homesteaded land defies the physical realities of homesteading itself. Consider the application of $L + \varepsilon$ units of labor to H units of land, where ε is arbitrarily small. With sufficient neglect, the H units of land will assuredly return to a state as natural as that which existed before homesteading was completed (when only $L-\varepsilon$ units of labor have been

---

[15] Rothbard ([1982] 2003, 65) starkly distinguishes between virgin land and that which has the "mark of former human use." However, if a labor-mixing paradigm is to be meaningfully distinguished philosophically from first possession, the division between land that has been utilized sufficiently to bestow a property right and homesteadable land is not so wholly apparent. This ambiguity still, in accordance with Rothbard, places the onus on the would-be homesteader to discover whether such *ostensibly* neglected land is indeed homesteadable, regardless of whether adverse possession is deemed permissible; to assume homesteadability is to risk reassertion of property rights and eviction by a pre-existing owner.

applied). Thus, a sliding scale of development exists between homesteaded and homesteadable land. To draw both a permanent and stark distinction at L is to imbue this last unit of homesteading labor with qualities bordering on the magical.

This is not to say that advocates of a perpetual retention position ignore the physical entropy of human improvements upon land or other property. Rothbard ([1982] 2003), as the preeminent modern example, rules out the permissibility of adverse possession but makes no significant attempt to justify precisely why property rights, once established, are unqualifiedly perpetual. That land, having once been taken out of the commons, is permanently private is, as I have previously argued, fundamentally tautological. In his attempt to rule out the (pragmatic rather than theoretical) continuous use doctrine of Ingalls, Rothbard ([1982] 2003, 64) likens all owned but idle resources to a watch sitting in a drawer.[16] If we return, however, to the example of a tract of land cleared and left idle centuries ago, the notion that such resources are, because of previous homesteading, non-appropriable is far less obvious at an intuitive level.[17]

Beyond the intuitive appeal of this extreme rehomesteading case, a significant merit of the labor-mixing paradigm in establishing property rights is that the physical reality of homesteading is reflected within the conceptual framework; mixing what is private (one's labor) with what is unowned creates privateness. While there is no reason why the particulars of a property rights system must necessarily overlap with physical reality, a more direct derivation of intangible rights (property and otherwise) from the tangible world and its characteristics is less intellectually precarious than rights created outside of or in opposition to objective reality. In this instance, we are presented with two alternatives in property retention, namely (i) that land once homesteaded is perpetually private and (ii) that land once homesteaded remains private by

---

[16] For a summary of Ingalls's philosophy, see Liggio (1981). The author is in no way attempting to justify mutualism or continuous use in their most extreme and absurd sense nor to rest any element of his case for adverse possession on the pragmatics of reappropriating idle land (except subordinately and where explicitly inferred from Locke).

[17] It is parenthetical but worthwhile to note that Kinsella (2008, 30) grounds his argument against intellectual property in its non-scarcity and potential for unlimited usage. Where we can both use the same good simultaneously (such as an ebook), conflict over rights to exclusive use (i.e., property rights) obviously do not obtain. Though not directly applicable to the case of adverse possession (in scarce resources), the same principle of usage is the yardstick by which property rights may be passively transferred from nonuser to user.

some measure of use by the owner. The latter is, as I have previously detailed, in better keeping with the criterion by which the land was initially made private (labor mixing). Placing the means of property acquisition and the means of retention under the same labor-mixing criterion makes for a more coherent system overall. Additionally, supposing the term "inalienable rights" is not a redundancy, property rights need not automatically imply unqualified rights in perpetuity. Thus, there is no reason to take perpetual retention as the default position, with the burden of justification upon those who would contest it. To assert that quasi-virgin land homesteaded a century ago remains private because of long-since-dissipated labor mixing is, to borrow a phrase from *The Ethics of Liberty* (p. 64), "so much empty verbiage and fantasy."

Indeed, even adherents to the perpetual retention position are faced with a temporal dilemma in property rights: the necessary speed by which land must be homesteaded for the homesteader to maintain an exclusive right to do so. Consider, for example, a man who wanders into a patch of thick wilderness and, every year, cuts the limb off of one tree. By any reasonable standard, he is not homesteading the land with sufficient speed to prevent others from clearing the wilderness and acquiring the right to its use. Were the same man to cut down a limb every ten minutes, the scenario would be drastically changed. As noted by Block (2004), the total quantity of labor may also vary by geography. For example, an acre of meadowland is more easily cleared than an acre of forest. Thus, the necessary homesteading criterion is not simply the quantity of labor but rather the conditional improvement that must be rendered (by labor) in some reasonable period.

Homesteading of land is, therefore, a matter of (loosely) continuous rather than episodic application of labor to nature. Accordingly, continuous ownership should require some measure of continuous mixing between labor and property. I qualify the previous statement with "some measure of continuous" to rule out the extreme position that any abatement of labor mixing would render land immediately rehomesteadable. Just as the timeframe of homesteading must adopt some reasonable period by which nature becomes privately owned, so must the prevailing temporal attitude follow some guideline of what is situationally reasonable.

Given previously discussed inconsistencies regarding the necessary validity of assertion (ii), I proceed with the description of a modest alternative. Having mixed a sufficiently large quantity of labor with a sufficiently small quantity of land over a sufficiently short period of time, the homesteader acquires exclusive ownership of that land for T periods into the future. The value of T is roughly proportional to the ratio L/H, reflecting the fact that more labor applied to the same quantity of land implies a more pronounced removal from the state of nature and thereby a greater temporal ownership claim. Having been homesteaded, the land can be continually rehomesteaded by the original owner through the continued application of labor.[18] If sufficiently little labor is applied for a sufficiently large number of periods, the land returns to something like a state of nature and may be rehomesteaded.[19]

Whether or not such revision of homesteading theory can be branded as libertarian, this conception of property rights nonetheless adheres to the spirit of John Locke's treatment of property, wherein wastage of resources is given nearly as much attention as the just acquisition of resources from nature. In Book I of his treatises of government, Locke makes a case for the natural right of the needy to the surplus of the rich: "God the Lord and Father of all, has given no one of his children such a property in his peculiar portion of the things of this world, but that he has given his needy brother a right to the surplusage of his goods; so that it cannot justly be denied him, when his pressing wants call for it."[20] Even at its most non-egalitarian, the previous passage would clearly grant the legitimacy of other (needy) homesteaders' claims to any unused property "surplusage" that, within the context of this discussion, can be very clearly (but conservatively) identified via the chronic neglect of the original owner.

In addition, the granting of perpetual property rights through continuous rather than episodic use ensures that, loosely speaking, resources will be better used to their capacity, in accordance with the following passage from Book II:

> It will perhaps be objected to this, that if gathering the acorns, or other fruits of the earth, etc. makes a right to them, then any one may *ingross* as much as he will. To which I answer, Not so. The same law of nature, that does by this means give us property, does also *bound* that *property* too. *God has given us all things richly,* 1 Tim. vi. 12. is the voice of reason confirmed by inspiration. But how far has he given it us? *To enjoy.* As much as any one can make use of to any

---

[18] The quantity of labor continuously applied to the land need not equal L. For example, occupying a house requires far less labor than building one, yet the occupancy of a house would, by any sensible scheme of property rights, constitute adequate usage of the land it is built upon.

[19] Note that this proposal does not rule out some form of compensation to the original homesteader or his heirs by the rehomesteader. However, practical applications of adverse possession would likely leave little remaining value in land or property that is capable of being rehomesteaded. If, to take an extreme position, land must return to a truly natural state to become rehomesteadable, the question is irrelevant.

[20] Locke ([1764] 2005), Book I, Chapter IV.

advantage of life before it spoils, so much he may by his labour fix a property in: whatever is beyond this, is more than his share, and belongs to others.[21]

The previous passage also provides a less problematic qualification to private property than the much-debated Lockean proviso taken alone. Those who allow their property to "spoil" have negated their "bond" to these resources and thereby forfeit this property. Supposing the Lockean proviso is not contradictory in and of itself, this qualification to ownership may therefore be recast as the principle of taking only as much as one can productively use, as evidenced by *one's own actions* so that "enough and as good" of *unused* resources are available to others. The common law principle of adverse possession adapts this philosophical argument to the realm of everyday legal practice.

III. Clarifications to a Revised Theory of Property Retention

Because homesteading theory is most readily applicable to land, I have focused solely on this resource in the previous section. Portable property such as cars, machinery, and so on can only be produced by applying labor to land. These objects have thus, by definition, been removed from the state of nature. That which is not part of the state of nature (and is therefore never homesteadable) could also not, by the logic of perpetual retention, be obtained other than by sale, gift, or explicit abandonment. If, however, one accepts the notion of "forestalling" in property rights, the argument for adverse possession previously described would apply to both property and land.[22]

One may also object to anything but a perpetual retention position on the grounds that such amendments to homesteading theory would rule out the possibility of savings. However, to save is merely to increase future consumption at the expense of present consumption. As such, savings implies nothing of use. To require some use of savings is to expose such savings to nontrivial risk and thereby create a positive obligation to risk.[23] Insofar as such savings are not held in readily perishable assets, they are also impervious to transfer of ownership by rehomesteading. In short, savings in nonperishable assets with incidental and somewhat trivial use value (such as

---

[21] Ibid., Book II, Chapter V.

[22] For a detailed exposition of the question of forestalling, see Block (2004).

[23] I refer to such trivial risks as the theft of one's savings (which is tautologically untrue of consumption). Thus, by savings I mean (conceptually) risk-free placeholders of wealth, such as titles to gold.

gold or diamonds) is perfectly compatible with a conception of property rights that admits of adverse possession on strictly philosophical grounds.[24]

Lastly, one might conclude that a conceptual framework wherein labor mixing retains a right to property would grant the renter of a property an eventual ownership claim. As I have previously discussed, this conclusion is incorrect under all but the most extreme, mutualist-type interpretations of "continuous use."[25] When a sharecropper farms land he does not own or a renter occupies a housing unit he does not own, he utilizes such land under the dispensation of the landowner, whether directly or indirectly. Embedded in the notion of neglect is an absence of attention, which certainly cannot be said of those who delegate their land and resources to others at their best use value. A child sent to boarding school is not neglected by his parents, even though the child is not under their immediate care. Thus, use of land extends to contracted surrogates with no ownership claim whatsoever in the land they use or occupy.

IV. Conclusions

I have briefly argued for the necessity of a temporal dimension to property rights on libertarian rather than utilitarian grounds by appealing to the nature of original acquisition rather than enforcement costs or legal traditions. As such, the duration by which neglected land or property becomes homesteadable is simply another continuum problem to be settled on a contextual basis, much like the necessary speed of homesteading, the necessary amount of labor per unit of land to establish a property right, and so on. Ellickson's utilitarian framework for adverse possession law, rooted in subjective costs to adverse possessor and original owner, is thereby supplanted by a libertarian framework rooted in the objective rate of deterioration to improvements that originally brought (and kept) the land out of the commons. As a matter of public policy, such a reimagination of the foundations for adverse possession law is likely to extend the prevailing timeframe (typically ten to twenty years) for transfer of property rights.

---

[24] While the holding of land strictly for the purposes of speculation may indeed be a form of savings, the original ownership of such virgin or near-virgin land is incompatible with the labor mixing necessary to bestow the property right upon the original speculator. Thus, a strict adherence to any Lockean-libertarian system of property rights actually renders the issue inapplicable.

[25] Typically, squatters seeking transfer of ownership via current adverse possession law must be occupying land without the original owner's awareness of their presence.

To view competing systems of individual property rights along a single temporal dimension fuses the left-libertarianism of Proudhon with the right-libertarianism of Rothbard and Nozick. In the former view, resources remain one's property insofar as they are used by the would-be owner. In the latter, resources remain one's unqualified property into the infinite future. A legal system that permits adverse possession (though potentially adopted on practical rather than philosophical grounds) simply takes a middle position. The inclusion of a temporal element thereby fortifies the whole of libertarian property theory; to the extent that libertarian and utilitarian positions overlap, utilitarianism fills in contextual gaps where principle would otherwise be ceded to pragmatism. In its aversion to waste and spoilage, a continuous use theory of property rights also meshes better with Locke, the forerunner of libertarian homesteading theory, than the perpetual retention position.

References

Block, Walter. 2004. "Libertarianism, Positive Obligations, and Property Abandonment: Children's Rights." *International Journal of Social Economics* 31(3): 275-286.

Casey, Gerard. 2012. "Ownership and Possession—Where Do You Draw the Line?" Unpublished manuscript.

Ellickson, Robert C. 1986. "Adverse Possession and Perpetuities Law: Two Dents in the Libertarian Model of Property Rights." *Washington University Law Quarterly* 64(3): 723-737.

Epstein, Richard. 1986. "Past and Future: The Temporal Dimension in the Law of Property." *Washington University Law Quarterly* 64(3): 667-722.

Hoppe, Hans-Hermann. 1989. *A Theory of Socialism and Capitalism*. Boston: Kluwer. Available from: http://mises.org/document/431 [Accessed 1 September 2012].

Kinsella, N. Stephan. 2008. *Against Intellectual Property*. Auburn, AL: Mises Institute. Available from: https://mises.org/library/against-intellectual-property-0 [Accessed 29 May 2018].

Liggio, Leonard P. 1981. "Ingalls: On Land and Liberty." *Literature of Liberty* 4(3): 55-56.

Locke, John. (1974) 2005. *Two Treatises of Government and a Letter Concerning Toleration*. Stillwell, KS: Digireads.com.

Miller, David. 1989. *Market, State, and Community*. Oxford: Oxford University Press.

Nozick, Robert. 1974. *Anarchy, State, and Utopia*. New York: Basic Books.

Posner, Richard A. 2007. *An Economic Analysis of Law*. 7th ed. New York: Aspen.

Proudhon, Pierre-Joseph. 1840. *What Is Property?* Trans. B. R. Tucker. New York: Dover.

Radin, Margaret J. 1986. "Time, Possession, and Alienation." *Washington University Law Quarterly*, 64(3): 739-758.

Roark, Eric. 2012. "Applying Locke's Proviso to Unappropriated Natural Resources." *Political Studies* 60(3): 687-702.

Rothbard, Murray N. (1982) 2003. *The Ethics of Liberty*. New York: NYU Press.

Sanders, John T. 1987. "Justice and the Original Acquisition of Property." *Harvard Journal of Law and Public Policy* 10(2): 367-99.

Schmidtz, David. 1990. "When Is Original Appropriation Required?" *Monist* 73(4): 504–19.

Book Review: *The Economics of Law, Order, and Action: The Logic of Public Goods*

Gerard Casey[*]

Jakub Bożydar Wiśniewski: *The Economics of Law, Order, and Action: The Logic of Public Goods*. London: Routledge, 2018, pp. 157; vi. ISBN-13: 978-0815367871.

JAKUB WIŚNIEWSKI'S *The Economics of Law, Order, and Action: The Logic of Public Goods* is surely handicapped by having the dullest of titles for what is a most exciting book. A work of economics exciting? Surely not! Surely yes!—if it is the kind of heterodox economics that Wiśniewski espouses, one that has radical implications for ethics and politics, and not economics as an esoteric branch of applied mathematics. When you have finished reading this book, you might be inclined to think that it is really a not-too-thinly disguised argument for libertarian anarchism, and in thinking this you would not be far wrong. However, although the book is strongly, very strongly, sympathetic to libertarian anarchist concerns, its point of departure is neither ethics nor politics but economics, specifically economics in the Austrian praxeological tradition. Only in its final chapter does the author turn his attention thematically to ethical concerns. In the interests of full disclosure, it should be revealed that this reviewer is a card-carrying libertarian anarchist so that any book that made a half-decent approach to bolstering the case for

---

[*]Gerard Casey is professor emeritus of philosophy at University College Dublin.

CITATION INFORMATION FOR THIS ARTICLE:

Gerard Casey. 2018. "Book Review: *The Economics of Law, Order, and Action: The Logic of Public Goods*. *Libertarian Papers*. 10 (1): 127-132. ONLINE AT: libertarianpapers.org. THIS ARTICLE IS subject to a Creative Commons Attribution 3.0 License (creativecommons.org/licenses).

libertarian anarchy would meet with his approval. Yet this is not a half-decent rehearsal of the much-travelled roads of libertarian anarchy but a full-blooded, sophisticated, dense, dialectical and deadly subversion of some of the sacred cows of standard economics and, through that, a not-so-indirect vindication of anarchy.

So, what is the point of the book? It is to exhibit the deficiencies in the classical and neoclassical arguments that underpin the claim that a territorial monopoly of force is both desirable and inevitable to ground the supposedly public goods of law and defence. In five dense chapters, Wiśniewski argues that the standard account of public goods is both artificial and arbitrary (chapter 2) and makes a strong case for the provision of defence and law—archetypal public goods if ever there were any—as private goods (chapters 3 and 4). But what if it were to be argued that territorial monopolies of force—in a word, governments—are not created primarily to provide the public goods of law and defence but instead emerge naturally and seemingly inevitably from the operation of a human nature that is inexorably predatory? Chapter 5 engages and rejects this realpolitik argument. In the final chapter, chapter 6, Wiśniewski broadens the scope of the enquiry to provide a critical discussion of some central aspects of praxeology, including the notions of the supposedly necessary rational character of our desires, moral objectivity, and a Rawlsian version of a public good.

There is little point to trying to provide a summary of all the arguments and claims that Wiśniewski makes—there is simply too much to cover adequately all of this even if it were otherwise desirable. The book's second chapter, which, from the perspective of Austrian economics, critiques the standard account of public goods, is perhaps its foundational chapter; the subsequent accounts of defence and law as private goods become operational only if the road block constituted by the standard account of public goods has previously been cleared out of the way. If we were to frame the argument that Wiśniewski intends to demolish, it might run as follows. There are goods, in particular, those of defence and law, that cannot be supplied (adequately) by the operation of the free market. These goods, public goods if there are any such things as public goods, are necessary for the functioning of any society and can only be supplied by an agency exercising a monopoly of force (in a given area), therefore, such an agency is both necessary and morally and politically justifiable.

The provision of law by private means has been proposed and defended by many writers and, although still controversial, it is not an intuitively unreasonable position to take. The provision of adequate public defence by private means, however, is quite another matter, so, for the purposes of this brief review, I am going to take the conclusion of the second chapter—the rejection of the standard economic idea of public goods—as given and focus my attention on the third chapter which deals with the idea of defence as a private good. Here, I can provide only the barest of sketches—the actual discussion is much more detailed and refined.

Wiśniewski deals with the question of public defence by private means on three levels: short-, mid- and long-range. The major economic problem facing the market for private provision of defence is the problem of free riders, free riders being those who benefit from the provision of a service but will not pay for it, leaving the cost to be borne by others. It is often argued that the problem of free-riders will lead either to the under-provision of a service or its complete non-provision whereas, the claim continues, where there is an agency with a monopoly of force, all are forced to pay and so there is no free-riding problem.

The short-range provision of private defence is relatively unproblematic. There are no obvious economic problems in any given individual's contracting with a private firm for their provision of services designed to protect the individual's life or property. These services can be provided in such a way as to be narrowly targeted at the client and his property so that there are minimal positive spillover effects to those not paying for this service. Whatever positive spillover effects there might be are not so great as to obviate the need for those other individuals to make their own arrangements for the protection of their lives and properties.

So much for narrowly-focussed entities in need of protection such as one's life and property. But what about mid-range services such as street patrols or surveillance cameras in areas used by the public? Would not the free-rider problem become a major issue at this level, with the prospect of multiple free-riders benefitting from the service but not prepared to pay for it threatening the profitability of supplying services of this kind? One solution might be the use of restrictive covenants. Restrictive covenants are legal obligations that 'run with the land', that is, which are attached to and are transferred with property ownership. Restrictive covenants are not in (legal) fashion at the moment but there is nothing in principle to prevent their reintroduction. However, there are problems with the establishment of restrictive covenants and even greater problems with the maintenance of such legal agreements. Perhaps the answer lies in the privatisation of areas used by the public in general and the levying of a charge on users for the use of such areas. Once again, such a solution while feasible in principle is likely to be effective only in the most favourable of circumstances. Perhaps the defence company could announce (and implement) a policy of not protecting those who had not paid for its services. Modern technology could be used to discriminate effectively between payers and non-payers so that the defence agency could decline to come to the aid of non-payers or do so only out of charity and then only occasionally, otherwise the deterrent effect would be diffused. Moreover, those who pay for the service could, if they were so inclined, ostracise the non-payers socially and economically, thus adding to the pressure on the non-payers to pay.

The provision of long-range (national) protection on the free market appears to be much more of a challenge than either the short or mid-range issues; it may even seem insurmountable. What are we talking about here? Well, the kind of services normally provided by the state security forces—ABM and nuclear weapons.

In the first place, a variety of general arguments for the superiority of the free market (which the experienced free-marketeer will recognise) can be provided (as by Gustave de Molinari) to make the case for the free-market provision of long-range defence, just as for any other good—competition reduces prices and improves quality of goods and service; voluntary transactions do not injure productive forces as do coercive methods; the rational allocation of resources is possible in a free market but not in a state of coercion; only the decentralised free market with a plethora of independent decision-making units can acquire and make use of the appropriate knowledge; only the free market can provide the capital resources needed for efficient and high productivity.

Because the costs of large-scale aggression would be borne by the aggressors and not externalised, a free-market world would be more peaceable than a monocentric one. Any socio-political grouping animated by free market principles would pose little or no threat to its neighbours.

But, still the question remains, what of those states that are stupidly aggressive and blind to the merits of the free market? How will one defend oneself from those? "...could it not be convincingly suggested," writes Wiśniewski, "that an ideologically fundamentalist dictatorship rich with natural resources might attempt to launch an all-out suicide attack against an enclave of libertarian legal polycentrism?" (52) Such an eventuality cannot be ruled out, of course. But why assume that the libertarian legal polycentrists would be any less effective in defence than the fundamentalist dictatorship in attack? There is no reason to think that whatever amenities are required for national defence could not be supplied in a libertarian legal polycentric polity as the result of negative and positive forces. Negatively, the libertarian legal polycentrists could rely on the tried and tested mechanism of ostracism. Those defence agencies and their subscribers that had a local-only remit could be excluded from the normal social and business relationships that all need in order to flourish. Positively, voluntary contributions to the cost of national defence could be expected from producers to create and sustain their reputations and to enhance their market desirability.

Would we be likely to run into the problem suggested (notoriously) by Ayn Rand, that of the various defence agencies engaging in inter-agency squabbles or, even worse, one defence agency's attempting to create a monopoly of force? Once again, it must be noted that the cost of aggression is extremely high and no non-coercive defence agency has the capacity to externalise its costs. These would have to be borne by its subscribers who would be obliged to pay for this aggression and to suffer the results of negative and positive ostracism from the subscribers of other agencies. But even in our world which is dominated by territorial monopolies of force, a thriving market in private protection exists and a multiplicity of various agencies manage to coexist without being forced into mutual aggression by irrational forces.

All in all, then, Wiśniewski's presentation of his thesis is commendably and forcefully dialectical, with argument, counter-argument, example and counter-example, all densely but coherently and lucidly intertwined. My bare summary of just a small part of this exciting work cannot capture the rationally coercive character of the work as a whole.

The book comes in at just over 150 pages but, if I can be excused a seeming paradox, it is longer than it looks! Being set in a small font size of Times New Roman (still eminently readable though), I reckon you are getting about 80,000 words for your money. And speaking of money, the cost of this book is astronomical! At the time of this writing, the book is priced at €120 on Book Depository, £115 on Amazon.uk, and $140 on Amazon.com. Pricing of this order seriously limits the book's potential readership, which is a shame, since it is a book that deserves to be widely read. Some may think a comment on pricing is out of order since it has nothing to do with the intrinsic merits or demerits of the book. But authors write to be read and not just to have a few hundred copies buried in crepuscular obscurity in a university library, to be read, if at all, by a handful of scholars and some fortunate students who stumble across it inadvertently.

Standard academic books generally generate little or no cash advances to the authors, who bear all the cost of writing the work and, increasingly, some share of the editorial costs. The costs of publishing have dropped significantly in the electronic era, with publishing on demand, outsourcing of copy-editing, and so on. It might be thought, well, this is a hard-cover version and hard-cover books cost more to produce. Yes, they do, but not that much more. Books priced in this way are clearly targeted at well-heeled university libraries which spend other people's money on other people, a category of which the comic writer P.J. O'Rourke has spoken trenchantly if scatologically.

Should you read this book? Yes, if you want to experience a well-argued presentation of the economic case for the rejection of economic and political orthodoxies. Should you buy this book? Not unless you have more money than sense, although, that said, the intellectual value of this book is such as to probably justify the ridiculous outlay required to purchase it.

Libertarian Papers

VOLUME 10, ISSUE 2 (2018)

A JOURNAL OF PHILOSOPHY, POLITICS, AND ECONOMICS

libertarianpapers.org

Executive Editor | Stephan Kinsella (Houston, Texas)

Editor | Matthew McCaffrey (University of Manchester)

Editorial Board

Walter Block
Loyola University New Orleans

Paul Cantor
University of Virginia

Gerard Casey
University College Dublin

Gary Chartier
La Sierra University

Anthony Gregory
Independent Institute

Robert Higgs
Independent Institute

Hans-Hermann Hoppe
Property and Freedom Society

Jesús Huerta de Soto
Universidad Rey Juan Carlos, Madrid

Jörg Guido Hülsmann
University of Angers, France

Jason Jewell
Faulkner University

Roderick T. Long
Auburn University

Allen Mendenhall
Faulkner University

Roberta Modugno
University of Roma TRE

Jan Narveson
University of Waterloo

Hiroyuki Okon
Kokugakuin University, Tokyo

Sheldon Richman
Future of Freedom Foundation

Butler D. Shaffer
Southwestern Law School

Josef Šíma
Prague University of Economics

Edward Stringham
Trinity College

Frank van Dun
University of Ghent

Jakub Wiśniewski
Ludwig von Mises Institute Poland

Thomas E. Woods
Ludwig von Mises Institute

Ed Younkins
Wheeling Jesuit University

Aims and Scope

Libertarian Papers is a peer-reviewed journal of libertarian scholarship established in 2009. Its purpose is to advance scholarly research in disciplines of particular interest to the libertarian community, broadly conceived. The journal is interdisciplinary in scope, publishing original research from a wide variety of fields, especially philosophy, politics, and economics, but also legal theory, history, literary criticism, and social or cultural analysis. Its broader mission is to continue the tradition established by publications such as the *Journal of Libertarian Studies*.

Colophon

The cover image for this volume is Canaletto's *View of the Entrance to the Arsenal*.

Table of Contents

Libertarian Papers, Volume 10, Issue 2 (2018)

1. "The Tenuous Foundations of the Sufficiency Proviso"
   by Lamont Rodgers 141

2. "Caring About Projects, Responsibility, and Rights: A Response to Rodgers"
   by Fabian Wendt 159

3. "The Still Tenuous Foundations of a Sufficiency Proviso: A Rejoinder to Wendt"
   by Lamont Rodgers 173

4. "Police Choice: Feasible Policy Options for a Safer and Freer Society"
   by Corey A. DeAngelis 179

5. "A Strategic Doctrine of Disproportionate Force for Decentralized Asymmetric Warfare"
   by Joseph Michael Newhard 207

6. "Innovative Dynamism Improves the Environment"
   by Arthur M. Diamond, Jr. 233

7. "Feasibility Claims in the Debate over Anarchy versus the Minimal State"
   by Brad R. Taylor 277

8. "On Banking, Credit, and Inflation"
   by Spencer Heath 295

9. "Deriving Rights to Liberty"
   by Scott A. Boykin 301

10. "The Use of Torrents in Society"
    by Radu Uszkai 343

11. "The Anatomy of Nationalism:
    A Fresh Appraisal Based on Recent Case Studies"
    by Jamin Andreas Hübner..373

12. "Review Essay: *Selfish Libertarians and Socialist
    Conservatives? The Foundations of the Libertarian-
    Conservative Debate*"
    by Aleksandar Novaković 415

13. "Ten Years of Libertarian Scholarship"
    by Stephan Kinsella 427

14. "Reflections on Ten Years of *Libertarian Papers*"
    by Matthew McCaffrey..429

THE TENUOUS FOUNDATIONS OF THE SUFFICIENCY PROVISO

LAMONT RODGERS[*]

FABIAN WENDT PROPOSES combining libertarian foundations with a proviso that requires a just system of private property to ensure that everyone has a sufficient amount of resources to pursue projects. He calls this proviso a sufficiency proviso. This proviso is said to have advantages over all rival provisos "because it better coheres with the most plausible rationale for endorsing a libertarian theory of justice in the first place" (Wendt 2018b, 169). Given these advantages, he expresses surprise that no other libertarians have defended a sufficiency proviso. In section 1, I present the rationale for the proviso. In section 2, I show that Wendt relies on a consequentialist justification of private property rights. Wendt regards this consequentialist justification as the most plausible rationale for endorsing private property rights, but he never defends that justification. I argue that this consequentialist derivation of property rights makes it an open question whether individuals have any of the rights libertarians take them to have. In section 3, I identify the problems that stem from divorcing justice from rights, as Wendt does. In the fourth section, I show that his consequentialist position leads to a serious attenuation of self-ownership. Finally, in the fifth section, I demonstrate that the notion of a system of private property is antiquated. I cast doubt on whether there is any plausible conception of a system of private property that matches the systems in which people actually live in our global economy. One could thus understand my discussion as

---

[*]Lamont Rodgers is professor of philosophy at Houston Community College.
CITATION INFORMATION FOR THIS ARTICLE:
Lamont Rodgers. 2018. "The Tenuous Foundations of the Sufficiency Proviso." *Libertarian Papers*. 10 (2): 141-157. ONLINE AT: libertarianpapers.org. THIS ARTICLE IS subject to a Creative Commons Attribution 3.0 License (creativecommons.org/licenses).

both an effort to explain why others have not defended a proviso such as Wendt's and as an attempt to show that the prospects of defending such a proviso are dim.

Before moving on, it is important to note my understanding of Wendt's project. I read Wendt as attempting to prove that his proviso, and more broadly his "moderate libertarianism," is what fits most comfortably with a very commonly accepted foundation of libertarian private property rights. I read him this way because of his explicit claims. However, he might actually mean something weaker; and indeed, he sometimes hints at this separate project. He might mean that there is a theory of rights and property that is broadly, but not quintessentially, libertarian and that, if one moves from a specific set of *nearly* libertarian assumptions, one can get to moderate libertarianism with a sufficiency proviso. In this paper, I read him only as pursuing the first project. The latter is not a problem for right-wing libertarians as it stands.[1] For it to be a problem, Wendt would need to show that the initial assumptions of that project are more plausible and less problematic than the assumptions right-wing libertarians actually make. That is a task Wendt never takes up.

1. The Rationale for a Sufficiency Proviso

Wendt seems to attempt to ground his proviso in a starting point ostensibly like that of many other libertarians. Wendt holds that the idea that persons are project pursuers is close to the starting point in the derivations of basic rights that one finds in Loren Lomasky and Eric Mack, for example. Wendt points to the general sort of derivation he accepts in the following passage:

> One powerful... argument for libertarianism as a theory of justice builds on the idea of project pursuit. Persons are purposive beings and have the capacity to pursue all kinds of projects. Trivially, all projects require the use of one's body and mind, and so persons should be conceived as self-owners. But almost all such projects also require external resources, in one way or another, and they require being able to count on one's resources. Hence persons as project-pursuers also need the opportunity to acquire private property in external resources... Therefore, a libertarian theory of justice should combine self-ownership with a second natural right, the right to the practice of private property. Now if one accepts the project pursuit

---

[1] Henceforth, when I say "libertarian" or "libertarians," I should be taken to refer to right-wing libertarians.

rationale for a libertarian theory of justice, then one should also care that everyone actually has sufficient resources to live as a project pursuer. Without sufficient resources, one is simply unable to live a life as a project pursuer. That is why a libertarian theory of justice should somehow try to incorporate sufficientarian concerns. (Wendt 2018b, 170–71)

Wendt is clear that this argument is a very rough sketch (Wendt 2018b, 171). Nonetheless, he finds it sufficient to motivate the inclusion of his sufficiency proviso within a libertarian theory of justice. He repeats essentially this idea elsewhere when he writes the following:

The rationale for granting persons a Hohfeldian moral power to acquire property in external resources in accordance with conventional practices of private property is that it allows them to securely pursue personal projects… If caring about people as project pursuers is the rationale for advancing a libertarian theory of justice that allows people to acquire property in accordance with conventional practices, it must also require that people indeed have sufficient resources for project pursuit. (Wendt 2018b, 174)

The fact that some lack sufficient resources to live as project pursuers is problematic, as Wendt sees it, because the whole point of private property is to facilitate the pursuit of projects. When individuals lack such resources, it is, at least prima facie, a problem for the system of private property in question. Since the point of private property is to facilitate project pursuit, Wendt denies that responsibility matters when it comes to determining whether the proviso is satisfied:

The proviso does not ask about the reasons why someone is below the sufficiency threshold. It does not require showing, for example, that someone is below the sufficiency threshold without any fault of his own, or because a practice of private property is in place. From the perspective of the project pursuit rationale for libertarianism, someone not having enough to be a project pursuer is always a concern, no matter what its cause is. (Wendt 2018b, 174)

The idea here is that if what really matters is that everyone has resources to pursue projects, then we must be motivated to supply those resources when others lack them. Here, Wendt has us reacting to important facts about others. I said that this is close to the starting point that one finds in Lomasky and Mack, and Wendt himself seems to welcome this comparison. He characterizes Lomasky's derivation as follows:

He imagines a state of nature with project pursuers who care a lot about their own projects, but are also empathetic with the concerns of others, have some disposition to behave altruistically, and are able to recognize impersonal value. He tries to show that from such a state of nature mutually acknowledged moral space will naturally emerge. (Wendt 2018a, 4)

Something like the idea that we can respond to impersonal value seems implicit in Wendt's suggestion that we should care about others as project pursuers. I do not wish to pin the belief in impersonal value on Wendt. He may well reject it. What matters is that his sketch of the rationale for the proviso clearly requires us to care enough about others not merely to leave them alone, but to furnish them with resources when doing so does not thwart the purpose of private property in the first place. This is why I said above that when individuals lack sufficient resources, it is a prima facie problem.

Wendt places an important limitation on the demands the proviso may place on property owners. He writes that "the sufficiency proviso cannot unconditionally require to bring everyone above the sufficiency threshold" (Wendt 2018b, 174). He holds that the proviso requires that a system of private property must be designed to bring everyone above the sufficiency threshold "if that is possible without undermining the point of the practice of private property in the first place" (Wendt 2018b, 174). The point of private property is to allow people to pursue their projects; if the demands of satisfying the proviso undermine that very point, then the system need not satisfy it.

Similarly, Wendt does not say that everyone must have sufficient resources to pursue any old project. Instead, the sufficiency proviso requires seeing that everyone's basic human needs are met. When possible, a just system of private property requires that everyone has "food, clothing shelter, etc." (Wendt 2018b, 175). Some people, such as the disabled, might need more than this. Again, the point is that if one cares about project pursuit, one must ensure that everyone has the resources to be able to pursue projects. In this vein, Wendt claims that survival itself is not to count as a "project" (Wendt 2018b, 175).

So far, I have sketched the rationale for the proviso. I have also pointed to two limitations Wendt places on it. There is one further limitation to note before moving on. Wendt applies his proviso not to original appropriations, but to systems of private property. There are two aspects of this claim. First, Wendt is not interested in offering an account of justice in original appropriation—at least not via the sufficiency proviso. He is pretty clear about this in several places.[2] Second, he writes that "what counts, from the point of view of the project pursuit rationale for libertarianism, is not that

---

[2] Wendt (2018b, 175; 2018a, 13).

everyone can initially acquire things, but that everyone can come to own and use sufficient things" (Wendt 2018b, 175). This justification of the sufficiency proviso is novel and provocative. If Wendt is correct, a much more extensive state than most libertarians are willing to tolerate could be justified. After all, someone has to fund, enact, and police the administration of the proviso. In the following section, I challenge the very foundations of Wendt's rationale for private property rights.

2. A Consequentialist Justification of the Proviso

There is a subtle difference between Wendt's characterization of the standard justification of rights, on the one hand, and that found in Nozick and Mack, on the other. Wendt writes the following:

> The rationale for granting persons a Hohfeldian moral power to acquire property in external resources in accordance with conventional practices of private property is that it allows them to securely pursue personal projects. But without actually succeeding to have sufficient resources for pursuing projects beyond mere survival, this power is not of much help. (Wendt 2018b, 174)

The first sentence seems to say that rights *allow* people to try to secure personal objects. Wendt then proceeds to talk of *actually succeeding* at having sufficient resources. This is why Wendt feels it is necessary to have a sufficiency proviso. He takes the rationale for private property rights to be that they are the best way to ensure that everyone has enough to pursue projects. But this is not the same as holding that private property rights exist as a means of allowing people to attempt to pursue their projects. Wendt either does not notice this difference between his position and that of other libertarians or he thinks that the way the libertarians he targets argue is wrong. However, if the latter is the case, Wendt never shoulders the burden of arguing against their starting point.

Robert Nozick treats rights as side constraints. He then asks us why we should accept side constraints (Nozick 1974, 30). His answer is that side constraints reflect the idea that people are not mere means to be used for the purposes of others (Nozick 1974, 31). Now, as pertains to the present discussion, Nozick clearly rejects the consequentialist rationale for rights. Wendt needs to enter this discussion and show why Nozick is wrong.

Now, Wendt is right that libertarian theorists have to say that we can respond to facts about others. Mack, for example, holds that each of us can and should respond to the fact that others have their own ends to pursue, just as each of us has such ends. However, Mack and Nozick both seem to hold that the response that best fits with the fact that each individual has his own ends to pursue is that each of us should not interfere with others to the greatest extent possible. This is usually the least costly manner of responding to important normative facts about others.

Cost also matters when it comes to Wendt's discussion of responsibility. As I mentioned above, when Wendt tries to insert sufficiency considerations into a theory of justice, he ignores part of the traditional rationale for mere rights of non-interference. Part of the rationale for rights is that deference is the least costly way of responding to the fact that others have their own projects to pursue. Once we must deliver goods or services to others, we bump up the cost. This departure is important because it allows Wendt to part ways with most libertarians in denying that responsibility matters in determining whether one should receive support vis-à-vis the proviso. This is a massive departure from the tradition in which Wendt is working. Indeed, some of the authors Wendt cites have spent a great deal of time exploring the role that responsibility plays in deciding whether libertarians should support a social safety net.

John Locke is clear that people who have sufficient *opportunities* should not complain because to do so would be to evince the desire "to benefit of another's pains" (Locke 1952, §34). While Locke is discussing original appropriations in this passage, there is no textual evidence that his view changes when it comes to systems of private property. Indeed, in his *Essay on the Poor Law*, Locke proposes implementing forced labor on those who refuse to make use of the opportunities available to them.[3]

Eric Mack argues that there may well be scenarios in which there is a libertarian-friendly rationale for taxation in order to aid people who are in dire straits. While he thinks that this road is "convoluted," he does think that it needs to be taken seriously by everyone, irrespective of their views of taxation. However, he is clear that this program would be aimed at aiding those who are living "faultlessly (or faultlessly enough)" (Mack 2006, 140).

These are just two examples among many. Within the libertarian tradition, it is common to hold that one's claim to aid from others *as a matter of justice* is contingent in part on the responsibility the recipient bears for his

---

[3] This essay is available in *Political Essays*, ed. Mark Goldie (New York: Cambridge University Press, 1997), 182–98.

or her condition.[4] One reason why libertarians hold this is that the cost of delivering goods and services to others is increased if the individual should receive those goods no matter why he or she needs them.

Wendt clearly does not think that focusing on cost is the right way to look at the matter. He believes that the attractiveness of rights is that they "enable everyone to actually live as a project pursuer" (Wendt 2018b, 171). This is a consequentialist justification of rights. If rights do not fulfill this purpose, they are unjustified. If there is a superior means of enabling people to live as project pursuers while eschewing or limiting rights, then *that* system would be superior to the system of rights libertarians tend to favor. If this is the view, then the argument for rights is subject to a purely empirical justification. Now, while it is wrong to see good derivations of rights as completely divorced from empirical concerns, it is also notoriously problematic to justify rights on entirely empirical grounds. Libertarians do not primarily oppose well-run European welfare states because they fail to allow everyone to live as a project pursuer. Libertarians oppose those states because they violate both bodily and private property rights, regardless of those states' success in allowing individuals to live as project pursuers.

Wendt's consequentialist justification of private property rights makes it an open question just how extensive the rights libertarians tend to endorse should be. This is true even of bodily rights. If rights are justified because they enable project pursuit, paternalism, for example, could be justified on the grounds that it sometimes does so too. But Wendt has not attempted to deal with paternalism and the challenge self-ownership poses to it—at least as far as I can tell. His claim that we show proper concern for others by seeing that they have sufficient resources is problematic in terms of cost. In the following section, I assess Wendt's claim without considering cost. I argue that we can show that we care for others in ways that are not as demanding as Wendt's proviso.

3. Justice and Care

The consequentialist justification of rights is actually at the heart of Wendt's fundamental departure from a standard libertarian theory of justice. Wendt characterizes the libertarian position as conceiving "justice in terms of

---

[4] There might be practical reasons for having a proviso that does not deal with responsibility. Perhaps the process of determining which claimants are responsible will be too unwieldly. For a discussion, see, among others, Zwolinski (2015). Wendt, though, is not offering a pragmatic case for his proviso.

private property" and holding "that persons are self-owners and have a moral power to acquire property rights in initially unowned external resources" (Wendt 2018b, 170). This seems right. However, Wendt is keen to argue that his proviso does not require assigning positive rights or welfare rights to persons (Wendt 2018b, 176). This is because the system of private property itself is unjustified if it fails to satisfy the rationale for private property in the first place. It is unfortunate that he does not say more about this, but it seems that there is no individual who has a claim right to reach the level of sufficiency. Instead, since the system is unjustified, the system should be reformed so as to make it justified (Wendt 2018b, 176).

Now, how Wendt sees these two ideas fitting together is unclear. Ostensibly, they are in conflict. Libertarianism defines justice in terms of rights; the sufficiency proviso says that a system of private property can be unjust even if no one's rights are violated.[5] It seems that Wendt agrees to a degree. He calls his theory "libertarian" in a sense distinct from that offered above: "I would insist that a theory should count as an overall 'libertarian' one when it gives considerable weight to self-ownership and the natural right to the practice of private property, even if it combines them with some additional principles of justice" (Wendt 2018b, 170).

Wendt is thus aware of this departure from the standard libertarian picture. Again, he has an argument to show that this departure is not merely permissible, but required. Part of the case for the sufficiency proviso is that it is more consistent with libertarian theory. For example, he rejects the egalitarian proviso found in the writings of left-wing libertarians such as Michael Otsuka and Peter Vallentyne. Wendt holds that an egalitarian proviso is not supported by libertarian considerations: "The rationale for a libertarian theory of justice does not speak in favor of an egalitarian proviso. In order to be able to securely pursue person projects, one need not have equal opportunities for welfare or natural resources. One needs to have sufficient opportunities and sufficient resources" (Wendt 2018b, 177).

Further, an egalitarian proviso "imposes unnecessarily harsh restrictions on legitimate project pursuit" (Wendt 2018b, 177). In this vein, he cites Loren Lomasky's observation that for an egalitarian to "insist that all persons are morally obligated to bring about the equal allocations of material goods is to ignore that each person has primary reason to supply for himself those

---

[5] Wendt mistakenly claims that Mack's anti-paralysis postulate can be used to argue for Wendt's proviso. But Mack's anti-paralysis postulate protects rights. Wendt never claims to be protecting rights.

goods which are needed for the advancement of his own projects" (Wendt 2018b, 177, citing Lomasky 1987, 122).

The egalitarian proviso is to Wendt's left, so to speak. It requires that people deliver much more to others than Wendt believes is defensible. But Wendt rejects at least two provisos to his right for reasons unrelated to rights.

First, he argues against Nozick's proviso. Nozick's requires that appropriations do not relevantly worsen the condition of others. Nozick seems to extend this proviso beyond mere appropriations to individual transactions, and possibly a system of private property itself.[6] Whatever the case, Wendt takes this proviso to be too weak. He writes: "That one's situation is not worsened by an appropriation or by the system allowing initial appropriation is simply not enough to grant the necessary external preconditions for living one's life as a project pursuer" (Wendt 2018b, 179). Why is this a problem? Wendt writes that "if the rationale for a libertarian theory of justice is to enable persons to live as project pursuers, then Nozick's proviso is too weak" (Wendt 2018b, 179).

What is his argument for the move from the antecedent to the consequent in this proposition? It seems to be this claim: "If one really cares about everyone being able to live as a project pursuer and regards this as the rationale to endorse libertarianism, then nothing less than the sufficiency proviso is adequate" (Wendt 2018b, 179). If one really cares that people live their lives as project pursuers, one must care that they have enough resources to do this. One must not only care, but form a program of private property rights so that those who lack enough to live as project pursuers see resources delivered to them.

Wendt says something similar about Eric Mack's proviso. Given this thick conception of "care," it is not surprising that Wendt rejects Mack's proviso. Mack's proviso requires that "persons not deploy their legitimate holdings, i.e., their extra personal property, in ways that severely, albeit non-invasively disable persons world-interactive powers" (Mack 1995, 187). The idea is that if we rightly attribute to others robust ownership, such as rights over their talents and faculties, then we must attribute to others not merely rights against invasive disablement, but also against non-invasive disablement. As Mack puts it, these world-interactive powers include the individual's "capacities to affect extra-personal environment in accord with her purposes" (Mack 1995, 186). Since these powers are "essentially relational… [t]he presence of an extra-personal environment open to being affected by those

---

[6] Nozick (1974, 179).

powers is an essential element of their existence" (Mack 1995, 187). The reason for attributing rights over talents and faculties to others in the first place is to allow them to "pursue their own good (or projects)" (Wendt 2018b, 180).

Wendt thinks that this proviso is too weak for two reasons. First, he writes that by requiring only that the uses of property do not disable the world-interactive powers of others, Mack "leaves out all cases where someone's world-interactive powers are severely limited, but not due to other persons, or not due to their uses of their property. This is unfortunate if one cares about people actually being able to live their lives as project pursuers" (Wendt 2018b, 181). Second, "persons whose world interactive powers are not severely disabled can still lack sufficient resources for being able to live their lives as project pursuers" (Wendt 2018b, 181). If one really cares about project pursuit, one should not allow this to happen.

Those familiar with right-wing libertarianism will wonder about Wendt's use of "care" in his justification of the sufficiency proviso. In particular, it is clear that Wendt fails on two fronts to justify employing this proposition in his argument: "If one accepts the project pursuit rationale for a libertarian theory of justice, then one should also care that everybody actually has sufficient resources to live as a project pursuer" (Wendt 2018b, 170–71).

The first front on which Wendt fails to justify this proposition is that he ignores other ways of showing concern for others. One way to see this is to consider how other provisos fail to get us to the consequent in the conditional proposition that ends the previous paragraph. Here are four stages one might move through before getting to Wendt's proviso. First, Eric Mack's proviso prohibits rendering nugatory the world-interactive powers of others (Mack 1995, 187–88). Mack specifically holds that if someone is culpably at a level of insufficient resources, that person is not entitled to redress (Mack 2006, 140–41). So imagine that I have the only fruit tree around. I enclose it with a fence. There is no other food in the area. Bob's powers are disabled *because* I deny him access to the fruit. Mack's proviso is violated. If I remove the fence and say that Bob may pick fruit, the proviso is not violated. This proviso requires mere deference.

Robert Nozick's proviso seems to require not lowering anyone's level of expected welfare. Return to the previous example of the fence around the tree. When I remove the barrier from the tree, I might satisfy Nozick's proviso. Provided that Bob endures no loss of expected welfare, I have satisfied it. However, if Bob does endure a loss of expected welfare, I seem to have violated the proviso. I might also have to use some of the seeds to plant more trees. After all, two of us are eating and not just one.[7] This proviso ostensibly requires a little more from us than Mack's, but it does not reach the level that Wendt requires.

Now suppose that we strengthen Mack's and Nozick's provisos with the stipulation that if some people are unable to achieve some sufficient level of opportunities or welfare, then others must provide it. However, if some are culpably lacking sufficient opportunities or welfare, then it is impermissible to force others to provide it. This is still weaker than Wendt's proviso because it matters why a person lacks sufficient resources. The four stages, then, are Mack's proviso, Nozick's proviso, Mack's proviso with a requirement that we deliver resources to those who cannot help themselves, and Nozick's proviso with a requirement that we deliver resources to those who cannot help themselves.

Again, suppose that Bob refuses to pick fruit and demands that I deliver some fruit to him. Mack's proviso does not require me to do any such thing. Ex hypothesi Bob is perfectly capable of getting the fruit himself. I am not creating a barrier. So he has to get it himself. Wendt seems to hold that I do not really care about project pursuit. When I removed the barrier, I did not demonstrate that I really care. The justification of that claim requires an extraordinary argument, especially since Wendt introduces it into a tradition that clearly does not agree with his view about "really caring."[8] Locke and Mack, for example, think that responsibility matters. My only claim here is that Wendt does not offer any sort of argument to show that they are wrong, let alone an extraordinary one.

Similarly, Nozick's proviso seems to require not lowering anyone's level of expected welfare. Suppose that I do not merely remove the fence, but plant some more trees. Under these conditions, we have enough fruit so that both of us are at the level of welfare we would have expected had the other not been around. If Bob refuses to harvest any apples, Wendt would have to say that I do not care about project pursuit. He would have to say this even though there are more apples precisely because I planted more to satisfy Nozick's proviso.

---

[7] This is not obviously part of Nozick's proviso, but I insert it for the purposes of demonstration.

[8] The story is to be constructed so that my ability to pursue projects is not undermined by Bob's demand. I can pursue my projects. The point is that we need to know why I do not care about project pursuit when I refuse to deliver fruit to Bob.

While I think most libertarian theorists hold that adjusting one's behavior to satisfy *any* of the four provisos mentioned above is indicative of *some* level of care, focus only on the two in which one would help those who cannot help themselves.[9] Suppose that I ask Bob whether he is unable to collect the fruit. If he says that he is not, I would help him. If he says that he is but wishes not to collect it, I do not help him. Wendt seems to hold that I do not really care about project pursuit in either case. I hope that this seems intuitively implausible, because it is.

One final means of showing concern for others is to treat sufficientarian concerns as part of a theory of virtue. Imagine that I agree with Wendt that people who really care about project pursuit should also really care that others have enough resources to pursue projects—at least when this does not interfere with the purpose of private property in the first place. However, I say that this shows that there are virtue-based reasons to see that everyone has enough to pursue projects. Nobody has a right ensuring that others keep him or her at a level of sufficiency; Wendt himself says this. Since he is a libertarian, he "conceive[s]… justice in terms of property rights" (Wendt 2017, 1). Because I too do this, I hold that the reasons for keeping everyone at a level of sufficiency are not part of a theory of *justice*, but part of a theory of *virtue*. I am not holding that there is no way of blocking this way of looking at things. I am saying that Wendt has done nothing to block it.

It seems that Wendt is aware that he is asking for a great deal more care than most libertarians do, at least as it pertains to the demands of justice. To justify this departure, Wendt claims that "it is most convenient to see the sufficiency proviso as part of the natural right to the practice of private property" (Wendt 2018b, 176). The key idea is that the "Sufficiency Proviso co-determines what a 'justifiable' practice of private property is—namely a practice that satisfies the sufficiency proviso" (Wendt 2018b, 176). A system of private property is unjust if it fails to satisfy the proviso, precisely because a system is just only when it does so. He denies that the reasons why one is in need of aid matter; a system cannot be justified to people who suffer under that system, especially when seeing to it that they have sufficient resources would not undermine the point of private property in the first place. He says that "private property is justified because private property is necessary for project pursuit, but practices of private property should work for all" (Wendt 2018b, 179). Apparently, a practice of private property should "work" for those who refuse to work at all.

---

[9] Some libertarians eschew a proviso entirely. See Rothbard (1998) and Machan (2009), among others. I am grateful to an anonymous reviewer for these examples.

Lurking behind my discussion up to this point has been self-ownership. The idea that individuals have a natural proprietorship over their bodies, talents, and faculties is both attractive and the hallmark of libertarianism. Self-ownership matters for many reasons, not the least of which is cost. If I own myself but owe you something—even mere deference—I endure a cost. The greater this cost, the more my ownership of myself is diminished. Wendt also accepts self-ownership. It is thus necessary to assess Wendt's claims about his proviso and self-ownership.

4. Mitigating Self-Ownership

Wendt characterizes the libertarian position as conceiving "justice in terms of private property" and holding "that persons are self-owners and have a moral power to acquire property rights in initially unowned external resources" (Wendt 2018b, 170). Wendt seems to wish to preserve self-ownership. However, in an effort to avoid "merely formal" self-ownership, he requires individuals to reform a system of private property even if it violates no one's rights.

Call self-ownership rights "merely formal" if they protect people against physically invasive actions but do nothing to prevent people from horrible non-invasive suffering at the hands of others. A standard case might look like this: Bob owns himself. Tom builds a wall around Bob, such that if Bob touches the wall, he will violate Tom's property rights. Bob, on the other hand, will starve to death, even though Tom never touched him.

I think we would all agree that Tom has wronged Bob. Many libertarians agree as well (Mack 2002; Block 2016; Dominiak 2017). I think we would also agree that there are good reasons to believe that the wrong Bob suffered is a violation of his rights. Wendt, though, goes beyond this and says that if there is no wall and Bob is going to die because he refuses to go and get some food, the problem vis-à-vis justice lies with *the system of private property* and not Bob.

With regard to what this might mean in practice, Wendt's treatment of this issue is perhaps intentionally vague. He writes that a system of private property should be reformed if some individual lacks sufficient resources to pursue projects, provided that doing so does not undermine the purpose of rights in the first place. He says also that this neither requires attributing positive rights to people nor delivering goods to others. However, it is obvious that "reforming" the practice can require work in order to see to it that others have sufficient resources. When one combines this possibility with Wendt's judgment that it does not matter why someone lacks sufficient resources, self-ownership is obviously weakened. If one individual must take the time to see to it that another has sufficient resources, his self-ownership rights are obviously weaker than if he did not have to do so. This is true even if, as Wendt says, no one must *deliver* resources to another.

Even if other individuals are kind enough to handle the delivery of those goods and services, the individual whose goods are taken must perform the labor of keeping records, making goods accessible, and so on. I am not arguing that there is no way of trimming away at the edges of self-ownership as Wendt is prepared to do. I am arguing that Wendt's proviso requires far more than Nozick's and Mack's provisos; and Wendt offers only a questionable conception of "care" and a consequentialist derivation of rights to justify doing so.

The worry about self-ownership is especially important in relation to Mack's proviso. Mack sees his proviso as improving on Nozick's because it puts the injustice in proviso violations back into a theory of rights (Mack 2002). Since Wendt sees libertarians as defining justice in terms of rights, Mack's proviso is more libertarian than Nozick's. But Wendt knocks the proviso right out of a theory of rights and back into a separate theory of justice. Once there is a theory of justice distinct from a theory of rights, the demands of that separate theory of justice mitigate self-ownership. The demands of satisfying that theory are costs; and they limit what individuals may do, even when their actions do not violate the rights of others. I take it as fairly obvious that this weakens self-ownership.

Wendt's efforts to avoid a merely formal conception of self-ownership amount to throwing the baby out with the bathwater. As long as people can pursue projects, Wendt denies that we need to factor in whether a needy individual is responsible for his or her lack of sufficient resources. But this allows—and welcomes—free riders to have a claim on the efforts of others.

I am sure that Wendt would respond here by holding that it simply is problematic for someone to have insufficient resources for project pursuit. That, after all, was his reason for rejecting Nozick's and Mack's provisos. The reason that lacking sufficient resources is *problematic* has to do with the foundations of rights, as Wendt sees it. Wendt's consequentialist justification of property rights subtends this response. I argued above that what Wendt says about both of those issues is problematic from a libertarian perspective. Unless he has a better argument up his sleeve than the care-based consequentialist rationale that he repeats throughout his writings on the issue, I contend that nothing he says is problematic for the libertarians in question.

5. The Bygone System of Private Property

Wendt follows Eric Mack in arguing that his proviso applies to a system of private property. The difference between the two is that Mack argues that it is unclear who has to do anything to help those who suffer a proviso violation. After all, no individual is doing anything that violates rights. Wendt argues that the whole system must be modified to see to it that those who suffer within it have sufficient resources, as long as doing so does not undermine the purpose of private property in the first place. I argue that Mack's judgment is far more reasonable than Wendt's because systems of private property in the real world are both inclusive and exclusive in ways that are problematic for Wendt's proviso.

Given the makeup of my family and our dietary habits, it is vastly more likely that we are more economically linked to workers in Maharashtra, India, than to the homeless in Muncie, Indiana. We buy goods produced by the former; I do not know how we might economically relate to the latter. The former cooperate with me in a system of private property insofar as I buy things from them. They are factually included in the system of private property within which I participate. The homeless in Muncie at least might not be.

The problem this example illustrates is that *systems* of private property are no longer local and easily identifiable. We can be involved in multiple systems that include far-flung and obscure individuals in some ways, but which exclude geographical neighbors in other ways. This makes it remarkably difficult to say which people's suffering is grounds for reforming any particular system of private property. The upshot is that it would be remarkably challenging to craft a system that aids those that it needs to aid. In this regard, Mack's judgment is superior to Wendt's. We do not know who is responsible for making changes to aid others.[10]

I have written thus far on the assumption that Wendt thinks that systems of private property are unjustified if people within them suffer because of the systems. My point is that individuals near me might not be part of the system of private property at all. A response to what I have said so far is that anyone subject to the laws of a system of private property is thereby an individual whose suffering can require an adjustment of the system. So, the local nonparticipants are still subject to the system. But this must also include the distant workers whose wares we buy. It also has to

---

[10] The fact that Mack links the need for changing the system to rights violations is also superior.

include the people who are near those whose wares we buy and thus subject to the rules of the system of private property.

The obvious problem here is that our global economy seems to extend the notion of "a system of private property" to include just about everyone. This also makes it hard to amend the system to make sure that everyone has sufficient resources. One might think that national governments should do so, but even that is challenging for several reasons. First, some governments simply lack the resources to do so. Second, there is no obvious reason why the local nonparticipant should receive resources while the distant participant should not (if that distant participant lacks sufficient resources). Third, if wealthy nations must somehow orchestrate the delivery of goods to those in need elsewhere, this can be very costly. It might be so costly that the point of private property could be undermined. Now, it never is clear what Wendt thinks the point of private property is beyond project pursuit. Nonetheless, we could imagine that ensuring that everyone has sufficient resources is costly enough to lower the standard of living of many in wealthy nations, but not so costly that no one can pursue projects. Where Wendt draws the line is unclear. Fourth, many of those local governments may lack the moral authority to oversee the distribution of resources for other reasons. Perhaps some governments are engaged in human rights violations such that they have forfeited any claim to be the architects of private property systems.[11] The first three points are conceptual in nature; they apply to any global economy. The last one applies to actual governments. In that regard, it is less significant.

I do not know how to show that these problems are insurmountable. What is clear is that the difficulties raised here are problematic for Wendt, but not for Mack. Once the proviso is divorced from rights violations, the need to specify what counts as problematic suffering arises. The fact that systems of private property are no longer local and geographically contained is particularly difficult for positions such as Wendt's.

If Wendt has a means of justifying either his consequentialist derivation of rights or his robust conception of "care," then there are reasons for libertarians to take the sufficiency proviso seriously. As it stands, the foundations of Wendt's proviso are weak in their own right and at odds with standard libertarian ideas.

---

[11] Litotes intentional.

References

Block, W. E. 2016. "Forestalling, Positive Obligations and the Lockean and Blockian Provisos: Rejoinder to Stephan Kinsella." *Ekonomia–Wroclaw Economic Review* 22 (3): 27–41.

Dominiak, Lukasz. 2017. "The Blockian Proviso and the Rationality of Private Property Rights." *Libertarian Papers* 9 (1): 114–28.

Locke, John. 1952. *Second Treatise of Government.* New York: Macmillan.

Locke, John. 1997. "Essay on the Poor Law." In *Political Essays*, edited by Mark Goldie, 182–98. New York: Cambridge University Press.

Lomasky, Loren. 1987. *Persons, Rights, and the Moral Community*. New York: Oxford University Press.

Machan, Tibor. 2009. "Self-Ownership and the Lockean Proviso" *Philosophy of the Social Sciences* 39 (1): 93–98.

Mack, Eric. 1995. "The Self-Ownership Proviso: A New and Improved Lockean Proviso." *Social Philosophy & Policy* 12: 286–315.

Mack, Eric. 2002. "Self-Ownership, Marxism, and Egalitarianism: Part I: Challenges to Historical Entitlement." *Politics, Philosophy and Economics* 1 (1): 75–108.

Mack, Eric. 2002. "Self-Ownership, Marxism, and Egalitarianism (Part 2): Challenges to the Self-Ownership Thesis." *Politics, Philosophy, and Economics* 12: 83–84.

Mack, Eric. 2006. "Non-Absolute Rights and Libertarian Taxation." *Social Philosophy and Policy* 23 (2): 109–41.

Nozick, Robert. 1974. *Anarchy, State, and Utopia*. New York: Basic Books.

Rothbard, Murray. 1998. *The Ethics of Liberty*. New York: New York University Press.

Wendt, F. 2018a. "Three Types of Sufficientarian Libertarianism." *Res Publica*. doi:10.1007/s11158–018–9400-y.

Wendt, Fabian. 2018b. "The Sufficiency Proviso." In *Routledge Handbook of Libertarianism*, edited by J. Brennan, B. van der Vossen, and D. Schmidt, 169–83. Routledge: New York.

Zwolinski, Matt. 2015. "Property, Coercion, and the Welfare State: The Libertarian Case for a Basic Income Guarantee for All." *Independent Review* 19, no. 4 (Spring): 515–29.

Caring about Projects, Responsibility, and Rights: A Response to Rodgers

Fabian Wendt[*]

I THANK LAMONT RODGERS for critically discussing my work and giving me the chance to clarify and elaborate a couple of points about the sufficiency proviso and moderate libertarianism in general. I hope this exchange will help us better understand where the main points of disagreement lie.

My response to Rodgers has six sections. After a very brief summary of what moderate libertarianism and the sufficiency proviso are (section 1), I try to answer his main allegations: that I advance a problematically "consequentialist derivation of rights" (section 2) and a questionably "robust conception of 'care'" (section 3). Both allegations invoke a good deal of misunderstandings, as I will explain. I then discuss the role of personal responsibility (section 4) and whether self-ownership rights are mitigated in a problematic way (section 5) and thereby try to refute arguments against my view that many not-so-moderate libertarians will be inclined to make. The last section provides a short discussion of an issue I did not take up earlier: how practices of private property are to be individuated (section 6).

---

[*]Fabian Wendt is a research associate at the Smith Institute for Political Economy and Philosophy at Chapman University.

CITATION INFORMATION FOR THIS ARTICLE:

Fabian Wendt. 2018. "Caring about Projects, Responsibility, and Rights: A Response to Rodgers." *Libertarian Papers*. 10 (2): 159-172. ONLINE AT: libertarianpapers.org. THIS ARTICLE IS subject to a Creative Commons Attribution 3.0 License (creativecommons.org/licenses).

1. A Very Brief Sketch of the View

Moderate libertarianism (see Wendt 2017, 2018) is a theory of justice. It starts with the idea that people should be able to live as project pursuers. Because people should be able to live as project pursuers, we should conceive them as endowed with self-ownership rights and a right to acquire external resources in line with justifiable conventional practices of private property. To be justifiable, a practice of private property has to satisfy the so-called "sufficiency proviso," among other things. The sufficiency proviso holds that a practice of private property has to be designed in a way such that everyone has sufficient resources to live as a project pursuer, if this is possible without undermining the point of having a practice of private property in the first place. The point of practices of private property is to allow people to live as project pursuers.

That people are to be able to live as project pursuers is thus an idea that has three functions: it grounds self-ownership and the right to acquire external resources in line with justifiable conventional practices of private property, it co-determines what a justifiable practice of private property is, and it serves as a telos for practices of private property (it specifies what their point is and allows us to evaluate different practices as better or worse).[1]

The view is a *moderate* version of libertarianism above all because it endorses the sufficiency proviso, which is weaker than the egalitarian proviso advocated by left-libertarians such as Hillel Steiner (1994) but stronger than the provisos advocated by Robert Nozick (1974) and Eric Mack (1995). It is also moderate in that it conceives practices of private property as conventional,[2] takes rights to be stringent, but not maximally stringent, and holds that rights do not exhaust political morality. But the main focus of my discussion will be on the sufficiency proviso.

2. A Consequentialist Justification of Rights?

In the last paragraph of his piece, Rodgers writes: "If Wendt has a means of justifying either his consequentialist derivation of rights or his robust conception of 'care,' then there are reasons for libertarians to take the sufficiency proviso seriously" (2018, 158). I take him to imply that I do not

---

[1] I emphasize the point about the telos of practices of private property in a work-in-progress paper.

[2] One could say that it is as Humean as a Lockean view could be (or the other way around).

have such a means. So let me begin my reply (in this and the next section) with these (allegedly) "tenuous foundations" of my view.

I am surprised that my (so far admittedly sketchy) justification of rights was read as a consequentialist justification.[3] I believe that self-ownership rights and the right to the practice of private property have a point and that this point is to enable everyone to live as a project pursuer. Why is this consequentialist? At least it does not seem more consequentialist than any other theory about the point of rights—be it to protect interests, to protect choices or autonomy, or to create spheres of jurisdiction.

Be that as it may, let us focus on why Rodgers regards my "consequentialist" justification of rights as *problematic*. He does not say very much, but one thing he suggests in this context and with reference to Nozick is that rights function as side-constraints (2018, 147). Yet I agree that rights function as side-constraints, albeit not as maximally stringent side-constraints. Rights can sometimes give way to other moral considerations, as even Nozick admits (1974, 30n). I do not see a reason why the project pursuit–based justification of rights should stand in the way of their functioning as side-constraints.[4]

A second problem with my justification of rights seems to be that it is, well, different from what some other libertarians would be prepared to say with regard to rights and project pursuit, namely that "private property rights exist as a means of allowing people to attempt to pursue their projects" (Rodgers 2018, 147). This is indeed different from what I say since being allowed to live as a project pursuer is compatible with not being able to live as a project pursuer. Now while I do not understand why this alternative justification of rights is supposed to be any less "consequentialist" than my own justification, I am happy to "[shoulder] the burden of arguing against [this alternative] starting point" (Rodgers 2018, 147).[5]

---

[3] Rodgers also writes that I give a "purely empirical" justification of rights (2018, 149), which puzzles me even more. The view is based on the axiological (i.e., non-empirical) idea that it is a good thing if people are enabled to live as project pursuers.

[4] Or at least why it should be any less compatible with conceiving rights as side-constraints than other accounts that spell out what the alleged point of rights is. *Any* such theory will have to deal with what is sometimes called the "paradox of deontology" (see Scheffler 1985; McMahon 1991; also Nozick 1974, 30–33), but this is by no means a problem that is specific to a project pursuit–based defense of rights as side-constraints.

[5] Relatedly, Rodgers says that if moderate libertarianism started from other assumptions than right-wing libertarianism, then I would need to show that my

As I pointed out before (Wendt 2017, 175), the alternative starting point is not very attractive because being formally allowed to live as a project pursuer is not of much value if you are not actually able to live as a project pursuer. That is why a theory of rights should not be based on the claim that people should be formally allowed to live as project pursuers, but on the claim that people should be able to live as project pursuers. Rodgers does not give us a reason to think otherwise.

A final note: In the introduction to his text, Rodgers writes that he will read me as attempting to prove that moderate libertarianism and the sufficiency proviso are "what fits most comfortably with a very commonly accepted foundation of libertarian private property rights" (2018, 144), which he apparently takes to be the claim that people are to be formally allowed to live as project pursuers. He says that he reads me this way because of "my explicit claims" (2018, 144). I do not know what he is referring to. In my 2017 piece, I argue that moderate libertarianism "better coheres with the most plausible rationale for endorsing a libertarian theory of justice in the first place" (2017, 169), but "most plausible" is certainly not the same as "commonly accepted." Moreover, I am not sure how "commonly accepted" the foundational claim that people are to be formally allowed to live as project pursuers really is. I do hope, though, that my sketchy project-pursuit rationale for moderate libertarianism does not sound completely alien to libertarian ears. In any case, if Rodgers wants to confine himself to showing that moderate libertarianism cannot be derived from the claim that people are to be formally allowed to live as project pursuers, then he is pushing at an open door. I am very willing to admit that moderate libertarianism—of course—cannot be derived from that claim. Luckily, for the most part Rodgers does not seem to read me the way he claims to read me.

3. A Robust Conception of Care

This brings me to Rodgers's worries about my questionably "robust conception of care." Rodgers quotes me saying that "[if] one really cares about everyone being able to live as a project pursuer and regards this as the rationale to endorse libertarianism, then nothing less than the sufficiency proviso is adequate" (2018, 151). Why is this false? According to Rodgers, I "fail to [justify] this proposition" because I ignore other ways of showing concern for others (2018, 152). What are these other ways? Maybe we care enough about people's ability to pursue projects by respecting the provisos

---

assumptions "are more plausible and less problematic than the assumptions right-wing libertarians actually make" (2018, 144).

advocated by Nozick or Mack (or variations of them).[6] Now luckily I discussed Nozick's and Mack's provisos extensively (2017, 176–80), and I think one can demonstrate that they are too weak if one accepts my starting point—that is, the idea that people should be able to live as project pursuers. As explained in the last section, being merely allowed to live as a project pursuer is not of much value if one is actually unable to live as a project pursuer; therefore a theorist who "really cares" about people's ability to pursue projects should accept the sufficiency proviso and nothing weaker. This is the thought.

Rodgers goes on to apply four relatively weak provisos—among them Nozick's and Mack's—and the sufficiency proviso to a case in which a person named Bob refuses to pick fruits himself and instead wants them freely delivered by someone else, maybe us, suggesting that it is not so clear that we do not "care" sufficiently about project pursuit if we opt for a proviso that is weaker than the sufficiency proviso and allows us to refuse to give our nice fruits to Bob (2018, 152–54).

But all this is misguided in two respects. Most importantly, my proviso works differently from the provisos of Mack and Nozick. My sufficiency proviso is a proviso regarding the justifiability of practices of private property, while Mack's proviso is a proviso on how to exercise one's property rights and Nozick's proviso is a proviso that concerns acts of initial appropriation and, as a historical shadow, transfers of property.[7] Thus only Mack's proviso and, in a different way, Nozick's proviso apply to the case of Bob. Second, the sufficiency proviso is not to make sure that everyone gets whatever they want or is able to succeed with any particular project they might fancy. It is to enable them to live as project pursuers—that is, to have the resources that are necessary to live as someone who is in a position to pursue projects and is not forced to struggle for survival every day. That ability is not at stake in the case of Bob. If he merely refuses to pick fruits, but could easily do it (or just eat the quinoa salad he bought at the grocery store instead), then he is able to live as a project pursuer.

I conclude, then, that while my "caring" about people's ability to pursue projects may be considered robust, Rodgers does not give us a reason to find it questionable.

---

[6] Rodgers also proposes that it may be considered virtuous to care about other people's ability to pursue projects (2018, 154). I do not disagree, but this certainly does not undermine the case for the sufficiency proviso.

[7] Nozick also seems to accept a proviso that applies to practices of private property as a whole (1974, 177), next to his proviso on acts of initial appropriation.

4. The Role of Personal Responsibility

One important issue raised by Rodgers is the issue of personal responsibility. In one of my articles Rodgers is referring to, I say: "From the perspective of the project-pursuit rationale for libertarianism, someone not having enough to be a project pursuer is always a concern, no matter what its cause is" (2017, 173–74). Rodgers replies that "denying that responsibility matters in determining whether one should receive support vis-à-vis the proviso" is a "massive departure" from the libertarian tradition (2018, 148), and, quite clearly, he takes the libertarian tradition to be correct on this point.

In response, it is important to get clear *for what* personal responsibility is to matter or not to matter. In my view, it does not matter for the assessment of the justice of practices of private property in one specific sense: a practice of private property should, if possible, be designed such that everybody has sufficient resources to live as a project pursuer, even people who do not have sufficient resources because of faults of their own, at least if they did not violate other people's rights and thus deserve punishment.[8] But what *institutions* are justifiable, from that point of view, is a separate issue.[9] As I put it in my earlier piece: "Considerations about responsibility are certainly important for designing the institutions that are to implement the proviso, but they do not matter at the level of a theory of justice" (2017, 174). Relevant institutions are all property-related laws and social norms as well as organizations, in particular organizations that are entitled to change, enact, or enforce property-related laws or social norms (possibly including state institutions).

Thus if responsibility-*insensitive* institutions of welfare provision—such as a state-provided basic income—would undermine the point of having a practice of private property in the first place, then moderate libertarianism would *not* support such institutions. Likewise, if responsibility-insensitive institutions of welfare provision would work so poorly that they would fail to live up to the sufficiency proviso, then moderate libertarianism would again *not* support such institutions. Why might either of these be the case? Maybe because such institutions would incentivize people to free ride on the efforts

---

[8] Rodgers says that, according to my view, if "Bob is going to die because he refuses to go and get some food, the problem vis-à-vis justice lies with the system of private property and not Bob" (2018, 155). I disagree, because if Bob just refuses to go and get food, even though he easily could, then he is perfectly able to live as a project pursuer.

[9] This sharp distinction between principles of justice on the one hand and the institutions that are to realize principles of justice on the other is also common among Rawls-inspired libertarians or classical liberals (see Tomasi 2012).

of others, as Rodgers puts it (2018, 156).[10] It is *possible* that the sufficiency proviso, although unconditionally demanding sufficient resources for everyone, is not satisfied by institutions that are designed to unconditionally provide everyone with sufficient resources (or that it is satisfied by them, but at the price of undermining the point of having a practice of private property in the first place). It is more plausible, though, that responsibility-insensitive institutions of welfare provision will usually meet the proviso (and not undermine the point of having a practice of private property in the first place), bad-incentive effects notwithstanding.

But that a certain set of institutions satisfies the sufficiency proviso does not imply that they are *required* by the sufficiency proviso. After all, it could be that both responsibility-sensitive and responsibility-insensitive institutions of welfare provision satisfy the sufficiency proviso (and do not undermine the point of having a practice of private property in the first place). What moderate libertarianism recommends, in the end, will depend on which of these institutions better lives up to the telos of practices of private property—that is, does a better job at enabling everyone to live as a project pursuer by creating clear-cut spheres of non-interference. As Rodgers acknowledges, some libertarians have advocated a basic income or a negative income tax already (Friedman 1962; Hayek 2012; Zwolinski 2015),[11] but moderate libertarianism is also compatible with advocating responsibility-sensitive institutions of welfare provision.

It should be noted that it is also possible that market anarchism—that is, a set of institutions that does not include *any* state-run provision of welfare—satisfies the sufficiency proviso and scores highest from the point of view of the telos of practices of private property. This is not my view, but it is a view that is compatible with moderate libertarianism.

Once one distinguishes the level of principles of justice and the level of institutions, it becomes clear that responsibility-related objections have to target the former, not the latter, if they are to target moderate libertarianism. So what could be objected against the view that, if possible, a *just* practice of private property has to be designed in a way such that everybody has

---

[10] Relatedly, David Schmidtz writes: "Our need for food, clothing, and shelter is beyond question; our need for guaranteed provision is not. Nor is guaranteed provision guaranteed to make people better off. After all, the guarantee does not mean the goods are free. What it means is someone else has to pay. It means people have to pay for other people's needs and other people's mistakes instead of their own" (1998, 9).

[11] For an overview, see Zwolinski (2017); for a critical discussion, see Rodgers and Rodgers (2016).

sufficient resources to live as a project pursuer, even people who do not have sufficient resources due to faults of their own, at least if they did not violate other people's rights and thus (arguably) deserve punishment?

One possibility would be to argue that people deserve to suffer when they lack sufficient resources because of faults of their own (even if they did not violate other people's rights). But this seems not quite congenial to what hopefully is the spirit of libertarianism. Libertarianism should be supportive of human flourishing and happiness (I think).

Another possibility would be to argue that justice cannot require taking from some to give to others, because the former have *property rights* over these resources and justice cannot sanction a violation of these property rights. It should first be noted, though, that this argument does not have much to do with personal responsibility. If it is wrong to take from some in order to give to others, then this arguably applies irrespectively of whether those on the receiving end need resources because of faults of their own or because of bad luck. Second, the argument is *based on* a rejection of the sufficiency proviso and is therefore unsuited to serve as a refutation of the sufficiency proviso. Why is it based on a rejection of the sufficiency proviso? Because it refers to property rights that are claimed to be violated by the sufficiency proviso. Yet according to moderate libertarianism, what property rights people have is to be determined by reference to justifiable practices of private property, and the sufficiency proviso co-determines what a justifiable practice of private property is.

To sum up: Responsibility-based objections can be accommodated by moderate libertarianism when they target institutions, not principles of justice. When they target principles of justice, they are either unconvincing or question-begging.

5. The Natural Duty of Justice and Mitigated Self-Ownership Rights

Rodgers worries that the sufficiency proviso leads to a multiplication of duties and hence to a problematically weakened conception of self-ownership (2018, 155–56). How so? He rightly notes that no individual has a *right* to reach the sufficiency threshold, according to moderate libertarianism (2018, 150). This, among other things, distinguishes my view from Loren Lomasky's view, in which modest welfare rights play a prominent role (1987; see Wendt 2018). The sufficiency proviso simply sets a standard that co-determines whether a practice of private property is justifiable. Nothing more or less. So duties to satisfy sufficiency-related *rights* are not the problem.

Yet moderate libertarianism is compatible with the assumption that people have a *natural duty of justice* to help bring about just institutions, even though it is *also* compatible with denying that there is such a duty (see Wendt 2018). A duty of justice would be a positive duty (i.e., a duty to *do* something), albeit not a duty that correlates with rights. Rodgers, in any case, worries that such a duty would mean that self-ownership rights are mitigated since "'reforming' the practice can require work in order to see to it that others have sufficient resources" (2018, 155).

A first reply is to concede the point but insist that nothing in moderate libertarianism and the sufficiency proviso forces us to accept that there is such a duty of justice. But I tend to think that in fact there is such a duty, so I am not quite happy with this first reply. It is arguably not a duty to work harder, though, but a duty to—in one way or other—help reform institutions in the direction of what justice requires. Of course this does not imply that this duty of justice is enforceable and should be enshrined as a *legal* duty.

A second reply is to again concede the point but deny that it is a worry if self-ownership is slightly weakened. After all, *all* moral duties limit self-ownership by specifying limits to what one may permissibly do. This holds for the negative duties to respect other people's self-ownership rights, it holds for duties that result from one's promises and contracts, and so on. So the mere fact that a duty of justice to help reform an unjustifiable practice of private property *is* a duty and therefore sets limits to self-ownership rights is not enough to discredit the assumption that there is such a duty.

A third reply is that the duty of justice would arguably not be an enforceable duty, and so it would limit self-ownership rights only in setting limits to what one may permissibly do, but it would not give others greater discretion to interfere with what one does.

Maybe the real objection is that duties and rights have to be *compossible* (see, e.g., Nozick 1974, 238; Rothbard 1998, 99–100; Narveson 1988, 127; Steiner 1994, 88).[12] Negative duties that correlate with other people's rights can be exercised simply by sitting at home, doing nothing. Fulfilling them cannot require the violation of other people's rights. Positive duties that are voluntarily incurred by way of promises or contracts—such as duties to help someone revising a manuscript—also cannot violate negative rights, simply because they are voluntarily incurred. And if someone should dare to promise to violate another person's negative rights, this promise would not be valid and thus would not generate positive duties to begin with. To fulfill positive

---

[12] For a recent discussion of compossibility, see Christmas (2019).

duties that are *not* voluntarily incurred, on the other hand, it can be necessary to infringe other people's negative rights. The only way to fulfil a duty to help to feed others may be to violate property rights, for example. That is why we should reject the existence of positive duties that are not voluntarily incurred, including the alleged duty of justice to help reform practices of private property that are not justifiable.

My first reply to this is the same as above: Concede the point, but insist that nothing in moderate libertarianism and the sufficiency proviso forces us to accept positive duties. But, again, since I think there is a positive duty of justice, I do not want to rely on this response.

A second reply is to claim that the positive duty of justice is not stringent enough to ever outweigh negative rights. This is certainly plausible for self-ownership rights; but what about the legal property rights that are constituted by an unjustifiable practice of private property? One could hold that practices of private property may only be reformed by legal means, such that the duty of justice never legitimizes the violation of legal property rights.[13] It seems to me that there is a good amount of truth to this, but I am skeptical that it is never ever possible for the duty of justice (or other positive duties) to outweigh negative rights, and so I will not rely on this reply either.

The third (and best) reply is to simply reject the claim that duties and rights have to be compossible. Consider that even negative rights and duties can get into indirect conflicts. Amartya Sen tells the (here slightly altered) story of A, who is about to be killed by B if we do not break into C's office to get to a telephone and warn him (1988). (This is obviously before the time of cell phones.) Only negative rights are at stake: A's self-ownership rights are in danger of being violated by B, and C's (or her bosses') ownership rights in the office are in danger of being violated by us. Now, in ideal circumstances—that is, without B's desire to kill—of course both A's and C's negative rights could easily be respected. But in the non-ideal circumstances in which B is about to violate A's negative rights, it seems permissible to infringe C's negative rights in the name of protecting A's more important negative rights. If that is right, even negative rights are not compossible in an important sense.

Now if that is right, then why should it not also be permissible, under certain circumstances, to infringe a person's negative rights for other reasons

---

[13] Violating legal property rights may be regarded as unjust even within unjustifiable practices of private property. But this is an issue that would deserve a deeper discussion than I can provide here.

(e.g., because of a positive duty)? Judith Thomson presents a case in which A has a drug in a locked box on his back porch and is out of town. Unfortunately right now a child needs exactly this drug to survive, and we would be in a position to give A's drug to the child (1981, 133). (We cannot contact A to ask for permission; again, no cell phones.) There is no indirect conflict of negative rights, since only A's negative property rights are at stake. Thomson writes: "But surely it is plain as day that property rights are not infinitely stringent. I suppose it hardly needs argument to show they are not. In any case, the fact that it is morally permissible for us to go ahead in [the case of the child] would show... that they are not" (1981, 138).

In the examples of Sen and Thomson, it is permissible to infringe property rights in external resources. But the same can happen to self-ownership rights. If the only way to get the drug to the child is by way of tickling someone gently, but against her will, for one minute (you can make up the background story yourself), then this certainly is permissible. Generally speaking, libertarians rightly emphasize the importance of negative rights and duties, but to claim that justice consists in a system of perfectly compossible rights and duties that never generates any conflicts—and thus never allows any permissible infringements of rights—is simply implausible.[14]

I conclude that one should not worry too much about the duty of justice to help bring about just institutions. But, recall, moderate libertarianism is compatible with a rejection of that duty anyway. So if you are skeptical about that duty, just accept moderate libertarianism without it.

6. Individuating Practices of Private Property

A final question raised by Rodgers is how practices of private property are to be individuated (2018, 157–58). The sufficiency proviso, recall, requires practices of private property to enable everyone to live as a project pursuer, if that is possible without undermining the point of having a practice of private property in the first place. To find out whether a practice of private property is justifiable, we thus have to *individuate* practices of private property. We need

---

[14] With regard to self-ownership rights, Rodgers also worries about paternalism (2018, 149), but since this has not much to do with the sufficiency proviso, I will only give a very brief answer. The hope is that the project-pursuit argument grounds self-ownership rights that are stringent enough to prohibit most instances of paternalism, while on the other hand permitting some forms of soft paternalism, such as saving someone's life by pushing him out of the way of a deadly threat (when he cannot be warned).

a criterion where one practice ends and another starts, so to speak. Rodgers writes that "*systems* of private property are no longer local and easily identifiable" (2018, 157) and that maybe in our globalized world there is just one system of private property that is to include just about everyone (2018, 158).[15]

This is not supposed to be a knock-down argument, I suppose, but it certainly requires some kind of answer. Here is what seems most plausible to me: What counts as an individual practice of private property should basically track *law*. The basic guideline should be that we have an individual practice of private property in a geographical area that is united by a common property law. Now sometimes there are several levels of law applying to the same geographical area. In a particular region in Europe, for example, there may at the same time apply local laws, federal laws, and EU laws. Since international law also legislates property issues, it can often be considered the top layer. One can ask the question whether a practice of private property is justifiable with regard to each of these levels and thereby count each level as one individual practice of private property. But one can also assess several levels together for a particular geographical region, when the region is united by a common property law at least on one level, and thus count the whole as *one* practice of private property. I do not think one has to decide between these two ways of individuating practices of private property. In any case, one can make a good case for the view that there are practices of private property below the level of the global economic system.

References

Christmas, Billy. 2019. "A Reformulation of the Structure of a Set Compossible Rights." *Philosophical Quarterly* 69: 221–34.

Friedman, Milton. 1962. *Capitalism and Freedom*. Chicago: University of Chicago Press.

Hayek, Friedrich. 2012 (1973, 1976, and 1979). *Law, Legislation and Liberty*. London: Routledge.

Lomasky, Loren. 1987. *Persons, Rights, and the Moral Community*. Oxford: Oxford University Press.

---

[15] He also points out that governments may lack the authority to oversee the distribution of resources (2018, 158). This is true, but it points at much more general worries about political authority that I cannot begin to discuss here.

Mack, Eric. 1995. "The Self-Ownership Proviso: A New and Improved Lockean Proviso." *Social Philosophy and Policy* 12: 186–218.

McMahon, Christopher. 1991. "The Paradox of Deontology." *Philosophy & Public Affairs* 20: 350–77.

Narveson, Jan. 1988. *The Libertarian Idea*. Philadelphia: Temple University Press.

Nozick, Robert. 1974. *Anarchy, State, and Utopia*. New York: Basic Books.

Rodgers, Lamont, and Travis J. Rodgers. 2016. "The Libertarian Case for a Basic Income Guarantee: An Assessment of the Direct Proviso-Based Route." *Libertarian Papers* 8(2): 235–46.

Rodgers, Lamont. 2018. "The Tenuous Foundations of the Sufficiency Proviso." *Libertarian Papers* 10(2): 143–59.

Rothbard, Murray. 1998 (1982). *The Ethics of Liberty*. New York: New York University Press.

Scheffler, Samuel. 1985. "Agent-Centred Restrictions, Rationality, and the Virtues." *Mind* 94: 409–19.

Schmidtz, David. 1998. "Taking Responsibility." In *Social Welfare and Individual Responsibility*, edited by D. Schmidtz and R. Goodin, 1–96. Cambridge: Cambridge University Press.

Sen, Amartya. 1988 (1982). "Rights and Agency." In *Consequentialism and Its Critics*, edited by S. Scheffler, 187–223. Oxford: Oxford University Press.

Steiner, Hillel. 1994. *An Essay on Rights*. Oxford: Blackwell.

Thomson, Judith J. 1981 (1977). "Some Ruminations on Rights." In *Reading Nozick*, edited by J. Paul, 130–47. Totowa: Rowman & Littlefield.

Tomasi, John. 2012. *Free Market Fairness*. Princeton: Princeton University Press.

Wendt, Fabian. 2017. "The Sufficiency Proviso." In *Routledge Handbook of Libertarianism*, edited by J. Brennan, B. van der Vossen, and D. Schmidtz, 169–83. London: Routledge.

Wendt, Fabian. 2018. "Three Types of Sufficientarian Libertarianism." *Res Publica* (online first).

Zwolinski, Matt. 2015. "Property, Coercion, and the Welfare State: The Libertarian Case for a Basic Income Guarantee for All." *Independent Review* 19 (4): 515–29.

Zwolinski, Matt. 2017. "Libertarianism and the Welfare State." In *Routledge Handbook of Libertarianism*, edited by J. Brennan, B. van der Vossen, and D. Schmidtz, 323–41. London: Routledge.

THE STILL TENUOUS FOUNDATIONS OF A SUFFICIENCY PROVISO: A REJOINDER TO WENDT

LAMONT RODGERS[*]

I AM GRATEFUL TO FABIAN WENDT for responding to my evaluation of his work on Moderate Libertarianism. Wendt's efforts are important because they focus on foundational issues of justice and there is a dearth of quality work on those issues these days. Due to lack of space, the most productive way to structure this brief rejoinder is to focus on two general issues before touching on one smaller point. First, I explain why Wendt offers something like an empirical justification of libertarianism. Here I will be clearer than I originally was about why this is a problem that Wendt needs to address better than he has. It is my hope that this initial discussion paves the way for me to demonstrate my second point—namely, that Wendt's statement of his own argument for the proviso is either question-begging or unsurprising. I conclude by saying a little bit about Wendt's discussion of positive obligations.

1. Contingent Libertarianism and Why it Matters

Wendt is surprised that I characterize his position as consequentialist (Wendt 2018c, 163). Perhaps it is more useful to call his position "Strongly

---

[*] Lamont Rodgers is professor of philosophy at Houston Community College.
CITATION INFORMATION FOR THIS ARTICLE:
Lamont Rodgers. 2018. "The Still Tenuous Foundations of a Sufficiency Proviso: A Rejoinder to Wendt." *Libertarian Papers*. 10 (2): 173-178. ONLINE AT: libertarianpapers.org. THIS ARTICLE IS subject to a Creative Commons Attribution 3.0 License (creativecommons.org/licenses).

Contingent Libertarianism" and explain what I mean by that.[1] Imagine an anarcho-capitalist regime that satisfies Mack's proviso, but not Wendt's. This regime requires no incursions into the available set of people's self-ownership rights to satisfy the proviso. Imagine that the only way to satisfy Nozick's stronger proviso is to move to a version of classical liberalism, say, where some 'public goods' are funded via taxation. This regime requires some incursions into people's self-ownership rights to satisfy the proviso. Yet, imagine that this does not satisfy *Wendt's* proviso. To do that, pretend that we must move to something like a modern welfare state. This requires substantial incursions into people's rights but does not undermine the point of private property in the first place. Wendt not only lacks the theoretical resources to block this sort of political arrangement—his position requires it.[2] Wendt knows this and seems to accept it (Wendt 2018c, 167).

It is important to see that Wendt's requirement that individuals are able to live as project pursuers even shapes the nature of rights (Wendt 2018c, 162). So, if we have individuals who can live as project pursuers only if they receive forced blood donations, Wendt's starting point seems to require that too (as long as those forced to donate blood can live as project pursuers).[3]

Why does it matter that Wendt has no principled commitment to what most of us would see as a libertarian regime? Wendt canvasses three potential reasons (Wendt 2018c, 163-64). However, he ignores what I take to be the gravamen of my discussion. I very clearly identify cost as *a* problem for Wendt's discussion of justice and responsibility (Rodgers 2018, 147-148). The problem is not, as Wendt suggests, that his starting point is *different* from that of other libertarians. The problem is that Wendt must show us why he is right about the *telos* of a system of private property. Wendt thinks he has an answer to this challenge and I think it is not a very good one.

Wendt responds to my challenge as follows: "the alternative starting point is not very attractive because being formally allowed to live as a project pursuer is not of much value if you are not actually able to live as a project pursuer" (Wendt 2018c, 164). Why is this not much of an answer to concerns

---

[1] Wendt does not see how his position is more consequentialist than rivals, but surely there is an obvious difference between his endorsement of a political system based on whether it facilitates project pursuit and a position that says we must simply leave others alone (Wendt 163, n4).

[2] He could, of course, block it on empirical grounds. That is because his endorsement of libertarianism *as a political system* rests on those empirical questions.

[3] Wendt might say that this obligation should not be enforced (Wendt 2018c, 169). Still, the possibility seems like a serious problem, especially vis-à-vis cost.

about cost? The issue of cost is introduced to question whether the *telos* of private property can be shown to be what Wendt says it is.[4] He is right that being able to live only as a formal project pursuer is unattractive. However, the fact that a position is unattractive is distinct from the question of whether we can derive an alternative—especially if the effort to avoid the position itself comes with unattractive implications. So Wendt is wrong about how much mileage he can get out of the observation that being formally allowed to live as a project pursuer is unattractive.

As the move through the political institutions that might satisfy the proviso demonstrates, satisfying Wendt's proviso could justify significant incursions into people's lives. And it is possible that this would mark an incursion into people's lives that may well be costlier and more unattractive *to them* than the failure to satisfy the sufficiency proviso.[5] This is important because Wendt must show that such individuals are guilty of an error. He cannot accomplish that task by reiterating what he takes the *telos* of a system of private property to be. This is question-begging. Nor can he accomplish this by reminding us that a "theorist who "really cares" about people's ability to pursue projects should accept the sufficiency proviso and nothing weaker" (Wendt 2018c, 165). What I am trying to challenge here is the very *telos* of a system of private property. Perhaps I was not clear enough about that in my initial paper.

2. Method

Wendt begins his discussion by citing arguments about justice from Nozick, Lomasky, and Mack. Those authors share roughly the same starting point: individuals are mutually disinterested and enjoy a prerogative to pursue their own ends. The challenge for a theory of justice that takes seriously the moral separateness of persons is to show how mutually disinterested individuals may properly be shown to have good reasons to constrain their behavior toward each other. This challenge arises because individuals properly pursue their own ends. So, we need an argument to bridge the gap between an agent's prerogative to pursue her own ends and the claim that she should not do this in ways that thwart the ends of others (in certain ways). If one thinks one can go beyond mere deference, one needs an argument for

---

[4] Alternatively, one could use cost to question whether the path to Wendt's proviso is as smooth and linear as he seems to think.

[5] Loren Lomasky grapples with this issue in Lomasky (1987), in particular pp. 80-83. David Gauthier seems willing to bite some serious bullets (Gauthier, 1986, pp. 285-286).

that conclusion too. One can see people like Lomasky, in particular, struggling to deliver just such an argument.

I read Wendt to be offering a means of bridging this gap.[6] It seems he is not attempting to bridge it (Wendt 2018c, 164).[7] He is up to a decidedly different task. Part of the reason I read Wendt the way I did is that in his response to me, his own characterization of his argument for the proviso makes his project seem either overtly question-begging or not particularly surprising. Wendt argues for a proviso that holds "that a practice of private property has to be designed in a way such that everyone has sufficient resources to live as a project pursuer, if this is possible without undermining the point of having a practice of private property in the first place" (Wendt 2018c, 162). How does he get to that proviso? He "starts with the idea that people should be able to live as project pursuers" (Wendt 2018c, 162). Once one accepts *that* stating point, it is all downhill to the Sufficiency Proviso. If we start with a position logically incompatible with other provisos, then those provisos look unattractive. This is certainly true. However, even as a mere justifying explanation for the proviso, Wendt's conclusion is not exactly startling.[8] There are questions about what we can show the *telos* of a system of private property to be. Wendt ignores them almost entirely. The *telos*, in short, is not an uncontroversial starting point.

3. Positive Obligations

Wendt suggests that my resistance to positive obligations might come from concerns of compossibility (Wendt 2018c, 169). However, I never mention the issue. Still, I wish to discuss some of what Wendt says. Wendt argues that there are good reasons to give up on compossibility. He adduces a series of thought experiments to show that rights sometimes give way to positive obligations. I think he is correct, but not in a way that helps him

---

[6] I think that anyone exercising something like the principle of charity would have read my arguments as an effort to show that Wendt fails to overcome this crucial gap. They would have remembered my very clear statement about how I read Wendt. Wendt ignores my initial statement in his rejoinder, save to say that I seem not to read him as I say I do (Wendt 2018, 164).

[7] If one reads him as attempting to bridge the gap, then he accomplishes the task in a manner that is entirely too easy. He simply fattens up the initial concerns that agents must have so that they really care about what Wendt does and, voila, he is across the gap. This is what my initial response attempted to say.

[8] Wendt mentions a work in progress that I have yet to read. Perhaps he addresses some of the challenges I raise in that piece (Wendt 2018c, 162 n1).

show what he must show. I think Wendt needs to argue that we may weaken self-ownership in a way that is not so costly that it gives us good reasons to doubt that he can defend his view of *telos* of a system of private property.

When Nozick discusses cases in which rights are overridden, he treats those rights as liability rules.[9] If you may break into my house to steal a drug that will save a child, you owe me compensation. Wendt might disagree with this, but he has not argued against it. He has only shown that we may sometimes not *fully* respect the rights of others. However, if even in (most of) those cases, we owe compensation, his argument does not go far enough. Nobody is compensated for being forced to uphold Wendt's proviso. Wendt must address this issue.

He suggests that those who oppose positive obligations may simply say that the proviso is unenforceable. However, this takes the teeth out of the argument for the proviso. If what matters is that not being able to live as a project pursuer is unattractive, then holding that this is precisely what might happen is required is at least problematic. Thus, I do not see how this move is available. If one finds positive obligations problematic—say, because they are costly—then one should be suspicious of the Sufficiency Proviso.

I hope these brief remarks clarify both my initial assessment of Wendt's proviso and some of the challenges I still think he faces in defending it.

References

Gauthier, David. 1986. *Morals by Agreement*. New York: Oxford University Press.

Lomasky, Loren. 1987. *Persons, Rights, and the Moral Community*. New York: Oxford University Press.

Nozick, Robert. 1974. *Anarchy, State, and Utopia*. New York: Basic Books.

Rodgers, Lamont. 2018. "The Tenuous Foundations of the Sufficiency Proviso." *Libertarian Papers*. 10(2): 143–59.

---

[9] Nozick does this both directly and indirectly. The argument in chapter 4 of Nozick 1974 directly employs liability rules. He also refers the reader to work on liability rules and rights. See Nozick, 1974, 338n6. Wendt is correct to note that Nozick does not know what to do in *some* cases of moral catastrophe, but we must not ignore the entire chapter in which he discusses cases in which rights become liability rules.

Wendt, F. 2018a. "Three Types of Sufficientarian Libertarianism." *Res Publica*.doi:10.1007/s11158–018–9400-y.

Wendt, Fabian. 2018b. "The Sufficiency Proviso." In *Routledge Handbook of Libertarianism*, edited by J. Brennan, B. van der Vossen, and D. Schmidt, 169–83. Routledge: New York.

Wendt Fabian. 2018c. "Caring about Projects, Responsibility, and Rights: A Response to Rodgers." *Libertarian Papers*.10 (2): 161-174.

POLICE CHOICE: FEASIBLE POLICY OPTIONS FOR A SAFER AND FREER SOCIETY

COREY A. DEANGELIS[*]

1. Introduction

THE SYSTEM OF POLICING in the United States is largely failing US citizens by providing low-quality services. Police response times[1] are slow, and, even more importantly, government police officers are frequently shown to be abusing their power (Lewis 1999). Perhaps because of advancements in social media technologies, citizens are noticing many more cases of police officers' abuse of power. Indeed, a simple Google Trends search reveals that public interest in the term "police brutality" reached all-time highs in each year from 2014 to 2016.[2] Furthermore, over 1,100 citizens were killed by police officers each year from 2014 to 2017.[3]

A recent viral video shows an intoxicated man from Arizona crying and begging for his life on his hands and knees before a police officer, Philip

---

[*]Corey A. DeAngelis is an education policy expert and received his Ph.D. in education policy from the University of Arkansas.

CITATION INFORMATION FOR THIS ARTICLE:
Corey A. DeAngelis. 2018. "Police Choice: Feasible Policy Options for a Safer and Freer Society." *Libertarian Papers*. 10 (2): 179-206. THIS ARTICLE IS subject to a Creative Commons Attribution 3.0 License (creativecommons.org/licenses).

[1] "In New Orleans, Call 911 and Wait for an Hour." *The Economist*. Retrieved from: https://www.economist.com/blogs/democracyinamerica/2015/12/police-response-times.

[2] "Police Brutality" (2018). Google Trends. Retrieved from: https://trends.google.com/trends/explore?date=all&geo=US&q=police%20brutality.

[3] "Killed by Police 2017." Retrieved from: http://www.killedbypolice.net/kbp2017.

Brailsford, shot and killed him.[4] While the victim, Daniel Shaver, was on the ground, the police officer continuously shouted at him and yelled things like, "I'm not here to be tactical and diplomatic with you. You listen. You obey." How did all of this start? The police officers came because they thought Daniel Shaver had a rifle; however, no rifle was ever found in the room. Philip Brailsford was acquitted of second-degree murder charges.

Surprisingly, according to data collected by Mapping Police Violence, 99 percent of all of the cases in 2015 did not result in the conviction of a police officer.[5] Perhaps even more disturbing is the fact that African Americans are over three times as likely to be killed by police as whites (Ross 2015). Citizens with darker skin color also report slower police response times, even after controlling for factors such as socioeconomic status and other demographic characteristics (Cohen, Zechmeister, and Seligson 2015), and African Americans report lower levels of trust and satisfaction with police departments (Brown and Coulter 1983; Van Ryzin, Muzzio, and Immerwahr 2004), perhaps because of racial discrimination in the use of police force (Fryer 2016).

Of course, the quality of police departments varies by location. For example, citizens are seven times more likely to be killed by police officers in Oklahoma than in Georgia. Police-quality levels are often positively correlated with per capita income within a given geographic location. Indeed, Cohen, Zechmeister, and Seligson (2015) find that individuals with more wealth report that police respond more quickly to their requests. This is likely because police departments are primarily funded through property taxes, and wealthy people can afford to purchase expensive houses with access to the best policing services.

Currently, one of the strongest pressures for police departments to improve is generated through residential selection, also known as Tiebout choice (Tiebout 1956). When citizens choose where they are going to live, they consider the bundle of publicly provided services they receive, including K-12 schooling, parks, fire departments, and policing. If a police department is using a substantial amount of tax dollars and is not keeping its citizens safe, individuals can move to a geographic location that has a more effective police force. When individuals leave an area, house prices decrease, property-tax

---

[4] "Graphic Video Shows Daniel Shaver Sobbing and Begging Officer for His Life before 2016 Shooting." *Washington Post*. Retrieved from: https://www.washingtonpost.com/news/post-nation/wp/2017/12/08/graphic-video-shows-daniel-shaver-sobbing-and-begging-officer-for-his-life-before-2016-shooting/?utm_term=.d622f2b20f34.

[5] "Mapping Police Violence." Retrieved from: https://mappingpoliceviolence.org.

revenue decreases, and police departments lose funding. Consequently, police departments theoretically have a financial incentive to improve quality levels. In addition, public police-force incentives may largely come from interbureau competition for public dollars (Baicker and Jacobson 2007; Benson, Rasmussen, and Sollars 1995).

However, since police departments are public entities, they do not face the same shutdown pressures that private organizations encounter. In addition, since the residential-selection decision includes consideration of a large bundle of public services, and transaction costs associated with switching residences are very high, Tiebout choice is a weak form of police accountability. The lack of competitive pressures to perform well might have something to do with the low quality levels of government policing in the United States (Forst 2000). In the schooling industry, for example, residential assignment is also a commonly cited reason for lackluster educational results in the United States (Chubb and Moe 1988; Friedman 1997).

The concept of school choice, made popular in the United States by Milton Friedman (1955), has arguably led to substantial quality improvements (DeAngelis 2017; Shakeel, Anderson, and Wolf 2016; Wolf 2007; Wolf et al. 2013) and cost reductions (Lueken 2016; Spalding 2014) in the K-12 education system. In theory, the ability to opt out of a residentially assigned government school provides additional competitive pressures for all schools, public or private, to perform well. Similarly, the ability to opt out of a residentially assigned government police force could provide additional incentives for all rights-protection firms to raise quality levels.

Today, police departments lack the incentives necessary to perform well. If a police department does an exceptional job at ensuring public safety, it is not financially rewarded for doing so. Property-tax revenues remain the same in the short run until enough people decide to move to the department's geographic area. However, at the same time, it is possible that the quality levels of other public services, such as parks and schools, go down. The net result may be that great police departments are financially punished in the short run for a job well done. In addition, police officers are often compensated based on seniority and credentials rather than their ability to handle potentially violent situations calmly (Bartel and Lewin 1981; Danielson 1967; Devine 1969; Hall and Vanderporten 1977). It should not surprise us that police quality is not where we would like it to be; police officers are simply responding to the incentives that exist within the current system of rights protection. Perhaps it is rational that police officers are using violence rather than difficult psychological techniques: if officers know they are not going to be rewarded for skillful de-escalation, and that they will not be punished for violent acts, they may be more likely to use violence since it minimizes their own risk of death.

In a system of private police choice, consumer choices would reward great police officers for their services. The police-choice system would also hold low-quality police departments accountable for their actions. Imagine that the video of the horrific death of Daniel Shaver was released in a system of police choice. The public relations disaster would lead to financial losses to the policing firm, and the officer would probably be out of a job. Public outrage would entice consumers of rights-protection services to leave the policing company for a more professional and safer firm. In addition, customers from different policing firms could compare police quality levels side-by-side by discussing with their network of acquaintances or by simply looking up quality statistics and customer-satisfaction ratings online.

In the following sections, I discuss examples of private policing, feasible public and private police-choice policy options, and the common (but generally invalid) criticisms of police choice. I conclude with recommendations. While one report has applied the concept of school vouchers to prisons (Volokh 2012), this is the first time (that I know of) that police choice has been discussed in the literature. Other scholars have theorized that private subscription-based patrol and restitution services could emerge as a free market alternative to government police when governments become fiscally unstable (Guillory and Tinsley 2009). Barnett (2014) similarly suggested that rights-maintenance organizations could provide legal services and patrol services. In addition, David Friedman (1989) and Murray Rothbard (1978) argued that law and order could be provided privately. However, Guillory and Tinsley (2009), Barnett (2014), Friedman (1989), and Rothbard (1978) did not discuss how present society could move toward a system of privately produced law enforcement. The current study provides a few politically feasible avenues.

2. Examples of Private Policing

This section outlines just a few of the historical examples of private rights protection. Although it is not a comprehensive account of all examples, since that would be largely redundant, these examples illustrate that rights protection can be privately provided and more desirable than the government-provided alternative.

2.1 England

The government did not create an official organization to provide law enforcement services in England until the Metropolitan Police Act of 1829, so policing was largely a privately produced service in the seventeenth and eighteenth centuries (Emsley 2014; Harris 2004; Old Bailey Proceedings 2015). Indeed, tracking down rights violators was not even an official duty of the government before 1829 (Beattie 2001).

Because the government did not adequately provide the essential service of rights protection, a private market emerged (Hitchcock and Shoemaker 2006). The private police in the seventeenth and eighteenth centuries, known as thief takers, would accept payments from the victims, and sometimes rewards from the government, for returning stolen property (Beattie 2001; Gilbert and Schichor 2000; Howson 1985; Wales 2000). To further incentivize the private service, starting in 1692 the government introduced statutory financial rewards for convictions (Beattie 2001; Wales 2000). In addition, citizens such as Henry Fielding paid weekly wages to groups of thief takers to catch criminals, investigate violations, and return stolen goods (Beattie 2012; Beattie 2017; McLynn 1989). Some evidence suggests that private-police groups such as the Bow Street Runners were effective. London's Old Bailey Proceedings (2015) indicate that the Bow Street Runners improved detection rates and decreased crime. News outlets such as the BBC[6] have contended that "the Bow Street Runners proved to be very effective" in that crime rates fell and conviction rates increased. In addition, the BBC claimed that "the success of the Bow Street Runners led to other initiatives" increasing private protection such as the Middlesex Justices Act of 1792 and the origin of the River Thames Police in 1798.

Of course, seventeenth-century England is not the only historical example of privately produced rights-protection services. There were also several forms of private rights protection in ancient Rome (Kelly 1988), and the United States in the eighteenth and nineteenth centuries (Dempsey 2010).

2.2 Detroit, Michigan

Detroit, Michigan, may be the best current-day example of a hard case for private rights protection in the United States. The most recent data from the US Census Bureau (2017a; 2017b) indicate that 39 percent of the Detroit population lives in poverty, with a per capita income level of $15,562.

---

[6] "The Establishment and Influence of the Bow Street Runners." BBC. Retrieved from: https://www.bbc.com/education/guides/z9y9fcw/revision/3.

Detroit's poverty level is almost three times the national average, while its per capita income level is 68 percent below the national average. Perhaps more importantly, according to the most recent statistics provided by the Federal Bureau of Investigation (2016), Detroit is the most violent city in the United States, with 13,705 violent crimes including 202 murders, 579 rapes, 9,882 aggravated assaults, and 2,941 robberies in 2016. Detroit's violent crime rate was 5.3 times the national average in 2016.

The low standard of living in Detroit could partially be because the city's safety issues have pushed companies to go elsewhere. After all, why would anyone want to invest in property in a place that does not successfully protect property? Detroit police have even issued public statements saying that since the city is so dangerous, visitors must "enter at [their] own risk.7" Perhaps because of the inability of the government police force to keep Detroit safe, private security agencies, such as Threat Management Center, have emerged. The founder of Threat Management Center, Dale Brown, has frequently pointed out that his employees are highly trained to use negotiation and de-escalation tactics based on knowledge of human psychology, rather than force, to de-escalate otherwise violent situations. He has also discussed how he provides security services for free, even with his company's currently strong monopoly power, to those that are unable afford the services, as well as senior citizens and victims of domestic violence and stalking. In addition, none of the employees have been killed, and none of his customers have been injured or killed since the company's inception over twenty years ago. Dale Brown also claims his services have reduced violent crime by 90 percent in some neighborhoods.[8]

Michigan senator Arlan Meekhof introduced Senate Bill 594, known as the Special Police Agency Act, on September 27, 2017. This bill would "permit legally organized entities to enter into contracts with special police agencies" (Michigan Legislature 2017). However, while this bill would allow for licensed private police forces, it would not provide a funding mechanism such as a voucher because it would not allow citizens to opt out of government police protection and take their share of the expenditures with them. The lack of a funding mechanism could create two significant problems for successful systems of police choice: (1) insufficient demand for a sustainable market, and (2) a lack of financial incentives for government-

---

[7] CBS Detroit (2012). "Enter at Your Own Risk: Police Union Says War-Like Detroit Is Unsafe for Visitors." Retrieved from: http://detroit.cbslocal.com/2012/10/06/enter-at-your-own-risk-police-union-says-war-like-detroit-is-unsafe-for-visitors.

[8] Threat Management Center. Retrieved from: www.threatmanagementcenter.com.

run police departments to improve. In addition, current government regulation could mean high barriers to market entry for private police firms even if public funding were to be made available (Meehan and Benson 2015; Stenning and Cornish 1975).

2.3 San Francisco, California

The California Gold Rush of 1849 enticed thousands of people to move to the West Coast. During that time, groups of criminals such as the Regulators and the Sydney Ducks attacked local businesses and households, but a government police force did not exist in 1849. Because the San Francisco inhabitants could not rely on a government police force to protect them, they had to privately provide the service. The private police force came into existence and protected San Franciscan households and neighborhoods without the need for coercive revenues. Private police firms such as the San Francisco Patrol Special Police still exist and provide valuable services to citizens (Stringham 2015). Scholars have noted that San Francisco's private police are more cost effective than off-duty police officers (Bechler 2011; Office of International Criminal Justice 1995).

2.4 Other Examples

These are not the only examples of private policing. Major railroads in the United States and Canada still have large private police forces (Benson 1998; Benson 2014). Private law enforcement officers, or security officers, in South Carolina are authorized by the state to make arrests, respond to service calls, and give traffic tickets.[9] Of course, the situation in South Carolina is unique in the United States, as other states tightly constrain the scope of activities private officers can perform (Meehan and Benson 2015). Because of heavy regulation in the current system, the police-choice programs I propose in this report would likely need to pass alongside deregulation legislation to be effective.

---

[9] South Carolina Code of Laws, Title 40, Chapter 18. Retrieved from: https://www.scstatehouse.gov/code/t40c018.php.

3. Policy Options

3.1 Vouchers

A well-known type of voucher system already exists in the United States today in sixteen states and in the nation's capital. If a family is not happy with the quality of its child's educational arrangements, it can opt out of its residentially assigned government school and take a fraction of its allocated public funding to the private school of its choice (EdChoice 2017a). Since private schools must attract their customers from traditional public schools, and public schools receive funding based on enrollment counts, all schools, public and private, have a strong incentive to educate children effectively (Chubb and Moe 1988; DeAngelis and Holmes Erickson 2018; Friedman and Friedman 1990; Hoxby 2003; Merrifield 2001).

While Milton Friedman (1955; 1962) is often thought of as the first person to propose a publicly funded school-choice voucher, the concept existed long before his lifetime. Thomas Paine (1791) contended that education ought to be privately provided and that government should "allow for each of these children ten schillings a year for the expense of schooling." Similarly, John Stuart Mill (1859) argued that while government might have an incentive to compel each child to receive an education, it "might leave to parents to obtain the education where and how they pleased, and content itself with helping to pay the school fees of the poorer classes of children, and defraying the entire school expenses of those who have no one else to pay for them."

Private-school voucher programs are usually tied directly to state education-funding formulas that are largely based on student-enrollment counts. For this reason, public schools already experience weak competitive pressures through residential, or Tiebout, choice (Tiebout 1956). In contrast, police departments in the United States are usually funded through a combination of local property taxes, sales taxes, and grants from state and federal governments (which are not based on formulas directly tied to population levels). However, police forces similarly have at least a weak incentive to perform well based on population levels. When people leave a given jurisdiction because of low police quality, the demand for, and price of, housing decreases, ultimately leading to an indirect reduction in property-tax revenues and police funding. While policing revenues and expenditures are not directly linked to a funding formula, it is still feasible to enact a publicly funded voucher system alongside our current system of policing.

A publicly funded police-choice voucher could be based on the average amount of public funding per citizen (or household) living in the jurisdiction.

For example, the city of Dallas estimates that total police funding for fiscal year 2016-17 was around $504 million.[10] The population in Dallas was estimated to be about 1.318 million in 2016.[11] This means that each citizen in the city of Dallas used around $382—about $1,528 for a family of four—in police expenses in 2016. Similarly, it is estimated that New York City's 2016 policing expenditures were $5.5 billion[12] for its population of 8.538 million.[13] In other words, New York City spent about $644 on each citizen—about $2,576 for a family of four—on policing in 2016. While every citizen in New York City ought to be allocated their total public-funding amount, a politically feasible solution (often used for school-choice vouchers) could be to allocate a fraction of the per-citizen funding amount to each citizen that opts out of their residentially assigned government police force. After all, the government-run police departments, a highly concentrated interest group, would likely lobby through the democratic process to continue to hold their monopoly on force. They would likely make the claim that since a large portion (let us assume 25 percent) of their costs are fixed, a 100 percent reduction in public funding per citizen leaving their protection would cause the department to close its doors, leaving several innocent families without means of protection. In that case, a family of four in New York City could receive 75 percent of the average public-police funding annual amount (or about $1,932 in 2016) to prevent short-run financial disasters in government-run police agencies. Alternatively, such a bill could simply limit the level of voucher-recipient growth from year to year.

A police voucher does not need to be publicly funded through the local police budget. The voucher could be privately funded (like tax-credit scholarships for education) through voluntary donations from individuals and corporations. People could send donations to government-authorized private-police voucher-granting organizations. Clearly, the tax credits would reduce overall tax revenue; however, the private donations would offset these losses by increasing the total amount of police funding available while

---

[10] City of Dallas. "Financial Transparency." Retrieved from: http://dallascityhall.com/departments/budget/financialtransparency/Pages/default.aspx.

[11] United States Census Bureau. QuickFacts. "Dallas, Texas." Retrieved from: https://www.census.gov/quickfacts/fact/table/dallascitytexas/PST045216.

[12] "Report on the Fiscal 2017 Preliminary Budget and the Fiscal 2016 Preliminary Mayor's Management Report." New York Police Department. Retrieved from: https://council.nyc.gov/budget/wp-content/uploads/sites/54/2016/05/056-NYPD.pdf.

[13] United States Census Bureau. QuickFacts. "New York City, New York." Retrieved from: https://www.census.gov/quickfacts/fact/table/newyorkcitynewyork/PST045217.

decreasing the variable costs allocated toward government-provided rights protection (see, e.g., Trivitt and DeAngelis 2017).

3.2 Savings Accounts

Much like an education savings account (ESA) or a health savings account, communities could implement a privately or publicly funded rights-enforcement savings-account program (RESA). Each individual citizen could receive an annual amount equal to a fraction of the per-citizen police funding level and use those funds to purchase private police services. These funds would likely mostly be allocated toward a private police department; however, we could imagine plenty of other privately produced goods and services that are used to ensure that rights are protected such as home security systems, safes for valuables, firearms, car alarm systems, private security guards, property-tracking GPS devices, self-defense courses, guard dogs, neighborhood-watch teams, and online identity-theft protection.

The RESA model has two important advantages over vouchers. First, RESAs allow citizens to customize their rights-protection service packages beyond police departments. Second, RESAs introduce stronger price signals into the market for rights protection. Because policing vouchers could only be used on one type of service, the voucher scenario essentially creates a price floor equal to the per-citizen police funding level determined by the state. In a New York City voucher scenario, we would expect the least expensive policing plan to be at the voucher amount of about $483 (75 percent of $644) per citizen in 2016. This price floor would not exist in a New York City RESA scenario, as individual citizens would have a strong incentive to economize on their spending on the private police department. If people paid less than $483 to have their rights protected, they would be rewarded by getting to save those funds for other types of rights-protection services.[14] To create additional incentives to economize, RESA plans could also include the ability of customers to roll over a portion of unused funds, as ESA legislation currently allows (EdChoice 2017b), from year to year.

3.3 Chartered Police Agencies

Although profit-seeking firms have a strong financial incentive to reduce use of violence and coercion, government actors may not yet feel

---

[14] DeAngelis, C. A. (2017). "This Kind of School Choice is Superior to Vouchers." *Foundation for Economic Education*. Retrieved from: https://fee.org/articles/this-kind-of-school-choice-is-superior-to-vouchers.

comfortable allowing private companies to use coercion at all. A more politically feasible option is public-police choice, much like public school choice (i.e., public charter schools). State or local governments could approve certain private entities to manage publicly funded police departments. These police departments would be free in the sense that customers would pay zero at the point of entry; however, they would need to be indirectly funded through the current public-police budget—likely from state and federal government grants and local sales and property taxes.

While the inability of these public police forces to charge an explicit fee would likely be politically advantageous, a few economic problems would arise. First, an explicit price of zero would guarantee there would not be any information or incentives gained from price differentiation. Great public police forces would not be financially rewarded for their excellent services; instead, they would be rewarded with a waitlist of customers. Obviously, since variation in police-department quality is bound to emerge, quantity demanded is likely to exceed quantity supplied for certain public police departments. To ensure fairness, government would likely resort to a random lottery whenever such a phenomenon occurs (as currently happens with public charter schools). Great police departments would recognize that their talents were not being financially rewarded and might lose motivation over time. In addition, the high-quality police departments with excess demand would learn that they could simply replace an unhappy customer with one of the many happy customers desperately waiting in the queue. In other words, persistent shortage conditions would likely lead to quality deterioration (Rockoff 1992).

4. Common Criticisms

Whenever the concept of police choice is raised, economists and everyday citizens respond with criticisms that can be summed up in six categories: (1) conflicts between customers of different agencies, (2) situations in which one agency prevents the rights of another company's customer from being violated, (3) rights protection as a public good, (4) rights protection having positive externalities, (5) certain types of violations' having costs that are spread out across several members of society, and (6) rights protection being too important to leave to private profit-seeking firms.

While some of these criticisms are stronger than others, none of them are legitimate reasons why anyone should expect the current system of government-run policing to outperform any of the systems of police choice I previously explained.

4.1 Conflicts between Customers of Different Agencies

The first response to the idea of private police choice is almost always related to a possible dispute between customers of different private police agencies. Imagine a situation in which someone protected by a competing agency steals your automobile out of your garage. Once you notice the incident, you tell your private police force. Your private police force (Firm A) looks at the video footage it installed in your garage to deter theft and identifies the violator as John Smith. Your private police force calls up John Smith and tells him it is quite certain he stole its customer's automobile and that he must return it and compensate the police force $50 for its time and effort, or else it will show up at his front door in a day or two to retrieve the automobile by force. John Smith points out he too has his own reputable private police force (Firm B) and that if Firm A shows up at his front door tomorrow, he will have Firm B show up to defend him. Of course, this kind of situation sounds like it is going to lead to a small war on John Smith's front lawn. Clearly, this would not be an improvement on the current government-run monopoly system (Friedman 1989).

However, as David Friedman (1989) argued, this situation would not likely occur. Since the two private police forces would be profit-seeking firms, they would avoid war because it is very costly. The firms would need to pay for any ammunition used, maintenance for weapons, and any damages accruing to their customers' property because of the skirmish. Perhaps more importantly, the firms would need to pay their employees a lavish salary for the elevated risk of death on the job. And, of course, their bottom lines would be negatively affected since their customers would not like firms that continuously waged war on their front lawns, damaged their property, and put their families in danger. A private firm that waged war would also have to charge a high price to its customers to cover unnecessary battle expenses, which would lead to lost customers and pressures to shut down. In addition, it would not be profitable for a private firm to engage in warfare, because other, peaceful private firms would have an incentive to avoid collaborating with aggressive firms. This is because (1) interactions with aggressive firms would be risky, and (2) peaceful firms would not want the bad reputation of dealing with aggressive firms. In contrast, government actors can wage expensive wars while remaining in business since it is nearly impossible for their customers (citizens) to opt out of paying for them (Tannehill and Tannehill 2007).

One way to avoid this problem altogether is for each firm to agree on fair private arbitrators that would settle these types of disputes (Friedman 1989). Firm A and Firm B could either agree on a settlement out of court or simply take the disagreement to arbitration. I would argue that the former would be much more likely because the time and effort put into taking the case to arbitration is highly costly (if a firm believed it would lose the arbitration case, it would be more profitable for it to accept the loss before pursuing the case further). If each firm believed it had a good chance of winning the case, the arbitrator would look at the evidence from each firm and determine the victor. With enough evidence to prove John Smith guilty, Firm B would have to pay Firm A for its time and effort used to fight the case, John Smith would have to return the automobile, and his firm would need to provide compensation to the owner. If Firm B did not listen to the verdict of the agreed-upon arbitrator, Firm A (and other firms that learn of Firm B's bad reputation) would likely discontinue doing business with it in the future, leading to either a war, a shutdown, or both. Since Firm B would have much stronger incentives to comply with the determined result of the case—even if it did not agree with the verdict—the loss in arbitration would likely simply mean Firm B would charge risky customers such as John Smith higher rates in the future (similar to what currently happens in the market for car insurance). If John Smith did not like the higher rates, he could switch to a different private police force or even return to the government-run police force. This would give rights violators an obvious financial incentive to obey the law.

This leads to another problem that could occur in the long run. Private police forces might be able to raise prices on their most costly customers and perhaps even proactively turn down customers they perceive to be risky. The result might be that the government-run police forces would get stuck with the costliest customers, whom the private police forces would not want. However, it is not hard to imagine police forces emerging that specialize in serving these types of customers. For example, several private schools exist that largely serve disadvantaged communities of color[15] and others exist that only serve children that are deaf[16] or blind. There are also private companies that help the absolutely least advantaged members of society—the homeless—get off the public streets and become productive citizens with drug-rehabilitation and vocational services.[17] In addition, while this criticism has been made about private school-choice programs in the United States, twenty of twenty-one studies have found that the disadvantaged students that

---

[15] *US News and World Report.* "Historically Black Colleges and Universities." Retrieved from: https://www.usnews.com/best-colleges/rankings/hbcu.

[16] Niche. "Horace Mann School." Retrieved from: https://www.niche.com/k12/horace-mann-school-bronx-ny.

[17] Volunteers of America. "Assisting Homeless People." Retrieved from: https://www.voa.org/homeless-people.

are left behind in traditional public schools actually do better academically because of the stronger competitive pressures for government-run schools to improve (Egalite 2013).

Nonetheless, a more politically feasible solution may be to include a provision in the private police-choice bill mandating that the public and private police forces must accept all customers and use a random lottery when a shortage arises. However, there are risks that come along with attempting to control a service industry in this way. After all, the highly regulated school-choice program in Louisiana that compelled participating private schools to surrender their admissions standards to the state experienced lower school-quality levels (DeAngelis and Hoarty 2018; Sude, DeAngelis, and Wolf 2018) and less specialization (DeAngelis 2018; DeAngelis and Burke 2017; DeAngelis and Burke forthcoming).

Further, in the US there are already jurisdictions that overlap (Friedman 1989). Federal, state, county, city, municipal, school, and park police already exist in almost any geographic location at any given time, and they do not go to war with one another when conflict arises. This may be because they are all government-run; however, they are currently commanded by different government agencies and different public officials. Nonetheless, another politically feasible option could be to use a system of choice among government-run alternatives. However, as I argued in the section on chartered police agencies, because of shortages and the lack of incentives and information otherwise provided by price signals the public police-choice arrangement would not be economically efficient.

It is also worth noting the conjecture that a system of private policing would mirror a system of organized crime. Friedman (1989) made a strong argument against this theory. Today, gangs acquire much of their power from their ability to bribe government police officers. Because government police departments are not profit-seeking firms that face shutdown conditions when expenses exceed revenues, and because they are unlikely to lose customers when crime rates increase (on the contrary, the citizens might vote to increase spending on government policing if crime rates increase), government police officers do not have strong financial incentives to turn down bribes. In addition, gangs have a financial incentive to engage in bribery because they can bribe police officers an amount below what they expect to collect through coercive activity such as robbery. Employees of private police agencies are less likely to accept bribes and turn a blind eye because they are in the business of protecting their customers' rights. As Friedman (1989) argued, "The only bribe it would pay the [private] agency to take would be one for more than the value of the goods stolen—a poor deal for the thief…

This reduces to the thief bribing the victim by more than the amount stolen, which is improbable."

4.2 Preventing Noncustomers' Rights from Being Violated

Another possible problem regarding customer overlap exists: if there is uncertainty about whether a potential victim is its customer, a given agency might spend less of its time and effort preventing rights violations. After all, it is more efficient and beneficial to prevent a person's rights from being violated in the first place than to seek out a violator after the fact.

There are three reasons why this criticism is probably invalid. First, police officers today allocate most of their resources toward responding to complaints and seeking out violators after they have already broken the law (Stevens 1999). Indeed, the Police Foundation conducted the Kansas City Preventative Patrol Experiment from 1972 to 1973 by randomly assigning levels of police patrol to geographic areas. It eliminated routine preventative patrol in five areas, meaning the police only entered these areas when they were called. The level of preventative patrol was increased by two or three times in five other areas, with five areas used as a control group with normal patrol levels. The Police Foundation found evidence to suggest that changing the levels of preventative patrol affected the incidence of crimes, meaning violators were not deterred by the police or that police currently spend most of their time responding to calls instead of preventing violations (Kelling et al. 1974). In fact, ride-along observers found that Kansas City patrol officers "spent a considerable amount of time waiting to respond to calls for service."[18] Furthermore, researchers have found that less than 5 percent of 911 calls lead to the prevention of a rights violations or even to an arrest (Witkin, Guttman, and Lenzy 1996).

Second, the current system's problems may be much deeper. After all, we need to compare the proposed system to the current system, which is far from perfect. Statute dictates that the government does not have a duty to protect its citizens or even to respond to its calls. For example, in 1975, two men broke into a house in the nation's capital and robbed, raped, and beat three women over a fourteen-hour period. One of the women was able to call the police twice, but the police did not stop the violators. When the women attempted to sue the city for negligence, the court determined that

---

[18] "The Kansas City Preventative Patrol Experiment." Police Foundation. Retrieved from: https://www.policefoundation.org/projects/the-kansas-city-preventive-patrol-experiment.

the government did not have a duty to protect the women (Stevens 1999; DC 1981). Similarly, a California appellate court (1997) indicated that "police officers have no affirmative statutory duty to do anything."

Third, private rights-protection firms could agree on what they would do if such a situation arose. If one firm proactively protected the rights of another firm's customer, the customer's firm could give the proactive firm a side payment. This already occurs in other industries. For example, imagine a customer belongs to a private bank (Bank A) and would like to use its services (specifically, withdrawal from an automated teller machine), but their nearest member bank is a hundred miles away. If the individual withdraws cash from another bank's (Bank B) automated teller machine, the individual pays a small service fee to Bank A. Bank A then pays Bank B for providing this service to its customers. With such agreements, it would similarly be profitable for each rights-protection firm to proactively assist customers from other agencies. Even if such an agreement did not exist, companies could assist noncustomers out of good will. Currently, police officers may help you when you are on vacation even if you do not pay them anything in taxes. The only difference from the private system is that the police officers from profit-seeking companies would have an additional incentive to help noncustomers. The proactive firm could attract noncustomers to its company by offering them superior service.

In addition, coordination among private policing agencies would be profitable if the sharing of information reduced the risk that individuals would be harmed by rights violators. Because information sharing improves security for customers, security firms have strong financial incentives to share intelligence with competitors. In theory, a system of police choice could lead to the establishment of private information-coordinating agencies that would operate along similar lines as Interpol.[19] Private police agencies would also have an incentive to share valuable information with competing firms because of the discipline of constant dealings (Friedman 1989). Firm A would give Firm B information to help Firm B protect its customers in the expectation that Firm B would share its information with Firm A in the future. Firm B would know that if it did not share its information with Firm A in the future, then (1) Firm A would no longer assist it and (2) Firm A could damage Firm B's reputation by showing other competitors that Firm B is not trustworthy. Because of the discipline of constant dealings, Firm B has a long-run financial incentive to help Firm A with information in the future.

---

[19] Interpol. "Connecting Police for a Safer World." Retrieved from: https://www.interpol.int/en.

4.3 Public Goods

Some critics make the claim that rights protection is a public good, and, since it is a public good, government force must be used to require everyone to pay their fair share. This argument is probably the weakest of the objections considered here, as rights protection obviously fails both of the standard economic conditions of a public good: (1) excludability, and (2) nonrivalrousness in consumption (Samuelson 1954). First, since it is possible for a rights-protection agency to exclude nonpayers from its protection, a free-rider problem does not arise. Since the free-rider problem does not arise, government force is not necessary to fund the service. That we historically had (e.g., England's thief takers in the eighteenth century; San Francisco's private police in the mid-nineteenth century), and currently have (e.g., private police in Detroit, San Francisco, and South Carolina; private mall security; private university police; private railroad police), private policing is concrete evidence that policing can be privately produced and provided.

Even if a free-rider problem did exist with policing, government force would not be the only way to fund the service. After all, even true public goods such as the radio are successfully funded through voluntary mechanisms such as advertisements. In addition, the free-rider problem has been eliminated through technological innovation in the radio industry. For example, satellite-radio companies, such as SiriusXM, have been able to solve the public-good problem by successfully excluding nonpayers from using their services. As Milton Friedman (1962) contended, private monopolies are preferable to government monopolies since (1) individuals can opt out of paying for a private service, and (2) private firms have a stronger incentive to solve the free-rider problem associated with true public goods such as the radio. Johnson and Libecap (1982) also argued that private entrepreneurs have stronger incentives to solve the public-good problem. Furthermore, policing fails the second, but perhaps less important, public-good condition since it is rivalrous in consumption. When one customer requires the assistance of a police officer, the rest of the customers served by the firm have fewer police officers at their disposal.

4.4 Positive Externalities

When people make the claim that rights protection is a public good, I believe they mean to say that rights protection is good for the public. In other words, what they mean to say is that rights protection produces large positive externalities, or uncompensated benefits to third parties. If I voluntarily purchase rights protection from the firm of my choice, I benefit from the transaction by having my rights protected, and the private firm benefits since it receives my money and earns a profit. However, other members of society that did not directly pay for the service benefit as well. If I feel safer because I know I have a great private police force, I will be more likely to trade with other individuals in the marketplace and more likely to produce valuable goods and services. Most economists agree that this type of market failure would produce a less than socially optimal level of rights-protection services, all else equal (Coase 1937; Pigou 1920).

However, the presence of positive externalities does not mean government must operate the rights-protection agencies; instead, it merely means that government might have an incentive to provide some additional funding of rights protection to push consumption up toward the socially optimal level. Milton Friedman (1955) made the same claim: government may have a reason to fund, but not operate, schools. Nonetheless, since none of us know what the truly socially optimal level of rights protection is, we do not know how much the government ought to subsidize rights protection. Indeed, in attempting to reach the socially optimal level of rights protection, we might miss the socially optimal level and end up further away from the optimal level than if we had taken no action at all (Friedman 1986; 2013). Either way, each of my proposed policy solutions that are publicly funded provides rights protection for every single citizen living in the geographic area. Furthermore, I argue that the level of rights protection would be higher (even with the same amount of tax dollars allocated) because of the incentive to economize (rather than the alternative incentive for bureaucrats to maximize budgets [Niskanen 1971]) in a choice setting. After all, Donahue (1989) found that public service providers are about 50 percent less efficient than private contractors because of less robust labor flexibility, incentives, and accountability, and a weaker focus on results (Pastor 2003).

4.5 Violations with Diffuse Costs

Certain rights violations disperse relatively small costs across many individuals within a society. If this is the case, individual consumers of private rights protection might consume a less than socially optimal level of these types of rights-protection services. For example, we might expect that speeding laws would not be enforced as much as we would like. When I hire a rights-protection agency, I will not be willing to pay as much for its police officers to reduce average driving speeds on the roads because the benefit of deterring one driver from going one hundred miles per hour is spread across all the other drivers, many whom may belong to alternative rights-protection agencies, on the road at the time. In other words, it may very well be that these types of laws would be enforced less than they are today.

However, no one knows the socially optimal level of speeding tickets. It could be that a reduction in the number of speeding tickets would bring us closer to the social optimum. After all, a recent audit found that police in Washington, DC, give out speeding tickets to citizens for "violations they don't commit and for vehicles they've never owned" and raise $179 million a year from traffic citations.[20] In addition, we could imagine certain ways that a given private rights-protection agency could compensate another agency's customers when its own customers drive too fast or recklessly. Rights-protection agencies could install cameras on the dashboards of their customers' automobiles, and their customers could make complaints whenever other drivers speed. If the two drivers were from different agencies, the case would go to arbitration, and if the evidence was strong enough, the reckless driver's agency would have to pay for the other agency's time and effort (Friedman 1989).

In addition, customers that drive recklessly have a larger risk of getting into an accident in which they are at fault. Since risky customers' agencies would have to compensate the victims' agencies for their losses, risky customers would have their protection rates go up and reputations go down. The clear incentive would be to drive as safely as possible so you would not have to bear all the costs of the damages you cause. In addition, if a class action lawsuit was filed against a certain reckless driver, the incentive to drive as safely (and politely) as possible would be strengthened even further.

4.6 Importance

Many people believe that certain aspects of life are too important to be left to faith in the self-interested decisions made by individual actors in the free market (Hebdon 1995; Linowes 1988; Shenk 1995; Wessel 1995). They believe that essential services such as policing need to be instead carefully controlled by supposedly benevolent actors within the government. However, this argument is invalid for three main reasons.

First, government actors are also rationally self-interested individuals; however, while self-interested individuals within the free market system demand goods and services that have the highest quality levels at the lowest

---

[20] "DC Is the Wild West When Enforcing Tickets for Traffic Violators, Audit Finds." *Washington Post.* September 8, 2014. Retrieved from: https://www.washingtonpost.com/local/trafficandcommuting/withering-inspector-general-report-criticizes-dc-parking-and-traffic-ticketing/2014/09/08/da6ae324-3781-11e4-8601-97ba88884ffd_story.html?noredirect=on&utm_term=.e286cefeab1d.

costs, individuals in the political system pursue their self-interest by catering to the needs of concentrated interest groups rather than each individual citizen. In addition, self-interested political actors use as many resources for their constituents as possible so they can politically profit (Niskanen 1971).

Second, many of the same people calling for a government monopoly on the highly important service of rights protection acknowledge that government should not have a monopoly on the most essential product that exists: food. The natural experiment has been implemented at least three times. The USSR controlled the production of food in the 1930s, leading to food shortages, starvation, and about seven million deaths (Graziosi 2017; Werth 2016). The Great Chinese Famine, from 1959 to 1961, killed between fifteen and thirty million citizens from starvation (Holmes 2009), and many scholars contend that Mao Zedong's policies that controlled the food industry were strong contributors to the problem (Dikötter 2010; Li and Yang 2005). More recently, in 2016, the Venezuelan government took control of the supply of food, and again, food shortages arose and have persisted (Dube, Vyas, and Kurmanaev 2018; Oré 2016).

Third, most people agree that the government is ineffective and inefficient at performing relatively simple tasks such as mail delivery and renewing drivers' licenses. Oddly, many of the same people also claim government somehow does a better job than the free market with the much more complex task of protecting rights. Instead, we should expect that governments that do a poor job with simple tasks would do an even less effective job at completing more intricate tasks (Free to Choose Network 2015). Of course, it is not that people holding government jobs are incompetent, lazy, or malevolent. On the contrary, the problem is that the set of incentives included within the political system make it as difficult as possible for government employees to produce high-quality products at low costs (Niskanen 1971). Furthermore, the absence of the invaluable information and incentives provided by price signals within government systems should only exacerbate the problem of ineffectiveness as tasks become more complex (Hayek 1945).

5. Conclusion

While the system of rights protection is highly costly and largely inefficient in the United States, it does not have to be. As with any other service industry, a monopoly on production leads to significant difficulties for customers. The big problem is that low quality in this service industry does not simply lead to inconveniences; monopoly power in rights protection means customers are more likely to be stolen from, harmed, or even killed.

What is worse in this specific scenario is that many of the deaths occur at the hands of the providers of the service.

Rights protection can be strengthened through each of the public or private police-choice options I have mentioned: charters, vouchers, and savings accounts. In theory, these policies should lead to substantial quality improvements and reductions in costs, especially because policing fails the economic definition of a public good. Furthermore, other common criticisms of the proposed policies have been addressed in this study; and while the proposed policies are not panaceas, I expect them to lead to substantial improvements over the status quo. In practice, private rights protection, even without any government funding, has been shown to be highly successful in environments as different as present-day Detroit and seventeenth- to eighteenth-century England. We should expect a publicly funded and privately produced system of police choice to perform even better.

References

Baicker, K., and M. Jacobson. (2007). "Finders Keepers: Forfeiture Laws, Policing Incentives, and Local Budgets." *Journal of Public Economics*, *91*(11-12), 2113-2136.

Barnett, R. E. (2014). *The Structure of Liberty: Justice and the Rule of Law*. Oxford, UK: Oxford University Press.

Bartel, A., and D. Lewin. (1981). "Wages and Unionism in the Public Sector: The Case of Police." *Review of Economics and Statistics*, 63(1), 53-59.

Beattie, J. M. (2001). *Policing and Punishment in London, 1660-1750: Urban Crime and the Limits of Terror*. Oxford, UK: Oxford University Press. pp. 226-256.

Beattie, J. M. (2012). *The First English Detectives: The Bow Street Runners and the Policing of London, 1750-1840*. Oxford, UK: Oxford University Press.

Beattie, J. M. (2017). "Early Detection: The Bow Street Runners in Late Eighteenth-Century London." In C. Emsley and H. Shpayer-Makov (eds.) *Police Detectives in History, 1750-1950* (pp. 15-32). London, UK: Routledge.

Bechler, R. E. (2011). "Private Police Ownership: Can It Possibly Happen?" *Journal of California Law Enforcement*, *45*(1), 12-16.

Benson, B. L. (1998). *To Serve and Protect: Privatization and Community in Criminal Justice*. New York: New York University Press.

Benson, B. L. (2014). "Let's Focus on Victim Justice, Not Criminal Justice." *Independent Review*, *19*(2), 209-238.

Benson, B. L., D. W. Rasmussen, and D. L. Sollars. (1995). "Police Bureaucracies, Their Incentives, and the War on Drugs." *Public Choice*, *83*(1-2), 21-45.

Brown, K., and P. B. Coulter. (1983). "Subjective and Objective Measures of Police Service Delivery." *Public Administration Review*, *43*(1), 50-58.

Chubb, J. E., and T. M. Moe. (1988). "Politics, Markets, and the Organization of Schools." *American Political Science Review*, *82*(4), 1065-1087.

Cohen, M. J., E. J. Zechmeister, and M. A. Seligson. (2015). *Those with Darker Skin Report Slower Police Response*. AmericasBarometer: Topical Brief. Vanderbilt University. Retrieved from: https://www.vanderbilt.edu/lapop/insights/ITB016en.pdf.

Danielson, W. F. (1967). *Police Compensation*. Center for Law Enforcement Research Information, Research and Development Division, of the International Association of Chiefs of Police.

DeAngelis, C. A. (2017). "Do Self-Interested Schooling Selections Improve Society? A Review of the Evidence." *Journal of School Choice*, *11*(4), 546-558.

DeAngelis, C. A. (2018). "Which Schools Participate? An Analysis of Private School Voucher Program Participation Decisions across Seven Locations." Unpublished Manuscript.

DeAngelis, C. A., and L. Burke. (2017). "Does Regulation Induce Homogenisation? An Analysis of Three Voucher Programs in the United States." *Educational Research and Evaluation*, *23*(7-8), 311-327.

DeAngelis, C. A., and L. Burke. (forthcoming). "Does Regulation Reduce Specialization? Examining the Impact of Regulations on Private Schools of Choice in Four Locations." *EdChoice*.

DeAngelis, C. A., and B. Hoarty. (2018). "Who Participates? An Analysis of School Participation Decisions in Two Voucher Programs in the United States." *Cato Institute Policy Analysis No. 848*.

DeAngelis, C. A., and H. Holmes Erickson. (2018). "What Leads to Successful School Choice Programs? A Review of the Theories and Evidence." *Cato Journal*, *38*(1), 247-263.

Dempsey, J. S. (2010). *Introduction to Private Security*. Belmont, CA: Cengage Learning.

Devine, E. J. (1969). "Manpower Shortages in Local Government Employment." *American Economic Review, 59*(2), 538-545.

Dikötter, F. (2010). *Mao's Great Famine: The History of China's Most Devastating Catastrophe, 1958-1962*. New York, NY: Walker Publishing Company.

Donahue, J. D. (1989). *Privatization Decision: Public Ends, Private Means*. New York, NY: Basic Books.

Dube, R., K. Vyas, and A. Kurmanaev. (2018). "Venezuela's Maduro, Clinging to Power, Uses Hunger as an Election Weapon." *Wall Street Journal*. Retrieved from: https://www.wsj.com/articles/venezuelas-maduro-clinging-to-power-uses-hunger-as-an-electoral-weapon-1521734622.

EdChoice (2017a). *Types of School Choice: What Are School Vouchers?* Retrieved from https://www.edchoice.org/school-choice/types-of-school-choice/what-are-school-vouchers-2.

EdChoice (2017b). *The ESAs in K-12 Education Are and How They're Different from Coverdell ESAs*. Retrieved from: https://www.edchoice.org/blog/esas-k-12-education-theyre-different-coverdell-esas.

Egalite, A. J. (2013). "Measuring Competitive Effects from School Voucher Programs: A Systematic Review." *Journal of School Choice, 7*(4), 443-464.

Emsley, C. (2014). *The English Police: A Political and Social History*. London, UK: Routledge.

Federal Bureau of Investigation (2016). *Uniform Crime Reporting. Michigan. Offenses Known to Law Enforcement by City, 2016*. Retrieved from: https://ucr.fbi.gov/crime-in-the-u.s/2016/crime-in-the-u.s.-2016/tables/table-6/table-6-state-cuts/michigan.xls.

Forst, B. (2000). "The Privatization and Civilianization of Policing." *Criminal Justice, 2*(24), 19-78.

Free to Choose Network (2015). *Free to Choose 1990 - Vol. 04: The Failure of Socialism—Full video* [Video file]. Retrieved from: https://www.youtube.com/watch?v=KFqJoY8GwWI.

Friedman, D. D. (1986). *Price Theory: An Intermediate Text*. Cincinnati, OH: South-Western Publishing Co.

Friedman, D. D. (1989). *The Machinery of Freedom: Guide to a Radical Capitalism*. Open Court Publishing Company.

Friedman, D. D. (2013). *Global Warming, Population, and the Problem with Externality Arguments*. London, UK: Libertarian Alliance. Retrieved from: https://www.youtube.com/watch?v=s-yJ3K9fNos.

Friedman, M. (1955). "The Role of Government in Education." In R. Solo (ed.), *Economics and the Public Interest*, pg. 123-144. New Brunswick, NJ: Rutgers University Press.

Friedman, M. (1962). *Capitalism and Freedom*. Chicago, IL: University of Chicago Press.

Friedman, M. (1997). "Public Schools: Make Them Private." *Education Economics*, 5(3), 341-344.

Fryer Jr, R. G. (2016). *An Empirical Analysis of Racial Differences in Police Use of Force*. National Bureau of Economic Research Working Paper No. 22399.

Gilbert, M. J., and D. Schichor. (2000). *Privatization of Criminal Justice: Past Present and Future*. Cincinatti, OH: Anderson Publishing Co.

Graziosi, A. (2017). "Political Famines in the USSR and China: A Comparative Analysis." *Journal of Cold War Studies*, 19(3), 42-103.

Guillory, G., and P. C. Tinsley. (2009). "The Role of Subscription-Based Patrol and Restitution in the Future of Liberty." *Libertarian Papers*, 1, 1-40. Retrieved from: http://libertarianpapers.org/12-role-subscription-based-patrol-restitution-future-liberty.

Hall, W. C., and B. Vanderporten. (1977). "Unionization, Monopsony Power, and Police Salaries." *Industrial Relations: A Journal of Economy and Society*, 16(1), 94-100.

Harris, A. T. (2004). *Policing the City: Crime and Legal Authority in London, 1780-1840*. Columbus, OH: Ohio State University Press.

Hayek, F. A. (1945). "The Use of Knowledge in Society." *American Economic Review*, 35(4), 519-530.

Hebdon, R. (1995). "Contracting Out in New York State." *Lab. Stud. J.*, 20, 3.

Hitchcock, T., and R. Shoemaker. (2006). *Tales from the Hanging Court*. London, UK: Hodder and Arnold. Retrieved from: http://uhra.herts.ac.uk/bitstream/handle/2299/104/003-Hanging%2520Court-cpp.pdf.

Holmes, L. (2009). *Communism: A Very Short Introduction* (Vol. 209, pg. 32). New York, NY: Oxford University Press.

Howson, G. (1985). *Thief-Taker General: Jonathan Wild and the Emergence of Crime and Corruption as a Way of Life in Eighteenth-Century England.* New Brunswick, NJ: Transaction Publishers.

Johnson, R. N., and G. D. Libecap. (1982). "Contracting Problems and Regulation: The Case of the Fishery." *American Economic Review, 72*(5), 1005-1022.

Kelling, G. L., T. Pate, D. Dieckman, and C. E. Brown. (1974). *The Kansas City Preventive Patrol Experiment.* Washington, DC: Police Foundation.

Kelly, M. A. (1988). "Citizen Survival in Ancient Rome." *Police Stud.: Int'l Rev. Police Dev., 11*, 195.

Lewis, C. (1999). *Complaints against Police: The Politics of Reform.* Sydney, AU: Hawkins Press.

Li, W., and D. T. Yang. (2005). "The Great Leap Forward: Anatomy of a Central Planning Disaster." *Journal of Political Economy, 113*(4), 840-877.

Linowes, D. F. (Ed.). (1988). *Privatization: Toward More Effective Government: Report of the President's Commission on Privatization.* University of Illinois Press.

Lueken, M. F. (2016). *The Tax-Credit Scholarship Audit: Do Publicly Funded Private School Choice Programs Save Money?* EdChoice. Retrieved from: https://eric.ed.gov/?id=ED570441.

McLynn, F. (1989). *Crime and Punishment in Eighteenth-Century Europe.* London, UK: Routledge.

Meehan, B., and B. L. Benson. (2015). "The Occupations of Regulators Influence Occupational Regulation: Evidence from the US Private Security Industry." *Public Choice, 162*(1-2), 97-117.

Michigan Legislature (2017). *Senate Bill 594.* Retrieved from: http://www.legislature.mi.gov/(S(gqcmlm0blnuy10orjea0rb5g))/mileg.aspx?page=GetObject&objectname=2017-SB-0594.

Niskanen, W. A. (1971). *Bureaucracy and Representative Government.* New Brunswick, NJ: Transaction Publishers.

Old Bailey Proceedings (2015). *Policing in London. The Role of Private Individuals before the Police.* Retrieved from: https://www.oldbaileyonline.org/static/Policing.jsp#individualstext.

Office of International Criminal Justice (1995). *Readings*. Collection of papers presented at the Ninth Annual Futures Conference on Privatization in Criminal Justice: Public and Private Partnerships, 13-15 March, University of Illinois at Chicago.

Oré, D. (2016). "Venezuela's Military to Coordinate Food, Medicine Distribution." Reuters. Retrieved from: https://www.reuters.com/article/us-venezuela-food-idUSKCN0ZS2BU.

Pastor, J. F. (2003). *The Privatization of Police in America: An Analysis and Case Study*. Jefferson, NC: McFarland & Company.

Rockoff, H. (1992). *Price Controls*. London, UK: Edward Elgar Publishing.

Ross, C. T. (2015). "A Multi-Level Bayesian Analysis of Racial Bias in Police Shootings at the County-Level in the United States, 2011-2014." *PloS One, 10*(11), e0141854.

Rothbard, M. N. (1978). *For a New Liberty: The Libertarian Manifesto*. Auburn, AL: Ludwig von Mises Institute.

Samuelson, P. A. (1954). "The Pure Theory of Public Expenditure." *Review of Economics and Statistics, 36*(4), 387-389.

Shakeel, M., K. P. Anderson, and P. J. Wolf. (2016). *The Participant Effects of Private School Vouchers across the Globe: A Meta-analytic and Systematic Review*. EDRE Working Paper No. 2016-07.

Shenk, J. W. (1995). "The Perils of Privatization." *Washington Monthly, 27*(5), 16-23.

Souza v. City of Antioch, 62 California Reporter, 2d 909, 916 (Cal. App. 1997).

Spalding, J. (2014). *The School Voucher Audit: Do Publicly Funded Private School Choice Programs Save Money?* Friedman Foundation for Educational Choice. Retrieved from: http://ocpathinker.org/wp-content/uploads/2017/06/The-School-Voucher-Audit.pdf.

Stevens, R. W. (1999). *Dial 911 and Die*. Hartford, WI: Mazel Freedom Press.

Stenning, P. C., and M. F. Cornish. (1975). *The Legal Regulation and Control of Private Policing and Security in Canada*. Centre of Criminology, University of Toronto. Retrieved from: https://www.ncjrs.gov/App/Publications/abstract.aspx?ID=49678.

Stringham, E. (2015). *Private Governance: Creating Order in Economic and Social Life*. Oxford University Press.

Sude, Y., C. A. DeAngelis, and P. J. Wolf. (2018). "Supplying Choice: An Analysis of School Participation Decisions in Voucher Programs in Washington, DC, Indiana, and Louisiana." *Journal of School Choice*, *12*(1), 8-33.

Tannehill, M., and L. Tannehill. (2007). *The Market for Liberty*. Auburn, AL: Ludwig von Mises Institute.

Tiebout, C. M. (1956). "A Pure Theory of Local Expenditures." *Journal of Political Economy*, *64*(5), 416-424.

Trivitt, J. and C. A. DeAngelis. (2017). *State and District Fiscal Effects of a Universal Education Savings Account Program in Arkansas*. EDRE Working Paper No. 2017-04.

United States Census Bureau (2017b). *Poverty*. Retrieved from: https://www.census.gov/topics/income-poverty/poverty.html.

United States Census Bureau (2017b). *QuickFacts. Detroit, Michigan*. Retrieved from: https://www.census.gov/quickfacts/fact/table/detroitcitymichigan/PST045216.

Van Ryzin, G. G., D. Muzzio, and S. Immerwahr. (2004). "Explaining the Race Gap in Satisfaction with Urban Services." *Urban Affairs Review*, *39*(5), 613-632.

Volokh, A. (2012). "Prison Vouchers." *University of Pennsylvania Law Review*, *160*, 779-863.

Wales, T. (2000). "Thief-Takers and Their Clients in Later Stuart London." In P. Griffiths and M. Jenner (eds.), *Londinopolis: Essays in the Cultural and Social History of Early Modern London*. Manchester, UK: Manchester University Press. pp. 67-84.

Warren v. District of Columbia, 444 A.2d 1, 4 (D.C. 1981).

Werth, N. (2016). "Food Shortages, Hunger, and Famines in the USSR, 1928-33." *East/West: Journal of Ukrainian Studies*, *3*(2), 35-50.

Wessel, R. H. (1995). "Privatization in the United States." *Business Economics*, *30*(4), 45-50.

Witkin, G., M. Guttman, and T. Lenzy. (1996). "This Is 911... Please Hold." *US News & World Report*, *120*(24), 30-37.

Wolf, P. J. (2007). "Civics Exam." *Education Next*, *7*(3), 67-72.

Wolf, P. J., B. Kisida, B. Gutmann, M. Puma, N. Eissa, and L. Rizzo. (2013). "School Vouchers and Student Outcomes: Experimental Evidence from Washington, DC." *Journal of Policy Analysis and Management*, *32*(2), 246-270.

A Strategic Doctrine of Disproportionate Force for Decentralized Asymmetric Warfare

Joseph Michael Newhard[*]

Newhard (2017) recommends that anarcho-capitalist societies acquire nuclear weapons and adopt aggressive territorial-defense postures. It argues that the defense of anarchist territory will require escalation, preemption, and offensive operations targeting hostile states. It thus rejects the doctrine of dogmatic nonaggression that might arise out of a desire to extend the nonaggression principle (NAP) to enemies and others outside the private defense network. Below, I substantiate the necessity of ruthlessness in the defense of anarchist territory. In doing so, I describe a strategic doctrine of disproportionate force, modeled after Israeli doctrine,[1] that I recommend private defense agencies adopt, given the likely decentralized and asymmetric character of their armed forces.

An anarchist society will face numerous disadvantages. It is likely to be small in size and population. A small territory means a lack of strategic depth. A small population means fewer soldiers and less output to allocate to defense, holding output per capita constant. Perhaps the society will see significant capital accumulation, enhancing productivity and providing

---

[*]Joseph Michael Newhard is assistant professor of economics at East Tennessee State University.

CITATION INFORMATION FOR THIS ARTICLE:
Joseph Michael Newhard. 2018. "A Strategic Doctrine of Disproportionate Force for Decentralized Asymmetric Warfare." *Libertarian Papers*. 10 (2): 207-231. ONLINE AT: libertarianpapers.org. THIS ARTICLE IS subject to a Creative Commons Attribution 3.0 License (creativecommons.org/licenses).

[1] In particular, I refer to Israel's doctrine concerning hostile state actors such as Syria, Iran, Egypt (preceding the 1979 peace treaty), and Jordan (preceding the 1994 peace treaty).

sufficient funds to cover the large fixed costs of modern defense. Yet it is not certain that corporations will invest in stateless societies. The societies' survival will require that corporations do invest: the societies being relatively small, both the workforce and fighting force must be capital intensive. However, the most efficient substitute for soldiers and the most effective deterrent available to small nations is probably nuclear weapons. Additionally, an anarchist society may have to research and develop its own weapons, as Western defense contractors in particular may embargo them.[2] Private defense agencies or their contractors must allocate costly weapons research to where they can maximize deterrence, and this likely means focusing on the development of nuclear weapons and appropriate delivery vehicles. Lastly, coordination costs may rise under the private provision of defense, especially if multiple agencies defend the same territory.[3] The decentralized and asymmetric nature of stateless warfare will present challenges to be overcome.

---

[2] The Arms Export Control Act (AECA) of 1976 gives the president of the United States the authority to control the import and export of weapons and defense services. Of particular concern are preventing the proliferation of weapons of mass destruction, minimizing the risk of outbreak or escalation of war, and reducing international terrorism. The act also prohibits the sale of certain sensitive weapon technologies. Foreign military sales (FMS) and export controls are governed by subpart 225 of the Defense Federal Acquisition Regulation Supplement of the Federal Acquisition Regulation. The Department of State approves individual countries on a case-by-case basis, and defense contractors must obtain a license from the department for direct commercial sales (DCS). Both FMS and DCS are subject to similar restrictions and to congressional notification and review. Along with the AECA, the International Traffic in Arms Regulations regime restricts the export of military technology. It seems unlikely that an anarchist society would satisfy the State Department's alleged concerns pertaining to proliferation, escalation, and terrorism. The United States also exerts pressure on allies not to sell arms to its adversaries, as with the canceled Falcon deal between Israel and China in 2000. In any case, the anarchists might be able to import weapons from China or Russia if not the NATO countries.

[3] My view is that the chain of command governing a single military increases efficiency and that splitting up the armed forces into several autonomous units each with its own high commander necessarily increases the cost of coordinating an operation relative to a combined force of the same size under one commander. As mentioned below, Napoleon apparently believed that alliances made for weaker opponents for this reason. In a working paper, I argue that defense is a natural monopoly and that private defense agencies are likely to merge and acquire each other for the sake of reducing costs.

In some important ways, the anarchist society I envision resembles modern Israel. Accordingly, Israel's approach to national defense, especially from the time of its establishment in 1948 through the 1980s, proves instructive for anarchists.[4] It is relatively small in size and population and lacking in natural resources but boasts a technologically advanced and capital-intensive economy and had gross national output of $320 billion in 2016. These features have molded the Israel Defense Forces (IDF) into a small but superlative military that has survived surprise attacks by Egypt, Syria, and Jordan while conquering new territory. Israel has built a powerful air force; maintains an effective defense shield against artillery shells, mortars, rockets, missiles, and planes; and is widely believed to wield a nuclear arsenal produced from its own nuclear reactor and nuclear-reprocessing plant. Israel's ability to survive in the face of large, hostile neighbors despite its disadvantages makes it an excellent template for anarchist defense.

One key difference between an anarchist society and Israel is the latter's superpower backing. It is doubtful that the anarchists will have any state benefactors, large or small.[5] This is not entirely negative: Israeli leaders have "generally felt that the combined and complementary pressure of the superpowers snatched away from the IDF an imminent clear-cut victory in August 1970 and again in October 1973" (Ben-Horin and Posen, 1981, 8–9). Although US taxpayers provide Israel with $3.8 billion annually in military aid, amounting to a quarter of its defense budget (Gazit, 2011, 1), this pressures Israel to accede to the demands of the US government, which has regional interests of its own. This relationship restricts Israel's ability to export arms to some countries, cultivates "a culture of dependence," and limits Israel's ability to cooperate with America's rivals such as China (Gazit, 2011). Furthermore, 75 percent of the military grants must be spent on American arms, even at the cost of higher prices and inferior quality while undermining the Israeli defense industry in the process (ibid., 5).

---

[4] This paper will focus on Israeli strategy from its founding through the 1980s, when the country's primary threats consisted of large neighboring states. Since then, "extreme, violent, and well-armed substate actors have replaced neighboring state armies as Israel's main military threat" (Herzog, 2015). Israel's armed conflicts remain asymmetric, but the power distribution is now in its favor as it combats militant groups such as Hamas and Hezbollah.

[5] There are possible scenarios in which a state would support an anarchist society, such as if Russia decided to back anarchists in the United States to destabilize the government or region. Murphy (2017, 226) entertains the same possibility: "One coalition of global powers might 'adopt and protect' the anarchist island from rival powers, the way the Soviet Union was allied with Cuba during the Cold War."

Consequently, "superpower intervention is regarded, overall, as an obstruction and diminution of Israeli advantages. In particular, it is seen to provide the Arabs an opportunity to wage wars of limited liability" (Ben-Horin and Posen, 1981, 9).[6] Other important differences between the anarchist society and Israel include the latter's military conscription, its central bank, and the power to tax.

Lastly, the stated goals of Israeli defense planners[7] are in general terms also the anarchists' goals. Anarchists seek to preserve their culture of private property and nonaggression and to attract capital and technology to enjoy high living standards. Fighting even victorious wars undermines these goals, so the highest priority must be deterrence. The most effective means of deterrence is to maintain a military force capable of defeating the enemy, preferably with a minimal loss of anarchist life, property, and output. Since aggressors are rational agents who weigh the costs and benefits of invasion, anarchists must advertise a willingness to impose great costs on them. This sometimes requires subordinating considerations of the NAP to those of military expediency.[8] If deterrence is successful, the NAP will remain in force because the threat of retaliation will discourage potential invaders from provoking the anarchists from the start; as in Israel, the objective is "deterrence ex ante, not revenge ex post" (Beres, 2016). Below, I argue that anarchists must reject the martyrdom of dogmatic nonaggression in foreign affairs and instead adopt a strategic doctrine of disproportionate force, modeled after Israeli doctrine. My guiding principle is that of Cicero two thousand years ago: "Let the safety of the people be the highest law."

---

[6] With a defense budget of $18.6 billion in 2015, Israel finds that US military aid constitutes a significant and important resource. Although American aid has allowed Israel to increase its military budget, it is also not thought to be reliable in the long run and is believed to foster dependence (Ben-Horin and Posen, 1981, 6). On a related note, the Israeli defense budget does show that the anarchists will not have to come anywhere near the $600 billion the United States spent on war and defense in fiscal year 2015 in order to effectively defend themselves.

[7] These are defined in Eizenkot (2016) as:
    1) Safeguarding its existence and defending its territory and its residents.
    2) Preserving its values and its character.
    3) Securing its social and economic power.
    4) Strengthening its international status and maintaining peace.

[8] Newhard (2017, 63) lists several such scenarios including preventive strikes, some preemptive attacks, the deliberate bombing of infrastructure and private property, and any attack involving collateral damage.

1. Constraints

The anarchist society will face certain disadvantages in its struggle for survival. The first of these pertains to population size. At present, it seems that any arising anarchist society would have few residents. Perhaps as few as one hundred people worldwide would abandon their homes, careers, and social networks to establish an anarcho-capitalist society today. Certainly a figure as high as one million seems excessively optimistic, yet this may be the minimum threshold to establish even a modest conventional defense apparatus, let alone the standing army and nuclear force of Newhard (2017).[9]

If the population is small, the territory will also be small. Lacking strategic depth, maneuverability will suffer. Invaders will have easier access to military assets and to residential and business investments. Defending a smaller area may also bring certain tactical advantages, discussed below. However, the territory defended must be contiguous, an outer buffer zone will be essential, and the anarchists must maintain air superiority. Geography will also play an important role in defense, even with advanced weapons.[10] Although it is difficult to speculate on the physical features of a country not yet in existence, we can posit some ideal features of anarchist territory: A mountain perimeter will provide a natural defense barrier. Fertile land, plentiful water, and a climate conducive to growing crops will be ideal.[11] Natural resources such as lumber, coal, oil, and even rare earth elements may be invaluable. Access to land and sea trading routes will allow the anarchists to exploit their comparative advantages. Yet, depending on location, we must also consider that the anarchist society may be cut off from trade altogether.

---

[9] Even assuming a sustained disintegration of the Westphalian system in the coming centuries, some sort of exogenous shock may be necessary to achieve the critical mass that allows a market-anarchist society to assume its rightful place among the powers of the earth.

[10] Journalist Ze'ev Schiff argues, "Speed and precision of modern weaponry actually increase the importance of topography and geography in the modern battlefield" (Ben-Horin and Posen, 1981, 28).

[11] To the extent that trade is impeded by state meddling or by geography, the anarchist society will have to become self-sufficient. However, if trade is unimpeded, land and climate become less important to survival. Much of Israel's land is not ideal for farming, but citrus fruits are among its major exports. Effective water management has allowed Israeli farmers to increase output in recent years. Grains, fruits, nuts, and beef are among the country's major imports (US Department of Commerce, 2017).

Although an island may be a tempting location since there are some uninhabited and unclaimed ones, it may be difficult to defend.[12] This will not matter if no state is interested in the island, but that is most likely to be the case only if the island's location or natural resources are of little strategic or economic value. If the island is uninhabited, it is likely a poor source of food, fresh water, and other necessities of life, not to mention oil, coal, iron, cotton, lumber, corn, rice, wheat, beef, or other major commodities. If the island is isolated, trade will be extremely costly, diminishing opportunities for specialization and reducing living standards. Regrettably, the same lands anarchists find appealing are likely to be of value to states. If the anarchists find an acceptable island, even a modest state navy may quietly cut it off from trade and communication, strangling it. An island may put the anarchists at greater threat of a hopeless siege unless they invest in a powerful navy of their own.[13]

Market anarchists expect that throwing off the state will result in unprecedented capital investment, technological advancement, and growth in output per capita. This productivity will attract even more residents, including statists who are only attracted to higher wages (if permitted entry).[14] However, it is possible that capital accumulation will be low, resulting in a largely agrarian society of farmers and homesteaders and low output per capita. The economic theory of regulation holds that many corporations do not prefer a free market, in which competition drives long-run profits down to zero. Corporations and the state thus enter into a symbiotic relationship by which the state imposes regulations, taxes, and monopoly privileges via patents, copyrights, and trademarks to diminish competition, allowing

---

[12] Murphy (2017) assumes an island throughout his analysis of libertarian defense.

[13] In my estimation, sieges will be more manageable for the anarchists on land than at sea. It seems that the larger the territory, the more difficult it becomes for the imperialist power to successfully cut off the defender from the outside world, but this is true only on land; islands seem easier to isolate with only a few boats and planes, as during the Cuban missile crisis. In contrast, even in Operation Rolling Thunder the United States was never able to prevent soldiers and supplies from traveling along the Ho Chi Minh Trail to supply the Viet Cong, for instance.

[14] A free and happy population and a modern, industrialized economy will provide advantages for defense, as in Israel, which seeks "to generate a more technically competent, and more highly motivated force than her adversaries. Differences in internal cohesion have also meant that all of Israel's power is 'usable' in war, whereas the Arabs have had to tie down forces for defense of the internal regime" (Ben-Horin and Posen, 1981, 10).

corporations to generate profits, in turn giving the state something to tax.[15] Furthermore, to attract foreign direct investment, capitalists must believe that the anarchists are capable of enforcing property rights and that their society carries low country risk and political risk. Defense agencies must provide capitalists with assurances that their capital will be safe from an invasion.[16] Yet to build formidable defenses sufficient to attract business capital investment, anarchists will require significant military capital. This feedback loop could impair the ability of a free society to achieve a critical mass. Since a lack of capital would rule out building a modern military, I assume below that the anarchists will be able to attract capital investment.

Lastly, private defense agencies will bear coordination costs not experienced by their statist rivals. If defense is decentralized—provided by multiple agencies—this will increase the cost of defense, rendering it slower and less decisive. As Ben-Horin and Posen (1981, 10) report, "Coalitions tend to have coordination problems in planning and running joint military operations. They are plagued by disputes about risks, costs, and the distribution of plunder." This is why Napoleon once stated that he preferred to wage war against alliances. Coordination among various private defense agencies may slow down defense and increase its costs relative to vertically integrated state armies. Fortunately, coordination costs will be offset to some extent by the greater efficiency that comes with private ownership of military assets and the profit motive. Modern defense may even be a natural monopoly, given the large fixed costs it entails, in which case the coordination costs would be further reduced if private defense companies merged. Given the superior efficiency of defense provision by private actors, the assumption of coordination costs will be relaxed in the remainder of the paper. In the next section, I will briefly discuss asymmetric warfare in light of the above constraints.

2. Asymmetric Warfare

Asymmetric warfare usually refers to irregular conflicts[17] between state and nonstate actors—the latter typically consisting of guerilla forces

---

[15] For more on the theory of regulation, see Stigler (1971), Peltzman (1976), Posner (1974), and Becker (1983).

[16] Even if corporations and their cash flows are fully insurable, insurance costs will escalate if defense is unreliable.

[17] "Irregular Warfare: A violent struggle among state and nonstate actors for legitimacy and influence over the relevant populations. Irregular warfare favors indirect and asymmetric approaches, though it may employ the full range of military and other

employing terrorism, sabotage, subversion, and insurgency (Jones, 2012, 1–2)—but, in its most general sense, concerns conflicts in which there is a disproportionate distribution of power.[18] Given that the anarchist economy is likely to be relatively small, its military apparatus will also be modest. Anarchists can compensate for the lack of soldiers with investments in capital, but as Israel has discovered, even the most technologically advanced weapons in the world are not a perfect substitute for boots on the ground (Ben-Horin and Posen, 1981, 5–6). Additionally, if technology and capital are lacking in the economy, it is difficult to provide cutting-edge defense, leaving anarchists reliant on guerilla forces and tactics (see Rothbard, 1999; Stromberg, 2003). The analysis of anarchist wars with states must therefore consider the likely-asymmetric nature of the conflict. Below, I assume that the anarchists are able to build a proper military rather than rely on guerillas and small arms alone. Accordingly, we may look to Israel as a model for national survival.

Israel has developed a unique defense strategy in light of its geography, relatively small population, and relatively meager natural resources. It lacks strategic depth,[19] given its shape and size, and "Israel's population, industry, and military infrastructure are heavily concentrated and within easy reach from the borders" (Ben-Horin and Posen, 1981, 5). Given these realities, military planners believe that Israel "must create artificial strategic depth by means of fortifications in depth… [and] all wars must be transferred to enemy territory as quickly as possible," requiring offensive forces and an "inclination to preempt" (ibid., 5). To survive a surprise attack, Israel maintains an advanced early-warning system and a large standing army (ibid., 6). Its small size also provides the advantage of interior lines, allowing it to concentrate forces on one front or shift between fronts rapidly (ibid., 10).[20]

---

capacities, in order to erode an adversary's power, influence, and will" (Department of the Army, 2008, Glossary-11).

[18] "Asymmetric warfare is generally understood to be a conflict in which the strengths and sizes of the opponents do not mirror each other. The side with the conventional disadvantage is probably incapable of winning through direct, conventional warfare. It must seek victory through other methods that exploit weaknesses in the superior conventional power's capacity to prevail" (Department of the Army, 2008, J-3).

[19] "A hostile fighter could fly across all of Israel (40 nautical miles wide from the Jordan River to the Mediterranean Sea) within four minutes, while traveling at 'only' subsonic speed" (Federation of American Scientists, 2000).

[20] Because of a probable lack of strategic depth, anarchists must maintain air superiority. This means developing a cutting-edge air force to prevent imperialists from waging war against them from the sky with drones and gunships. They may also opt for

Its small population leads Israel to assume calculated risks to end wars more quickly. It desires short wars for three reasons: First, "a speedy victory forestalls the intervention of other Arab states" (ibid., 38). Second, there is a "fear that indecisive warfare could result in snowballing material, human, and political costs" (ibid., 38). Third, "short wars that forestall Arab mobilization of superior quantitative resources, satisfies the Israeli aversion to 'wars of attrition'" (ibid., 38). A long, drawn-out war favors large countries in which injured and killed soldiers are more readily replaced. This desire for short and decisive wars compels a more offensive approach to defense; thus Major General Israel Tal asserts that "the 'few' must adopt the principle of delivering the first blow" (ibid., 34).[21]

Defending Israel's home front entails "enabling the continuity of the use of military force both for defense and offence... protection of vital national infrastructure... [and] protection of population centers" (Eizenkot, 2016, 26). The overarching aim is "the establishment of extended periods of security calm to enable the development of society, economy, and science" and to improve preparedness for war (ibid., 10). The first element of effective territorial defense is having "defensible borders." Former foreign minister Abba Eban describes these as "borders which can be defended without a preemptive initiative" (Ben-Horin and Posen, 1981, 26).

The importance of border defense for small countries rests on the fact that defending a small territory means one cannot afford to cede any of that territory to the enemy. Writing on Israel, Ben-Horin and Posen (1981, 19)

---

defense shields similar to Israel's Iron Dome, which intercepts artillery shells and rockets, and its David's Sling, which intercepts planes, drones, and missiles.

[21] Small size also means no absolute end to all wars. Major General Israel Tal states that Israel "did not have the option of gaining a final and definite national decision by means of the military defeat of our enemies" (Ben-Horin and Posen, 1981, 4), requiring eternal vigilance to ensure national survival. It is understood that "mere frustration of Arab efforts to destroy Israel will not in itself suffice to deter their continuation. The tremendous disparity in size and resources will sustain hopes of future success," and "denial of sudden destruction does not foreclose the possibility of material and moral attrition to the same end" (Ben-Horin and Posen, 1981, 13). Israel seeks to compel enemies to accept "resignation to the permanent existence" of itself (ibid.). Despite the IDF's small size, its relative advantages include maneuverability, efficiency, high-quality intelligence gathering, and defense against high-trajectory fire (Eizenkot, 34–35). Its defense is based on "flexibility in the use of IDF forces within Israel's borders, reduction of civilian vulnerability... [and] intelligence gathering and early warning systems" (Eizenkot, 25–26).

suggest, "Perhaps the most tangible and least disguisable among the necessarily imprecise criteria for 'victory' is the territorial factor. It is also the most symbolic. The Israelis therefore regard it as crucial that the Arabs not make territorial gains in a war, at the very least." Thus IDF doctrine holds that "the entire border region must be treated as a permanently threatened region" (Eizenkot, 2016, 38). Borders that are more difficult to defend may invite attack and contribute to instability, as Ben-Horin and Posen (1981, 27) explain: "In the absence of defensible borders… there would be less slack to exploit in a crisis. Israel could not afford to accept the first blow. The tendency to preempt would rise, with concomitant problems for crisis stability."[22] The requirements of effectively defending the borders begin with a large standing army backed by reserve forces that can mobilize quickly.

3. The Standing Army

Murphy (2017, 223–24) suggests that the profit motive will lead private defense agencies to forgo standing armies in favor of small, capital-intensive fighting forces. In fact, he recommends it, fearing that a standing army might be turned against consumers.[23] The evidence suggests the possibility that a free society could survive without a standing army. About two dozen countries lack standing armies, including Iceland, Costa Rica, Dominica, Haiti, Granada, and Panama (Military Branches, 2017). Not that they are all defenseless: Faroe Islands and Greenland, for instance, are under the protection of Denmark and thus NATO, and the Vatican City is implicitly protected by Italy and NATO. Iceland is also in NATO, having joined on the

---

[22] From Ben-Horin and Posen (1981, 26), the benefits of defensible borders are as follows:
1) Provide a margin of safety in surprise attacks.
2) Make the anarchist territory a more difficult target.
3) Enhance military options and increase flexibility.

[23] Whether capital intensive or labor intensive, whether in possession of conventional or nuclear weapons, any army capable of defending against foreign invaders is also capable of crossing the Rubicon and attacking its own people. The problem is not eliminated by substituting capital for labor or by abstaining from weapons of mass destruction. How to ensure that the incentives of private defense agencies will be such that they will refrain from aggressing against their own people for money and power remains up for discussion. Bizarrely, Murphy (2017, 229–30) recommends that the anarchists merely "cut a deal" with potential invaders in the absence of a defensive force. Clearly this approach will produce the opposite of the intended effect by encouraging aggressors to invade for the sake of extortion.

condition that it need not build a standing army of its own.[24] Liechtenstein, however, is not in NATO and has no standing army of its own, instead relying on Austria and Switzerland for its defense (Macias, 2018). Of the countries that do maintain standing armies, many possess only token forces by Western standards, yet they generally have maintained their autonomy over time. So perhaps a free society could survive with little or no military defense, under certain conditions: to state the obvious, the key to surviving without a standing army is to not be attacked.[25] The pertinent question is whether, having built no standing army, including a proper air force and coast guard, the anarchist society would remain at peace.

For reasons I describe in section 4, I believe an attack is reasonably likely.[26] I therefore reiterate my position in Newhard (2017, 60), which calls for reserve forces in support of a large standing army serving the roles of training, intelligence gathering, monitoring borders, repelling invasion, and activating the reserves. Unfortunately, mobilization of a large reserve force entails a high opportunity cost of lost output. In Israel, "the country's economy is strained to the limit in times of emergency by the absence of the majority of all able-bodied civilian men, who constitute two-thirds of the IDF's wartime strength" (Ben-Horin and Posen, 1981, 7). Yet, in contrast

---

[24] Major mutual-defense treaties and alliances include the Collective Security Treaty Organization; North Atlantic Treaty Organization; Council of South American Defense; the ANZUS Treaty; US defense treaties with Japan, the Philippines, Taiwan, and South Korea; and the United States–Israel Strategic Partnership Act of 2014 and the 2016 Memorandum of Understanding. The memorandum, approved by the Obama administration, provides Israel with $38 billion over ten years with $33 billion for foreign military financing and $5 billion for missile-defense assistance. In the name of Israeli security, the United States has also provided billions of dollars in military and economic aid to Egypt since the 1979 Camp David Accords. US military aid to Jordan dates to 1957. In the Middle East, the United States also provides military aid to Israel's northern neighbors Lebanon and Syria, and sells arms to Israel, Lebanon, Iraq, Jordan, Kuwait, Egypt, Saudi Arabia, the U.A.E., Bahrain, Qatar, and Oman (Bearak and Gamio, 2016). This support is seen as greatly diminishing the benefits of the grants to Israel (Gazit, 2011, 4).

[25] Small countries that have been invaded by larger ones in recent years include (at the hands of the United States) Afghanistan, Iraq, Syria, the Philippines, the Sahara, the Horn of Africa, Pakistan, Yemen, Libya, and Cameroon, and (at the hands of Russia) Georgia, Ukraine, and Afghanistan.

[26] I concur with Kahn (1960, 642): "Insofar as the enemy is willing to gamble that [a country] will not go to war because it lacks an adequate civil or air defense program, war is brought nearer."

with what Murphy recommends, Israel discovered a need for "substantially larger air and ground forces" after the 1973 war (ibid., 5–6) despite its technologically advanced military. Even with a heavy reliance on 450,000 reserve personnel, Israel maintains a standing force of 180,000.

A small population and army would make the anarchist society particularly sensitive to casualties. Israel faces a similar situation because "small population renders it psychologically and materially vulnerable to manpower losses," leading it to emphasize minimization of casualties (ibid., 21). According to Ben-Horin and Posen (1981, 5–6), "Israel has always been vastly outnumbered in potential manpower," and its small size and population make it vulnerable to surprise attacks and "extended strategies of attrition." This has left it "searching for even more efficient use of an almost maximally tapped pool of manpower." It has been able to reduce loss of life in combat by building more capital-intensive forces.[27]

Murphy (2017, 226) observes that even if the United States invaded anarchist land, "the relevant metrics would not be the entire U.S. military budget versus the funds spent by the private defense agencies" since the former is spread out across the globe (and, I would add, suffers significant waste). Strategic sufficiency holds that "it is not necessary to match a nuclear-armed competitor in every measure of strategic nuclear capability," and that the key to deterrence is maintaining a capability to retaliate after a surprise first strike (Denmark and Wirtz, 2005). It is an alternative to strategic superiority, which will not be attainable versus large empires such as the United States.[28] Yet, even if attacked by only a small part of the American armed forces, the invading society's forces—even if only a single aircraft carrier—will still be formidable.[29]

---

[27] The United States has done the same: "It is well known that the American military has sought to minimize casualties whenever possible by the substitution of firepower, even in cases such as Vietnam where firepower may have been inappropriate" (Ben-Horin and Posen, 1981, 21–22).

[28] Maintaining a second-strike capability is critical to achieve stability. As described by Hoeber (1972), sufficiency entails four objectives:

1) Maintain an adequate second-strike capability to deter surprise first strikes.
2) Provide no incentive for the enemy to strike first.
3) Prevent the enemy from being able to cause greater destruction than one's own country can.
4) Defend against small attacks.

[29] It is commonly said that each US aircraft carrier alone is more powerful than the air forces of 70 percent of the countries of the world. If the war in Afghanistan is

4. The Threat of Invasion

Newhard (2017, 58) asserts, "State invasion of anarchist territory should be considered inevitable." Murphy (2017, 225–26) counters that states would only have one chief motive to invade: to destroy the anarchist society as a positive example to the world of the free market at work. He adds that such a motive would be a tough sell to that country's citizens. Murphy underestimates the power of the propaganda that has led the United States to enter wars around the world in which the public had no legitimate interest. The invasion of Iraq is only one recent example. The explosion of the USS Maine, which may have originated internally, led to the Spanish-American War and the Philippine-American War. False stories about Central Powers' soldiers were spread among the allied powers in World War I. The Gulf of Tonkin incident escalated the Vietnam War. Operation Northwoods, a proposed false flag against Cuba calling for violence against American civilians and soldiers, and Operation Washtub, in which the United States planted fake Soviet arms in Nicaragua, demonstrate that the government considers false-flag operations to be on the table and effective. Most Americans are rationally ignorant of foreign intervention including ongoing US operations in Africa and may be just as unaware of such operations directed against the anarchist society. The masses seem overwhelmingly uninterested in military operations that do not affect them directly. The state may also employ covert black operations to undermine the anarchist society, and dictators who do not answer to their people may also be a threat.

There are numerous reasons why a state might invade even a small anarchist society. If a state views the latter's territory as a strategic location given the state's geopolitical interests, it may want to invade. This may be particularly true if it views the anarchist society as weak, worrying that a power vacuum exists for a rival state to exploit. As a free society, the anarchist society may also become a major point of origin for drugs and

---

any indication, the anarchists could expect an initial airstrike followed by a land invasion. The airstrike of cruise missiles and bombs would target military bases, anti-aircraft weapon systems, communications, and radar. Cruise missiles could be launched from vehicles on land, airplanes, surface ships, and submarines. Bombs would be delivered by such aircraft as the B-1, B-52, F-15, and the B-2 stealth bomber. Once air superiority was achieved, Predator drones and AC-130 gunships might be used to kill anarchists from the air and ground troops could invade to expel defense agencies from the cities and seize assets such as air bases for themselves. To prevent this, anarchists must maintain superiority in the airspace above them with fighter jets and surface-to-air missiles.

weapons trafficking, provoking military action similar to US involvement in Latin America including Operation Just Cause, Plan Colombia, and the Merida Initiative. Potential prostitution, pornography, and unconventional hedonistic behavior in anarchist societies might also be cited to justify foreign intervention while concealing the imperialists' true motives. Recall that in addition to arms dealing, rumors of sexual irregularities perpetrated by David Koresh against children at Mount Carmel were enough to justify in the public's eye the mass murder of all the Branch Davidians, including the children.

Starting up an anarchist society on land claimed by a state would invite a response by the latter's military. For this reason, anarchists might want to start up in a weak state with no allies, or on uninhabited land, though this may leave them with less valuable land. If the anarchists desire a standard of living resembling what we now enjoy in the West, they will choose territory with fertile land, plentiful water, low-cost access to sea and land trading partners, and natural resources such as lumber, coal, and oil. These features also make the location desirable to states.[30] The anarchists will have to optimize, as choosing a better location means a greater likelihood of conflict.[31]

If the society is as productive as anarchists hope and statists fear, it may accumulate a significant amount of wealth including gold and silver; the incentive to control or invade would therefore increase over time. If gold alone does not motivate an attack, it will surely be confiscated after being attacked for other reasons. The discovery of valuable natural resources may also provoke an attack, especially if the find includes rare earth elements vital to defense systems or consumer products, or even just oil.

Murphy (2017, 227) argues that acquiring nuclear weapons could provide a casus belli for states to attack.[32] He refers to the Cuban missile crisis as evidence that nuclear arms would provoke an invasion despite the fact that the presence of nuclear missiles in Cuba successfully deterred one. He also seems to believe a conventional force would not similarly provoke an attack despite the fact that the Bay of Pigs invasion and Operation Mongoose were directed at a nuclear-free Cuba. In recent years, surely nuclear weapons

---

[30] Some anarchists speak of seasteading, which I do not believe is a viable alternative. Anarchists do not want a country that can be destroyed with a single torpedo.

[31] The founding of Israel from 1947 to 1948 may be instructive, but that is beyond the scope of this paper.

[32] "A casus belli is an event that may be the cause and alleged justification of a general war or a large-scale military action" (Ben-Horin and Posen, 1981, 16).

have played a role in the hesitancy of the United States and South Korea to invade North Korea. It is doubtful that the United States would have invaded Iraq if Saddam Hussein had had nuclear weapons. The allegation of chemical weapons in Iraq was one of the justifications for invading, and also reveals that states do not fear all weapons of mass destruction equally: nuclear weapons are still the gold standard of deterrence.[33]

A standing army does not guarantee a society's survival if the society is attacked. If there are enemies to engage, the probability of survival is certainly higher with an army than without one. The particular circumstances matter: Liechtenstein survives with no military of its own, yet it would be just as absurd for Israel to adopt Liechtenstein's military posture as it would be for Liechtenstein to adopt Israel's. The question is which scenario anarchist society will more closely resemble. Above I make the case that in many ways relevant to national defense it will resemble modern Israel and that the anarchist society would therefore benefit by adopting Israeli weapons and tactics. In the next section, I describe Israel's strategic doctrine in detail.

5. Disproportionate Force

Israel's strategic doctrine calls for a "defensive strategy, executed offensively" (Ben-Horin and Posen, 1981, 12). Major operational elements of the doctrine include "a strong commitment to the offensive" and "high regard for the advantages of preemption and speed in conduct of wars," among other things (ibid., 29). Lacking strategic depth and surrounded on three sides by powerful rivals, Israel relies on taking the initiative to survive. Emphasizing the importance of "decisive victory," it believes "that the enemy cannot be defeated through defense. Therefore, offensive force is needed to achieve clear military results" (Eizenkot, 2016, 10). As noted by Ben-Horin and Posen (1981, 29), "Offensive operations are believed by the IDF to compensate for Israel's overall numerical inferiority. By seizing the operational initiative it can dictate the place and pace of events. The IDF would concentrate forces at chosen points, attain local parity or even superiority, and seek decisive operational victory by swift disruption or destruction of enemy forces at critical junctures."

---

[33] Responding to the claim that "defenses will be destabilizing because they will increase incentives for one side to strike first in a crisis," a study by the RAND Corporation finds this to be false if offensive forces are small and invulnerable (Thomson, 1984, 2). At worst, the effect is ambiguous since the perceived benefit of attacking is higher but so is the perceived cost.

The authors add that pursuing defense in an offensive manner "[renders the enemy] reactive, always a step behind the action or away from it." Israeli brigadier general A. Kahalani advises,

> Our doctrine believes that the best defense is a good offense. Most of our training was on how to attack. Our ideology preaches that if you attack, you have more of a chance for success. Israeli tacticians teach that you really can't achieve a victory through defense, so it was not emphasized in our service schools. The defense is very dangerous because it gives the initiative to the attacker. We, the defender, are forced to react to all the actions that the attacker makes (ibid., 32).

At the heart of this ostensible aggressiveness is a desire for peace through deterrence. As Ben-Horin and Posen (1981, 30) note, "It is only through a demonstrated capability for offensive operations that Israel can credibly threaten the decisive operational victories that are central to her deterrence doctrine. The same capability is also seen as the only assured Israeli means of forcing an end to a war, thus reducing its costs." If deterrence fails, it is Israel's desire to return to peacetime quickly. Aggression is embraced out of the belief that wars "would otherwise continue indefinitely, or end only temporarily" until the enemies were resupplied and new allies brought into their coalition (ibid., 30).

Similarly, with the ultimate aim of deterrence, Newhard (2017, 63) calls for aggressive defense tactics including "preemptive attacks on troop buildups on the outskirts of anarchist lands… [and] engaging individual enemy units that have not yet attacked in a battle." It also calls for "[taking] the fight to an approaching potential enemy" and first-strike counterforce attacks, noting that "the element of surprise improves the kill ratio and permits one to knock out some of the enemy's weapons before they can be used in the counterattack" (ibid., 68–71). Likewise, "Israeli strategists have long stressed the importance of striking first in the face of a major imminent threat," referred to as a "preemptive counter-offensive" or "anticipatory counter-attack" (Ben-Horin and Posen, 1981, 34). Its enemies with large standing armies are "potentially capable of making a swift transition to attack from their peacetime positions in order to exploit the small size of Israel's standing army and disrupt the mobilization of the reserves" (ibid., 5). Preemption transfers the battle to enemy territory, increasing the enemy's costs; it denies the enemy the opportunity to use its battle plans and forces it to improvise; and it disrupts or prevents the mobilization of enemy forces. These outcomes "neutralize the numerical advantage of the enemy coalition" (ibid., 34).

History reveals the importance of taking the initiative rather than waiting until the enemy aggresses. "Between 1948 and 1967, major Israeli interests were vulnerable to "nonviolent" actions, such as diversion of the Jordan River tributaries in the north... The Israelis [also] considered their borders "indefensible" in the event of Arab concentration of offensive forces along them" (Ben-Horin and Posen, 1981, 17), a scenario in which Newhard (2017, 63) calls for preemption even if aggression is not certain or imminent. A stated policy of preemption also warns enemies to avoid threatening behavior since such behavior could cause a war even if their intent is only to intimidate the anarchists into assuming costly defensive measures. Private defense companies may draw lines in the sand warning rivals of what kind of actions they consider provocative. Such warnings "lessen the possibilities of miscalculation leading to unintentional escalation, ... provide a clear signal to [the people] that 'the deterrence system' is no longer effective and that military action is called for, [and] lay the basis for international legitimization of military action" (Ben-Horin and Posen, 1981, 16–17). Additionally, "the more geographically vulnerable Israel becomes, the more it can be expected to rely on hard-nosed *casus belli* to bridge the gap between a policy that aims to deter the outbreak of war and an operational doctrine that stresses the advantages of preemption or 'anticipatory' offensive war" (ibid., 18).

The disadvantages of a purely defensive posture are heightened if the defender lacks strategic depth, in which case it is of even greater importance that the battle be taken to the enemy's homeland. Newhard (2017, 63–64) therefore proposes that anarchists "take the fight to the enemy territory to minimize the destruction of their own territory," reasoning that "allowing statist invaders to fight their wars away from home spares them the worst costs of war." He adds, "The anarchists may find that taking the battle to the invader's home country is preferable, the NAP be damned." Regardless of Murphy's (2017, 221) objection, Israel's experience has led it to embrace exactly this: Ben-Horin and Posen (1981, 33) report that statements by soldiers and politicians indicate that "the IDF will swiftly carry the battle deep into enemy territory" and that "the standing forces of the IDF have been enlarged to facilitate "prompt counter-offensive operations" or even a "substantial preemptive strike." The authors also cite former Israeli defense minister E. Weizman as asserting, "If they fight us on the eastern front we shall not sit there in our bunkers and shoot from them at the attacking tanks, but rather [we shall] cross the lines. This is the minimum we have to do, especially in view of the quantities of modern weaponry the other side possesses." Similarly, Israel Tal insists on the principle of "first strike" and "offensive operations" deep in enemy territory, once the country is seriously threatened (ibid., 33). According to Ben-Horin and Posen (1981, 30), "Offensive action deep inside enemy territory is seen as the only strategic defense option available to the IDF… It seeks to concentrate its efforts against the enemy who poses the greatest immediate threat and vanquish him by means of offensive operations."[34] This strategy has contributed to Israel's security and prosperity for seventy years. The same goes for the United States, where many Americans take for granted the strategic advantage of their uniquely isolated position, far from the battlefields of most of the wars the country has waged.

Recognizing the utility of aggressiveness,[35] Israel relies on intelligence and early-warning systems so they may respond to attacks before they begin. Israel exhibits a "willingness to use violent force as a first option," such as in the Six-Day War in 1967, when "Israel responded to Arab troop buildup with an effective pre-emptive strike against Egyptian airfields." After observing warning signs of an impending strike, Israel destroyed Egypt's air force before Egypt could attack it:

> Egypt announced hostility to Israel; set its military to its highest alertness level; expelled UN emergency forces from the shared Sinai Border; strengthened its forces on the same border; closed the important Straits of Tiran to Israeli ships; and fomented a more favorable balance of power by signing alliances with Iraq, Jordan, and Syria…. The response to these threats was a swift and decisive attack in which 90% of Egypt's air force was suddenly destroyed without warning. A similar attack was also conducted in Syria. (Goldstein, 2016)

In the 1973 Yom Kippur War, Israel was caught off guard by a surprise attack as Egypt crossed the Suez Canal and Syria invaded the Golan Heights. In the first day, hundreds of Israeli soldiers were killed, and fifty fighter jets and five hundred tanks were destroyed. Defense Minister Moshe Dayan proposed the nuclear option, which was rejected by Prime Minister Golda Meir. Instead, Israel was able to achieve victory with conventional weapons thanks in part to Operation Nickel Grass, the US airlift arranged by US secretary of state Henry Kissinger (see Cohen, 2003), which included one hundred F-4 Phantom fighter jets as well as tanks, artillery, and ammunition.

---

[34] Ben-Horin and Posen (1981, 29): "The maxim of 'carrying the battle into the enemy's territory' embodied Israel's solution to the vulnerability of the long 1949 armistice lines and the absence of strategic depth. Defense was judged either impossible or too risky in view of the potentially disastrous consequences of even tactical retreat from those lines. The offensive was therefore seen by the Israelis as not only 'the best form of defense,' but—for them—the *only* one."[34]

[35] "In all situations the Israelis rely either on preventive attacks or massive retaliation" (Brown, 1981).

Israel also plans for operations in countries with no common borders, including strikes on facilities in target countries (Eizenkot, 2016, 30). On June 7, 1981, in Operation Babylon, Israel carried out a surprise air strike destroying the Iraqi nuclear reactor under construction near Baghdad. This attack commenced the Begin doctrine, Israel's policy of preventive strikes on the weapons of mass destruction of their enemies. The following day, a statement from the government asserted, "On no account shall we permit an enemy to develop weapons of mass destruction against the people of Israel" (Reuters, 1981).

Israel also emphasizes the importance of achieving "decisive victory" when deterrence fails to avoid drawn-out wars of attrition and to deter further attacks. Although it is known that no single military victory will ever solve its security problem, it is important to clearly defeat the enemy in any military encounter: "crushing defeat of their adversaries by offensive operations in the enemy's own territory is seen by the Israelis as their only reliable means of ending a war altogether, to prevent its becoming a drawn out slugging match" (Ben-Horin and Posen, 1981, 18). This explains the sentiment that "we must conclude our wars with the advantage clearly on our side. The Arabs must be the losers" (ibid., 19). Israel seeks to "project both the capability to deny, by defensive and disarming operations, and the capability to punish, by substantial destruction of Arab armies and occasional infliction of strategic damage beyond the battlefield" (ibid., 14).[36]

Of course, the ultimate aim of this strategic doctrine is to deter. Lieutenant General Yigal Allon believes "only an army capable of winning would have the power to deter... The hope to deter depended not on military strength alone but on the credibility of using it at the proper time and in a decisive way" (ibid., 20), up to and including totally destroying the

---

[36] "Israelis have come to put increasingly greater emphasis on IDF punishment of the enemy, militarily and economically... and escalate hostilities where necessary to avoid 'playing' on Arab terms" (Ben-Horin and Posen, 1981, 15). Failure to communicate the will to respond to provocations is believed by some to have diminished the credibility of Israeli deterrence (ibid., 15). The authors continue, "War outcome itself becomes an integral element of future deterrence... Both the short run and the long run require *clear IDF conventional military superiority* over its adversaries" (ibid., 16). This requires that the IDF "apply its superiority, whenever deterrence fails, in an offensive operational mode and in pursuit of indisputable military victory" (ibid., 16). The last line of anarchist defense should be modeled after the rumored Samson Option, in which the Israeli armed forces would launch a massive retaliatory attack with weapons of mass destruction against an invading country as a last resort.

enemy.[37] Since war would be so destructive,[38] successfully deterring invasions is of the utmost importance.

In summary, anarchists are well advised to follow Israel's example, which has empowered it to overcome existential threats since its founding in 1948. As with Israel, the anarchists' objective is first to deter, and second to achieve quick and decisive victory when attacked. To this end, they must build a military of shields and swords, developing both defensive and offensive weapons. They must acquire nuclear weapons while openly rejecting the doctrine of "no first use," and accept the necessity of taking the battle to the homeland of any invading force. They must clearly communicate to the world that even nonviolent provocation will be considered a casus belli justifying preemption. Establishing a reputation for responding to intimidation, threats, and attacks with preemptive and preventive strikes and massive retaliation will deter most provocations and maximize the probability of David defeating Goliath if attacked.[39] Once hostilities have commenced, the anarchist society must work to quickly achieve decisive victory. By rejecting the doctrine of dogmatic nonaggression and adopting a strategic doctrine of disproportionate force, anarchists will reduce the likelihood that they will be attacked at all, leaving them free to live their lives productively and in peace.

---

[37] This is known as the Dahiyah doctrine. Gadi Eisenkot asserts, "We will wield disproportionate power against every village from which shots are fired on Israel, and cause immense damage and destruction. From our perspective, these are military bases… This isn't a suggestion. This is a plan that has already been authorized." He adds, "This strike has to be carried out as quickly as possible, through prioritizing strikes at its assets, rather than chasing after launch sites. Such a response is likely to be remembered by decision makers in Syria and Lebanon for many years, thus deepening deterrence" (Harel, 2008).

[38] Lack of a capital city or government assets would mean targeting by enemy forces would be of private defense headquarters, field offices, bases, and perhaps industry, civil structures, and infrastructure; they might wage what from the anarchists' perspective would effectively be a total war. The lack of a capital city would not deter attack: the invader would simply bring a defenseless civilian population to its knees and then set up its own police state, controlling roads and utilities. States would demand submission and offer the alternative of starvation.

[39] "Since the emphasis has to be on making certain that in the event of enemy attack some bombs at least are delivered in retribution one wants these bombs to be, and thus to appear before the event, as horrendous as possible" (Brodie, 1958, 26). The more horrendous retaliation can be made, the less likely an invasion becomes.

6. Final Thoughts

Conflict comes with living in a world of scarcity. Anarchists cannot wish away threats to their autonomy nor base their strategic doctrine on the assumption that they are immune from attack. The possibility of being invaded will always exist. A single defeat in battle could mean the end of the free society, and no single victory could secure it forever. Yet the anarchists wish to live in peace. To do so, they must have a defense force capable of defeating the enemy, and they must credibly threaten its use; this is the most reliable means of deterring attacks altogether. In this paper, I argue that the requirements of such a force include a standing army, nuclear weapons, and a strategic doctrine of disproportionate force. The anarchists must be willing to launch preventive and preemptive strikes, escalate conflicts, take the fight to the enemy's homeland, and achieve quick and decisive victory. Although this precludes extending the NAP to rivals, the ultimate objective is deterrence: such a military might see no hostilities at all as long as it is viewed by rivals as powerful and credible.

A strategic doctrine of disproportionate force will not be without its critics among anarchists, and some will also object to invoking Israel as a model to be emulated. However, Israel's continued survival since 1948 demonstrates the doctrine's effectiveness even when defending a relatively small territory of only a few million residents (in 1970, Israel's population was just under 3 million, compared to 35 million in Egypt and over 6.3 million in Syria). Detractors must either counter that Israel at the time of the Six-Day War and the Yom Kippur War does not parallel what anarchists will face or explain how Israel's adoption of a more passive strategic doctrine would have been superior when Egypt amassed its military along Israel's border in the Sinai Peninsula in 1967, for example. Could Israel have achieved victory after the two-front surprise attack of the Yom Kippur War in 1973 with a defense budget along the lines of what Murphy (2017, 226) proposes, or through nonviolent resistance (ibid., 229–30)? Does the possession of nuclear weapons, or preventive strikes on the nuclear facilities of rivals, somehow undermine Israel's security? Anarchists opposed to the ruthless foreign policy outlined above should explain why a doctrine of dogmatic nonaggression would be superior to what has been proven to be effective in the real world even when Israel faced off against much larger enemies who were supplied with advanced weapons by the Soviet Union.

Like Israel's military planners, this paper advocates a realpolitik worldview, holding that "states cannot be entirely sure of the actions of other states… [and] the way to ensure continued existence against such uncertainty is through power" (Goldstein, 2016). As General Ehud Barak put it, "Until the wolf shall lay with the lamb, we'd better be wolves" (ibid., 2016). This paper also concurs with George Washington: "To be prepared for war is one of the most effectual ways of preserving peace." This same principle was also known to the Romans: *Si vis pacem, para bellum* ("He... who desires peace, prepare for war"; Vegetius, 2011).[40] To survive, the anarchist society must become a gentle giant: powerful enough to deter or respond to attacks, yet civilized enough to refrain from needlessly attacking others.

Lastly, at the time of writing it does not appear that market anarchism is imminent. At best, anarchist theory describes a society of the future, not the present. As a result, my analysis of such a society's feasibility relies in part on projections of the future conditions under which it might arise. One of my assumptions is that the current multistate system is unsustainable in the long run and will give way to a world government. This government will monopolize weapons of war including nuclear weapons and will not allow independence or peaceful secession. In this scenario, only war can preserve an anarchist society or any free and independent state. In the long run, both Israel and any emergent anarchist lands will face security threats from such a government. Consequently, I am interested in whether pockets of freedom can be preserved for the few while the rest of the world submits to a supreme authority, especially if the combined powers of the world work together to erase from history any independent holdouts. For the future of freedom, one can only hope that these future rebels adopt a strategic doctrine that puts the defense of their families, nations, culture, and liberties above all else.

References

Bearak, Max, and Lazaro Gamio. 2016. "The U.S. Foreign Aid Budget, Visualized." *Washington Post,* October 18. Available at: https://www.washingtonpost.com/graphics/world/which-countries-get-the-most-foreign-aid.

Becker, Gary S. 1983. "A Theory of Competition among Pressure Groups for Political Influence." *Quarterly Journal of Economics* 98, no. 3: 371–400.

Ben-Horin, Yoav, and Barry Posen. 1981. "Israel's Strategic Doctrine." RAND Corporation (R-2845-NA).

---

[40] Another Latin phrase, *Nemo me impune lacessit* ("No one attacks me with impunity"), would make for an appropriate private-defense-company slogan.

Beres, Louis Rene. 2016. "Understanding Israel's Nuclear Strategy." Israel Defense. December 1. Available at: http://www.israeldefense.co.il/en/node/27760.

Brodie, Bernard. 1958. "The Anatomy of Deterrence." RAND Corporation (RM-2218).

Brown, William R. 1981. "Israel's Defense Policy." *Christian Science Monitor*, July 8. Available at: https://www.csmonitor.com/1981/0708/070831.htm.

Cohen, Avner. 2003. "The Last Nuclear Moment." *New York Times*, October 6. Available at: http://www.nytimes.com/2003/10/06/opinion/the-last-nuclear-moment.html.

Department of the Army. 2008. *Army Special Operations Forces Unconventional Warfare* (FM 3–05.130).

Denmark, Abe, and James J. Wirtz. 2005. "Sufficiency." *Weapons of Mass Destruction: An Encyclopedia of Worldwide Policy, Technology, and History*, edited by Eric Croddy, James J. Wirtz, and Jeffrey A. Larsen. Santa Monica, CA: ABC-CLIO.

Eizenkot, Gadi. 2016. "The IDF Strategy." Israel Defense Force.

Federation of American Scientists. 2000. "Strategic Doctrine." FAS.org. May 25. Available at: https://fas.org/nuke/guide/israel/doctrine.

Gazit, Yarden. 2011. "Economic and Strategic Ramifications of American Assistance to Israel." Jerusalem Institute for Market Studies.

Goldstein, Adam. 2016. "Understanding the Bellicosity of Israel's Defense Policy." The World Mind. October 13. Available at: https://edspace.american.edu/theworldmind/2016/10/13/understanding-the-bellicosity-of-israels-defense-policy.

Harel, Amos. 2008. "Analysis: IDF Plans to Use Disproportionate Force in Next War." *Haaretz*, October 5. Available at: https://www.haaretz.com/analysis-idf-plans-to-use-disproportionate-force-in-next-war-1.254954.

Herzog, Michael. 2015. "New IDF Strategy Goes Public." Washington Institute for Near East Policy. August 28. Available at: http://www.washingtoninstitute.org/policy-analysis/view/new-idf-strategy-goes-public.

Hoeber, Francis P. 1972. "SALT I: The Morning After." RAND Corporation (P-4867).

Jones, Seth G. 2012. "The Future of Irregular Warfare." RAND Corporation (CT-374).

Kahn, Herman. 1960. *On Thermonuclear War*. Princeton, NJ: Princeton University Press.

"Military Branches." 2017. *The World Factbook*. Central Intelligence Agency.

Macias, Amanda. 2018. "From Aruba to Iceland, These 36 Nations Have No Standing Military." *CNN*. April 18. Available at: https://www.cnbc.com/2018/04/03/countries-that-do-not-have-a-standing-army-according-to-cia-world-factbook.html.

Murphy, Robert P. 2017. "Libertarian Law and Military Defense." *Libertarian Papers* 9, no. 2: 213–32.

Newhard, Joseph Michael. 2017. "Minimum Deterrence as a Vulnerability in the Market Provision of National Defense." *Libertarian Papers* 9, no. 1: 56–76.

Peltzman, Sam. 1976. "Toward a More General Theory of Regulation." *Journal of Law and Economics* 19, no. 2: 211–40.

Posner, Richard A. 1974. "Theories of Economic Regulation." *Bell Journal of Economics and Management* 5, no. 2: 335–58.

Reuters. 1981. "Israeli and Iraqi Statements on Raid on Nuclear Plant." *New York Times*, June 9. Available at: http://www.nytimes.com/1981/06/09/world/israeli-and-iraqi-statements-on-raid-on-nuclear-plant.html.

Rothbard, Murray N. 1999. *Conceived in Liberty*, vol. IV. Auburn, AL: Ludwig von Mises Institute.

Stigler, George J. 1971. "The Theory of Economic Regulation." *Bell Journal of Economics and Management* 2, no. 1: 3–21.

Stromberg, Joseph R. 2003. "Mercenaries, Guerillas, Militias, and the Defense of Minimal States and Free Societies." In *The Myth of National Defense*, edited by Hans-Hermann Hoppe. Auburn, AL: Ludwig von Mises Institute.

Thomson, James A. 1984. "Strategic Defense and Deterrence." RAND Corporation (P-6985).

US Department of Commerce. 2017. "Israel—Agriculture." Available at: https://www.export.gov/apex/article2?id=Israel-Agriculture.

Vegetius. 2011. *The Military Institutions of the Romans (De Re Militari)*, edited by Major Thomas R. Phillips and translated by John Clarke. Mansfield Centre, CT: Martino Publishing.

INNOVATIVE DYNAMISM IMPROVES THE ENVIRONMENT

ARTHUR M. DIAMOND, JR.[*]

1. Introduction

"INNOVATIVE DYNAMISM" is the economic system that has brought us the new goods and process innovations that over the last 250 years have spectacularly improved life (McCloskey 2010, pp. 2 and 48; see also Diamond 2019a). The system has previously been called "entrepreneurial capitalism," but that name is misleading because capital is not the system's salient feature and because "capitalism" is also sometimes used to name the very different system in which entrenched cronies reward and protect each other. Joseph Schumpeter suggested that the phrase "creative destruction" is a better label for what is most important in "capitalism" (1950, p. 83). Schumpeter's label is better than "capitalism" because it emphasizes how goods that are new and better add to, and partly replace, old goods. But Amar Bhidé and others have noted that the "destruction" in "creative destruction" misleadingly exaggerates the costs of innovation (Bhidé 2008, pp. 341–55; 2009, p. 17).

---

[*] Arthur M. Diamond, Jr. is Professor of Economics at the University of Nebraska Omaha. Some of the issues in this paper are discussed, though more briefly, in his book *Openness to Creative Destruction: Sustaining Innovative Dynamism* (expected in 2019). In a few places, the discussion overlaps. The author is grateful to Mark Wohar for discussing, and providing a reference on, the robustness of his and McMillan's results on the effect of carbon dioxide on temperature. I also appreciate thoughtful and constructive comments from the editor and from two anonymous referees.

CITATION INFORMATION FOR THIS ARTICLE:

Arthur M. Diamond, Jr. 2018. "Innovative Dynamism Improves the Environment." *Libertarian Papers*. 10 (2): 233-275. ONLINE AT: libertarianpapers.org. THIS ARTICLE IS subject to a Creative Commons Attribution 3.0 License (creativecommons.org/licenses).

Innovations often add to our choices rather than replace our earlier choices. Even buggy whips are still made, sold, and used. When innovative new goods replace older goods, the replacement is rarely total, is often gradual, and usually occurs with significant warning that allows those who are alert some time to adapt. A better phrase to describe "capitalism" or "creative destruction" is "innovative dynamism." "Dynamism" suggests change broad enough to include change that adds to, as well as change that replaces, what has come before. "Innovative" suggests that the change is not merely directionless churn but positive change that improves life.

Some of us want the new goods and processes but fear that they come at too high a cost in terms of damage to the environment. Here I take the fear seriously and respond. Those who fear the environmental effects of innovative dynamism are most afraid that some new goods and process innovations may greatly harm humanity by increasing global warming. I will devote much of the discussion of the environment to addressing that issue. But because a full accounting should include the often beneficial effects of innovative dynamism on other aspects of the environment, I start there.

Although this is a long paper, it still does not answer all questions a scholar might ask related to the environment. For instance, it treads lightly, or not at all, on some important theoretical issues as to how a system of innovative dynamism can and should affect the environment. There have been many useful theoretical papers on issues such as how property rights should affect policies on the environment, and how a market economy is intergenerationally sustainable in the sense of leaving a better environment to future generations. Some of the papers that at least in part discuss how property rights should affect policies on the environment include Rothbard (1982), Cordato (2004), Pennington (2005), Dawson (2009), McCaffrey (2012), Carden (2013), Hebert (2013), Block (2014), and Dolan (2014). Other papers have, in whole or part, addressed other important topics, such as how a market economy is intergenerationally sustainable (Diamond 1987; Dawson 2008) and how public choice theory can help us to understand the rise of environmentalism (Yandle 2013).

In contrast to the papers just mentioned, my paper focuses mainly on empirical issues. I empirically defend the claim that the system of innovative dynamism has been friendly to the environment in the past and will continue to be friendly to the environment in the future. Theoretical issues of political philosophy, institutions, and policies are important and are worthy of considerable discussion, but my approach also tells us something important.

The contribution of this paper is not to gather new data or to develop new techniques for analyzing old data. Rather the contribution is synthetic: to compile and organize a wide array of previously isolated evidence, examples, and arguments that together present a more optimistic view of the past, present, and potential effects of innovative dynamism on the environment.

Some readers may mostly share my optimistic view but believe that some of the claims of environmentalists may be true or partly true. These readers may then conclude that we should agree to environmentalist policies either for the sake of social harmony or as putative insurance against a worst-case environmental scenario.

Before buying the environmentalists' putative insurance, these readers should consider the price of insurance actually offered in the market. Part of Warren Buffett's company Berkshire Hathaway sells "super-cat" reinsurance, which insures other insurance companies against the occurrence of very large (i.e., super) catastrophes ("cat"), including those that some worry will result from global warming. When the price of such insurance is high, that implies market participants with a lot to gain or lose judge the probability of global warming catastrophes to be correspondingly high. But in actual fact the price of super-cat insurance is low and falling. This implies that the market assigns a low and falling probability to global warming catastrophes. Warren Buffett, in an annual shareholder letter, concludes: "When you are thinking only as a shareholder of a major insurer, climate change should not be on your list of worries" (Buffett 2016, p. A9).

While real global warming insurance may be a bargain, the faux insurance consisting of environmentalist government policies is not. Money, time, and effort spent to implement environmentalist policies have opportunity costs in terms of forgone economic growth that could feed the poor or cure the sick. Those who are regulated or taxed to pay for the insurance have fewer funds, and have less freedom of action, for pursuit of their own projects and dreams. As Bastiat taught us (1995, pp. 1–50) and Hazlitt reminded us (1952, pp. 17–21), we see the windmills and solar panels from environmental policies but do not see the projects and dreams that would have been made real if individuals had been left more of their own funds and the freedom of how to spend those funds.

Some of the direct costs can easily be measured. We can measure the over $8 billion budget of the Environmental Protection Agency.[1] We can measure how subsidies for renewable energy in Germany increased the cost for a German middle class family to heat its home in winter (Reed 2017, pp. B1-B2). We can measure the roughly 15,000 British poor who lost their lives

---

[1] See the EPA's website: http://www.epa.gov/planandbudget/budget.

in the winter of 2014–15 because of higher fuel costs from environmental policies such as renewable-energy mandates (Lomborg 2018, p. A15). It is much harder to measure the cost of entrepreneurial dreams forgone.

But the costs of anti–fossil fuel environmental policies are even higher than that. If fossil fuels were banned, as many environmentalists demand, we would not just stagnate, we would regress (Broughton 2014, p. A15; Epstein 2014, p. 87). We still might choose regress if it was necessary to fend off some worse threat to humanity or even to life on earth. But what if we could have progress and our dreams and still have a better environment, with life on earth flourishing? The evidence and argument of this paper is that progress, our dreams, the environment, and life on earth can indeed all flourish together.

2. How Innovative Dynamism Improves the Environment

Innovations have changed the environment, more often for the better than for the worse. One of our great innovations is the car, which has often been accused of being a cause of increased pollution. But cars put an end to the pollution from huge quantities of horse manure in city streets, which was not only unpleasant to walk in and smell, but was also unhealthy. Cars can produce noise, but clanking horse hooves were not quiet (Preston 1991, p. 51). Replacing horses with cars reduced horse manure in cities, just as replacing gas lighting with electric lighting reduced soot in homes.

Cancer has sometimes been attributed to aspects of modern life that result from innovations. But archeological discoveries show that cancer has been part of human life at least since the age of the Egyptian pharaohs, and probably much earlier (Mukherjee 2010, pp. 40–43 see also Zimmer 2018, p. A9; Krause-Kyora et al. 2018; Mühlemann et al. 2018). Increases in cancer in modern times are probably largely due to practices having nothing to do with innovation, such as smoking, and due to increasing longevity, which has allowed more people to reach an age at which they are at greater risk of cancer. If you doubt that preindustrial cooking and heating methods exposed humans to more cancer-causing toxins than the cooking and heating methods resulting from modern innovations, then you should "try cooking over an open fire burning half-rotten wood, or sitting in a cave warming yourself with a peat or dung fire, and you will know what pollution really is" (Selinske 2011, p. D4). Hunter-gatherers had dubious environmental credentials in other respects too. Kevin Kelly has pointed out that hunter-gatherers had the ultimate disposable culture, in which every tool and shelter was temporary (Kelly 2010, p. 30).

The innovation of creating fertilizer from nitrogen in the air increased food production per acre, allowing more of our land to be left in an uncultivated, green state (Ridley 2013, p. C4; see also Hager 2008). Lush vegetation worldwide is also promoted by increasing temperatures and higher levels of carbon dioxide (Ridley 2013, p. C4).

The many computer and communication innovations of recent decades have allowed us to produce goods digitally that previously required material versions. Books, videos, music, and mail are increasingly digital rather than material (Kelly 2010, p. 67). This dematerialization allows us to produce more goods, while at the same time making use of fewer resources and less energy (Ridley 2012, p. C4; see also Diamandis and Kotler 2012).

One cause of air pollution has been city drivers who must drive in circles to find free parking spaces. Innovations in information technology and communications now allow variable pricing in parking meters, so that the price will increase when most parking spaces are occupied, reducing the quantity demanded and ensuring that spaces will always be available without the circling (Cooper and McGinty 2012, p. A1).

3. Population, Resources, and Organic Farming

One of the first prophets of environmentalism was Robert Malthus in the late 1700s and early 1800s. In his account, humans were doomed to live at the margin of starvation because population increases faster than food supplies. Malthus was wrong (Fox 2014; Mayhew 2014). Partly through new technologies, population increased more slowly and food production increased more quickly, allowing humans, especially in the West, to enjoy huge improvements in the length and quality of life. Fertility rates have actually declined throughout the world and are expected to continue to modestly decline.

In the 1960s and 1970s, neo-Malthusians worried about a "population bomb," but they were just as wrong as their mentor (Ehrlich 1968). The United Nations (UN) provides a range of estimates, which it occasionally tweaks, but its rough expectation is that the rate of growth of world population will continue to fall until world population reaches a peak sometime before the end of this century (Ridley 2011, p. C4; see also Wattenberg 2004; Adamy 2016, p. A2; Soble 2016, p. A12). One respected analyst believes that the UN is overestimating fertility and that world population will peak as early as 2055 (Norris 2013, p. B3).

Part of the neo-Malthusian position is that as population increases, natural resources will become scarcer and more expensive. Economist Julian

Simon understood that with the advances from innovative dynamism, we learn how to find more resources and we find new ways to use materials that were previously considered useless (Simon 1996; see also Diamandis and Kotler 2012, p. 4; Ridley 2014b). In 1980, Julian Simon bet that the sum of the prices of five commodities would actually decline in the following ten years; Paul Ehrlich bet that the sum would increase (Last 2013, p. C6; Sabin 2013). In 1990, Paul Ehrlich paid Julian Simon.

The exhaustion of oil and gas has long been predicted, and with increasing urgency (Zuckerman 2013, p. 257). But as prices rose, many were surprised (Julian Simon would not have been among them, if he had lived long enough) by how innovations in the fracking process are allowing us to cheaply recover oil and gas that were thought to be beyond our reach (Burrough 2013, p. 7; Zuckerman 2013), and to do so without harm to drinking water (Gold and Harder 2015, p. A5).

With innovation, old resources lose value and new resources gain value. Whale oil was growing scarce until the little-used gunk percolating up through the oil seeps of Pennsylvania could efficiently be turned into kerosene by innovators such as John D. Rockefeller (Applebome 2008, p. 20; Dolin 2007). More recently there have been fears about limited supplies of rare earth metals, and about China monopolizing the known supplies. As prices rose, mine investors located new sources of supply, and some users of rare earth metals found substitute materials to use in place of them (Taylor 2015, pp. 265–266; Gholz 2014; Jakab 2017, p. B14; see also Norton 2017, p. B6; Fountain 2016a, p. A8).

The organic-food movement suggests that food grown without chemicals or genetic modification is more nutritious, healthier, and avoids spreading toxins to the environment. But actually in most cases organic and nonorganic food have similar levels of nutrition, and in some cases the nonorganic varieties have substantially higher levels of nutrition (Brody 2013, p. D7; Schwarcz 2012). A nonorganic, genetically modified tomato, for instance, "contains nearly 80 times the antioxidants of conventional tomatoes" (Brody 2013, p. D7). In a metastudy of the literature, Stanford scientists found that organic fruits and vegetables generally had no greater nutrition, but were much more expensive, than nonorganic fruits and vegetables (Chang 2012, p. A20; Smith-Spangler et al. 2012, pp. 348 and 357). The metastudy did find that organic foods on average had less pesticide residue and smaller quantities of antibiotic-resistant bacteria (Smith-Spangler et al. 2012, p. 358). However, a later study found that neither organic nor kosher chicken had fewer antibiotic-resistant bacteria than standard, nonorganic chicken (Strom 2013, p. D3; Millman et al. 2013). Organic foods are increasingly being recalled because of bacterial contamination, including "salmonella, listeria and hepatitis A" (Strom 2015, p. B3; see also Stewart 2016, p. B1).

So the benefits of organic food are more limited than is often believed. At the same time, the costs are larger than is often believed. The lower yields of organic farming imply that more labor, land, and water must be used to produce the same amount of food, hardly a prescription for greening the planet or feeding the hungry (Cowen 2013, p. 6). And a metastudy from Britain concluded that "ammonia emissions, nitrogen leaching and nitrous oxide emissions per product unit were higher from organic systems" (as quoted in Miller 2014, p. A13; see also Tuomisto et al. 2012).

I have nothing to say about the relative taste of organic and nonorganic food except to report that after partaking of the vegan organic food at his friend Steve Jobs's house, Rupert Murdoch was alleged to have commented, "Eating dinner at Steve's is a great experience, as long as you get out before the local restaurants close" (Murdoch's alleged comment as quoted in Isaacson 2011, p. 509).

4. Extinction and Resilience

Some environmentalists hold the view that we must preserve the earth in some particular state. But which state? In appearance, composition, and climate, the earth has always been in flux (Botkin 2012). Since life began, species have arisen, thrived (or not), and gone extinct. The vast majority of these extinctions occurred before humans existed. For instance, Stephen Jay Gould described an intriguing array of long-gone Burgess Shale creatures in his *Wonderful Life* (1989).

Often, we overestimate the negative effects of human activities on aspects of the environment. Many clusters of events for which humans are assigned blame are random (David Hand as quoted in Chozick 2014, p. 12; see also Hand 2014). Humans were initially blamed for bee-colony-collapse disorder; now the collapse is over, and we must admit that we do not understand why it came or why it left (Wilson-Rich 2014, p. A27). Where humans have intervened in major ways, life often has proven surprisingly resilient.

Birds have adapted to radiation from Chernobyl by producing more antioxidants that protect them from genetic damage (Fountain 2014a, p. D2; Galván et al. 2014). Animal life is thriving close to the Chernobyl site, and no long-term increase in human cancer has been demonstrated in the Chernobyl region (Hale 2011, p. C6; Moynihan 2012, p. C11; Blackwell 2012). In Montana, an abandoned copper mine has filled with water, creating a small, extremely toxic lake. Yet some hardy micro-organisms have evolved that can survive in the lake. Initially through self-funding, a pair of entrepreneurs with lowly academic positions have found unique chemicals produced by a couple of these micro-organisms that show promise in fighting cancer (Maag 2007, p. A21). We are beginning to understand that part of the reason for the greater resilience of life may be the "variable gene expression" that allows our genes to respond more flexibly to changes in our environment (Dobbs 2014, p. 11; Moalem 2014).

Our knowledge of the extent and resilience of life remains imperfect. Mark Twain, upon hearing of his obituary, once said that rumors of his death were premature. If they could speak, the same would be said by the oblong rocksnail and the Santa Marta sabrewing, both of which had long been considered extinct, only to be observed alive many years later (Bhanoo 2012b, p. D3; Whelan, Johnson, and Harris 2012; Fountain 2010b, p. D3). The rediscovery of the latter led a vice president of the American Bird Conservancy to conclude that "the ecosystem is more intact than you might have feared" (Michael Parr as quoted in Fountain 2010b, p. D3). Not only are species once thought extinct being rediscovered, but a large number of new species are identified for the first time each year. Often these new species are small, but sometimes they are large, as with the discovery by scientists in 2010 of the six-foot-long *Varanus bitatawa* lizard species (Fountain 2010a, p. D3; Welton et al. 2010).

Since the extinction of old species and the efflorescence of new species are part of the ebb and flow of the natural order (or maybe it should be called "natural disorder"), it is not clear how morally culpable humans are for extinctions that may be partly caused by human activity (Thomas 2017). And it is important to remember that humans are not necessarily responsible for every extinction that has occurred on our watch. For instance, the extinction of woolly mammoths roughly ten thousand years ago has been blamed on overhunting, but recent evidence suggests it may have been more due to the disappearance of a flower source of protein called "forbs" (*New York Times* 2014, p. D2; Willerslev et al. 2014) or to inbreeding and related difficulties during pregnancy (Bhanoo 2014, p. D2; Reumer, Broek, and Galis 2014).

More recent human activity is often blamed for the decline of Australia's Great Barrier Reef, but roughly half of the decline is due to a poorly understood increase in predation of the coral by starfish (Kwai 2018, p. A9; De'ath et al. 2012). Coral elsewhere have been found to be resilient to warmer water temperatures (Weintraub 2016, pp. D1 & D6), and scientists have successfully bred coral to be even more resilient (Cave and Gillis 2017, p. A6). Although the overall harm to coral from global warming is not yet known, we should note that any harm may partially be compensated by global warming's benefits to the thriving cuttlefish, squid, and intelligent octopus (St. Fleur 2016, p. A7; Doubleday et al. 2016).

Some extinctions have indeed been caused by humans, for instance the passenger pigeon. But is the world necessarily much worse off as a result? I remember that as a child, my great-grandmother told me how she, as a child, had seen the Indiana skies filled with passenger pigeons, and that passenger pigeon pie was delicious (Diamond 1987, p. 271). But passenger pigeons were viewed by farmers as a menace, descending and devouring their crops in enormous flocks (Greenberg 2014, pp. 74–78). Stanford scholar Henry Greely notes that the flocks of passenger pigeons were so large that they could take three days to cross a city, leaving the city "covered in an inch of guano" (Greely as quoted in Kolata 2013, p. A16). And are passenger pigeons anyone's idea of a Rawlsian primary good (Rawls 1971), required as a nonsubstitutable building block of the good life?

If we decide that humans treated the mammoths or the passenger pigeons unjustly, or if we decide the benefits of their presence are greater than the costs, then it appears increasingly likely that continued innovations in biology and chemistry will allow us to bring the mammoths, the passenger pigeons, and some other species back from extinction (Kolata 2013; Wade 2010, p. D3; Campbell et al. 2010; Shapiro 2015).

Stephen Jay Gould long ago noted that all of our genomes contain currently inactive sequences that code for traits of our ancestors that we no longer possess. Sometimes mutations accidentally activate these strands, resulting in horses with toes and hens with teeth (Gould 1983). If we could control these accidental activations, we would have another pathway to increased diversity of creatures, and perhaps of bringing back some of the traits (if not the species itself) of species that are now extinct. Inexpensive technology to recombine pieces of DNA is already within the reach of breeders and inventors, suggesting to Princeton physicist and futurist Freeman Dyson that we will enjoy "an explosion of diversity of new living creatures" (Dyson as quoted by Gorman 2012, p. D4).

Evidence of the diversity and resilience of nature can be found in many directions. In 2013, scientists were concerned about record-low water levels in the Great Lakes; in 2014, the scientists were "startled" to observe that the lakes were a foot higher, and rising (Bosman 2014, p. 16). Large stretches of the American West remain as wild and rugged as they were before Europeans arrived on the continent (Stark 2014, pp. 311–12). Most of us would be shocked to learn how quickly the planet would "return to its pre-human condition" if humans were to suddenly disappear (Shermer 2013, p. C10; see also Weisman 2007).

5. Does Government Intervention Help or Hurt?

Those who allege that the innovative entrepreneur often harms the environment usually propose government actions that constrain the innovative entrepreneur, either through regulations or through government programs funded by taxes that reduce the funds available for entrepreneurial innovation. So it is useful to consider the benefits and costs of such government programs.

As we have already seen, since the environment is constantly changing, with or without human actions, it is not immediately clear what static snapshot of earth should be preserved by those who want the government to save the environment. But apart from that key issue, government actions may not always have the effects desired by those who want to protect the environment. A startling example occurred in 1964, when the United States Forest Service chopped down the oldest tree in existence, a 4,900-year-old flourishing, dignified, defenseless bristlecone pine known to its friends as "Prometheus" (Robbins 2017, p. D9).

For an earlier historical example, in the early decades of the twentieth century, the Department of Agriculture encouraged farmers to settle in the Great Plains, in spite of the evidence that the region was subject to recurring severe droughts, and Congress doubled down by subsidizing banks that agreed to offer generous loans to those who credulously followed the department's advice (Egan 2006, pp. 50 and 126). In recent decades, government mandates for ethanol have raised prices for food and increased the amount of land under cultivation, reducing land left as natural habitat for native species (Martin 2008, p. 5). Surprisingly, the mandates also actually *add* carbon dioxide to the atmosphere since plowing additional land to grow corn for ethanol releases carbon dioxide from the soil (Matthews 2016, p. A9).

Another current example is the government-subsidized crop insurance for farmers that reduces the incentive farmers would otherwise have to adapt their farming practices to global warming and so increases the costs of global warming (Annan and Schlenker 2015, p. 266). Another unintended consequence arises when local governments limit the use of plastic bags at stores on the grounds that manufacturing the bags hurts the environment: reused plastic or cotton bags have been found to be contaminated with bacteria (Gruen 2014, p. A13; Klick and Wright 2012; Williams et al. 2011). Advocates of bag banning suggest that bags only be reused after they are washed. But is that consistent with conserving water and energy, not to mention human time?

Innovation in the construction and architecture professions could result in using land in ways that provide housing and services to a wider part of the population, but instead "environmental" regulations often freeze neighborhoods in a way that serves the preferences and interests of the incumbent long-term residents of the neighborhood (Dewan 2014; see also Glaeser 2011).

Or consider the Amish, who prefer to use simpler machines on their farms. If their corn stalks are broken by the corn borer pest, then their simple machines cannot pick up the stalks, and they must pick them up by hand, which is hard, tiring work (Kelly 2010, p. 222). So they prefer corn seed that is genetically modified to repel the corn borer. The Amish do not want government regulations against genetically modified seed innovations, because the innovations allow them to preserve other forms of stasis on their farms that they prefer.

6. Global Warming

What humans can achieve depends crucially on being able to use energy beyond our own muscles. Gasoline-powered cars and electricity-powered machines have extended our reach. The question here is whether those innovations have harmed the environment and, if so, how much. The main concern is that the production of energy increases global warming. I will consider that concern shortly. But before considering the possible costs, we should remember the benefits. The Amish, and some environmentalists, try to avoid electricity, both to encourage a simpler life for humans and to protect the environment. But it turns out that the only way to totally avoid electricity is to die: electricity flows in crucial biological processes and is literally "the spark of life" (Bynum 2012, p. C9; Ashcroft 2012).

Whatever our life plans, many of us increasingly want to guard against lapses in our electricity. We are buying home generators to protect us against lapses in electric-utility service that would deprive us of the safety and productivity of our lights, the freshness of our refrigerated food, the comfort of our air conditioning, and the knowledge and human connections of our computers and smart phones (Belson 2013, p. F8; Quindlen 2013, p. M14).

a. *Are We Getting Warm? Data and Models*

The alleged certainty of a scientific consensus on the causes, magnitude, and dire effects of global warming is based on the implications of some formal econometric models. Models of this kind are often called "integrated assessment models," or "IAMs" for short. MIT environmental economist Robert Pindyck summarizes what such models can tell us about the social cost of carbon ("SCC" for short) as a guide for policy choice:

IAMs are of little or no value for evaluating alternative climate change policies and estimating the SCC. On the contrary, an IAM-based analysis suggests a level of knowledge and precision that is nonexistent, and allows the modeler to obtain almost any desired result because key inputs can be chosen arbitrarily (Pindyck 2013, p. 870; see also Pindyck 2015).

In an eye-opening account, former Environmental Protection Agency (EPA) modeler Robert Caprara describes how he was pressured to tweak his model until it produced the result his boss desired. He was assigned to model the environmental benefits of an EPA program to subsidize sewage-treatment plants. When he presented his results to the EPA, they were rejected and he was told to revise the model. So he "reviewed assumptions, tweaked coefficients and recalibrated data" (Caprara 2014, p. A13). But the final estimate of total benefits for the EPA program did not change much, and the EPA continued to reject his analysis. In talking with the EPA administrator, he writes,

> [A]fter three iterations I finally blurted out, 'What number are you looking for?' He didn't miss a beat: He told me that he needed to show $2 billion of benefits to get the program renewed. I finally turned enough knobs to get the answer he wanted, and everyone was happy" (Caprara 2014, p. A13; see also Cragg and Caprara 1991).

Caprara's account is fully consistent with the public choice literature that suggests that administrators in government bureaucracies can be understood to be maximizing their power, as partly proxied by their budgets. (Niskanen 1971).

Steven Koonin, former professor of theoretical physics at Caltech and undersecretary of science in Barack Obama's Energy Department, has concluded that "we often hear that there is a 'scientific consensus' about climate change. But as far as the computer models go, there isn't a useful consensus at the level of detail relevant to assessing human influences" (Koonin 2014, p. C2). Even heavily tweaked models must eventually confront the evidence, if they are to have any claim to scientific credibility. So far, the evidence has not been fully consistent with the models' predictions.

The most prominent climate models predict increasing temperatures at a steady or increasing rate. But from about 2000 until about 2015, the rate of increase substantially decreased (Ridley 2014a, p. A13; see also McKitrick 2014). This slowdown in global warming was variously called a "pause," a "lull," and a "plateau" (Ridley 2014a, p. A13; Gillis 2013c, p. D3). As a result, some climate modelers lowered their "high end" and "best guess" estimates of how high temperatures will rise in the future (Gillis 2013b, p. D6; Revkin

2013). *New York Times* environmentalist reporter and blogger Andrew Revkin, with wistful chagrin, noted that the new estimates were trending toward those supported in the past by some libertarians, but he suggests that evidence be respected, writing that "nonetheless, the science is what the science is" (Revkin 2013).

The lull posed a practical setback for those who counted on the models, such as Shell Oil and the federal government. Shell shelled out several billion dollars for drilling rights from the federal government, and for equipment to drill in the Arctic, but has been stymied because the ice has not melted as quickly, or for as long, as they expected (Fowler 2012, p. B1; see also Gillis 2013a, p. A8). Also consistent with the general lull was the very cold winter of 2014 in the United States (Gillis 2014, p. D3). Global warming advocates increasingly relabeled "global warming" as "climate change" in order to distract attention away from the lukewarm empirical support that the lull provided for their models.

Nate Silver, who is famous for his success at statistical forecasting, believes that the lull is consistent with a long-term increase in global temperatures due to human actions (Scheiber 2012, p. 12; see also Silver 2012). But he also believes the lull demonstrates how hard it is to accurately forecast temperatures decades into the future. As a result, he suggests that global warming advocates and activists are unjustified in expressing their views with so much certainty. Where there is uncertainty, scientific progress might be best served by global warming advocates engaging, rather than dismissing, global warming skeptics (Garud, Gehman, and Karunakaran 2014, p. 62; see also Pearce 2011, p. 237; Hulme 2012, p. 224).

The reaction of some climate scientists to the lull was to double down on defense of the models by vilifying those who criticized the models (Wines 2014b, p. A14). The vilification took place partly through calling the critics pejorative names such as "denier" to try implicitly to associate the global warming "deniers" with Holocaust deniers. The vilification also took place through blacklisting climate skeptics from receiving research grants and from having their articles published in leading journals. But some scientists resist vilification.

Freeman Dyson is often viewed as one of the most important physicists of the second half of the twentieth century and has been on the faculty of the School of Natural Sciences at the Institute for Advanced Study in Princeton, New Jersey. Dyson has a lot of experience with mathematical models and believes that climate scientists exaggerate the precision of their models' forecasts, saying that "they come to believe models are real and forget they are only models" (Dyson as quoted in Dawidoff 2009, p. 36).

According to Dyson, increases in carbon dioxide mainly improve the environment by encouraging the growth of forests and crops. Any increases in temperatures will be modest, localized, and mainly benign. He observes that, for many, climate science has become a religion in which "belief is strong, even when scientific evidence is weak" (Dyson as quoted in *New York Times* 2015, p. 8).

"Science" is not the body of doctrine endorsed by a majority of those who are credentialed as scientists. Science is a process of open-minded, skeptical inquiry. Science is the activity of looking through Galileo's telescope, even when a majority of credentialed scientists refuse to look. When science is operating progressively, consensus is reached by the continuous accumulation and evaluation of evidence. But the evidence is rarely completely definitive, which is why the scientific attitude is one of tolerance toward those who hold different views. Not only does the evidence accumulate, but the methods of analyzing and weighing it differ and evolve.

The predictive accuracy of climate models on issues of practical importance remains tenuous, even for short-run predictions, let alone for predictions extending several decades. For example, climate-science models have been spectacularly wrong in predicting the following year's number of Chesapeake blue crabs (Suri 2015, p. 4). Harvard cognitive-bias expert Daniel Gilbert explains that conscientious scientists have major disagreements on how to collect, verify, and analyze data, which explains "why scientists disagree about the dangers of global warming" (Gilbert 2006, p. 162).

b. Humans and Nonhumans Adapt

More deaths are caused by cold days than by hot days, so global warming, which reduces the number of cold days and similarly increases the number of hot days, should result in an overall reduction in deaths (Gasparrini et al. 2015, p. 369). As a result of a highly variable climate during human evolution, natural selection gave a survival advantage to those of our ancestors who were more adaptable to quick and large climate change (Switek 2017, p. A15; Ungar 2017). Pre-industrial Icelanders, who had fewer modes of adaptation, substantially reduced their population growth rates in response to global *cooling* (Turner et al. 2012, pp. 254–55). Today humanity can survive and thrive if the global climate warms by a few degrees, so long as we do not abandon the policies and institutions that permit entrepreneurial innovation and adaptation. Economic historians who have studied past adaptability of United States agriculture to climate changes are generally optimistic about the ability of the US economy to adapt to global warming (Swoboda 2012, p. 222; see also Libecap and Steckel 2011). Consider an illustrative example. The maple-syrup tapping season consists of the range of days when nights are freezing and daytime temperatures are higher than 40 degrees Fahrenheit. In Vermont, the average tapping season is about five days shorter than it was fifty years ago, possibly partly because of global warming. In response, syrup producers have developed tubing technologies to more efficiently pull sap from the trees, with the result that, even with a shorter tapping season, they can now pull in roughly twice as much sap as they could fifty years ago (Scott 2013, p. 11).

Optimism for the future of cities can be defended by adaptations that will occur within cities, but also by migration to cities such as Minneapolis and Detroit that will become more appealing as the climate warms (Kotchen 2011, pp. 777–78; see also Kahn 2010). Major cities, such as Rotterdam, Tokyo, and St. Petersburg, have designed defenses against encroaching water, and such defenses could also be deployed in cities such as New York if the threat increases (Hotz 2012b, p. C3). In terms of individual comfort and productivity, individuals in the United States have increasingly protected themselves against the costs of hot weather, for example through the adoption of air conditioning, which has reduced heat-related mortality (Barreca et al. 2015, p. 251; see also Diamond 2017). More generally, John Christy, a University of Alabama distinguished professor of atmospheric science, believes that the modest temperature increases that are likely can be readily handled by adaptation strategies (Wines 2014b, p. A14).

In some areas of the earth, partly through human adaptation, warming brings some substantial benefits. For example, it would reduce the costs of shipping (Kramer and Revkin 2009; Goldman 2017, p. 12), communicating in (Joling 2010) and retrieving oil and minerals from (Kramer and Krauss 2011; Revkin 2008; Mouawad 2008; Krauss et al. 2005) the Arctic. It would increase agriculture and animal husbandry in Greenland (Faris 2008; Etter 2006); increase the opportunities for golf in Alaska (Dean 2009, p. A1) and sparkling-wine cultivation in England (Naik 2010, pp. A1 and A18); make Chicago winters milder (Kramer 2013, p. B1; Shteir 2013, p. 20); and make colorful fall foliage last longer (Smith 2016, p. A20). Roughly 80 percent of Americans live in counties where the weather has become more pleasant than it was forty years ago, back when global warming started to become an issue of debate (Egan and Mullin 2016a, p. 9; Egan and Mullin 2016b; see also Popovich and Migliozzi 2018, p. A11). The greatest benefit from global warming, however, may be in the very long run.

Palaeoclimatologist William Ruddiman believes an ice age that would have occurred about eight thousand years ago was prevented by global warming caused by carbon dioxide released from the soil when humans switched to agriculture (Kelly 2010, p. 38; Ruddiman 2005, p. 12). In the prestigious journal *Science*, earth scientist Shaun Marcott and his colleagues have reconstructed temperatures for the past 11,300 years and forecast that in the next several thousand years the North American continent would freeze over if past patterns continued (Gillis 2013d, p. A15; see also Marcott et al. 2013). This massive and disastrous freeze would be prevented by global warming (Gillis 2013d, p. A15).

It may be natural for us to care more about the adaptability of human beings to potential global warming than we care about the adaptability of other species. But many of us have some level of goodwill toward other species as well, and so we may also wonder whether they will have any ability to adapt to global warming. Fortunately, there is evidence that many of them can and will. For example, some scientists investigated how tropical flies would fare if their environment changed from very high humidity to a humidity of just 35 percent. For one of the species they investigated, after only five generations, the fifth generation was able to survive 23 percent longer than had the first generation (Zimmer 2014, p. D7; see also van Heerwaarden and Sgrò 2014). In England, as the climate has warmed somewhat, the brown argus butterfly has extended its range by fifty miles toward the North over a period of twenty years (Bhanoo 2012a, p. D3; Chen et al. 2011). As the annual temperature lows increase, Florida mangrove swamps have been found to greatly expand their range, which is good not only for the mangroves, but for the many fish and other organisms that spawn and thrive in the mangrove habitat (Gillis 2013e, p. A14; see also Cavanaugh et al. 2014).

Toward the poles, the Stony Brook ecologist Heather Lynch and her colleagues were "surprised" to find "a 53% increase in abundance globally" of the Antarctic's Adélie penguin population (Lynch as quoted in Hotz 2014, p. A3; see also Lynch and Schwaller 2014). The Adélie penguin, whose population is in the millions and is growing, is "considered a bellwether of climate change" (Hotz 2014, p. A3). Scientists recently discovered an additional 1.5 million Adélie penguins they had previously missed (Weintraub 2018, p. D2). Lest it be objected that this was a fluke, it is consistent with the latest count of 595,000 Antarctic emperor penguins, which was a substantial increase from the previous high-end estimate of 350,000 (Hotz 2012a, p. A2; Fretwell, LaRue et al. 2012; see also Fretwell 2012; Fretwell et al. 2014). Adaptability is not limited to penguins in the Antarctic. Toward the opposite pole, in the Arctic, as some ice has melted, perhaps because of global warming, polar bears are spending more time on land and less on ice, and so have switched their diets somewhat away from seal pups and toward caribou and snow-goose eggs (Bhanoo 2014, p. D2; see also Gormezano and Rockwell 2013a, 2013b; Iles et al. 2013).

c. *Causes of Warming*

Global warming is usually blamed on increases in carbon dioxide due to human activities. Among those activities are the production of many of the new goods that are among the benefits of innovative dynamism, such as air conditioning and the car, since these innovations use energy that emits carbon dioxide. Other results of innovative dynamism reduce carbon dioxide in the atmosphere, such as the process innovations that make manufacturing more efficient and that allow more food to be grown on less land. We do not yet know whether, on balance, innovative dynamism increases or reduces carbon dioxide in the atmosphere. If it turns out that on balance innovative dynamism increases carbon dioxide in the atmosphere, then those of us making a case for innovative dynamism would want to learn the extent to which carbon dioxide causes global warming.

However, William Happer, Princeton University physics professor and former director of the Office of Energy Research at the Department of Energy, coauthored a commentary in which he points out that the effects of carbon dioxide on temperature are ambiguous and that the main effect of increased carbon dioxide is the benefit of increased agricultural productivity, concluding that,

> [W]e know that carbon dioxide has been a much larger fraction of the earth's atmosphere than it is today, and the geological record shows that life flourished on land and in the oceans during those times. The incredible list of supposed horrors that increasing carbon dioxide will bring the world is pure belief disguised as science (Schmitt and Happer 2013, p. A19).

The benefits of carbon dioxide for plant life have been widely confirmed. For example, researchers at Columbia University found that oak trees in high–carbon dioxide Central Park weighed eight times as much as equally old oak trees in low–carbon dioxide rural areas (Gugliotta 2012, p. D3; see also Ziska et al. 2012; Searle et al. 2011). Other, more general empirical research also has confirmed the ambiguous effect of carbon dioxide on temperature. For example, a sophisticated econometric analysis using a very long time-series dataset on carbon dioxide and temperature found that carbon dioxide has little, if any, effect on temperature (McMillan and Wohar 2013). A different study using other econometric techniques and shorter time-series datasets finds a stronger positive relationship, but also finds that the previously discussed lull in global warming is genuine, not a statistical artifact, and is largely due to human actions reducing greenhouse emissions (Estrada and Perron 2017).

One feature of some climate models is that they include a tipping-point effect in which beyond some threshold, climate change accelerates. The potential costs implied by climate catastrophes in such models can be large and sudden. One geohistorical illustration sometimes given of the effects of passing a tipping point is the desertification of the Sahara. But evidence from geological and archeological research indicates that both the change in climate and the related human migrations occurred "over millennia, not just in a few desperate decades" (Naik 2014, p. C3; see also Francus et al. 2013).

Journalists and the public often assume that every destructive weather event is at root caused by global warming. But some phenomena often attributed to global warming may be due to periodic and hard-to-predict natural variations (Bhanoo 2009; Hansen 2009). One example is the warming of the American Northwest. Recent research suggests that the warming is almost entirely due to the effect of winds on the waters of the Pacific, winds little affected by human activity (Wines 2014a, p. A19; see also Johnstone and Mantua 2014).

d. *What We Should Do*

The main relevance of global warming to the case for innovative dynamism is that if global warming justifies restricting the production of carbon dioxide, then it will be much harder to reap the benefits of many of the innovations that otherwise make life better. James Payne has written a clear and persuasive article arguing that each of six claims must be true to justify carbon dioxide–limiting policies (Payne 2014, p. 265). These six claims are as follows:

1. Global temperature over the past century has risen.

2. Temperature will continue to rise over the next century and impact climate.

3. The main cause of this continuing temperature rise is the emission of carbon dioxide due to consumption of fossil fuels.

4. The future rise in global temperature will have extremely high human costs (the great-net-harm proposition).

5. The cost of governmental programs for restricting the use of fossil fuels will be significantly less than the net harm of carbon-dioxide-induced global warming (the benefit-cost proposition).

6. Governments are effective and responsible problem-solving machines and can therefore implement a robust, consistent, and worldwide policy of restricting the use of fossil fuels (the government-efficacy proposition).

To these six claims, I add a seventh:

7. Geoengineering, either by government or done privately, cannot effectively and efficiently mitigate a large increase in temperatures.

Of these I judge that claim 1 is true; claim 2 is likely true, though a recent lull raised doubts; claim 3 is likely true, though some recent econometric analysis is ambiguous; claim 4 is likely false, based mainly on humanity's proven ability to adapt through entrepreneurial technological innovations and other means; claim 5 is likely false, based on the sort of evidence presented by Ridley (2010) and Lomborg (2007). On claim 5, among the important costs of government programs are their opportunity costs. Other problems, including poverty, disease, and war, exceed in severity any problems caused by global warming (Lomborg 2009a, 2009b; 2009c, 2009d; Henderson and Cochrane 2017, p. A17).

Claim 6 is almost certainly false, based partly on the theory and evidence of the public choice literature. Bjørn Lomborg calculates that the $11 billion spent by Spain to produce more energy without releasing carbon dioxide, has "delayed the impact of global warming by roughly 61 hours, according to the estimates of Yale University's well-regarded Dynamic Integrated Climate-Economy model" (Lomborg 2013, p. A17). That $11 billion is roughly 1 percent of Spain's GDP and is more than the country spends on higher education. Such a large expenditure, with such high opportunity costs and small reduction in global warming, is not evidence of government effectiveness or efficiency. Another example is government mandates on the use of biofuels, such as the US mandate on ethanol use. Farmers switching land from food crops to biofuel increases the price of food crops, which leads farmers in countries such as Brazil to cut down carbon dioxide–absorbing rainforests to grow the now-higher-priced crops (Power 2008, p. A13; see also Fargione et al. 2008; Searchinger et al. 2008).

Claim 7 is likely false, based mainly on humanity's proven ability to develop technological innovations. A variety of geoengineering solutions are in various stages of development (Wagner and Weitzman 2015a, 2015b). One of the best-known solutions is from physicist, information technologist, inventor, and entrepreneur Nathan Myhrvold, who proposes to benignly simulate the earth-cooling effects of past major volcanic eruptions (Stephens 2009, p. A19; Levitt and Dubner 2010, pp. 180–203; see also Porter 2017a, pp. B1 & B4; Fountain 2018b, p. D3).

Another approach being applied in a variety of forms is to sequester carbon dioxide, meaning to take it from the air and store it as part of some liquid or, usually, solid mixture or compound. Dr. Olaf Schuiling, a retired geochemist, is exploring the use of the mineral olivine, which naturally absorbs carbon dioxide from the environment (Fountain 2014b, p. A1). Ants naturally break down minerals into olivine through a process that may be emulated by humans (Akst 2014, p. C4; see also Dorn 2014). Algae are being developed that absorb carbon dioxide and produce oil (Catsoulis 2010, p. C8). Carbon dioxide is being drawn from the air to sequester in forms of carbonate in Iceland (Fountain 2016b, p. A6; Matter et al. 2016) and Oman (Fountain 2018a, p. A10). Carbon dioxide can be sequestered in forests (Gillis 2016, p. D6; Chazdon et al. 2016) and in the soil (Leslie 2017, p. 7; Hansen et al. 2017). Finally, the FuelCell Energy firm is developing a new fuel cell that may efficiently both sequester carbon dioxide and produce energy (Schwartz 2016a, p. B2).

Of the seven claims then, one is almost certainly true, two are likely true, three are likely false, and one is almost certainly false. Since all the claims must be true to justify government policies restricting carbon dioxide, such policies are not justified.

Humans have a long history of successful adaptation to climate change. (For example, on the adaptability of Paleolithic humans to major climate change, see Rothstein (2010).) In modern times under a system of innovative dynamism, creative inventors find ways to reduce global warming (*Economist* 2010; Stephens 2009; Hotz 2007), and innovative entrepreneurs find ways to adapt to it (Ouroussoff 2010; Sengupta 2009; Dell, Jones, and Olken 2009, p. 203) or make use of it (Revkin 2009).

But what if I am wrong, and all seven claims are true? Would that justify having the government subsidize or mandate greater use of renewable-energy technologies such as solar and wind? Even more ominously for the flourishing of innovative dynamism, would that justify restricting development and use of energy-consuming innovations such as cars, air conditioning, and computers? First, consider alternative energy technologies.

These technologies are not free of problems. For example, wind power is land intensive: it takes three hundred square miles of windmills to generate sufficient electricity to power a city of seven hundred thousand, and that is assuming enough wind for the turbines to generate electricity 100 percent of the time, instead of the roughly 30 percent of the time that they actually do (Lehr 2013, p. A17; see also Porter 2017b, pp. B1-B2; Sweet 2015, p. B1). And whether wind turbines are friendly to the environment depends on which aspects of the environment you focus on. They are noisy, not everyone enjoys seeing them in their landscape, and they kill birds in large numbers: in 2013, Duke Energy agreed to pay $1 million for killing golden eagles and other birds at two of its Wyoming wind farms (Bryce 2013, p. A17; see also Schwartz 2016b, p. D2; Lintott et al. 2016).

If renewable-energy technologies are not promising, then are we left with no choice but to restrict the development and use of energy-consuming innovations that produce carbon dioxide? I argue that even then, there would be better ways of limiting carbon dioxide. I highlight one of the most obvious: nuclear power. Nuclear power generates minimal carbon dioxide, allows us to continue to benefit from technological innovations, and has risks that are lower than often thought and can readily be reduced even further. The worst nuclear-power accident to date occurred at Chernobyl. I have already cited evidence that the effects of this accident on both human and nonhuman life have been less than was expected and is commonly believed. The Yucca Mountain storage facility for spent nuclear fuel has multiple barriers to ensure that radioactive materials will be isolated for the long term (Wald 2014a, p. A20). If an alternative to Yucca Mountain is desired, the deep, thick salt beds near Carlsbad, in New Mexico, would provide a self-sealing repository expected to encapsulate the waste for millions of years (Wald 2014b, p. A9). New designs for smaller nuclear reactors would greatly increase the efficiency and safety of reactors, especially in comparison to the one in Chernobyl, but also in comparison to those operating in countries such as the United States and Japan (Wald 2013, p. B6).

7. Conclusion: Three Shades of Green

The goals of environmental activists vary: some seek to protect the vitality and beauty of nature, others seek to appear noble, and still others seek to end innovative dynamism. In short, there are three shades of green: Scout green, sanctimonious green, and watermelon green.

Many of us enjoy spending time in nature, hiking or camping or driving through scenic vistas. We are Boy Scouts at heart (I once was a Scout, and am not embarrassed to admit it). We do not litter, and we vote with our dollars for parks or organizations that take the adventure, wonder, and beauty of nature seriously. These would include Disney's Epcot, Omaha's Henry Doorly Zoo, and the Nature Conservancy. We are Scout green.

Sanctimonious green was embodied by Henry David Thoreau, a hero to many. Yet he carelessly, and unrepentantly, started a fire in a dry forest near Concord that destroyed over three hundred acres of the forest (Glaeser 2011, pp. 199–200). Also, Thoreau apparently was only comfortable in the tame, civilized forests such as those near Concord, since he became "near hysterical" with stress when he once encountered a true wilderness forest (Bryson 1999, p. 45). Thoreau was not the only one whose practice was not aligned with his preaching. Thomas Edison went on famous camping trips with Henry Ford as a "feeble protest against civilization," but he installed electric lights in his tent (Freeberg 2013, pp. 296).

Many modern environmentalists are proud to recycle and to use fluorescent or LED bulbs, but stop short of unplugging their refrigerators or washing machines (Kurutz 2009, p. D4; Rosling 2010). Greenpeace activists unfurled a banner extolling renewable energy, and in the process damaged an ancient etching of a hummingbird in the Peruvian desert (Neuman 2014, p. A17). On the other hand, there is Mexican ecologist Jesús Manuel García-Yánez, who grew up living a "sustainable" life only because his family was too poor to do anything else. He worked hard and got an education in order to "get out of that life" (García-Yánez as quoted in Tortorello 2012, p. D6).

Green is traditionally the color of environmentalists, and red is traditionally the color of communists and the left. Watermelons are green on the outside and red on the inside (Delingpole 2012). Watermelon environmentalists support environmentalism mainly as a tactic in their deeper goal of destroying innovative dynamism (Klein 2014; Porter 2015, p. B9; Roberts 2018). While the vast majority of environmentalists are not adopting environmentalism as a strategy to undermine innovative dynamism, the watermelon environmentalists make up in shrewdness what they lack in numbers. They understand that by increasing regulations and costs, they can undermine entrepreneurial innovations, reducing the benefits of innovative dynamism and thereby undermining the system they seek to destroy.

A perceptive analysis of watermelon greens was penned by Deirdre McCloskey, in part quoting from Joseph Schumpeter's *Capitalism, Socialism and Democracy* (McCloskey 2007; Schumpeter 1950, p. 144). Those who benefit from stagnation or cronyism have over time strategically alleged a variety of harms from innovative dynamism. They alleged that innovative dynamism impoverishes workers. When that claim was refuted, they shifted to alleging that innovative dynamism colonized the underdeveloped countries. When this was refuted, they began alleging that innovative dynamism will destroy the environment. When that is refuted, they will shift to alleging some other harm; there is already talk of a robot apocalypse (Diamond 2019b).

Schumpeter and McCloskey's insightful analysis might discourage us from investing the time and effort to show how innovative dynamism improves the environment. But that would be a mistake. Unless the evidence is shown and the case is made, many conscientious citizens will support policies that will shackle innovative dynamism, stopping the flow of new goods and processes that would otherwise make their lives longer and better. Unjustified environmental policies are not insurance bought; they are opportunities lost.

References

Adamy, Janet. "Low Birth Rate Poses Economic Challenge." *Wall Street Journal* (Weds., May 11, 2016): A2.

Akst, Daniel. "R and D; Are Ants Cooling the World?" *Wall Street Journal* (Sat., Aug. 16, 2014): C4.

Annan, Francis, and Wolfram Schlenker. "Federal Crop Insurance and the Disincentive to Adapt to Extreme Heat." *American Economic Review* 105, no. 5 (May 2015): 262–66.

Applebome, Peter. "Our Towns; Once They Thought Whale Oil Was Indispensable, Too." *New York Times*, First Section (Sun., Aug. 3, 2008): 20.

Ashcroft, Frances. *The Spark of Life: Electricity in the Human Body*. New York: W. W. Norton & Company, 2012.

Barreca, Alan, Karen Clay, Olivier Deschenes, Michael Greenstone, and Joseph S. Shapiro. "Convergence in Adaptation to Climate Change: Evidence from High Temperatures and Mortality, 1900–2004." *American Economic Review* 105, no. 5 (May 2015): 247–51.

Bastiat, Frédéric. "What Is Seen and What Is Not Seen." In *Selected Essays on Political Economy*. Irvington-on-Hudson, NY: The Foundation for Economic Education, Inc., 1995, pp. 1–50.

Belson, Ken. "Power Grids Iffy, Populous Areas Go for Generators." *New York Times* (Thurs., April 25, 2013): F8.

Bhanoo, Sindya N. "Observatory; In Extra Rib, a Harbinger of Mammoth's Doom." *New York Times* (Tues., April 1, 2014): D2.

Bhanoo, Sindya N. "Observatory; Snails Appear Reborn, or Were Overlooked." *New York Times* (Tues., Aug. 14, 2012b): D3.

Bhanoo, Sindya N. "Observatory; A Butterfly Takes Wing on Climate Change." *New York Times* (Tues., May 29, 2012a): D3.

Bhanoo, Sindya N. "Mt. Kilimanjaro's Ice Cap Continues Its Rapid Retreat, but the Cause Is Debated." *New York Times* (Tues., Nov. 3, 2009): A6.

Bhidé, Amar. "The Venturesome Economy: How Innovation Sustains Prosperity in a More Connected World." *Journal of Applied Corporate Finance* 21, no. 1 (Winter 2009): 8–23.

Bhidé, Amar. *The Venturesome Economy: How Innovation Sustains Prosperity in a More Connected World*. Princeton, NJ: Princeton University Press, 2008.

Blackwell, Andrew. *Visit Sunny Chernobyl: And Other Adventures in the World's Most Polluted Places*. New York: Rodale Books, 2012.

Block, Walter E. "Comment on Dolan on Austrian Economics and Environmentalism." *Quarterly Journal of Austrian Economics* 17, no. 2 (Summer 2014): 224–48.

Bosman, Julie. "Creeping up on Unsuspecting Shores; the Great Lakes, in a Welcome Turnaround." *New York Times*, First Section (Sun., June 29, 2014): 16 & 20.

Botkin, Daniel B. *The Moon in the Nautilus Shell: Discordant Harmonies Reconsidered*. New York: Oxford University Press, 2012.

Brody, Jane E. "Personal Health; What You Think You Know (but Don't) About Wise Eating." *New York Times* (Tues., Jan. 1, 2013): D7.

Broughton, Philip Delves. "Bookshelf; Go Ahead, Fill 'Er up; Renouncing Oil and Its Byproducts Would Plunge Civilization into a Pre-Industrial Hell—a Fact Developing Countries Keenly Realize." *Wall Street Journal* (Tues., Dec. 2, 2014): A15.

Bryce, Robert. "Wind Power Is Brought to Justice; Duke Energy's Guilty Plea for Killing Protected Birds Is an Ominous Sign for Renewable Energy." *Wall Street Journal* (Fri., Nov. 29, 2013): A17.

Bryson, Bill. *A Walk in the Woods: Rediscovering America on the Appalachian Trail*. Pb. ed. New York: Broadway Books, 1999.

Buffett, Warren. "Notable & Quotable: Warren Buffett on Climate." *Wall Street Journal* (Tues., March 1, 2016): A9.

Burrough, Bryan. "Off the Shelf; the Birth of an Energy Boom." *New York Times*, SundayBusiness Section (Sun., Nov. 2, 2013): 7.

Bynum, William. "Singing the Body Electric." *Wall Street Journal* (Sat., Sept. 29, 2012): C9.

Campbell, Kevin L., Jason E. E. Roberts, Laura N. Watson, Jörg Stetefeld, Angela M. Sloan, Anthony V. Signore, Jesse W. Howatt, Jeremy R. H. Tame, Nadin Rohland, Tong-Jian Shen, Jeremy J. Austin, Michael Hofreiter, Ho Chien, Roy E. Weber, and Alan Cooper. "Substitutions in Woolly Mammoth Hemoglobin Confer Biochemical Properties Adaptive for Cold Tolerance." *Nature Genetics* 42, no. 6 (June 2010): 536–40.

Caprara, Robert J. "Opinion; Confessions of a Computer Modeler; Any Model, Including Those Predicting Climate Doom, Can Be Tweaked to Yield a Desired Result. I Should Know." *Wall Street Journal* (Weds., July 9, 2014): A13.

Carden, Art. "Economic Calculation in the Environmentalist Commonwealth." *Quarterly Journal of Austrian Economics* 16, no. 1 (Spring 2013): 27–43.

Catsoulis, Jeannette. "Global Warming and Common Sense." *New York Times* (Fri., Nov. 12, 2010): C8.

Cavanaugh, Kyle C., James R. Kellner, Alexander J. Forde, Daniel S. Gruner, John D. Parker, Wilfrid Rodriguez, and Ilka C. Feller. "Poleward Expansion of Mangroves Is a Threshold Response to Decreased Frequency of Extreme Cold Events." *Proceedings of the National Academy of Sciences (PNAS)* 111, no. 2 (Jan. 14, 2014): 723–27.

Cave, Damien, and Justin Gillis. "Building a Reef Tough Enough to Survive a More Perilous Sea." *New York Times* (Sat., Sept. 30, 2017): A6.

Chang, Kenneth. "Stanford Scientists Cast Doubt on Advantages of Organic Meat and Produce." *New York Times* (Tues., Sept. 4, 2012): A20.

Chazdon, Robin L., Eben N. Broadbent, Danaë M. A. Rozendaal, Frans Bongers, Angélica María Almeyda Zambrano, T. Mitchell Aide, Patricia Balvanera, et al. "Carbon Sequestration Potential of Second-Growth Forest Regeneration in the Latin American Tropics." *Science Advances* 2, no. 5 (May 13, 2016). DOI: 10.1126/sciadv.1501639.

Chen, Ching, Jane K. Hill, Ralf Ohlemüller, David B. Roy, and Chris D. Thomas. "Report; Rapid Range Shifts of Species Associated with High Levels of Climate Warming." *Science* 333, no. 6045 (Aug. 2011): 1024–26.

Chozick, Amy, interviewer. "'The Wonder Is Still There'; the Statistician David J. Hand on Eerie Coincidences and Playing the Lottery." *New York Times Magazine* (Sun., Feb. 23, 2014): 12.

Cooper, Michael, and Jo Craven McGinty. "A Meter So Expensive, It Creates Parking Spots." *New York Times* (Fri., March 16, 2012): A1 & A3.

Cordato, Roy. "Toward an Austrian Theory of Environmental Economics." *Quarterly Journal of Austrian Economics* 7, no. 1 (Spring 2004): 3–16.

Cowen, Tyler. *Average Is Over: Powering America Beyond the Age of the Great Stagnation.* New York: Dutton Adult, 2013.

Cragg, Steven T., and Robert J. Caprara. "Effects of Analytical Data Gathering and Handling Techniques on Calculated Risk Levels at Superfund Sites." In *Risk Analysis: Prospects and Opportunities*, edited by Constantine Zervos, Kathleen Knox, Lee Abramson and Rob Coppock. New York: Springer U.S., 1991, pp. 723–30.

Dawidoff, Nicholas. "The Civil Heretic." *New York Times Magazine* (Sun., March 29, 2009): 32–39, 54 & 57–59.

Dawson, Graham. "Privatising Climate Policy." *Economic Affairs* 29, no. 3 (Sept. 2009): 57-62.

Dawson, Graham. "The Economic Science Fiction of Climate Change: A Free-Market Perspective on the Stern Review and the IPCC." *Economic Affairs* 28, no. 4 (Dec. 2008): 42–47.

Dean, Cornelia. "Higher Seas? As Alaska Glaciers Melt, Land Rises." *New York Times* (Mon., May 18, 2009): A1 & A11.

De'ath, Glenn, Katharina E. Fabricius, Hugh Sweatman, and Marji Puotinen. "The 27-Year Decline of Coral Cover on the Great Barrier Reef and Its Causes." *Proceedings of the National Academy of Sciences of the United States of America* 109, no. 44 (Oct. 30, 2012): 17995–99.

Delingpole, James. *Watermelons: How Environmentalists Are Killing the Planet, Destroying the Economy and Stealing Your Children's Future*. London: Biteback Publishing, 2012.

Dell, Melissa, Benjamin F. Jones, and Benjamin A. Olken. "Temperature and Income: Reconciling New Cross-Sectional and Panel Estimates." *American Economic Review* 99, no. 2 (May 2009): 198–204.

Dewan, Shaila. "It's the Economy; Rent Asunder." *New York Times Magazine* (Sun., May 4, 2014): 16 & 18–19.

Diamandis, Peter H., and Steven Kotler. *Abundance: The Future Is Better Than You Think*. New York: Free Press, 2012.

Diamond, Arthur M., Jr. *Openness to Creative Destruction: Sustaining Innovative Dynamism*. New York: Oxford University Press, forthcoming 2019a.

Diamond, Arthur M., Jr. "Robots and Computers Enhance Us More Than They Replace Us." *The American Economist* (forthcoming 2019b).

Diamond, Arthur M., Jr. "Keeping Our Cool: In Defense of Air Conditioning." *Economics & Business Journal: Inquiries & Perspectives* 8, no. 1 (Oct. 2017): 1–36.

Diamond, Arthur M., Jr. "The Intergenerational Invisible Hand: A Comment on Sartorius's "Government Regulation and Intergenerational Justice"." *Journal of Libertarian Studies* 7, no. 2 (Summer 1987): 269–74.

Dobbs, David. "The Fault in Our DNA." *New York Times Book Review* (Sun., July 13, 2014): 11.

Dolan, Edwin. "The Austrian Paradigm in Environmental Economics: Theory and Practice." *Quarterly Journal of Austrian Economics* 17, no. 2 (Summer 2014): 197–217.

Dolin, Eric Jay. *Leviathan: The History of Whaling in America*. New York: W. W. Norton & Company, Inc., 2007.

Dorn, Ronald I. "Ants as a Powerful Biotic Agent of Olivine and Plagioclase Dissolution." *Geology* 42, no. 9 (Sept. 2014): 771–74.

Doubleday, Zoë A., Thomas A. A. Prowse, Alexander Arkhipkin, Graham J. Pierce, Jayson Semmens, Michael Steer, Stephen C. Leporati, Sílvia Lourenço, Antoni Quetglas, Warwick Sauer, and Bronwyn M. Gillanders. "Global Proliferation of Cephalopods." *Current Biology* 26, no. 10 (Mon., May 23, 2016): R406-R07.

Economist. "Bacteria and Climate Change; Invisible Carbon Pumps; a Group of Oceanic Micro-Organisms Just Might Prove a Surprising Ally in the Fight against Climate Change." *Economist* (Sat., Sept. 11, 2010): 96–97.

Egan, Patrick J., and Megan Mullin. "Gray Matter; Global Warming Feels Quite Pleasant." *New York Times*, SundayReview Section (Sun., April 24, 2016a): 9.

Egan, Patrick J., and Megan Mullin. "Recent Improvement and Projected Worsening of Weather in the United States." *Nature* 532, no. 7599 (April 21, 2016b): 357–60.

Egan, Timothy. *The Worst Hard Time: The Untold Story of Those Who Survived the Great American Dust Bowl*. Boston: Houghton Mifflin, 2006.

Ehrlich, Paul R. *The Population Bomb*. New York: Sierra Club/Ballantine Books, 1968.

Epstein, Alex. *The Moral Case for Fossil Fuels*. New York: Portfolio, 2014.

Estrada, Francisco, and Pierre Perron. "Extracting and Analyzing the Warming Trend in Global and Hemispheric Temperatures." *Journal of Time Series Analysis* 38, no. 5 (Sept. 2017): 711–32.

Etter, Lauren. "Feeling the Heat for Icy Greenland, Global Warming Has a Bright Side as Temperatures Inch up, Melting Glaciers Bring New Life to a Frozen Land but Could Polar Bears Vanish?" *Wall Street Journal* (Tues., July 18, 2006): A1 & A12.

Fargione, Joseph, Jason Hill, David Tilman, Stephen Polasky, and Peter Hawthorne. "Land Clearing and the Biofuel Carbon Debt." *Science* 319, no. 5867 (Feb. 29, 2008): 1235–38.

Faris, Stephan. "Phenomenon; Ice Free; Will Global Warming Give Greenland Its Independence?" *New York Times Magazine* (Sun., July 27, 2008): 20.

Fountain, Henry. "How Oman's Rocks Could Help Save the Planet." *New York Times* (Sat., April 28 2018a): A10-A11.

Fountain, Henry. "A Volcanic Idea for Cooling the Earth." *New York Times* (Tues., Feb. 6, 2018b): D3.

Fountain, Henry. "A New Way to Search out Elusive Helium." *New York Times* (Weds., June 29, 2016a): A8.

Fountain, Henry. "Project in Iceland for Storing Carbon Shows Promise." *New York Times* (Fri., June 10, 2016b): A6.

Fountain, Henry. "Adapting to Chernobyl." *New York Times* (Tues., May 6, 2014a): D1 & D2.

Fountain, Henry. "Climate Cures Seeking to Tap Nature's Power." *New York Times* (Mon., Nov. 10, 2014b): A1 & A6.

Fountain, Henry. "Observatory; A New Lizard? Well, New to Science." *New York Times* (Tues., April 13, 2010a): D3.

Fountain, Henry. "Observatory; Rare Bird, Alive and Well and Living in Colombia." *New York Times* (Tues., April 13, 2010b): D3.

Fowler, Tom. "Shell Races the Ice in Alaska; Delays Put $4.5 Billion Arctic Drilling Plan in Danger of Missing Window before Next Freeze." *Wall Street Journal* (Mon., Aug. 20, 2012): B1-B2.

Fox, Justin. "Head Count." *New York Times Book Review* (Sun., Aug. 3, 2014): 20.

Francus, Pierre, Hans von Suchodoletz, Michael Dietze, Reik V. Donner, Frédéric Bouchard, Ann-Julie Roy, Maureen Fagot, Dirk Verschuren, Stefan Kröpelin, and Daniel Ariztegui. "Varved Sediments of Lake Yoa (Ounianga Kebir, Chad) Reveal Progressive Drying of the Sahara During the Last 6100 Years." *Sedimentology* 60, no. 4 (June 2013): 911–34.

Freeberg, Ernest. *The Age of Edison: Electric Light and the Invention of Modern America, Penguin History American Life*. New York: The Penguin Press, 2013.

Fretwell, Peter T., Michelle A. LaRue, Paul Morin, Gerald L. Kooyman, Barbara Wienecke, Norman Ratcliffe, Adrian J. Fox, Andrew H. Fleming, Claire Porter, and Phil N. Trathan. "An Emperor Penguin Population Estimate: The First Global, Synoptic Survey of a Species from Space." *PLoS ONE* 7, no. 4 (April 2012): 1–11.

Fretwell, Peter T., Phil N. Trathan, Barbara Wienecke, and Gerald L. Kooyman. "Emperor Penguins Breeding on Iceshelves." *PLoS ONE* 9, no. 1 (Jan. 2014): 1–9.

Fretwell, Peter. "The Emperor Strikes Back." *Significance* 9, no. 3 (June 2012): 4–7.

Galván, Ismael, Andrea Bonisoli-Alquati, Shanna Jenkinson, Ghanem Ghanem, Kazumasa Wakamatsu, Timothy A. Mousseau, and Anders P. Møller. "Chronic Exposure to Low-Dose Radiation at Chernobyl Favours Adaptation to Oxidative Stress in Birds." *Functional Ecology* 28, no. 6 (Dec. 2014): 1387–403.

Garud, Raghu, Joel Gehman, and Arvind Karunakaran. "Boundaries, Breaches, and Bridges: The Case of Climategate." *Research Policy* 43, no. 1 (Feb. 2014): 60–73.

Gasparrini, Antonio, Yuming Guo, Masahiro Hashizume, Eric Lavigne, Antonella Zanobetti, Joel Schwartz, Aurelio Tobias, et al. "Mortality Risk Attributable to High and Low Ambient Temperature: A Multicountry Observational Study." *Lancet* 386, no. 9991 (July 25, 2015): 369–75.

Gholz, Eugene. "Rare Earth Elements and National Security." Council on Foreign Relations working paper, Oct. 2014.

Gilbert, Daniel. *Stumbling on Happiness*. New York: Alfred A. Knopf, 2006.

Gillis, Justin. "In Latin America, Forests May Rise to Challenge of Carbon Dioxide." *New York Times* (Tues., May 17, 2016): D6.

Gillis, Justin. "By Degrees; Freezing out the Bigger Picture." *New York Times* (Tues., Feb. 11, 2014): D3.

Gillis, Justin. "Arctic Ice Makes Comeback from Record Low, but Long-Term Decline May Continue." *New York Times* (Sat., Sept. 21, 2013a): A8.

Gillis, Justin. "By Degrees; A Change in Temperature." *New York Times* (Tues., May 14, 2013b): D1 & D6.

Gillis, Justin. "By Degrees; What to Make of a Warming Plateau." *New York Times* (Tues., June 11, 2013c): D3.

Gillis, Justin. "Global Temperatures Highest in 4,000 Years." *New York Times* (Fri., March 8, 2013d): A15.

Gillis, Justin. "Spared Winter Freeze, Florida's Mangroves Are Marching North." *New York Times* (Tues., Dec. 31, 2013e): A14 & A16.

Glaeser, Edward L. *Triumph of the City: How Our Greatest Invention Makes Us Richer, Smarter, Greener, Healthier, and Happier.* New York: Penguin Press, 2011.

Gold, Russell, and Amy Harder. "Fracking's Harm to Water Not Widespread, EPA Says." *Wall Street Journal* (Fri., June 5, 2015): A5.

Goldman, Russell. "No Icebreaker Needed: Thaw Lets Tanker Traverse Arctic." *New York Times* (Sun., Aug. 27, 2017): 12.

Gorman, James. "Side Effects; D.I.Y. Biology, on the Wings of the Mockingjay." *New York Times* (Tues., May 15, 2012): D4.

Gormezano, Linda J., and Robert F. Rockwell. "Dietary Composition and Spatial Patterns of Polar Bear Foraging on Land in Western Hudson Bay." *BMC Ecology* 13, no. 51 (2013a).

Gormezano, Linda J., and Robert F. Rockwell. "What to Eat Now? Shifts in Polar Bear Diet During the Ice-Free Season in Western Hudson Bay." *Ecology and Evolution* 3, no. 10 (Sept. 2013b): 3509–23.

Gould, Stephen Jay. *Hen's Teeth and Horse's Toes: Further Reflections in Natural History.* New York: W. W. Norton & Co., Inc., 1983.

Gould, Stephen Jay. *Wonderful Life: The Burgess Shale and the Nature of History.* New York: W. W. Norton & Co., Inc., 1989.

Greenberg, Joel. *A Feathered River Across the Sky: The Passenger Pigeon's Flight to Extinction.* New York: Bloomsbury USA, 2014.

Gruen, Judy. "Becoming a Bagless Lady in Los Angeles." *Wall Street Journal* (Sat., March 8, 2014): A13.

Gugliotta, Guy. "Looking to Cities, in Search of Global Warming's Silver Lining." *New York Times* (Tues., Nov. 27, 2012): D3.

Hager, Thomas. *The Alchemy of Air: A Jewish Genius, a Doomed Tycoon, and the Scientific Discovery That Fed the World but Fueled the Rise of Hitler.* New York: Harmony, 2008.

Hale, Mike. "In Dead Zone of Chernobyl, Animal Kingdom Thrives." *Wall Street Journal* (Weds., Oct. 19, 2011): C6.

Hand, David J. *The Improbability Principle: Why Coincidences, Miracles, and Rare Events Happen Every Day.* New York: Scientific American/Farrar, Straus and Giroux, 2014.

Hansen, James, Makiko Sato, Pushker Kharecha, Karina von Schuckmann, David J. Beerling, Junji Cao, Shaun Marcott, et al. "Young People's Burden: Requirement of Negative CO2 Emissions." *Earth System Dynamics Discussions* 8 (2017): 577–616.

Hansen, Matthew. "UNO Scientists Pinpoint Global Warming Oddity in Himalayas." *Omaha World-Herald* (Thurs., Dec. 17, 2009): 1A-2A.

Hazlitt, Henry. *Economics in One Lesson.* Irvington-on-Hudson, NY: Foundation for Economic Education, Inc., 1952.

Hebert, David J. "Property Rights: Private or Public? Evidence from the Boston Frozen Water Trade." *Journal of Private Enterprise* 28, no. 2 (Spring 2013): 111–23.

Henderson, David R., and John H. Cochrane. "Climate Change Isn't the End of the World; Even If World Temperatures Rise, the Appropriate Policy Response Is Still an Open Question." *Wall Street Journal* (Mon., July 31, 2017): A17.

Hotz, Robert Lee. "Antarctic Penguins Thrive." *Wall Street Journal* (Fri., July 11, 2014): A3.

Hotz, Robert Lee. "Emperor Penguins Are Teeming in Antarctica." *Wall Street Journal* (Sat., April 14, 2012a): A2.

Hotz, Robert Lee. "Keeping Our Heads above Water; What Can New York Learn from Other Great Cities Battling Rising Tides and Sinking Land?" *Wall Street Journal* (Sat., Dec. 1, 2012b): C3.

Hotz, Robert Lee. "Dinosaur Hunter Seeks More Than Just Bare Bones; Prof. Horner Searches for Traces of Blood, DNA; Lucky Break from T. Rex." *Wall Street Journal* (Fri., Aug. 24, 2007): A1 & A12.

Hulme, Mike. "An Unwinnable Fight." *Nature Climate Change* 2, no. 4 (April 2012): 223–24.

Iles, D. T., S. L. Peterson, Linda J. Gormezano, D. N. Koons, and Robert F. Rockwell. "Terrestrial Predation by Polar Bears: Not Just a Wild Goose Chase." *Polar Biology* 36, no. 9 (Sept. 2013): 1373–79.

Isaacson, Walter. *Steve Jobs*. New York: Simon & Schuster, 2011.

Jakab, Spencer. "Will a Shortage of Cobalt Kill Electric-Vehicle Makers?" *Wall Street Journal* (Thurs., Nov. 30, 2017): B14.

Johnstone, James A., and Nathan J. Mantua. "Atmospheric Controls on Northeast Pacific Temperature Variability and Change, 1900–2012." *Proceedings of the National Academy of Sciences* (Sept. 22, 2014).

Joling, Dan. "Loss of Arctic Ice Opens up New Cable Route." *Omaha World-Herald* (Fri., Jan. 22, 2010): 4A.

Kahn, Matthew E. *Climatopolis: How Our Cities Will Thrive in the Hotter Future*. New York: Basic Books, 2010.

Kelly, Kevin. *What Technology Wants*. New York: Viking Adult, 2010.

Klein, Naomi. *This Changes Everything: Capitalism vs. The Climate*. New York: Simon & Schuster, 2014.

Klick, Jonathan, and Joshua D. Wright. "Grocery Bag Bans and Foodborne Illness." *University of Pennsylvania, Institute for Law and Economics Research Paper*, 13-2. Nov. 2, 2012.

Kolata, Gina. "So You're Extinct? Scientists Have Gleam in Eye." *New York Times* (Tues., March 19, 2013): A1 & A16.

Koonin, Steven E. "Climate Science Is Not Settled." *Wall Street Journal* (Sat., Sept. 20, 2014): C1-C2.

Kotchen, Matthew J. "Review of Kahn's Climatopolis." *Journal of Economic Literature* 49, no. 3 (Sept. 2011): 777–79.

Kramer, Andrew E., and Clifford Krauss. "Russia Embraces Arctic Drilling." *New York Times* (Weds., Feb. 16, 2011): B1-B2.

Kramer, Andrew E., and Andrew C. Revkin. "Arctic Shortcut Beckons Shippers as Ice Thaws." *New York Times* (Fri., Sept. 10, 2009): A1 & A3.

Kramer, Andrew E. "Polar Thaw Opens Shortcut for Russian Natural Gas." *New York Times* (Thurs., July 25, 2013): B1 & B6.

Krause-Kyora, Ben, Julian Susat, Felix M. Key, Denise Kühnert, Esther Bosse, Alexander Immel, Christoph Rinne, et al. "Neolithic and Medieval Virus Genomes Reveal Complex Evolution of Hepatitis B." *eLife* 7 (2018): e36666.

Krauss, Clifford, Steven Lee Myers, Andrew C. Revkin, and Simon Romero. "As Polar Ice Turns to Water, Dreams of Treasure Abound." *New York Times* (Mon., Oct. 10, 2005): A1 & A10-A11.

Kurutz, Steven. "Trashing the Fridge." *New York Times* (Thurs., Feb. 5, 2009): D1 & D4.

Kwai, Isabella. "A Voracious Starfish Is Destroying the Great Barrier Reef." *New York Times* (Sat., Jan. 6, 2018): A9.

Last, Jonathan V. "A Prediction That Bombed; Paul Ehrlich Predicted an Imminent Population Catastrophe; Julian Simon Wagered He Was Wrong." *Wall Street Journal* (Sat., Aug. 31, 2013): C6.

Lehr, Jay. "Opinion; the Rationale for Wind Power Won't Fly; Physical Limitations Will Keep This Energy Source a Niche Provider of U.S. Electricity Needs." *Wall Street Journal* (Tues., June 18, 2013): A17.

Leslie, Jacques. "Soil Power! The Dirty Way to a Green Planet." *New York Times*, SundayReview Section (Sun., Dec. 3, 2017): 7.

Levitt, Steven D., and Stephen J. Dubner. *Super Freakonomics: Global Cooling, Patriotic Prostitutes, and Why Suicide Bombers Should Buy Life Insurance*. pb ed. New York: Penguin Books, 2010.

Libecap, Gary D., and Richard H. Steckel, eds. *The Economics of Climate Change: Adaptations Past and Present, National Bureau of Economic Research Conference Report*. Chicago: University of Chicago Press, 2011.

Lintott, Paul R., Suzanne M. Richardson, David J. Hosken, Sophie A. Fensome, and Fiona Mathews. "Ecological Impact Assessments Fail to Reduce Risk of Bat Casualties at Wind Farms." *Current Biology* 26, no. 21 (Nov. 7, 2016): R1135-R36.

Lomborg, Bjørn. "Climate-Change Policies Can Be Punishing for the Poor; America Should Learn from Europe's Failure to Protect the Needy While Reducing Carbon Emissions." *Wall Street Journal* (Sat., Jan. 5, 2018): A15.

Lomborg, Bjørn. "Green Energy Is the Real Subsidy Hog; Renewables Receive Three Times as Much Money Per Energy Unit as Fossil Fuels." *Wall Street Journal* (Tues., Nov. 12, 2013): A19.

Lomborg, Bjørn. "Climate Change and Malaria in Africa; Limiting Carbon Emissions Won't Do Much to Stop Disease in Zambia." *Wall Street Journal* (Mon., Nov. 2, 2009a): A17.

Lomborg, Bjørn. "Global Warming as Seen from Bangladesh; Momota Begum Worries About Hunger, Not Climate Change." *Wall Street Journal* (Mon., Nov. 9, 2009b): A17.

Lomborg, Bjørn. "Opinion; Time for a Smarter Approach to Global Warming; Investing in Energy R&D Might Work. Mandated Emissions Cuts Won't." *Wall Street Journal* (Tues., Dec. 15, 2009c): A21.

Lomborg, Bjørn. "The View from Vanuatu on Climate Change; Torethy Frank Had Never Heard of Global Warming. She Is Worried About Power and Running Water." *Wall Street Journal* (Fri., Oct. 23, 2009d): A19.

Lomborg, Bjørn. *Cool It: The Skeptical Environmentalist's Guide to Global Warming*. New York: Alfred A. Knopf, 2007.

Lynch, Heather J., and Mathew R. Schwaller. "Mapping the Abundance and Distribution of Adélie Penguins Using Landsat-7: First Steps Towards an Integrated Multi-Sensor Pipeline for Tracking Populations at the Continental Scale." *PLoS ONE* 9, no. 11 (Nov. 2014): 1–8.

Maag, Christopher. "In the Battle against Cancer, Researchers Find Hope in a Toxic Wasteland." *New York Times* (Tues., Oct. 9, 2007): A21.

Marcott, Shaun A., Jeremy D. Shakun, Peter U. Clark, and Alan C. Mix. "Report: A Reconstruction of Regional and Global Temperature for the Past 11,300 Years." *Science* 339, no. 6124 (March 8, 2013): 1198–201.

Martin, Andrew. "The Feed; the Man Who Dared to Question Ethanol." *New York Times*, SundayBusiness Section (Sun., July 13, 2008): 5.

Matter, Juerg M., Martin Stute, Sandra Ó Snæbjörnsdottir, Eric H. Oelkers, Sigurdur R. Gislason, Edda S. Aradottir, Bergur Sigfusson, Ingvi Gunnarsson, Holmfridur Sigurdardottir, Einar Gunnlaugsson, Gudni Axelsson, Helgi A. Alfredsson, Domenik Wolff-Boenisch, Kiflom Mesfin, Diana Fernandez de la Reguera Taya, Jennifer Hall, Knud Dideriksen, and Wallace S. Broecker. "Rapid Carbon Mineralization for Permanent Disposal of Anthropogenic Carbon Dioxide Emissions." *Science* 352, no. 6291 (June 10, 2016): 1312–14.

Matthews, Merrill. "The Corn-Fed Albatross Called Ethanol." *Wall Street Journal* (Weds., Jan. 6, 2016): A9.

Mayhew, Robert J. *Malthus: The Life and Legacies of an Untimely Prophet.* Cambridge, MA: Belknap Press, 2014.

McCaffrey, Matthew. "Five Erroneous Ways to Argue About Resource Economics." *Quarterly Journal of Austrian Economics* 15, no. 1 (Spring 2012): 120–42.

McCloskey, Deirdre N. *Bourgeois Dignity: Why Economics Can't Explain the Modern World.* Chicago: University of Chicago Press, 2010.

McCloskey, Deirdre N. "Creative Destruction Vs. The New Industrial State." *Reason* 39, no. 5 (Oct. 2007): 58–64.

McKitrick, Ross R. "HAC-Robust Measurement of the Duration of a Trendless Subsample in a Global Climate Time Series." *Open Journal of Statistics* 4 (2014): 527–35.

McMillan, David G., and Mark E. Wohar. "The Relationship between Temperature and CO2 Emissions: Evidence from a Short and Very Long Dataset." *Applied Economics* 45, no. 26 (2013): 3683–90.

Miller, Henry I. "Organic Farming Is Not Sustainable; More Labor with Lower Yields Is a Luxury Only Rich Populations Can Afford." *Wall Street Journal* (Fri., May 16, 2014): A13.

Millman, Jack M., Kara Waits, Heidi Grande, Ann R. Marks, Jane C. Marks, Lance B. Price, and Bruce A. Hungate. "Prevalence of Antibiotic-Resistant E. Coli in Retail Chicken: Comparing Conventional, Organic, Kosher, and Raised without Antibiotics." *F1000Research* 2 (July 11, 2013).

Moalem, Sharon. *Inheritance: How Our Genes Change Our Lives--and Our Lives Change Our Genes.* New York: Grand Central Publishing, 2014.

Mouawad, Jad. "Oil Survey Says Arctic Has Riches." *New York Times* (Thurs., July 24, 2008): C1 & C4.

Moynihan, Michael C. "A Guided Tour of Catastrophe." *Wall Street Journal* (Sat., May 26, 2012): C11.

Mühlemann, Barbara, Terry C. Jones, Peter de Barros Damgaard, Morten E. Allentoft, Irina Shevnina, Andrey Logvin, Emma Usmanova, et al. "Ancient Hepatitis B Viruses from the Bronze Age to the Medieval Period." *Nature* 557, no. 7705 (May 9, 2018): 418–23.

Mukherjee, Siddhartha. *The Emperor of All Maladies: A Biography of Cancer*. New York: Scribner, 2010.

Naik, Gautam. "Warmer Climate Gives Cheer to Makers of British Bubbly; Thanks to Milder Summers, England Takes Some Air out of France's Famous Tipple." *Wall Street Journal* (Tues., May 11, 2010): A1 & A18.

Naik, Gautam. "Climate Clues in the Sahara's Past; a Geologist's Findings in Africa Challenge the Way Scientists Think About the Threat of Desertification." *Wall Street Journal* (Fri., May 31, 2014): C3.

Neuman, William. "Peru Is Indignant after Greenpeace Makes Its Mark on Ancient Site." *New York Times* (Sat., Dec. 13, 2014): A7.

New York Times. "Freeman Dyson: By the Book." *New York Times Book Review* (Sun., April 16, 2015): 8.

New York Times. "Observatory; Tiny Plants' Loss May Have Doomed Mammoths." *New York Times* (Tues., Feb. 11, 2014): D2.

Niskanen, William A. *Bureaucracy and Representative Government*. Chicago: Aldine-Atherton, 1971.

Norris, Floyd. "Population Growth Forecast from the U.N. May Be Too High." *New York Times* (Sat., Sept. 21, 2013): B3.

Norton, Steven. "Rio Digs Deeper for Copper." *Wall Street Journal* (Thurs., June 8, 2017): B6.

Ouroussoff, Nicolai. "Architecture Review; the Future: A More Watery New York." *New York Times* (Fri., March 26, 2010): C21 & C23.

Payne, James L. "The Real Case against Activist Global Warming Policy." *Independent Review* 19, no. 2 (Fall 2014): 265–70.

Pearce, Fred. "Sceptical About Scepticism." *Nature Climate Change* 1 (Aug. 2011): 237–38.

Pennington, Mark. "Liberty, Markets, and Environmental Values." *Independent Review* 10, no. 1 (Summer 2005): 39–57.

Pindyck, Robert S. "Climate Change Policy: What Do the Models Tell Us?" *Journal of Economic Literature* 51, no. 3 (Sept. 2013): 860–72.

Pindyck, Robert S. "The Use and Misuse of Models for Climate Policy." *NBER Working Paper* # 21097, April 2015.

Popovich, Nadja, and Blacki Migliozzi. "Where Are America's Winters Warming the Most? In Cold Places." *New York Times* (Sat., March 17, 2018): A11.

Porter, Eduardo. "Economic Scene; To Curb Global Warming, Science Fiction May Become Fact." *New York Times* (Weds., April 5, 2017a): B1 & B4.

Porter, Eduardo. "Why Slashing Nuclear Power May Backfire." *New York Times* (Weds., Nov. 8, 2017b): B1-B2.

Porter, Eduardo. "Economic Scene; No Growth, No World? Think About It." *New York Times* (Weds., Dec. 2, 2015): B1 & B9.

Power, Stephen. "If a Tree Falls in the Forest, Are Biofuels to Blame? It's Not Easy Being Green." *Wall Street Journal* (Tues., Nov. 11, 2008): A13.

Preston, Richard. *American Steel: Hot Metal Men and the Resurrection of the Rust Belt*. New York: Simon & Schuster, 1991.

Quindlen, Anna. "House Call; a Message Delivered by Tornado; after Five Days without Power, a Desperate Writer Calls Her Contractor to Say: 'Generator. Please. Soon.'." *Wall Street Journal* (Fri., April 12, 2013): M14.

Rawls, John. *A Theory of Justice*. Cambridge, MA: Harvard University Press, 1971.

Reed, Stanley. "$222 Billion Shift Hits a Snag." *New York Times* (Thurs., Oct. 7, 2017): B1-B2.

Reumer, Jelle W.F., Clara M.A. ten Broek, and Frietson Galis. "Extraordinary Incidence of Cervical Ribs Indicates Vulnerable Condition in Late Pleistocene Mammoths." *PeerJ* (2014).

Revkin, Andrew C. "Climate Change; a Closer Look at Moderating Views of Climate Sensitivity." In *Dot Earth: New York Times Opinion Pages Climate Blog*, Feb. 4, 2013, URL: http://dotearth.blogs.nytimes.com/2013/02/04/a-closer-look-at-moderating-views-of-climate-sensitivity/?_r=0 .

Revkin, Andrew C. "Global Warming Is Delaying Ice Age, Study Finds." *New York Times* (Fri., Sept. 4, 2009): A17.

Revkin, Andrew C. "A Push to Increase Icebreakers in the Arctic." *New York Times*, First Section (Sun., Aug. 17, 2008): 6.

Ridley, Matt. "Opinion; Whatever Happened to Global Warming? Now Come Climate Scientists' Implausible Explanations for Why the 'Hiatus' Has Passed the 15-Year Mark." *Wall Street Journal* (Fri., Sept. 5, 2014a): A13.

Ridley, Matt. "The Scarcity Fallacy; Ecologists Worry That the World's Resources Come in Fixed Amounts That Will Run out, but We Have Broken through Such Limits Again and Again." *Wall Street Journal* (Sat., April 26, 2014b): C1-C2.

Ridley, Matt. "Mind & Matter; How Fossil Fuels Have Greened the Planet." *Wall Street Journal* (Sat., Jan. 5, 2013): C4.

Ridley, Matt. "Mind & Matter; The Future Is So Bright, It's Dematerializing." *Wall Street Journal* (Sat., Jan. 26, 2012): C4.

Ridley, Matt. "Mind & Matter; Who's Afraid of Seven Billion People?" *Wall Street Journal* (Sat., Oct. 29, 2011): C4.

Ridley, Matt. *The Rational Optimist: How Prosperity Evolves*. New York: Harper, 2010.

Robbins, Jim. "In a Strange Land; One of the Country's Least-Hyped Nature Preserves, Nevada's Great Basin National Park Has a Weird, Wild Beauty All Its Own." *Wall Street Journal* (Sat., March 11, 2017): D9.

Roberts, Sam. "Dr. Joel Kovel, a Founder of Ecosocialism, Is Dead at 81." *New York Times*, First Section (Sun., May 6, 2018): 26.

Rosling, Hans. "The Magic Washing Machine." In *TEDWomen*. Washington, D.C., 2010.

Rothbard, Murray N. "Law, Property Rights, and Air Pollution." *Cato Journal* 2, no. 1 (Spring 1982): 55–99.

Rothstein, Edward. "Exhibition Review; Hall of Human Origins; Searching the Bones of Our Shared Past." *New York Times* (Fri., March 19, 2010): C25 & C32.

Ruddiman, William F. *Plows, Plagues, and Petroleum: How Humans Took Control of Climate*. Princeton, N.J.: Princeton University Press, 2005.

Sabin, Paul. *The Bet: Paul Ehrlich, Julian Simon, and Our Gamble over Earth's Future*. New Haven, Conn.: Yale University Press, 2013.

Scheiber, Noam. "Known Unknowns." *New York Times Book Review* (Sun., Nov. 4, 2012): 12.

Schmitt, Harrison H., and William Happer. "Opinion; in Defense of Carbon Dioxide; the Demonized Chemical Compound Is a Boon to Plant Life and Has Little Correlation with Global Temperature." *Wall Street Journal* (Thurs., May 9, 2013): A19.

Schumpeter, Joseph A. *Capitalism, Socialism and Democracy*. 3rd ed. New York: Harper and Row, 1950 (first edition was 1942).

Schwarcz, Joe. *The Right Chemistry: 108 Enlightening, Nutritious, Health-Conscious and Occasionally Bizarre Inquiries into the Science of Daily Life*. Toronto, Ontario: Doubleday Canada, 2012.

Schwartz, John. "Exxon in Deal with Company to Advance Carbon Capture Technology." *New York Times* (Fri., May 6, 2016a): B2.

Schwartz, John. "Kind to the Planet, Not to Bats." *New York Times* (Tues., Nov. 15, 2016b): D2.

Scott, Julia. "Maple Syrup; Old-Fashioned Product, Newfangled Means of Production." *New York Times*, First Section (Sun., March 31, 2013): 11.

Searchinger, Timothy, Ralph Heimlich, R. A. Houghton, Fengxia Dong, Amani Elobeid, Jacinto Fabiosa, Simla Tokgoz, Dermot Hayes, and Tun-Hsiang Yu. "Use of U.S. Croplands for Biofuels Increases Greenhouse Gases through Emissions from Land-Use Change." *Science* 319, no. 5867 (Feb. 29, 2008): 1238–40.

Searle, Stephanie Y., Danielle S. Bitterman, Samuel Thomas, Kevin L. Griffin, Owen K. Atkin, and Matthew H. Turnbull. "Respiratory Alternative Oxidase Responds to Both Low- and High-Temperature Stress in Quercus Rubra Leaves Along an Urban-Rural Gradient in New York." *Functional Ecology* 25, no. 5 (Oct. 2011): 1007–17.

Selinske, Carol. "Letters; Cancer, Then and Now." *New York Times* (Tues., Jan. 4, 2011): D4.

Sengupta, Somini. "In Silt, Bangladesh Sees Potential Shield against Sea Level Rise." *New York Times* (Fri., March 20, 2009): A6.

Shapiro, Beth. *How to Clone a Mammoth: The Science of De-Extinction*. Princeton, N.J.: Princeton University Press, 2015.

Shermer, Michael. "Menace to the Planet?" *Wall Street Journal* (Sat., Oct. 5, 2013): C10.

Shteir, Rachel. "Chicago Manuals." *New York Times Book Review* (Sun., April 21, 2013): 1 & 20–21.

Silver, Nate. *The Signal and the Noise: Why So Many Predictions Fail — But Some Don't*. New York: The Penguin Press, 2012.

Simon, Julian L. *The Ultimate Resource 2*. Princeton, N.J.: Princeton University Press, 1996.

Smith, Craig S. "How a Changing Climate Helps Add Color to a Leaf Peeper's Paradise." *New York Times* (Thurs., Nov. 3, 2016): A20.

Smith-Spangler, Crystal, Margaret L. Brandeau, Grace E. Hunter, J. Clay Bavinger, Maren Pearson, Paul J. Eschbach, Vandana Sundaram, Liu Hau, Patricia Schirmer, Christopher Stave, Ingram Olkin, and Dena M. Bravata. "Are Organic Foods Safer or Healthier Than Conventional Alternatives?" *Annals of Internal Medicine* 157, no. 5 (2012): 348–66.

Soble, Jonathan. "Japan Lost Nearly a Million People in 5 Years, Census Says." *New York Times* (Sat., Feb. 27, 2016): A12.

St. Fleur, Nicholas. "One Resident of the Sea, Unlike Many, Is Thriving." *New York Times*, (Weds., May 25, 2016): A7.

Stark, Peter. *Astoria: John Jacob Astor and Thomas Jefferson's Lost Pacific Empire: A Story of Wealth, Ambition, and Survival*. New York: Ecco, 2014.

Stephens, Bret. "Freaked Out Over Superfreakonomics; Global Warming Might Be Solved with a Helium Balloon and a Few Miles of Garden Hose." *Wall Street Journal* (Tues., Oct. 27, 2009): A19.

Stewart, James B. "Common Sense; New Chipotle Mantra: Safe (and Fresh) Food." *Wall Street Journal* (Fri., Jan. 15, 2016): B1 & B4.

Strom, Stephanie. "Private Analysis Shows a Sharp Increase in the Number of Organic Food Recalls." *New York Times* (Fri., Aug. 21, 2015): B3.

Strom, Stephanie. "A Science Project with Legs." *New York Times* (Tues., Nov. 5, 2013): D3.

Suri, Manil. "Mathematicians and Blue Crabs." *New York Times*, SundayReview Section (Sun., May 3, 2015): 4.

Sweet, Cassandra. "High-Tech Solar Plants Fail to Deliver." *Wall Street Journal* (Sat., June 13, 2015): B1 & B4.

Switek, Brian. "Bookshelf; Chewing over History." *Wall Street Journal* (Weds., May 31, 2017): A15.

Swoboda, Aaron. "Review of: The Economics of Climate Change: Adaptations Past and Present." *Journal of Economic Literature* 50, no. 1 (March 2012): 222–24.

Taylor, Timothy. "Recommendations for Further Reading." *Journal of Economic Perspectives* 29, no. 2 (Spring 2015): 259–66.

Thomas, Chris D. *Inheritors of the Earth: How Nature Is Thriving in an Age of Extinction*. New York: PublicAffairs, 2017.

Tortorello, Michael. "Seeds of an Era Long Gone." *New York Times* (Thurs., Nov. 22, 2012): D1 & D6.

Tuomisto, H. L., I. D. Hodge, P. Riordan, and D. W. Macdonald. "Does Organic Farming Reduce Environmental Impacts?—a Meta-Analysis of European Research." *Journal of Environmental Management* 112 (Dec. 15, 2012): 309–20.

Turner, Matthew A., Jeffrey S. Rosenthal, Jian Chen, and Chunyan Hao. "Adaptation to Climate Change in Preindustrial Iceland." *American Economic Review* 102, no. 3 (May 2012): 250–55.

Ungar, Peter S. *Evolution's Bite: A Story of Teeth, Diet, and Human Origins*. Princeton, NJ: Princeton University Press, 2017.

van Heerwaarden, Belinda, and Carla M. Sgrò. "Is Adaptation to Climate Change Really Constrained in Niche Specialists?" *Proceedings of the Royal Society B: Biological Sciences* 281, no. 1790 (Sept. 7, 2014): 1–1.

Wade, Nicholas. "Mammoth Hemoglobin Offers More Clues to Its Arctic Evolution." *New York Times* (Tues., May 4, 2010): D3.

Wagner, Gernot, and Martin L. Weitzman. "Book Excerpt: Climate Shock." *Milken Institute Review* 17, no. 2 (Second Quarter 2015a): 26–33.

Wagner, Gernot, and Martin L. Weitzman. *Climate Shock: The Economic Consequences of a Hotter Planet*. Princeton, N.J.: Princeton University Press, 2015b.

Wald, Matthew L. "Calls to Use a Proposed Nuclear Site, Now Deemed Safe." *New York Times* (Fri., Oct. 17, 2014a): A20.

Wald, Matthew L. "Nuclear Waste Solution Seen in Desert Salt Beds." *New York Times* (Mon., Feb. 10, 2014b): A9-A10.

Wald, Matthew L. "Deal Advances Development of a Smaller Nuclear Reactor." *New York Times* (Thurs., Feb. 21, 2013): B6.

Wattenberg, Ben J. *Fewer: How the New Demography of Depopulation Will Shape Our Future*. Chicago: Ivan R. Dee, Publisher, 2004.

Weintraub, Karen. "Black and White: Big Colony of Penguins Is Spotted near Antarctica." *New York Times* (Tues., March 13, 2018): D2.

Weintraub, Karen. "In Splash of Colors, Signs of Hope for Coral Reefs." *New York Times* (Tues., Aug. 16, 2016): D1 & D6.

Weisman, Alan. *The World Without Us*. New York: Thomas Dunne Books, 2007.

Welton, Luke J., Cameron D. Siler, Daniel Bennett, Arvin Diesmos, M. Roy Duya, Roldan Dugay, Edmund Leo B. Rico, Merlijn Van Weerd, and Rafe M. Brown. "A Spectacular New Philippine Monitor Lizard Reveals a Hidden Biogeographic Boundary and a Novel Flagship Species for Conservation." *Biology Letters* (April 7, 2010).

Whelan, Nathan V., Paul D. Johnson, and Phil M. Harris. "Rediscovery of *Leptoxis Compacta* (Anthony, 1854) (Gastropoda: Cerithioidea: Pleuroceridae)." *PLoS ONE* 7, no. 8 (Aug. 2012): 1–6.

Willerslev, Eske, John Davison, Mari Moora, Martin Zobel, Eric Coissac, Mary E. Edwards, Eline D. Lorenzen, Mette Vestergård, Galina Gussarova, James Haile, Joseph Craine, Ludovic Gielly, Sanne Boessenkool, Laura S. Epp, Peter B. Pearman, Rachid Cheddadi, David Murray, Kari Anne Bråthen, Nigel Yoccoz, and Heather Binney. "Fifty Thousand Years of Arctic Vegetation and Megafaunal Diet." *Nature* 506, no. 7486 (Feb. 6, 2014): 47–51.

Williams, David L., Charles P. Gerba, Sherri Maxwell, and Ryan G. Sinclair. "Assessment of the Potential for Cross-Contamination of Food Products by Reusable Shopping Bags." *Food Protection Trends* 31, no. 8 (Aug. 2011): 508–13.

Wilson-Rich, Noah. "Are Bees Back Up on Their Knees?" *New York Times* (Thurs., Sept. 25, 2014): A27.

Wines, Michael. "Human Role in Warming of Northwest Played Down." *New York Times* (Tues., Sept. 23, 2014a): A19.

Wines, Michael. "Though Scorned by Colleagues, a Climate-Change Skeptic Is Unbowed." *New York Times* (Weds., July 16, 2014b): A14.

Yandle, Bruce. "How Earth Day Triggered Environmental Rent Seeking." *Independent Review* 18, no. 1 (Summer 2013): 35–47.

Zimmer, Carl. "In Ancient Skeletons, Scientists Discover a Modern Foe: Hepatitis B." *New York Times* (Thurs., May 10, 2018): A9.

Zimmer, Carl. "Matter; Study Gives Hope of Adaptation to Climate Change." *New York Times* (Tues., July 29, 2014): D7.

Ziska, Lewis H., James A. Bunce, Hiroyuki Shimono, David R. Gealy, Jeffrey T. Baker, Paul C. D. Newton, Matthew P. Reynolds, Krishna S. V. Jagadish, Chunwu Zhu, Mark Howden, and Lloyd T. Wilson. "Food Security and Climate Change: On the Potential to Adapt Global Crop Production by Active Selection to Rising Atmospheric Carbon Dioxide." *Proceedings of the Royal Society B: Biological Sciences* 279, no. 1745 (Oct. 22, 2012): 4097–105.

Zuckerman, Gregory. *The Frackers: The Outrageous Inside Story of the New Billionaire Wildcatters.* New York: Portfolio/Penguin, 2013.

FEASIBILITY CLAIMS IN THE DEBATE OVER ANARCHY VERSUS THE MINIMAL STATE

BRAD R. TAYLOR[*]

1. Introduction

Feasibility is a concept often invoked but rarely defined in political argument. We hear claims such as "Your ideas are good in principle, but wouldn't work in practice" or "Sure, but that's never going to happen," but the precise content of such claims is often unclear. Feasibility or practicality is obviously important and must in some sense be a hard constraint on political argument if political argument is meant to serve a practical purpose. It does not matter how good the proposed solution would be; the fact of infeasibility acts as a trump card removing any need for a balancing of feasibility against desirability. We need not entertain impossible ideas, even really good ones.

The idea of feasibility as a constraint on institutions and policy has played an important role in the argument for libertarian institutions. Buchanan's (1984) characterization of public choice theory as "politics without romance" and Munger's (2014) gentle mocking of "unicorn governance" have been powerful responses to those putting excessive faith in the willingness and ability of government to solve social problems. It may be possible to imagine an ideal set of policies through which a wise and

---

[*]Brad R. Taylor is lecturer in economics and political economy at the University of Southern Queensland.

CITATION INFORMATION FOR THIS ARTICLE:

Brad R. Taylor. 2018. "Feasibility Claims in the Debate over Anarchy versus the Minimal State." *Libertarian Papers*. 10 (2): 277-293. ONLINE AT: libertarianpapers.org. THIS ARTICLE IS subject to a Creative Commons Attribution 3.0 License (creativecommons.org/licenses/).

benevolent dictator can produce a desirable result, but any real-world proposal relying on such assumptions is rightly dismissed as infeasible.

Feasibility arguments have also divided libertarian scholars. Anarchists and minarchists routinely accuse each other of making utopian arguments. I here consider these disagreements in light of the philosophical literature on political feasibility with the aim of both clarifying the points of disagreement in the debate on anarchy versus limited government and interrogating the role of feasibility considerations in political argument. I suggest that anarchists and minarchists often talk past each other because they are adopting different concepts of feasibility without clearly specifying their meaning. The dispute here is not merely a verbal one, but the argument turns on a variety of positive and normative questions that are often masked by loose talk about feasibility. This has lessons for the concept of feasibility more generally. The diversity of feasibility claims we see in political argument is too great to be captured by a single formulation, despite what recent work in political philosophy has attempted. I suggest that the concept of feasibility should be disaggregated using the method of elimination, and I show how this helps structure political argument and reveals sources of disagreement.

2. Feasibility in Political Theory

Political theorists have traditionally drawn a sharp distinction between questions of desirability and feasibility, roughly how good something would be if brought about versus how realistic it is to expect it could be brought about (Raikka 1998). For the most part, what precisely we mean by "feasibility" has been ignored, but a number of analytic political philosophers have recently become interested in the concept and sought to provide some conceptual clarity. Brennan and Southwood (2007, 10) consider a feasible action to be one with a "reasonable probability of success conditional upon trying." Gilabert and Lawford-Smith (2012, 4) see feasibility as a four-place predicate: "It is feasible for X to φ to bring about O in Z," with X being some agent, φ being some action, O being some outcome, and Z being some context. Wiens (2015) provides a vision of feasibility as a generalization of the familiar production possibility frontier from economics.[1]

Although these accounts differ in detail, they are united by an attempt to construct a general formulation of the concept of feasibility. It is this project I reject. I instead argue that the concept of feasibility should be

---

[1] See also Brennan (2013), Lawford-Smith (2013b, 2013a), Southwood and Wiens (2016), and Wiens (2013).

disaggregated rather than clarified as a singular concept in political argument. In similar spirit, Hamlin (2017) considers the extant philosophical literature on feasibility and finds four distinct types of feasibility claim not easily reduced to a simple formulation. I am in basic agreement with Hamlin's analysis but take his argument a step further. Whereas Hamlin provides a more nuanced conceptualization of feasibility, I suggest that political argument would proceed more smoothly if we were willing to give up the term "feasibility" (and related terms such as "realistic," "practical," and "utopian") altogether and instead say what we mean using more precise causal or counterfactual language. I lay out this method of elimination in section 6.

Consider the Gilabert and Lawford-Smith (2012) formulation of feasibility outlined above, for example. If this formulation is to capture the variety of feasibility claims we see in political argument, each predicate will be able to take on wildly different sorts of value. As I will show below, some but not all feasibility claims are agent relative, meaning that agent X will sometimes be undefined or at least defined rather vaguely. Actions φ can be made by individuals, but to fit many feasibility claims into this schema we would also need to include policies and policy proposals into this formulation. Outcomes can also be quite different, ranging from political and policy outcomes to social and economic ones. Considering all the dimensions along which feasibility claims can vary, I contend, a general formulation of feasibility that helps rather than hinders political argument is, if not strictly impossible, at least infeasible.

3. Feasibility Claims in the Anarchy vs. Minimal-State Debate

As a case study in feasibility claims made in political argument, I examine the debate between free market anarchists and small-government libertarians. This is a useful case study for two reasons. First, within these debates there is a reasonably strong (although not perfect) agreement on desirability, meaning that disagreements are primarily grounded in feasibility issues. Secondly, there is a rich source of written material, from academic journals and books to magazines and blog posts. This frequent back and forth provides a solid data source.

Anarchists claim we should have no state at all (e.g., D. Friedman 1989; Rothbard 1973; Stringham 2015); minarchists claim that we should have a minimal state restricted to a few basic functions (e.g., Buchanan 1975; M.

Friedman 1962; Nozick 1974; Rand 1964).[2] Both anarchists and minarchists have accused their opponents of being utopian (i.e., advocating the infeasible). In this section, I outline these feasibility arguments. I make no attempt to evaluate the arguments; the purpose is simply to tease out what exactly is being claimed when the concept of feasibility is deployed. My aim here is to sample the arguments made by a few influential libertarian scholars rather than conduct a comprehensive review of the literature.

4. Anarchy as Utopian

Any (outcome-sensitive) libertarian anarchist will presumably accept the following propositions:

(i) If implemented and maintained, the "policy outcome" of statelessness is sufficiently likely to produce a situation in which individual rights are respected.

(ii) If implemented, the policy outcome of statelessness is sufficiently likely be maintained (i.e., it is stable).

(iii) Statelessness can be implemented.

Each of these propositions can be disputed on feasibility grounds. Someone philosophically opposed to libertarian anarchism could deny that anarchism is desirable even while endorsing (i)–(iii) as true, because they do not consider the (factually undisputed) outcomes of statelessness preferable to the relevant alternatives.[3] This is not a feasibility claim, but rather a desirability claim. A minarchist could also endorse (i)–(iii) as true but reject anarchism on the grounds that they see a minimal state as more desirable than orderly anarchy. This is likewise not a feasibility claim, since such claims must in some sense take desirability as given. In broad terms, we might say that any argument against (i), (ii), or (iii) is a feasibility argument.

---

[2] Minimal-government libertarians differ a great deal in terms of just what the state can legitimately do. Nozick and Rand restrict the minimal state to a basic law-and-order function, while others such as Buchanan and Hayek allow for the production of public goods and even some basic redistribution. Since I am here interested in feasibility concerns, I set aside these differences in this paper.

[3] Someone concerned with social justice or moral purity, for example, might accept completely the economic argument that anarchy promotes efficiency or liberty but deny that this makes anarchy more desirable than the relevant alternatives because anarchy produces distributional patterns or allows behaviour that their nonlibertarian value system deems undesirable (and sufficiently so to outweigh any positive weight given to efficiency or liberty).

There will of course be differences of opinion on the level of likelihood required to meet conditions (i) and (ii). Two libertarians might agree on the desirability of orderly anarchy and on the probability of anarchy becoming disorderly or producing a de facto state while disagreeing on whether such a gamble is worth the risk. Such a disagreement would come down to risk preference, and this is an issue of desirability rather than feasibility. The method of elimination endorsed here can be used to tease out which disagreements are due to differences in probability judgements and which are due to differences in risk preference. The statement "Anarchy would be good if orderly, but it is too risky" is vague and can be made more precise by eliminating the term "too risky." For the statement to be taken seriously, some probability judgment and probability standard must be specified.[4] If thus reformulated, the statement would be made more precise and argument could focus on the real grounds of disagreement; if not, the statement can be conditionally rejected as meaningless until it is reformulated in more precise terms.

Each of these propositions has been attacked by non-anarchist libertarians. We can classify these arguments as (a) policy-effect arguments (those rejecting [i]); (b) policy-stability arguments (those rejecting [ii]); and (c) political-accessibility arguments (those rejecting [iii]). Below I discuss prominent examples from each category.

a) Policy effect

Anarchists argue that voluntary transactions will secure an acceptable level of social order and liberty. This claim has, to put it mildly, received a good deal of criticism, even among fairly radical libertarians. The criticism I am interested in here is the claim that anarchism, if realized (in the sense that anarchists have their way and the state ceases to exist), would produce, with certainty or with unacceptably high probability, violence and disorder. I take this to be a feasibility argument in the sense that it claims a political outcome would not produce the social outcome intended by its advocates. In political theory, the idea is normally traced to Hobbes; among libertarians and classical liberals, Ayn Rand and James M. Buchanan hold variants of this view.

---

[4] These need not be precise point estimates or standards. For example, the claim "Anarchy would certainly be too risky if there were a 5 percent chance of disorder, and although I am not confident of the exact probability I am confident it is greater than 5 percent" would be a meaningful statement that would allow productive argument on both the estimate and the threshold.

Rand (1964, ch. 14) argues that anarchy is incapable of protecting individual rights. She gives two reasons for this view. First, lacking a centralized coercive power, individuals would be vulnerable to the whims of nasty people. Rand (1964, 104) concludes that "if a society left the retaliatory use of force in the hands of individual citizens, it would degenerate into mob rule, lynch law and an endless series of bloody private feuds or vendettas." Second, decentralized enforcement is inconsistent with the enforcement of "objective law": "Even a society whose every member were fully rational and faultlessly moral, could not function in a state of anarchy; it is the need of objective laws and of an arbiter for honest disagreements among men that necessitates the establishment of a government" (Rand 1964, 107).

There are two feasibility claims here:

> **Rand's Hobbesian social undesirability**: Anarchy would lead to constant violence and rights violations. Thus, the anarchist's proposed policy of statelessness is an infeasible means of securing the desired social outcome of liberty.[5]
>
> **Rand's imperfect liberty**: There is no possible way for the anarchist's policy proposal to perfectly achieve the desired social outcome of respect for libertarian rights.

Buchanan's argument against anarchism is more developed than Rand's and more explicitly based on the Hobbesian state of nature and feasibility concerns. Buchanan (1975, 5) endorses anarchism as a philosophical doctrine: "To the individualist, the ideal or utopian world is necessarily anarchistic in some basic philosophical sense." Although the utopian anarchist vision of everybody respecting each other's rights is appealing, Buchanan sees it as a "conceptual mirage" since absent a unanimously agreed set of rights, there can be no perfect respect for those rights. This argument is similar to Rand's "imperfect liberty" argument, but Buchanan is not willing to hold up objective law as a meaningful standard of comparison. Buchanan's point is simply that utopian (i.e., conflict-free) anarchy is a logical impossibility as long as there is some disagreement over the assignment of rights and the boundaries of individual autonomy. Rand treats this as an argument for government because she believes there is an objective law that the government ought to enforce; Buchanan makes no such claim and sees

---

[5] It is not entirely clear whether Rand thinks the Hobbesian outcome is a certainty or merely very likely. Her use of terms such as "cannot" and "would" suggests the former, but interpretation is complicated by the fact that Rand reacted to criticisms of her argument against anarchy by cancelling the critic's subscription to the *Objectivist* rather than responding to the arguments (see Stringham 2007, 6–7).

disagreement over rights as a problem that does not disappear with the emergence of a state. The comparison is, as always, between two imperfect alternatives (Buchanan 1984; Demsetz 1969).

Buchanan does, however, argue that disagreement in anarchy would produce disorder for basically Hobbesian reasons: without external enforcement mechanisms, individuals would have incentives for predation rather than production, and this makes everybody worse off (Brennan and Buchanan 1985, ch. 1; Buchanan 1975, ch. 2; Buchanan 2005). Thus, according to Buchanan, the anarchist's claim that statelessness produces high levels of social order is mistaken. Although philosophically appealing on classical liberal grounds, it is unrealistic to expect anarchy to be orderly.

> **Buchanan's Hobbesian social undesirability:** Anarchy would lead to constant conflict and little cooperation. Thus the anarchist's proposed policy of statelessness would not produce the desired social outcome of Pareto nondominance by government.

b) Policy instability

Others have argued that although the Hobbesian view is overly pessimistic, libertarian anarchy would endogenously lead to the re-emergence of the state.[6] Cowen (1992, 268), for example, argues that "libertarian anarchy is not a stable equilibrium." Cowen accepts for the sake of argument that the Hobbesian jungle can be avoided through cooperation among competing protection agencies but claims that this ability to cooperate will itself lead to the emergence of a de facto state.[7] Similarly, Holcombe (2004, 326) argues that government is "unnecessary but inevitable" on the grounds that

---

[6] This view is sometimes attributed to Nozick (1974), though that is not quite correct. Nozick argued that a minimal state *could* emerge through voluntary interaction and used this as a normative justification for the minimal state. This does not imply that actual anarchy *would* lead to the re-emergence of the state.

[7] See also Cowen and Sutter (1999). Cowen's argument is perhaps best interpreted as the claim that anarchy would either be disorderly (if protection agencies cannot cooperate) or unstable (if they can). Caplan and Stringham (2003) respond by arguing that avoiding interagency war requires less cooperative efficacy than collusion since agreements to avoid war are self-enforcing whereas collusion is not. This gives rise to an anarchist "sweet spot" of intermediate interagency cooperation. Cowen and Sutter (2005) admit that such a sweet spot exists but argue that it will be small and thereby insist that orderly anarchy is unlikely. This is a slightly more complicated feasibility argument in that it states that depending on some uncertain conditions anarchy is either disorderly or unstable.

"without government—or even with a weak government—predatory groups will impose themselves on people by force and create a government to extract income and wealth from these subjects."

> **Cowen's political instability**: The proposed political outcome of statelessness is not a stable equilibrium. Even if the policy were implemented and would produce desirable social outcomes for as long as it existed, it would not exist for long.

Some libertarians accept that neither anarchism nor minimal-state libertarianism is a stable equilibrium, though minimal-state libertarianism is in some sense more stable. In a 1995 interview with *Reason* magazine, for example, Milton Friedman makes this claim (Doherty 1995):

> **Reason:** Why aren't you [a zero-government libertarian]?
>
> **Friedman:** Because I don't think it's a feasible social structure. I look over history, and outside of perhaps Iceland, where else can you find any historical examples of that kind of a system developing?
>
> **Reason:** One could argue the same thing about minimal-state libertarianism: that historically it seems to not be stable.
>
> **Friedman:** I agree. I wrote an article once arguing that a free society is an unstable equilibrium. Fundamentally, I'm of the opinion that it is. Though we want to try to keep that unstable equilibrium as long as we can! The United States from 1780 to 1929 is not a bad example of a limited-government libertarianism that lasted for a long time.

This raises the question of just how long an institution must survive to be considered stable, and as with the riskiness issue considered above, the method of elimination does not provide a definite answer but can be used to make stability claims more precise. Cowen's claim above would need to be reformulated in a way that specifies a time horizon. If anarchy lasted for only a day, it would surely be deemed unstable by any reasonable person, but requiring that a stateless society maintain itself for all time is an unreasonably high standard (Newhard 2016). To make an instability claim meaningful through the method of elimination, it must be reformulated in terms of the expected lifetime of the institution and a standard by which to judge it. As with riskiness, this reformulation need not make a definite prediction but needs to set reasonable parameters that can be debated openly.

c) Policy accessibility

Though it has received less attention in the academic literature than the other two categories of argument, a common argument in less formal debates among libertarians is the extent to which anarchy is achievable as a political goal. This is related to arguments about gradual versus radical change and the relative merits of activism within or outside existing political structures, though it is a distinct issue. Non-anarchist libertarians will often claim that anarchism is an infeasible proposal because it is unlikely to come about given current political realities; there is no path from here to there.

This is a feasibility argument in a sense quite different from the other two categories. Whereas rejecting (i) and (ii) would provide reasons against implementing anarchy if given a decisive choice,[8] rejection of (iii) provides no such reason but perhaps provides a reason not to waste one's time endorsing anarchism. If there is no way to bring anarchy about and we take action-guidingness to be a hard constraint on political theory, rejection of (iii) would lead us to exclude statelessness from the feasible set.

Though economists and political theorists tend to ignore in their formal writings the question of how to get "from here to there" in a practical sense, disagreements among libertarian academics on such matters are common in less formal settings such as dinner parties and non-academic essays. Holcombe's (2007) contribution to the *Cato Unbound* exchange on anarchy, for example, makes the argument that anarchism is not within the politically feasible set: "I have no quarrel with people who make those arguments [that anarchy is desirable], but from a policy perspective they are irrelevant. Government will be with us for the foreseeable future, so the real policy issue is not whether government should be eliminated but how to make it better." Holcombe sees the major barrier to implementation of anarchy in industrialized countries as the preferences of citizens: "American support for their government is the main reason why anarchy is completely infeasible from a policy perspective. Americans have it pretty good today, and they are not going to give up a reasonably comfortable status quo in exchange for an experiment in statelessness. So, regardless of its merits, anarchy has no prospect as an actual policy option. The bottom line is: in developed nations, most people support their government."

Many anarchists, such as the target of Holcombe's remarks, Peter Lesson, accept that anarchy is not a feasible option in this sense but see this as irrelevant to their position. In response, Leeson (2007a) writes: "I have not

---

[8] Some would dispute that instability is any argument against experimenting with anarchy. Rothbard, for example, argues that if the worst that can happen is that we get back to where we are, anarchy is a costless gamble that any rational person would take. As Cowen and Sutter and Holcombe emphasize, however, the state that re-emerges from anarchy could be much worse (i.e., less libertarian) than the one we abandon.

said anything that could be construed as identifying steps we could take to achieving anarchy in the U.S. Nor will I attempt to suggest how we might do this here. This is not because I do not think it is an important question. It is because I am not a political strategist, and this question of the political expediency of anarchy is really a question of political strategy." Later, Leeson (2007b) summarizes his response to the charge of infeasibility: "The political feasibility of anarchy does not in any way bear on the question of anarchy's superiority (or inferiority, depending upon one's position) to government." Leeson evidently does not see proposition (iii) as essential to his anarchism.[9]

5. The Minimal State as Utopian

Minarchists presumably endorse the following claims:

(i) If implemented and maintained, the "policy outcome" of the minimal state is sufficiently likely to produce a situation in which individual rights are respected.

(ii) If implemented, the policy outcome of a minimal state is sufficiently likely to be maintained (i.e., it is stable).

(iii) A minimal state can be implemented.

Many anarchists would reject (i) were it not for the qualification that the undesirability of other options is undisputed. There is little disagreement among libertarians on the desirability of a minimal state if that policy outcome can be implemented and maintained. Feasibility arguments against the minimal state are thus directed at propositions (ii) and (iii). As before, I label these "policy stability" and "policy accessibility" arguments.

a) Policy stability

Many anarchists (and pessimistic libertarians) see the idea that government can be limited to anything close to the size and scope imagined by minarchists as entirely fanciful. David Friedman (1989, 146–47), for example, concedes that a seriously restricted government capable of providing national defense and other public goods might be preferable to anarchy, but insists that no such limited government is possible:

---

[9] There are some related issues here about whether it's worthwhile advocating anarchy even if it's not a feasible option. In his contribution to the *Cato Unbound* conversation, Bruce Benson (2007) claims that having an ideal end-goal in mind is useful in structuring evaluations of incremental steps even if we think there is no chance of the goal ever being fully realized. We do not discuss these issues here.

> One cannot simply build any imaginable characteristics into a government; governments have their own internal dynamic. And the internal dynamic of limited governments is something with which we, to our sorrow, have a good deal of practical experience. It took about 150 years, starting with a Bill of Rights that reserved to the states and the people all powers not explicitly delegated to the federal government, to produce a Supreme Court willing to rule that growing corn to feed to your own hogs is interstate commerce and can therefore be regulated by Congress.

The logic of limited governments is to grow. There are obvious reasons for this in the nature of government, and plenty of evidence. Constitutions provide, at the most, a modest and temporary restraint. As Murray Rothbard is supposedly said, the idea of a limited government that stays limited is truly Utopian. Anarchy at least might work; limited government has been tried.

Here we seem to have a social-imperfection or political-instability claim as discussed above combined with the claim that we cannot be certain that anarchy has similar problems. Thus, we have a claim similar to but subtly different in form from those presented above.

b) Policy accessibility

Anarchists have argued that a minimal state is inaccessible in at least two ways: such an outcome is very unlikely or no individual has the capacity to bring about such an outcome. These are very different views of feasibility. The former is not agent relative and is essentially a probability claim. The latter is agent relative and more in line with Brennan and Southwood's (2007, 10) conception of feasibility as a "reasonable probability of success conditional upon trying." Here, it is not enough that the relevant outcome occurs, but that the relevant individual plays a sufficient role in bringing the outcome about. Patri Friedman (2009) makes both types of claim in his *Cato Unbound* essay "Beyond Folk Activism." His probability claim is that "libertarians are a minority, and we underperform in elections, so winning electoral victories is a hopeless endeavor." Thus, given the current political context, a minimal state is extremely unlikely. Instead of working within the system, Friedman argues libertarians should find ways to "make systemic changes, outside entrenched power structures, that could realistically lead to a freer world." For Friedman, this involves efforts to escape the power of the state geographically or economically. Friedman and Taylor (2010 2012) expand on this argument from a public choice perspective, arguing that since a single vote has virtually no chance of deciding an electoral outcome and very few people are capable of making a significant impact through political campaigning, the expected return of political activism is higher when working "outside the system" to undermine or sidestep government rather than attempting to influence policy.

6. Eliminating Feasibility

As we can see from the brief discussion above, anarchists and minarchists have deployed a number of different feasibility claims against one another in political argument. Some of these are agent relative, while others are not. Some concern the likely effects of a political outcome, others the accessibility or sustainability of an outcome. Rather than attempting to fit this diversity into a single formulation, I argue, we should take each argument on its own terms to determine whether its application of terms such as "feasibility" and "practicality" is covering for a lack of substantive argument.

The approach I take is the method of elimination. This was mentioned in passing by Richard Feynman (1969) as a way of determining whether an explanation of some phenomenon has been truly grasped. If an explanation using a scientific term such as "energy" or "gravity" cannot be rephrased in simpler language, then the explanation is a faulty one. Saying "Energy causes the car to move" does not mean anything unless the physical process through which this happens is to some sense understood in more basic terms. Chalmers (2011) introduces the method as a way of resolving philosophical disputes, and Bosworth (forthcoming) extends this to political argument. If there is disagreement on a proposition containing a vague term, the proposition should be capable of being rephrased until the vagueness is removed. If a political proposition cannot be rephrased once key terms are eliminated, this is proof of its nonsubstantiveness.

If an advocate of the minimal state accuses an anarchist of advocating the infeasible, we should demand that they rephrase their assertion in more basic terms. If they are making a meaningful statement, this should be possible. If they are unable to rephrase their statement without using vague terms such as "practical" or "feasible," the method of elimination tells us to reject the proposition as empty rhetoric, at least until somebody does find an acceptable rephrase of the argument in question. A single round of elimination will not resolve all disagreement, of course, but as the process is repeated, vagueness is reduced and the real grounds of disagreement are laid bare.

Thus the claim that orderly anarchy is unstable must be rephrased as a claim that some specific state of affairs meets some (presumably comparative) threshold of probability conditional on some action or event. This does not resolve the disagreement, of course, but helps reveal its source. Do the participants disagree on what constitutes a reasonable standard of feasibility or on the probabilities? If the former, we could have a disagreement on desirability rather than feasibility (e.g., on risk preference) or a merely verbal dispute. If a participant is unable to reformulate their argument in agreed-upon language, we either have a meaningless statement or an irreconcilable breakdown in political argument.

This is not to say that the use of terms such as "feasible" is completely off limits, only that anyone using them should be willing to rephrase in simpler terms if challenged. Many uses of the concept of feasibility remain useful. For example, Newhard (2016, 221) argues that "the emergence of a single stateless pocket of effective, privately provided defense for a 'reasonable' length of time is sufficient to affirm feasibility." By defining "feasibility," Newhard has in a sense pre-emptively eliminated it.[10] However, not everyone would agree that this is an appropriate definition of "feasibility," and this could lead to a debate over which definition better captures everyday usage or the relevant considerations for political argument. The method of elimination allows us to avoid this battle over definitions and instead focus on substantive differences in factual or normative judgements.

7. Conclusion

Feasibility is a crucial element of practical ethics and political theory, and I agree with theorists arguing that more precision and analytical rigor is required when making feasibility claims. I disagree, however, on the feasibility of constructing a general formulation of feasibility. As the above analysis has shown, feasibility claims take a variety of forms and are not easily reduced to a common formulation. Rather than defining "feasibility" as a general concept, I have argued that the term should be capable of being eliminated in political argument, with the claims deploying the concept rephrased in more basic terms agreed on by the parties to the argument.

For those engaged in debates over the feasibility of anarchy and the minimal state, this paper has outlined a useful tool for clarifying the source of disagreement and enforcing substantive argument rather than empty rhetoric or conceptual gerrymandering (Bosworth forthcoming; Dowding and Bosworth forthcoming). Anarchists and minarchists often talk past one another when using vague terms such as "practicality" and "utopian." A willingness to eliminate such loose talk and rephrase in mutually agreeable

---

[10] This definition remains vague, most obviously in what constitutes a reasonable length of time, and these terms may also be subject to elimination if they give rise to confusion or disagreement.

language can redirect argument to the real grounds of disagreement, which may be empirical or normative.

My claim that the term "feasibility" ought to be eliminated in certain circumstances should not be taken to mean that the concept is meaningless or unimportant. Rather, my claim is that, like the concept of desirability, it is too rich and contested to be adequately captured by a single conception precise enough to evaluate alternative policies or institutions. There are a number of concerns that can usefully be thrown in the feasibility bucket, and these are often closely related to one another. As the examples above have shown, however, there is no consensus even among libertarians on what policies and institutions count as feasible or infeasible. Arguments over definitions can obscure the real source of disagreement. To make progress, we should be willing to empty the bucket and consider the contents on their own terms.

References

Benson, B. L. 2007. "Anarchical Policy Analysis." *Cato Unbound*, August 17. http://www.cato-unbound.org/2007/08/17/bruce-l-benson/anarchical-policy-analysis.

Bosworth, W. forthcoming. "An Interpretation of Political Argument, an Interpretation of Political Argument." *European Journal of Political Theory*.

Brennan, G. 2013. "Feasibility in Optimizing Ethics." *Social Philosophy and Policy*, 301–2, 314–29.

Brennan, G., and J. M. Buchanan. 1985. *The Reason of Rules: Constitutional Political Economy*. Cambridge: Cambridge University Press.

Brennan, G., and N. Southwood. 2007. "Feasibility in Action and Attitude." In *Hommage a Wlodek: Philosophical Papers Dedicated to Wlodek Rabinowicz*, edited by T. Ronnow-Rasmussen, B. Petersson, J. Jonefsson, and D. Egonsson. http://www.fil.lu.se/hommageawlodek/index.htm.

Buchanan, J. M. 1975. *The Limits of Liberty: Between Anarchy and Leviathan*. Chicago: University of Chicago Press.

Buchanan, J. M. 1984. "Politics without Romance: A Sketch of Positive Public Choice Theory and Its Normative Implications." In *The Theory of Public Choice II*, edited by J. M Buchanan and R. D. Tollison, 11–22. Ann Arbor, MI: University of Michigan Press.

Buchanan, J. M. 2005. "Before Public Choice." In *Anarchy, State and Public Choice*, edited by E. Stringham, 77–87. Cheltenham, UK: Edward Elgar.

Caplan, B., and E. Stringham. 2003. "Networks, Law, and the Paradox of Cooperation." *Review of Austrian Economics* 164: 309–26.

Chalmers, D. J. 2011. "Verbal Disputes." *Philosophical Review* 1204: 515–66.

Cowen, T. 1992. "Law as a Public Good: The Economics of Anarchy." *Economics and Philosophy* 82: 249–67.

Cowen, T., and D. Sutter. 1999. "The Costs of Cooperation." *Review of Austrian Economics* 122: 161–73.

Cowen, T., and D. Sutter. 2005. "Conflict, Cooperation and Competition in Anarchy." *Review of Austrian Economics* 181: 109–15.

Demsetz, H. 1969. "Information and Efficiency: Another Viewpoint." *Journal of Law and Economics* 121: 1–22.

Doherty, B. 1995. "Best of Both Worlds: An Interview with Milton Friedman." *Reason*, June. http://reason.com/archives/1995/06/01/best-of-both-worlds.

Dowding, K., and Bosworth, W. Forthcoming. "Ambiguity and Vagueness in Political Terminology: On Coding and Referential Imprecision." *European Journal of Political Theory*.

Feynman, R. 1969. "What Is Science?" *Physics Teacher* 76: 313–20.

Friedman, D. D. 1989. *The Machinery of Freedom: Guide to a Radical Capitalism*. 2nd ed. La Salle, IL: Open Court Publishing.

Friedman, M. 1962. *Capitalism and Freedom*. Chicago: University of Chicago Press.

Friedman, 2009, April 6. "Beyond Folk Activism." *Cato Unbound*. http://www.cato-unbound.org/2009/04/06/patri-friedman/beyond-folk-activism/.

Friedman, P., and B. R. Taylor. 2010. "Seasteading: Institutional Innovation on the Open Ocean." Presented at the Australasian Public Choice Society Conference, University of Canterbury.

Friedman, P., and B. R. Taylor. 2012. "Seasteading: Competitive Governments on the Ocean." *Kyklos* 652: 218–35.

Gilabert, P., and H. Lawford-Smith. 2012. "Political Feasibility: A Conceptual Exploration." *Political Studies* 604: 809–25.

Hamlin, A. 2017. "Feasibility Four Ways." *Social Philosophy and Policy* 341: 209–31.

Holcombe, R. G. 2004. "Government: Unnecessary but Inevitable." *Independent Review* 83: 325–42.

Holcombe, Randall G. 2007. "Anarchy from a Policy Perspective." *Cato Unbound*, August 13. http://www.cato-unbound.org/2007/08/13/randall-g-holcombe/anarchy-policy-perspective.

Lawford-Smith, H. 2013a. "Non-ideal Accessibility." *Ethical Theory and Moral Practice* 163: 653–69.

Lawford-Smith, H. 2013b. "Understanding Political Feasibility." *Journal of Political Philosophy* 213: 243–59.

Leeson, T. 2007a. "Clarifying Matters." *Cato Unbound*, August 20. http://www.cato-unbound.org/2007/08/20/peter-t-leeson/clarifying-matters.

Leeson, T. 2007b. "A Stock-Taking." *Cato Unbound*, August 21. http://www.cato-unbound.org/2007/08/21/peter-t-leeson/stock-taking.

Munger, M. 2014. "Unicorn Governance." Foundation for Economic Education. https://fee.org/articles/unicorn-governance/.

Newhard, J. M. 2016. "On the Conspicuous Absence of Private Defense." *Libertarian Papers* 82: 221–34.

Nozick, R. 1974. *Anarchy, State, and Utopia*. New York: Basic Books.

Raikka, J. 1998. "The Feasibility Condition in Political Theory." *Journal of Political Philosophy* 61: 27–40.

Rand, A. 1964. *The Virtue of Selfishness*. New York: New American Library.

Rothbard, M. N. 1973. *For a New Liberty*. New York: Macmillan.

Southwood, N., and D. Wiens. 2016. "'Actual' Does Not Imply 'Feasible.'" *Philosophical Studies* 17311: 3037–60.

Stringham, E. 2015. *Private Governance: Creating Order in Economic and Social Life*. Oxford: Oxford University Press.

Stringham, E. 2007. "Introduction." In *Anarchy and the Law: The Political Economy of Choice*, edited by E. Stringham, 1–17. New Brunswick, NJ: Transaction Publishers.

Wiens, D. 2013. "Demands of Justice, Feasible Alternatives, and the Need for Causal Analysis." *Ethical Theory and Moral Practice* 162: 325–38.

Wiens, D. 2015. "Political Ideals and the Feasibility Frontier." *Economics & Philosophy* 313: 447–77.

On Banking, Credit, and Inflation

Spencer Heath[*]

IT IS OFTEN SAID that what anyone doesn't know doesn't hurt him. Where ignorance is bliss 'tis folly to be wise. But ignorance is not bliss. Ignorance is almost always fear, and our most constant fears are our fears of the unknown. It is what we do not know that gives us most anxiety and pain. We feel helpless in the presence of that which we do not understand. In the world of making a living, in the world of business, that is, perhaps nothing is less understood and, therefore, nothing more feared than inflation. Let us take a look at it. What is it that gets swelled up—inflated?

Now business has to do with wealth, and with the services that create wealth, and all proper business transactions consist in the exchanging of wealth and services for other people's wealth and services. And, during the course of these exchanges, wealth that is of low value (like raw or only partly finished materials) comes to have higher and higher value by reason of more and more services being incorporated in it, or in some way performed upon it, until, at last, there is nothing more to be done to it, and it is then, and not until then, a finished product; for it is then in the hands of its consumer and is then, literally, the consumer's own goods.

So, over the full course of production, there is rising value in a commodity, and in the course of its consumption there is a corresponding decline. During all the complex changes that lead to the final production of

---

[*]This fragment is Item 138 from the *Spencer Heath Archive*. According to a pencil notation, this article was never published. There is no date, but there is a notice of "Copyright Pending," so a date might be found by inquiring at the Copyright Office.

CITATION INFORMATION FOR THIS ARTICLE:
Spencer Heath. 2018. "On Banking, Credit, and Inflation." *Libertarian Papers*. 10 (2): 295-299. ONLINE AT: libertarianpapers.org. THIS ARTICLE IS subject to a Creative Commons Attribution 3.0 License (creativecommons.org/licenses).

the goods into the hand of the consumer, it is necessary that a record be kept of their value at each point of sale or transfer. If this could not be done, all exchange would have to be by barter and not by sale, for it is only by assigning values to them that goods can be sold; and markets are places where these values are assigned.

Barter is a transaction that is completed in one act—a completed exchange of goods for goods. But selling and buying divides the exchange transaction into two parts, with an interval of time in between. Goods are first delivered and then, after a time and usually in much variety, other goods are received in exchange. During this interval an account must be kept, and this account is kept either by a transfer of currency or by a transfer of bank credits from the receiver of the goods to him who has delivered them. When, finally, the exchange of goods for goods has been completed by other goods being received in exchange, there is a further transfer of the currency or credits to those who supply the goods finally received and completing the exchange.

Thus we see that currency and credits are only the records—the account keeping—of uncompleted exchanges. They are the symbols of the values of goods, and with every transfer of goods in one direction there is a flow of corresponding currency or credits in the reverse direction. The soundness of the accounts—the honesty of the currency or credits—therefore, depends, first, upon the goods having been given, of which the credits are merely the record (although we call them purchase price) and, second, their soundness depends upon further goods being produced and delivered to support the value, that is, the purchasing power, of the currency or credits.

Now, so long as currency and credits, which are called the instruments of exchange, are created only by the delivery of goods and services they will go hand in hand with such goods and services and will serve as the equitable instruments and measurement for other goods to be received in exchange, and in all this there will be neither inflation nor deflation. But let the account be falsified by any action that increases the amount of currency or credits or obligations, without supplying or performing any corresponding goods or services, and we have inflation. Our books of record do not correspond with our wealth, our increased obligations cannot be met in goods, and our currency and credits lose their value as instruments of exchange, for we do not have the goods in adequate amount to satisfy the increase of credits or obligations. Conversely, any action that cuts down the production of wealth has the same inflationary effect, for it makes a disproportion between the existing currency and credits and the amount of wealth coming into being to satisfy them.

Essentially, then, any action is inflationary that tends to cause disparity between the amount of wealth being produced and exchanged and the currency and credits which are the records of uncompleted exchanges and are, therefore, the measuring instruments by which exchanges of wealth and services are completed. These instruments come into being through the need of keeping accounts in trade and exchange. Traders always create them, hand in hand, with their uncompleted transactions in goods and services. When so created they are called credits.

Credits created by governments are called money and currency. Currency is not issued as the record of any uncompleted exchanges. Unless it has some intrinsic or redemption value, it is wholly fiat and inflationary, and it operates to transfer wealth without giving any wealth in exchange. And by positive enactments of law, nothing but currency is legal tender when public power and authority is invoked to enforce private obligations. Since very few obligations are disputed and very few of these are sought to be enforced by law, it happens that nearly all obligations are met by voluntary transfers of private credits in reverse direction to the flow of goods and services in the course of their exchange. It is here that the system of private banks functions, by its credits and debits, to keep the records and accounts so that goods and services can be freely exchanged.

This has almost entirely superseded their original and primitive function as depositories for the safe-keeping of gold and other valuables. Modern banks keep credits and not actual deposits. Yet they are under legal obligation to pay out actual coin or currency to the amount of all the credits they keep. The anomaly of this is shown in the fact that if the banks of New York City had in their vaults all of the United States currency that there is in circulation, they would not even then be able to meet the claims of their depositors in full. They would fall short about one and three quarters billions of dollars. It is as keepers of the accounts, of the credits and charges, and not as depositaries of money, much less of wealth, that the banks play their important role in the general exchanging of services and goods for other goods and services in which all employment and all production consists.

A merchant or tradesman buys goods and then sells the same goods. But this is only a partial transaction. It is a service, but it is not a completed exchange. The profit he makes is his wages for his services. This profit is in the form of credit in the bank, and it shows what amount or value of goods and services he is entitled to have in return for the services he has given. His piling up of credits is the result not of his accumulation of wealth but of his services in the distribution of goods. There is no completed exchange until the merchant finally receives goods and services in exchange for the services he has put out. In the interval between his giving services and his receiving, it is the function of the banks to keep the necessary account so that the goods and services he finally receives may be justly of the same value as what he has given. What is true of the merchant is also true of every person who gives services or goods and takes money or other credits. His transaction is not completed until he has received goods and services in return. The basic function of the whole system of banking and finance is to keep fair accounts of the uncompleted transactions.

All instruments of credit are the instruments of exchange because they are measuring instruments. They record the measure of the value of what has been given and fix the measure of the value that is to be received. When these instruments are increased in quantity or volume, either by currency inflation or by credit inflation, they become false measures of exchange and, therefore, unfair instruments for that purpose. The result is the same as falsification of any other system of accounts. But as inflation can be perpetrated only by public authority acting directly or indirectly, it cannot be reprobated in the same way, and its injurious effects must fall upon the public at large.

The normal and legitimate creation of credits is through giving goods and services. It is the service we contribute that gives us the credits wherewith we buy, and all our proper deposits in the banks are the records of what we have given and, therefore, of what we are entitled to receive. But governments do not create credits in this way. By taxation, they take existing credits from persons who have become entitled to them by giving goods and services, and transfer them to persons who have not given goods or services. All taxation is merely a transfer of purchasing power. It transfers from those who have given to those who have not given.

Governments make many attempts not only to transfer purchasing power, but also to create it. When they do this, they create obligations without creating any wealth to meet these obligations. They do this by borrowing against the future wealth of their taxpayers. When these public obligations outrun the prospect of the private production of wealth being able to meet them through taxation, they cannot continue to be issued. When this point is reached, either much public spending must stop or government must print and issue the currency that it spends. Such issues are artificially created debts, immediate charges against all present-existing goods and services. It becomes impossible for wealth and services to multiply as fast as the debts against them are created. The debts cannot be met; the credits cannot be made good; and all their value is lost for want of wealth to sustain them. Whenever credits are created without creation of wealth, that is inflation. And unless the production of wealth can keep up with the creation of credits and debts, such debts can never be paid.

The only rightful receiver, receiving as a matter of right and obligation to him, is he who has first been a giver. The only rightful buyer is he who has first been a seller. It is only by the selling or pledging of goods and services that credits can properly be created. Such credits become the records of the sales and are the proper instruments wherewith to complete the exchange by the purchase of other goods and services in lieu of those that have been sold.

Every artificial issuance of credits is a violation of the process and the principle of exchange, for such credits are not based on any goods or any services that have been sold. They assume to create purchasing power other than by exchange. They make those who produce wealth the debtors of those who do not produce. Such debts cannot continue indefinitely to be paid. In the end, there can be no credits or purchasing power but that which comes from the production of wealth and services and the putting of these into the course and channels of exchange. It is, at the last, only by freedom of production and freedom of exchange in unrestricted markets that authentic credits can be established as instruments of exchange. It is only in this way—by freedom of production and exchange—that just and rightful purchasing power can be created and maintained. When this truth becomes well understood, it will be practiced; and all the mystery and all the menace of inflation will have passed away.

Deriving Rights to Liberty

Scott A. Boykin[*]

IN WHAT FOLLOWS, I defend the moral rights to liberty associated with classical liberal and libertarian political thought. I focus initially on the idea that persons are separate and that, while this is a statement of fact rather than of value, the fact that persons are separate and distinct beings is a condition of human life that is critically important for moral and political philosophy. The separateness of persons is a feature of human life that is inextricably bound up with the meaningfulness of justice as an ethical and practical problem. If human beings were not separate and distinct beings with ends and interests of their own, there would be no place for principles of justice to mediate conflict and resolve disputes.

I turn next to practical reason. Our separateness is an important fact about us, and so is our capacity for practical moral judgment. Here I argue for a contractualist model of practical reasoning that shows how persons seeking not only to be rational in accomplishing their own ends but also to be consistently reasonable in their conduct toward other persons will adopt moral constraints on their conduct, which in my account are traditional classical liberal or libertarian rights to liberty. In the model of practical reason that I advance, our ability to justify our conduct to others through principled argument among free and rational persons is a means of identifying what moral constraints on our conduct we have in relation to other persons because they are separate, free, and rational beings.

---

[*]Scott A. Boykin is interim associate dean and associate professor of political science at Georgia Gwinnett College.

CITATION INFORMATION FOR THIS ARTICLE:
Scott A. Boykin. 2018. "Deriving Rights to Liberty." *Libertarian Papers*. 10 (2): 301-341. ONLINE AT: libertarianpapers.org. THIS ARTICLE IS subject to a Creative Commons Attribution 3.0 License (creativecommons.org/licenses).

The model of contractualist moral reasoning I propose enables us to identify and support principles of justice. These take the form of moral constraints on our conduct toward other persons that can perhaps fairly be described as natural rights insofar as they arise from conditions of human social life that are grounded in our nature as separate and distinct beings who are also free and equal moral agents. I argue that legitimate principles to govern social interaction are those that could not be reasonably rejected by all who would be subject to them and that agents must consider the reasons that can be offered for and against a proposed principle with a view to the separate existence of other persons. The consideration of proposed principles in this way yields general principles of just conduct that take the form of rights to liberty.

In section 1, I discuss how the separateness of persons infuses the circumstances of justice outlined historically by David Hume and taken up by more recent theorists. In section 2, I argue that persons who are presented with the values and ends of other persons cannot reasonably reject the idea that each is bound by moral constraints on their own actions, and in section 3 I show how this approach can be used to justify abstract and specifically articulated rights. What I have in mind in sections 1 through 3 is the general form of an argument of the type that Nozick suggested would be a "best explanation" for moral constraints on action. His sketch included a "strong statement of the distinctness of individuals" and a suggestion along the lines of Kant's second formulation of the categorical imperative, which maintained that persons should be viewed as ends in themselves and not principally as means to the ends of others.[1] This, as Nozick indicated, was merely a "sketch," but my aim here is to present a more complete statement of an argument of this type, and this is my chief focus.[2] While moral constraints do follow from the separateness of persons, they are not entailed directly by the separateness of persons in my account. That is, one might proceed by arguing that the separateness of individual persons is itself a moral idea from which moral principles follow directly. I argue instead that the separateness of individuals is part of the factual data that figure in practical moral judgment, and it is the latter, the nature of moral reasoning, from which we reach moral principles. My chief concern here is with practical reason as a method to arrive at principles of justice, and that is what I show in section 2, on practical

---

[1] Robert Nozick, *Anarchy, State, and Utopia* (New York: Basic Books, 1974), 32–34.

[2] Nothing hinges on whether what I am doing here is related to Nozick's suggested project. I do think, nonetheless, that what I outline here is one way to move his suggested project forward.

reasoning and contractualist justification in ethics. In section 3, I present an account of rights to liberty based thereon, identifying first abstract rights to liberty and then the means by which those may be specified in applicable forms.

1. The Separateness of Persons

The idea of the separateness of persons has often appeared as a critique of utilitarianism.[3] Utilitarianism aggregates individual preferences into a social preference for the choice that yields the greatest utility, and individuals are morally obligated to prefer that choice regardless of its consistency with their individual preferences. As a result, utilitarianism fails to acknowledge that persons are separate and distinct individuals by aggregating individual preferences into a social preference ordering. Utilitarianism, as Rawls puts it, treats a society as if it were a single person making a rational choice and thus "does not take seriously the distinction between persons."[4]

Furthermore, the aggregation of individual preferences means that the social choice may sacrifice some individuals' preferences on behalf of the preferences of others that happen to be consistent with the choice that satisfies the utilitarian standard. Utilitarianism thus morally requires individuals to prefer a social choice that runs counter to their own ends. That is, a utilitarian ethics may demand that we reject our commitment to our own ends (which is destructive of our integrity as individuals), not because these are morally deficient or inferior to the ends of others reflected in the social preference that yields the greatest aggregate utility, but solely because our ends are overruled by the social choice that yields a greater utility than one in which our ends are included. The ends of individuals are important for utilitarianism only insofar as they are pieces of a social preference ordering, and the fact that they are, individually, the ends of individual persons is morally insignificant. In the familiar argument offered by Nozick, Rawls, Williams, and others, utilitarianism denies the separateness of persons

---

[3] Nozick, *Anarchy, State, and Utopia*, 28–35; John Rawls, *A Theory of Justice* (Cambridge, MA: Harvard University Press, 1971), 22–27; Samuel Scheffler, *The Rejection of Consequentialism*, rev. ed. (Oxford: Oxford University Press, 1994), 6–13; Bernard Williams, "A Critique of Utilitarianism," in *Utilitarianism: For and against*, eds. J. J. C. Smart and Bernard Williams (Cambridge: Cambridge University Press, 1973), 108–18; Loren Lomasky, *Persons, Rights and the Moral Community* (Oxford: Oxford University Press, 1987), 52–55.

[4] Rawls, *A Theory of Justice*, 27.

because, first, it treats their individual ends as part of a social aggregate, and second, because it assaults the integrity of persons by morally compelling them to favor a social choice that maximizes aggregate utility but that denies their own ends.

For these reasons, utilitarianism fails even on its own terms because it fails to take seriously the distinction among persons. By aggregating their preferences, it disregards the very fact that gives us moral standing: our capacity to feel pleasure and pain in the satisfaction or frustration of our own ends. Utilitarianism does this because it regards the individual's preferences as valuable only insofar as they figure into the social calculation that promotes the greatest aggregate utility. In so doing, utilitarianism sidesteps or overlooks the separateness of persons that makes justice among persons a meaningful concept. This is why Rawls suggests that utilitarianism treats society as if it were one individual making a rational decision to promote its own ends rather than as a group of separate persons with distinct ends of their own.

1.1. The Objective Conditions for Justice

Part of the force of the critique of utilitarianism based on the separateness of persons arises from the fact that problems of justice are social problems among persons rather than rational maximizing choices for single individuals. The separateness of persons is part of what makes justice a meaningful concept, because principles of justice are means of resolving conflicts and disputes among separate and distinct individuals. When I use Hume's phrase "circumstances of justice," I mean that these are necessary conditions for justice in that they must obtain in order for justice to be meaningfully investigated as a topic of political consideration. In Hume's account, these circumstances include a rough equality of abilities, limited scarcity, and limited altruism.[5] If persons were not separate individuals, none of these conditions would make justice meaningful. Only separate persons can have a rough equality of abilities, demands for shares of scarce resources, and a limited altruism toward their fellows.

The three circumstances of justice outlined by Hume are those that make justice useful to human beings and are part of his explanation as to why social conventions of justice arise among us. Hart and Rawls, drawing on

---

[5] David Hume, *Enquiries concerning Human Understanding and concerning the Principles of Morals*, eds. L. A. Selby-Bigge and P. H. Nidditch, 3rd rev. ed. (Oxford: Clarendon Press, [1977] 1975), 183–92; David Hume, *A Treatise of Human Nature* (New York: Penguin, [1740] 1969), 546–47.

Hume, also maintain that these conditions are among those that give rise to a need for principles or rules of justice in society because under these conditions principles of justice enable us to cooperate with each other.[6] If any of these conditions are absent, we have no reason to expect others to cooperate with us, and principles of justice are not only not useful, but have no sensible function to perform.

In the accounts offered by Hume, Hart, and Rawls, each of these circumstances describes or reflects features that we share with one another and make us similarly situated. The rough equality of persons means that no one has powers so superior to others that he or she may regard others as beings of a lesser or different type than himself or herself. As far as our powers are concerned, we are similar to one another. That similarity in the form of rough equality means that there will regularly be conflicts among individuals that appear, in part, because we are generally equal to one another. Our general equality of powers also underscores our distinctness from one another. The second circumstance, limited scarcity, gives rise to competition and conflicts over material goods, but because scarcity is limited, principles that mediate competition and conflict have a function to perform. If there were a generalized extreme scarcity, so that one may survive only if another dies, principles of justice would have no expected function to perform to mediate competition and conflict between those concerned. The conflicts arising from both limited and extreme scarcity also underscore the separateness of individuals. The third circumstance, limited benevolence, also points to our distinct existence as persons. If benevolence were not limited, principles of justice would have no function to perform because there would be no competition or conflict among people. Our benevolence is limited because we accord greater weight to our own ends than to the different ends of other people. In doing so, we manifest our separate and distinct nature as individual human beings.

This does not mean we have a limited quantum of benevolence to bestow on other persons. Rather, it means that we tend to be partial to our own ends and interests as defined by us. These may even be directed toward benefiting others, such as when religious and moral beliefs inspire our ends. What does matter is that we place greater weight on the accomplishment of our own ends and advancement of our self-defined interests than we place on the advancement of other persons' ends and interests as defined by them. One might argue that moral theories are intended to overcome this

---

[6] Rawls, *A Theory of Justice*, 126–30; H. L. A. Hart, *The Concept of Law* (London: Oxford University Press, 1961), 189–95.

circumstance. Utilitarianism, for example, morally requires a person to place more weight on the collective choice than his or her personal ends and interests. But limited benevolence, or altruism, as one of the circumstances of justice is neither moral nor immoral, but part of the factual data in the background from which principles of justice are to be justified.[7]

Hume, Hart, and Rawls employ the circumstances of justice in different ways. For Hume, these circumstances of human social life help to explain why conventions emerge that enable us to live together and cooperate with one another. Conventions that protect property and freedom from physical harm are practically necessary for us to live in society with one another. For Hart, these circumstances show why, for human beings as we know them, there must be some prohibitions on conduct that protect us from physical harm and that enable us to make plans based upon our use of property in objects and agreements with others that dictate that some basic rules that must exist in order to ensure voluntary compliance with an order of rules that have a coercive sanction and enable human beings to live in society with one another. Hart regards such prohibitions as natural law in the sense that they are necessary for social cooperation among human beings as they are in our experience of them.[8]

These circumstances of justice reflect facts about human nature. They do not require any special insight into the essence of humanness or make any speculative metaphysical claims about what it means to be human. Further, the circumstances of justice do not of themselves make any moral claims or specify any particular moral principles. One may say, with Hart, that these circumstances show that a practicable legal system among human beings as we know them must include some prohibitions on physical aggression and theft. While this is a sound conclusion, it does not of itself show why we should assent to such a legal system or preserve our commitment to such a system when doing so does not advance our interests. Rather than being moral conclusions, the circumstances of justice consist of factual observations about human beings across time and cultures. A world in which any of these circumstances did not obtain would be very different from the

---

[7] As I argue later, we are entitled to bestow greater weight on our own ends because we are free and equal persons and other persons' ends do not of themselves have a special claim on our devotion. Their ends are important to them, and while we are morally obligated to recognize the special importance their ends have for them, that does not make them our ends too.

[8] Hart, *The Concept of Law*, 189–95.

one we know. The circumstances of justice are facts rather than moral principles, but they are facts that make justice a meaningful concept.

1.2. The Subjective Circumstances of Justice

Also bound up with the circumstances that make justice meaningful and with the separateness of persons is the idea that all individuals necessarily occupy different positions and have a personal point of view. Each individual sees the world through his or her own eyes. We each make decisions based upon the knowledge we have at the time we make them, as understood by us in light of our experiences and personality. Furthermore, as a result of our perspectival nature we necessarily find ourselves in conditions in which people have reasonable and good faith disagreements with one another about the value of the ends we and they wish to pursue.[9] Rawls regards these as "subjective circumstances of justice" because each person choosing principles of justice knows about themselves that they have ends, commitments, and a

---

[9] This is a different question from the one presented by the debate over the question whether intellectual peers with the same information can rationally disagree with each other over matters of belief involving facts and philosophical issues. See, e.g., Richard Feldman and Ted A. Warfield, *Disagreement* (Oxford: Oxford University Press, 2010). This issue arises under special conditions in which people with the same expertise or capacity have the same information before them and reach different conclusions. Those conditions are unlikely ever to be present in the kind of situation being considered here. The subjective circumstances of justice also present an issue that differs from that raised by either benign or coercive forms of paternalism. These theorists argue that since people are so prone to making mistakes in advancing their own interests, even as defined by themselves, political authorities should either incentivize better decisions or prohibit bad decisions. Common examples of such bad decisions involve health habits and debt. For a coercive form of paternalist argument, see Sarah Conly, *Against Autonomy* (New York: Cambridge University Press, 2013). For a more liberal or benign paternalism, see Richard H. Thaler and Cass R. Sunstein, *Nudge*, rev. ed. (New York: Penguin, 2009). Rather than addressing these issues, the less controversial point made here is that one of the subjective circumstances of justice is the observation that people have different conceptions of the good and that these differ from one another. On the one hand, this gives rise to conflict because the ends and plans of individuals may clash. On the other hand, this means that principles of justice should take into account the fact that persons' ends and plans compete and sometimes conflict with each other.

view of their own good when they choose principles of justice.[10] They are indeed part of the circumstances that make justice a meaningful concept because it is undeniable that human beings understand that they have ends, commitments, and a sense of their own good, that these differ among persons, and that these differences give rise to disputes and conflicts that principles of justice may mediate and resolve. Our differences on these matters make principles of justice both necessary and meaningful. Our ends may conflict, and our ends may be mutually exclusive. These facts are part of the circumstances of justice.

The separateness of persons is embedded in the circumstances of justice because separate persons have separate ends. In any society, persons will have some ends of their own, which they have by virtue of their individual position, personality, capacities, and desires. It is inevitable that in virtually any group, the individuals composing the group will have some separate ends, even if they have a common end that makes them a group. In a larger society, it is certain that most of the ends that individuals have will be their separate ends that they do not share with every other person in society.

What is important above all about the separate ends of persons is that they are not universally shared. A person may share ends with others and may form part of a group with a shared commitment. A common culture, religious idea, or political objective may unite people in an effort to achieve a shared end. None of these conditions overcome the fact that in any society, persons will have some ends that they do not share with everyone else in society. This means there are likely to be separately, and mutually exclusively, valued ends always present among persons in any society. It is the presence of competing valued ends that is one of the conditions that makes justice a meaningful issue to be resolved.

Persons are separate in that they are capable of choosing personally valued ends, pursuing those ends, and reaping the benefits of that pursuit. They are separate and distinct in their self-driven pursuit of self-chosen ends. This can readily be construed as a moral idea, but it is not necessary to do so to reach the more parsimonious conclusion that, as a matter of fact, persons have their own ends, commitments, and sense of their own good, and that this fact is one of those that makes the concept of justice a meaningful one.

---

[10] Rawls, *A Theory of Justice*, 127.

2. Reasonableness and Rights

The preceding section described the circumstances of justice as a factual account of human relations but did not set forth a theory of the good to be advanced by moral reasoning. In fact, I expressly rejected the notion that there is a scale of value to be maximized and that justice exists to serve. In this section, I offer a model of practical reason similar to others that have been termed "neo-Kantian" or "weak" contractualism,[11] by which we can identify and support principles of justice that establish rights as constraints on our conduct toward others. The circumstances of justice are the background data that provide substance from which to consider proposed principles of justice, but what is needed is a model of moral reasoning to show why some principles, and not others, could not be reasonably rejected by agents concerned with justice and not solely with their own ends and interests. Embedded within contractualism, which requires that we be able to justify our conduct by principles that other persons could not reasonably reject, is the acknowledgement of "the value of persons in the capacity for rational self-governance in pursuit of a meaningful life."[12] The circumstances of justice, factual rather than moral in nature, demonstrate not only the facts that make justice a meaningful concept but also the separateness of persons, which, in turn, supports the free and equal nature of moral agents whose claims must be justified to one another because none have inherent authority over other persons. The latter considerations do have moral significance, and these in turn indicate the kinds of reasons that support contractualism as a means of justifying moral principles. In order to reasonably reject a principle that allows or prohibits some act, persons must refer to the circumstances of justice, the separateness of persons, and the free and equal nature of moral agents in their objection to a moral principle. These are substantive categories of reasons that serve to narrow the range of reasons that can be offered for or against proposed principles of justice.

Contractualism as I outline it here requires us to take into account the interests of other persons, but it also limits the interests that we must take into account when considering principles of justice. These interests that we must take into account are those that we share as free, equal, and separate

---

[11] Gary Watson, "Some Considerations in Favor of Contractualism," in *Rational Commitment and Social Justice*, eds. Jules L. Coleman and Christopher W. Morris (Cambridge: Cambridge University Press, 1998), 177; Gerald F. Gaus, *Social Philosophy* (Armonk, NY: M. E. Sharpe, 1999), 92.

[12] Rahul Kumar, "Reasonable Reasons in Contractualist Moral Argument," *Ethics* 114, no. 1 (October 2003), 15.

moral persons seeking to cooperate with others under the circumstances of justice. We are free in that the default mode of human interaction is one of freedom. That is, where there are no moral constraints, we are free to act as we choose. We are equal in that no ordinary adult has any natural claim of authority over any other ordinary adult. We are separate persons under the circumstances of justice for the reasons I offered in the first section. We are moral persons insofar as we intend that our actions toward others be justifiable in accordance with principles that no one can reasonably reject. Moral persons seeking to cooperate may reasonably reject principles that do not serve the interests of free, equal, and separate persons under the circumstances of justice—that is, the interests they share with all other such persons. These are limited in scope but powerful where they are present. My aim in this section and the next is to unwrap these ideas.

This model of moral reasoning requires some minimal idealization of the agents. That is, some features of the reasoning of people as we know them must be controlled for in the model so that we are considering a process of moral decision-making under the circumstances of justice. We could insist upon actual dialog among people as we know them, even if their dialog is governed by conditions designed to yield general moral principles. This is the approach of Jürgen Habermas's discourse ethics.[13] The kind of process Habermas envisions seems unlikely to yield determinate principles and instead establishes a democratic procedure that might produce very different principles among different groups of people. Habermas expressly recognizes this about his approach.[14] A highly idealized moral point of view, on the other hand, yields determinate results, but we may question the results of a highly idealized hypothetical exercise if the persons imagined in it are very different from people as we know them.[15] A third approach is a modestly idealized one. The aim of this approach is to model moral reasoning in a way that is, as Gerald Gaus put it, "accessible" to ordinary people because the model constructed is not too far removed from people as we know them.[16] This kind of model is idealized to the extent necessary to

---

[13] Jürgen Habermas, *Moral Consciousness and Collective Action*, trans. Christian Lenhart and Shierry Weber Nicholsen (Cambridge, MA: Massachusetts Institute of Technology, 1990).

[14] Ibid., 92–109.

[15] Joseph Raz, "Facing Diversity: The Case of Epistemic Abstinence," *Philosophy & Public Affairs*, 19, no. 1 (1990): 3–46.

[16] Gerald Gaus, *The Order of Public Reason* (Cambridge: Cambridge University Press, 2011), 276–78.

describe moral reasoning among persons who seek to agree on the claims they may justly make upon each other. The model must make the participants consider the claims of other persons in good faith with the aim of seeking agreement on principles of interpersonal conduct they regard as just. This is idealized because it excludes the kind of self-interested hard bargaining and dishonesty we observe in real-world political debate.[17] The features of this model should include those needed to purge moral reasoning of considerations other than those aimed at deliberating on principles reflecting the claims that persons can make on other persons' conduct toward them. This is a model of moral reasoning, which human beings are capable of but do not always do in fact. It is true that people are often unreasonable.[18] That people do not always reason morally is not an embarrassment to a model of moral reasoning, which necessarily limits itself to that purpose and not a general account of human psychology and behavior.

The model of practical reasoning employed here leans heavily on the concept of reasonableness.[19] Reasonableness is a distinct concept from rationality: "There is no thought of deriving one from the other; in particular, there is no thought of deriving the reasonable from the rational."[20] Rationality refers to the methods by which we reach conclusions from the information we have, and full rationality requires not only flawless reasoning but also possession of complete relevant information to obtain the objective the reasoner has in view.[21] Reasonableness, on the other hand, involves a person's taking into account all of the reasons for or against some action (or principles allowing or forbidding the action). These will include not only the interests of the person making a judgment about the proposed action or principle, but also the interests of other persons as well. A rational person

---

[17] Gaus, *Order of Public Reason*, 331–32; John Rawls, *Political Liberalism* (New York: Columbia University Press, 1993), 48; T. M. Scanlon, *What We Owe to Each Other* (Cambridge, MA: Harvard University Press, 1998), 192.

[18] Shaun Young, "Rawlsian Reasonableness: A Problematic Presumption?," *Canadian Journal of Political Science* 39, no. 1 (March 2006): 164–65.

[19] I do not argue that rationality alone supports rights and duties to observe them. Alan Gewirth, in *Reason and Morality* (Chicago: University of Chicago Press, 1978), makes that argument, which suffers from the defect that, while I as a rational person may require and seek for myself the freedom to act on behalf my own ends, I may, rationally though unreasonably, seek to deny other persons that same freedom.

[20] Rawls, *Political Liberalism*, 51.

[21] Scanlon, *What We Owe to Each Other*, 31–32.

may seek to maximize what he or she values, but a reasonable person will recognize the force of norms that exclude some actions prohibited thereby.[22]

2.1. Reasonableness and Practical Reason

The circumstances of justice are conditions that obtain generally among strangers, or even among neighbors: limited scarcity, limited benevolence, and a rough equality of persons. It is these conditions that make principles of justice, characterized as rules of fair cooperation, meaningful to people who would adhere to them and be called upon to adhere to them. Reasonableness is a key concept in identifying such principles. In the context of articulating and defending proposed principles of justice, reasonableness is the quality of taking into account the interests of other persons.[23] Limited benevolence, limited scarcity of means, and rough equality of persons make justice a meaningful concept. If persons are to live together under such conditions, and if they recognize the separateness of others in their capacity to define and pursue their own valued ends and have a sense of justice about their relations to other people, claims that can be justified to them and that they can justify to others become the subject matter of justice and therefore of rights.

Reasonable persons "are ready to propose principles and standards as fair terms of cooperation and to abide by them willingly, given the assurance that others will likewise do so."[24] Reasonableness is a "moral point of view," though the phrase "moral point of view" is perhaps a misnomer. A specific point of view involves an individualized way of ranking or including and excluding particular interests, reasons, or considerations, and this is different than "evaluations 'all things considered,' with all relevant points of view taken

---

[22] To borrow Joseph Raz's terms, a "mandatory norm" is an "exclusionary reason." Exclusionary reasons are "second-order" reasons that rule out some acts not by outweighing or overriding first-order reasons but by excluding acts based upon those reasons. Joseph Raz, *Practical Reason and Norms* (New York: Oxford University Press, 1999), 73–76. Rights perform this function: "Deontological constraints might exhibit this same phenomenon. By grouping actions together into a principle forbidding them—'do not murder'—an action is removed from separate utilitarian (or egoist) calculation of *its* costs and benefits." Robert Nozick, *The Nature of Rationality* (Princeton: Princeton University Press, 1993), 62.

[23] Scanlon, *What We Owe to Each Other*, 33.

[24] Ibid., 49.

into account and each one given its due weight."[25] Thus there is not a moral point of view that is just one additional point of view among other points of view. Rather, a moral judgment is one that takes into account all relevant considerations and reasons and resolves conflicts among them. In this sense, it is not made from any particular point of view.

But as reasonable persons, we are not obligated to consider just any asserted interest or reason that other persons have but only interests or reasons that we share with them. The reasons and interests that other persons assert as bases for their claims must be reasons or interests that we share with them because they are reasons or interests that are comprehensible to us and that are the basis for free and equal persons to recognize as the bases for the reasonable rejection of principles for cooperation under the circumstances of justice. That is why moral obligation involves reciprocity among persons with equal moral authority. We are reasonable when we take into account the interests or reasons other persons have that we have too. The reciprocity of fairness delimits the range of interests that may be reasonably considered in principles of justice. These must be interests that we share. "I must justify my conduct in terms of some principle capable of being appealed to by all parties concerned, some principle from which we can reason in common."[26] The interests one can appeal to in considering principles of justice are generic or higher-order interests that are abstracted from the specific goals that individuals have and that are also held by other persons who have different goals and projects.[27] On the other hand, particular interests that I have, that I do not share with others, are not matters of justice. While they may be important to me in my conception of a good life, they are not matters of justice that I may employ as reasons to make demands upon other people. Stephen Darwall argues that the interests we share as free, equal, and rational persons are "in living self-directed lives on terms of mutual respect with

---

[25] James Rachels, "Evaluating from a Point of View," *Journal of Value Inquiry* 6 (1972): 144–57.

[26] W. M. Sibley, "The Rational versus the Reasonable," *Philosophical Review* 62, no. 4 (October 1953): 557.

[27] Though I do not intend by implication to adopt anything else Alan Gewirth argues, his description of the "generic-dispositional view of goods" is similar to what I mean here: "Where the particular purposes for which different persons act may vary widely, the capabilities of action required for fulfilling their purposes and for maintaining and increasing their abilities are the same for all persons." Gewirth, *Reason and Morality*, 59.

others,"[28] which are comparable to what Rawls calls the "moral powers" of a sense of justice and the capacity to "form, revise, and rationally pursue a conception of the good."[29] Moral principles are those that persons fitting this description could not reasonably reject, given the mutual aim of finding principles that they and other persons could not reasonably reject to govern their interaction.

There are some minimal criteria that qualify persons as being capable of reasonableness. Reasonable persons can make normative demands on other persons, and they can reasonably accept those demands, when the persons involved are free and equal agents, each of whom has the equal moral authority to make moral claims on others and to accept the moral claims others make on them. We are free and equal in that the circumstances of justice do not place anyone in a position of authority over others. Instead, the authority we possess is to make moral claims on others. It is not a position from which persons are bargaining for advantage, because the aim of reasonable persons considering principles to govern their interpersonal conduct is to realize fair terms of cooperation. This does not mean that people making moral decisions are radically different from ordinary people. What it does mean is that the kinds of reasons they can offer for or against proposed principles of justice are constrained by the concept of reasonableness.[30] Further, it means that the kinds of motivation people can have when engaged in normative discourse include being disinterested and impartial and do not include seeking advantages over others. Real people are often unreasonable, and when they are unreasonable they are not engaged in moral judgment. Seeking to win an argument for the sake of winning or for advantage of some kind over other persons is not moral decision-making.[31]

---

[28] Stephen Darwall, *The Second-Person Standpoint: Morality, Respect, and Accountability* (Cambridge, MA: Harvard University Press, 2006), 308.

[29] Rawls, *Political Liberalism*, 525; see also Darwall, *Second-Person Standpoint*, 309.

[30] As I discuss below in the section on cognitive biases and heuristics, persons are constrained by principles of rational decision in deciding upon matters of fact. A willingness to adopt principles of rational decision-making in deciding upon matters of fact is associated with reasonableness as a disposition, notwithstanding the distinction between the rational and the reasonable in ethical theory. If, for example, one insists in ethical disputation that the world is flat despite ample empirical evidence to the contrary, one is being unreasonable.

[31] Certainly, there are some theories that take an approach based upon rational self-interest and agreement as the source of rights and duties. In contrast to "weak" or "neo-Kantian" contractualism, these are inspired more by Hobbesian

Reasonable and fair terms of cooperation are reversible. Kurt Baier and Gerald Gaus employ the concept of reversibility to help define what kinds of principles can be considered as candidates for principles of justice. Baier says of reversibility that behavior is reversible when it is "acceptable to a person whether he is at the 'giving' or 'receiving' end of it."[32] Gaus defines reversibility as follows: "A person's advocacy [of a proposed principle] must not depend on her knowledge that she will only occupy specific roles or positions."[33] But even if we know what role we will occupy, our judgment about a proposed principle cannot depend solely on how it affects us as opposed to other persons: If "I object to a principle's being universally governing because of the way it affects my interests as an equal member, though I wouldn't if it were someone else, then this is also an objection of the wrong kind to a candidate moral principle."[34] Reversibility is a concept of reciprocity. It means that no one can defend as fair a principle that they are unwilling to have applied to them.

Reasonableness means that I must take into account the interests of other persons. Reversibility means I must take my own interests into account, because the principle that is agreed upon is one that I am willing to have applied to me. I take my own interests into account because my interests are those at stake if I concede that a claim is reversible against me. If I make this claim reasonably, I must take your like interests into account as well because reasonableness means I am taking the interests of others into account. Reversibility is an idea of reciprocity. It means that the interests I have at stake on the proposed principle are interests that you also have. Because fairness requires reversibility, I take my interests into account, and because reasonableness means I must take the interests of others into account, fairness understood as reversibility means that I must consider the interests that I share with other persons.

---

contractarianism. See, e.g., David Gauthier, *Morals by Agreement* (Oxford: Oxford University Press, 1986); Jan Narveson and James Sterba, *Are Liberty and Equality Compatible?* (Cambridge: Cambridge University Press, 2010), 123–68; Jan Narveson, *The Libertarian Idea* (Philadelphia: Temple University Press, 1988).

[32] Kurt Baier, *The Moral Point of View* (New York: Cornell University Press, 1958), 202.

[33] *Order of Public Reason*, 300.

[34] Darwall, *Second-Person Standpoint*, 308.

Rights as principles of justice are reversible. I claim against you the right to X, which imposes upon you a Hohfeldian duty[35] not to interfere with my Xing. To defeat my claimed right to X, you must offer a reason to reject that right as a fair term of cooperation under the circumstances of justice. One way to do that would be to show that the claim is not reversible in that the person making the claim is not willing to accept the same right to X being possessed by other persons. If it is not reversible in this sense, the person's claim is not fair. Every person making a claim to a right to X must be willing to accord the same right to other persons. To fail to do so would be unfair and thus unreasonable. Put in another way, it would be unreasonable for a person to reject others' right to X when they would prefer to have such a right themselves to not having such a right at all. Here we could consider a reason related to terms of cooperation why no one should have the right to X. This would enable you to reasonably reject a right to X if a right frustrates cooperation among persons. Thus, for example, a right to commit fraud or violent acts that interfere with the agency of other persons may be reasonably rejected because it frustrates cooperation among persons. Put differently, I make a claim to limit your liberty by denying you have the moral right to X. To defeat my claim, you must offer a reason against this restriction on your liberty that I cannot reasonably reject as a principle for fair cooperation under the circumstances of justice. While reversibility focuses on fairness, this question asks whether the asserted right prevents cooperation under the circumstances of justice. Anyone can reject a principle or right that would prevent cooperation under the circumstances of limited scarcity, limited benevolence, and rough equality of persons. For example, principles that grant ordinary adults different rights to liberty or grant special privileges to some and deny them to others would seem to do this. Likewise, principles that prevent persons from making rational financial or economic decisions would seem to do this as well. Further, principles that require more than a limited benevolence to other persons would seem to do this too where they compel us to serve others to our detriment. Anyone could reject as unreasonable principles that would frustrate terms of cooperation among persons under the circumstances of justice.

2.1.1. *What Happens When Reasonable People Disagree?*

Reasonable people may disagree. They may do so for a number of reasons. Rawls suggests the following: evidence may be hard to evaluate, we

---

[35] Wesley Hohfeld, "Some Fundamental Legal Conceptions as Applied in Judicial Reasoning," *Yale Law Journal* 23, no. 1 (November 1913): 30.

may disagree about the weight of different kinds of evidence or considerations, the concepts we use may be vague or indeterminate, the way reasonable persons "assess and weigh moral and political values" may differ because we have had different life experiences, it can be difficult to weight conflicting values against one another, and some considerations may not be vetoed, because there must be some limit to the range of considerations that can be counted.[36] A criticism of some forms of "weak" or neo-Kantian contractualism is that they seek to establish a procedure that will always yield a unique answer to moral problems, when a more defensible aim would be to establish an account of the kinds of reasons that are properly admissible in moral deliberation, accepting something less than a fully specified and determinate set of answers to all moral problems.[37] When someone reasonably rejects a principle, it cannot be the basis for fair terms of cooperation among persons seeking agreement on such terms. The result is what Gerald Gaus calls "blameless liberty," meaning there is no rule at all.[38]

Our cultural background and personal experiences influence our perceptions and values. One might suggest that the centrality of reasonableness is culturally biased because, for example, a particular culture might insist that women's proposals should not be considered. Another culture might insist that the proposals of some other racial, ethnic, or religious group should not be considered. Women could reasonably reject a standard of evaluation that discounted the proposals of women, as could persons who were members of other groups that a cultural perspective maintained should be discounted.[39]

Because we are considering whether one can defend universal rights, it is necessary that persons from multiple cultures who have different worldviews be included. With the objective of determining whether there are universal principles of justice—that is, human or natural rights—it is necessary that persons engaged in argument over asserted principles consider the norms of their own cultures or societies in a hypothetical and detached way so that they can view them critically.[40] Since our cultural and personal

---

[36] Rawls, *Political Liberalism*, 56–57.

[37] Gerald F. Gaus, *Social Philosophy* (Armonk, NY: M. E. Sharpe 1999), 107–8.

[38] Gaus, *Order of Public Reason*, 321.

[39] This would be true for views with another basis, such as ideology or religion, that hold that some groups of persons are somehow less than human or not worthy of consideration.

[40] As Habermas argues, this requires that persons engaged in ethical discourse have realized a certain degree of socio-cognitive development. Specifically, they must

backgrounds contribute to our understanding of reasons, and reasonableness as I have defined it involves shared reasons, we must consider how persons from diverse backgrounds with different reasons and values can have a common standard for evaluating proposed rights as principles of justice. A reason, or "evaluative standard," as Gaus puts it, may be intelligible to us in the sense that we understand it as a reason.[41] Intelligibility means that we can recognize that X is a reason for another person even though it is not a reason for us. This alone is not particularly helpful in reaching agreement on proposed norms. That X is a reason for you does not make it a reason for me in any sense, including a reason I would include in reaching a conclusion about the validity of a proposed norm. Gaus suggests the similar but distinct concept of shared reasons, or "evaluative standards," as he puts it, which are standards of reasoning that you and I both use, even though we may place more or less weight on them than other persons do.[42] These are more helpful in the sense that we both actually use them, so the standard is not foreign to us, even if we do not agree with the weight another person puts upon it.

Gaus rejects the shared-standards model because it excludes some standards that are important to many, such as religious considerations that others reject. This is indeed problematic if our standard requires persons to endorse the validity of the norms being considered. It is less problematic if the standard requires that persons offer reasons to reject the rule under consideration that no one can reasonably reject. Reasonableness requires that persons offer reasons to reject a rule that other persons share. Here, it will not do to assert, as Gaus suggests, religious conscience or other conceptions of the good to defeat a proposed norm, because it is not required that all endorse the proposed norm. Instead, they must offer a reason to reject the proposed norm couched in terms of reasons that everyone has under the circumstances of justice.

This has the effect of reducing the number and kinds of claims that can be considered. It definitely eliminates what Rawls calls "comprehensive doctrines," which include a broad range of belief systems that include different moral and religious ideas.[43] Rawls's idea of the "burdens of judgment" relates to justifying substantive principles in particular political

---

have reached the postconventional level of moral development in Kohlberg's categories of moral development. See *Moral Consciousness and Communicative Action*, 175–80.

[41] Gaus, *Order of Public Reason*, 283.

[42] Ibid., 286.

[43] Rawls, *Political Liberalism*, 13.

societies and seeking an "overlapping consensus" among comprehensive doctrines that most people in a society can accept. Recognizing the limits of the demands we can place on one another is a central part of a reasonable disposition, and it is supported by our moral equality.[44]

It is true that to consider one's own cultural norms and values in a hypothetical and detached way, as Habermas suggests, requires a high level of socio-cognitive development, higher in fact than most normal adults achieve in their lives. Does this mean that the contextualized reasons and values that persons who have not achieved such a level of development are to be disregarded? No, it does not, and in fact, their objections to proposed principles must be considered, as the impact of proposed principles on all persons concerned must be considered. But if their asserted rejection of a proposed principle is not a reasonable one, because it is one that does not reflect the generic interests of free, equal, and separate persons seeking terms of cooperation under the circumstances of justice, their asserted rejection need not be adopted and cannot be the basis for rejecting a proposed principle.

Are we able to hold persons responsible for observing principles that no one can reasonably reject if those persons are unable to consider proposed principles from outside the contextualized norms and values of their societies? Yes, and this is something that human societies do constantly and with good reason. Persons with a conventional level of socio-cognitive development are able to understand the content of principles of right and wrong and to govern their behavior accordingly. Prisons are full of persons who have a modest level of socio-cognitive development and yet committed horrible and violent crimes, knowing these to be wrong. After the Second World War, persons who unreasonably believed they were excused or justified in committing atrocious crimes against humanity were held responsible for them at Nuremburg, and the unreasonable beliefs these persons held that their actions were excused or justified were not reasons to not hold them accountable for their actions. Their unreasonable beliefs or principles do not excuse or justify their actions.

Approaches such as Rawls' that seek to present a fully determinate set of principles built upon assumptions fall prey to the argument that they are culturally contingent.[45] The contractualism I advance here remains aware of

---

[44] Allyn Fives, "Reasonableness, Pluralism, and Liberal Moral Doctrines," *Journal of Value Inquiry* 44 (June 2010): 331–33.

[45] John Gray, *Post-liberalism: Studies in Political Thought* (New York: Routledge, 1993), 48–50.

cultural differences and their practical importance, which is reflected in the partial indeterminacy of abstract principles and their specification as parts of systems of rules that I examine in section 3.

2.1.2. The Problem of Cognitive Biases or Heuristics

People may disagree about factual matters, such as the likelihood of some event, and this is a reason they may also disagree about norms, insofar as disagreement about norms arises from disagreement about beliefs regarding matters of fact or likelihood. It is well established as an empirical matter that cognitive biases and the use of cognitive heuristics infect our ordinary reasoning and lead us to make systematic errors of judgment about many matters.[46] For example, one common cognitive bias is to misconceive chance. Considering coin flips, people are likely to consider clusters of heads or tails as unlikely and to expect alternating heads and tails to be more likely when, in fact, such clusters are entirely attributable to chance.[47] There are many such cognitive biases and heuristics (or mental shortcuts) people make that lead them to erroneous judgments of fact because these are based upon various kinds of misconceptions.

While it is humbling to recognize that our hunches are so often wrong, these researchers tell us that not all hope is lost. One reason for studying cognitive biases and heuristics is to learn how to overcome shortcomings in our capacity for reasoning well.[48] Ariely suggests that "although irrationality is commonplace, it does not necessarily mean that we are helpless. Once we understand when and where we may make erroneous decisions, we can try to be more vigilant, force ourselves to think differently about these decisions, or

---

[46] See, e.g., Daniel Kahneman, et al., *Judgment under Uncertainty* (Cambridge: Cambridge University Press, 1982); Thomas Gilovich, *How We Know What Isn't So* (New York: Free Press, 1991); Dan Ariely, *Predictably Irrational*, rev. ed. (New York: Harper, 2010).

[47] See Amos Tversky and Daniel Kahneman, "Introduction: Judgment under Uncertainty: Heuristics and Biases," in *Judgment under Uncertainty: Heuristics and Biases*, eds. Daniel Kahneman, Paul Slovic, and Amos Tversky (New York: Cambridge University Press, 1982), 7–8; Thomas Gilovich, *How We Know What Isn't So: The Fallibility of Human Reason in Everyday Life* (New York: Free Press, 1991), 18–19.

[48] See Daniel Kahneman and Amos Tversky, "On the Study of Statistical Intuitions," in *Judgment under Uncertainty*, 494; Gilovich, *How We Know What Isn't So*, 185–94. See also the discussion in Gerald F. Gaus, *Justificatory Liberalism* (New York: Oxford University Press, 1996), 60–62.

use technology to overcome our inherent shortcomings."[49] We cannot expect people as we encounter them to have rid themselves of common defects in reasoning, but we can modestly idealize persons engaged in moral thinking about principles of justice to be willing not to rely on known cognitive biases or heuristics that lead to systematic errors of judgment. This is a degree of idealization and makes our agents different from the people we encounter on the street. On the other hand, it is at least in principle possible for people to recognize many kinds of errors in judgment. Since this degree of idealization is one that people can in principle achieve, it is not too far removed from the real people who would examine principles of justice. Gerald Gaus's "members of the public" are "idealized members of the actual public, but they are not so idealized that their reasoning is inaccessible to their real-world counterparts."[50] A modest degree of idealization is defensible where the idealized persons' thought processes are accessible to people as we encounter them. These are accessible in that people can in principle escape them, even if they fail to do so in fact.

Another way to see how it is defensible to invoke this cognitive idealization is that there are proponents of public policies that would institute corrective measures for these cognitive biases and heuristics. One extant policy supported by Thaler and Sunstein, for example, is the Pension Protection Act, a federal law in the United States that gives employers an incentive to automatically enroll their employees in defined-benefit plans, match their employees' contributions to those plans, and increase the amounts contributed to the plans over time.[51] The rationale behind this law is that employees often fail to take advantage of defined-benefit plans at work at all, much less take full advantage of these plans, and thereby save less for retirement than is optimal. To help those of us whose savings strategies are less than fully rational, this policy structures choices in such a way that people act more rationally in terms of saving for retirement.[52] The authors of this

---

[49] Dan Ariely, *Predictably Irrational: The Hidden Forces That Shape Our Decisions*, rev. ed. (New York: Harper-Collins 2009), 322.

[50] Gaus, Order of Public Reason, 276.

[51] Richard H. Thaler and Cass R. Sustein, *Nudge: Improving Decisions about Health, Wealth, and Happiness*, rev. ed. (New York: Penguin 2009), 117–18.

[52] Can someone reasonably reject an intervention such as the Pension Protection Act, which requires employers to structure their defined-benefit plans for their employees in such a way as to make their employees act in a manner that is more rational (or, better put, perhaps more rational, depending upon one's discount rate of future to present benefits)? Employers (or anyone) can reasonably reject this

policy can be deemed to have become sufficiently aware of the cognitive bias against sufficient saving for the future to design a way to remedy the effects of that bias. In doing so, they have demonstrated why a modest degree of cognitive idealization in deciding upon policies is defensible. In the sense that articulating rights is akin to policy making, it is likewise defensible to invoke this degree of cognitive idealization.

Can we obligate people to adhere to principles that more ideally rational versions of themselves cannot reasonably reject? Consider the influence of cognitive biases and heuristics that lead to erroneous conclusions about states of affairs, probabilities, or decisions. To the extent that these types of conclusions figure into reasoning about normative principles of action, leaving these biases or heuristics in place means that there is a greater likelihood that the person will reach an erroneous conclusion. In this context, this would mean that the person might reject a principle that they cannot reasonably reject if they are reasoning correctly. If a person were to deny their obligation by a normative principle on the basis that they are entitled to reason incorrectly, those who reason correctly are likewise entitled to disregard the person's denial of their obligation. The person who insists upon maintaining their unjustifiable biases or heuristics has not removed themselves from the moral community of persons who may be held accountable for their actions and whose (relevant, as in the sense defined above) interests must be considered, but they fail to offer reasons for rejecting a proposed principle that no one can reasonably reject. Those who reason without those biases or heuristics can reasonably reject the account offered by a person who insists on including their unjustifiable reasons or heuristics. In a word, reasonable persons can justifiably ignore bad reasoning. This does not conflate reasonableness and rationality, which remain distinct concepts. Insofar as determinations of matters of fact figure in consideration of principles of justice, it is unreasonable to insist upon some factual matter that has been shown to be false so that no rational person, in the modestly idealized sense contemplated here, would insist upon it. Thus, if I insist in moral disputation with you that when a coin has been flipped and turned up heads five times in a row, there is now a greater than 50 percent chance that it will turn up tails on the next flip, my insistence is unreasonable because it can be conclusively demonstrated as a matter of mathematical probability that the likelihood of tails is always 50 percent on any such coin toss. My belief to the contrary is a failure of rationality for me, but it becomes

---

requirement, which imposes burdens on the employers for the sake of a purported aggregate social benefit. For this reason, it is immoral to compel employers to structure their defined-benefit plans in this way.

unreasonable only when I insist upon this demonstrably false belief in moral disputation with you. It does not conflate rationality and reasonableness to maintain that insistence in moral discourse upon a factual matter that is demonstrably false is unreasonable.

Does modest idealization place too great a weight on practical reason as a feature of human life? Eric Mack argues that contractualism is flawed because it unjustifiably privileges human epistemic capacity, which is one of a number of important human capacities.[53] It is true that contractualism lays great stress on epistemic capacity. There are other human capacities that are important for other purposes, such as physical courage or strength, for example. While such capacities are important in other areas of human life, epistemic capacity has special relevance to the human activity of moral reasoning, so the stress that contractualism lays upon this capacity is warranted. Contractualism as I conceive it here does not unjustifiably privilege epistemic capacity above others. Instead, it reflects our understanding of human beings in the social conditions that make justice a meaningful concept to us. In this way it is rooted in the reality of our lives rather than simply a contractual agreement,[54] so agreement is not the basis for our rights. Rather, agreement is the affirmation of antecedently existing moral rights that we discover and articulate through contractualist reasoning. To show how it does not privilege epistemic capacity, contractualism as I am using it here to ground rights to liberty does not depend upon the epistemic capacity of the person having those rights. These rights can still be affirmed by other persons observing the objectionable conduct or acceptable conduct. Thus, for example, a person can object to conduct toward persons who, due to a cognitive defect, cannot defend themselves. Furthermore, people who lack certain epistemic abilities can still be held morally accountable for their conduct.[55] What is necessary is not the ability to engage in ethical reasoning at

---

[53] Eric Mack, "Scanlon as Natural Rights Theorist," *Philosophy, Politics & Economics* 6 (1): 68. It is a defensible interpretation of Scanlon that he, as Mack argues, understands the agreement on what is rejected to be what makes conduct wrong. See also Thaddeus Metz, "The Reasonable and the Moral," *Social Theory & Practice* 28, no. 2 (April 2002) 277–78.

[54] This is a key distinction between contractualism of the "weak" or "neo-Kantian" variety and the contractarianism inspired by Hobbes's political thought, in which promises supported solely by rational self-interest are taken to be the basis for moral rights and duties.

[55] Incidentally, Anglo-American law gives effect to this moral principle because it only excuses adult persons from criminal liability if they are unable to appreciate

the highest level of socio-cognitive capacities. Rather, it is the ability to know that something is wrong in the conventional sense. It is correct to say, as Gerald Gaus does,[56] that the conventional level of socio-cognitive development is sufficient for his "members of the public," or public reasoners. This is enough for them to know what is wrong, and it is not necessary for them to be able to engage in the highest levels of ethical reasoning. This is what enables them to hold other persons accountable for their conduct.

2.2. Rights Are Not a Value to Be Maximized or Optimized against Other Values

One might think of rights as an instrument to promote a general value of liberty that can be weighed against other values and thereby produce morally superior consequences, all things considered. But the standard of reasonable rejection does not include aggregated social values. What matters is not whether we are maximally or optimally producing a certain kind of value but whether the principles of justice we hold persons accountable to observe cannot be reasonably rejected by anyone. For this reason, rights thus established are constraints on conduct and not an instrument for producing a general value of liberty as part of a calculus of social value.[57] In this section, I consider paternalistic consequentialism, social welfare, and economic equality as competing values that might be alleged to defeat rights to liberty. Because having these values as competitors in a calculus of rights against a generalized value of liberty produces principles that anyone could reasonably reject, none of these are candidates for abrogating or limiting rights that no one can reasonably reject as the basis for fair terms of cooperation under the circumstances of justice.

2.2.1. Paternalistic Consequentialism

The problem of cognitive biases and heuristics points toward other problems that arise from bad individual reasoning. It is clear that many people make bad decisions involving such matters as health habits, debt, and many other things. For this reason, some theorists argue that they should be

---

the wrongful nature of their conduct. See, for a classic example, *Queen v. M'Naghten*, 8 Eng. Rep. 718 (1843).

[56] Gaus, *Order of Public Reason*, 214–16.

[57] See also Nozick, *Anarchy, State, and Utopia*, 28–30; Narveson, *Libertarian Idea*, 59.

prevented from making bad choices or compelled to make better ones.[58] Others argue instead that government should find ways to encourage people to make better choices.[59] Rights to liberty may allow people to make choices that harm themselves. Should we allow them to do that?

These paternalist arguments are based on consequentialist ethics, and similar considerations apply to both liberal and illiberal forms of paternalism that apply to utilitarianism (see section 1). Defects in human rationality may seem to justify intrusions on individual decision-making to produce superior results. For example, people may consume unhealthy foods, eat too much, or fail to save adequately for retirement. We can see how they may obtain better results if they are prevented from doing these things, or at least offered disincentives to do them. Policies that disregard the separateness of persons constitute intrusions on the integrity and freedom of persons for the sake of an aggregate benefit in much the same way that utilitarianism does. Integrity includes agent-relative reasons for action,[60] and these reasons can also be relative over time in a single person's life.[61] It is highly likely that some individuals' agent-relative reasons among a group of persons will differ from one another and that some, at least, will differ from the policy's chosen preference. A policy that breaches the integrity of persons' agent-relative reasons for action that is justified on the basis of getting it right most of the time is going to suffer from the same kind of defect as utilitarianism: it violates the integrity of some persons on behalf of an aggregate benefit.

One moral problem with these forms of paternalism is that they are concerned with consequences only and are thus plagued by some of the same problems as their cousin, utilitarianism. They disregard agency and ignore how the exercise of agency, apart from any inherent value it may have, also has consequences that may be desirable for the persons who experience them. For example, let us say that I have made various poor decisions in my life and, looking back on those decisions, I have learned from them. I have become wiser as a result of my mistakes, and I value the wisdom I have

---

[58] See Sarah Conly, *Against Autonomy* (New York: Cambridge University Press, 2013).

[59] See Richard H. Thaler and Cass R. Sunstein, *Nudge: Improving Decisions about Health, Wealth, and Happiness*, rev. ed. (New York: Penguin, 2009).

[60] This is a key part of Williams's critique of utilitarianism. See J. J. C. Smart and Bernard Williams, *Utilitarianism: For and Against* (Cambridge: Cambridge University Press, 1973), 108–17.

[61] Derek Parfit, *Reasons and Persons* (Oxford: Oxford University Press, 1984), 192–93.

gained in this way. Had I been prevented from making these mistakes by a benevolent dictator, I would indeed have avoided the negative consequences of my poor decisions, but I would be no wiser today than I was before. This is a bad result for me from my point of view, and it is a result that the benevolent dictator has imposed upon me, purportedly for my own benefit. I am on solid ground if I assert that the dictator's actions are unreasonable, regardless of the dictator's intention to act for my benefit, and anyone may reasonably reject them.

Sarah Conly argues that we are likely to reason poorly when presented with challenges in the moment and should bind ourselves with rules designed by someone in a planning mode not faced with the need for a hasty decision.[62] She notes that "in *Nudge*, Sunstein and Thaler refer often to the doer and the planner: the planner is able to think about decisions where he is not subject to, for example, temptation—he decides on the day's food purchases while he is at home, not when he is standing hungrily in front of the bakery counter."[63] Anyone who wishes to improve their diet for health purposes will soon learn that planning is important to success. If they succeed in learning to do this, that person will have strengthened their capacity for choice through the exercise of their agency. The paternalist seeks to deprive us of such opportunities to enhance our capacities through the exercise of our agency, and it is for this reason that paternalism breaches our separateness and why any person can reasonably reject such interventions. The stakes, of course, may be larger than in the foregoing example. Suppose I value teaching my children frugality and saving, which I regard as virtues. My children and I must have the freedom to make mistakes to develop and practice these virtues. The paternalist seeks to impose barriers to my ability to pursue this end I value, and I, or any other person, can reasonably reject such barriers and the principles on which they are erected.

2.2.2. *Welfare Economics*

Even sound individual choices may in some cases produce socially suboptimal results. Should we override rights to liberty where some kinds of actions, taken in the aggregate, have a collective impact that reduces social welfare? If we regard rights to liberty as part of a calculus of social well-being and employ, say, a criterion of Pareto optimality as our moral yardstick, we would certainly override rights to liberty to produce socially optimal outcomes. Thus, for example, Robert Frank defends cash subsidies to

---

[62] Conly, *Against Autonomy*, 38–39.
[63] Ibid., 38.

farmers "who cannot make ends meet" compared to other, less efficient programs such as price supports.[64] More generally, individual action that is not wrong in itself may lead to collective results that no one prefers, such as individual contributions to malinvestment that lead to economic effects that are harmful in the aggregate.[65]

But there are very powerful reasons not to think of rights in the way someone such as Frank suggests. To explain these, I borrow some concepts from F.A. Hayek, who was not himself a theorist of rights. Hayek distinguishes between two kinds of social order: *cosmos* and *taxis*.[66] *Cosmos* is a social order that exists, not to attain specific goals, but rather to facilitate the pursuit of individuals' goals. *Cosmos* itself does not have a goal. *Taxis*, on the other hand, is an organization designed to achieve some known and specified goal or goals. Hayek also distinguishes the following categories of rules: *nomos* and *thesis*.[67] *Nomos* consists of principles that facilitate cooperation among persons and facilitate the pursuit of individuals' ends that are not known to others. Such principles are end-independent rules of conduct. *Thesis* consists of rules that are characteristic of organizations and that are designed to achieve known specific purposes.

It is clear that a welfare economist regards a social and political system as having the goal of attaining socially optimal outcomes, even if they do not consider such a system itself as a type of organization in the sense that a business or public bureaucracy is an organization. As a result, consequentialist ethical approaches that seek to produce a particular pattern[68] of social outcome, such as welfare economics, suffer from the same kind of defect that plagues utilitarianism in that these will compromise the integrity of individuals and treat a social decision as if it were a rational decision-making process for an individual. Individuals must regard the socially optimal outcome as their preferred choice even if that requires them to forgo opportunities to increase their own well-being or exercise their freedom in ways that might lead to a less-than-optimal social outcome. Thus, I am

---

[64] Robert H. Frank, *The Darwin Economy: Liberty, Competition, and the Common Good* (Princeton: Princeton University Press, 2011), 115–16.

[65] John Cassidy, *How Markets Fail* (New York: Picador, 2010), 177–91.

[66] Friedrich A. Hayek, *Rules and Order*, vol. I of *Law, Legislation and Liberty* (Chicago: University of Chicago Press, 1973), 35–52. Cf. Michael Oakeshott's distinction between "civil" and "enterprise" associations in *On Human Conduct* (Oxford: Clarendon, 1975), 108–19.

[67] Ibid., 94–144.

[68] Nozick, *Anarchy, State, and Utopia*, 155–60.

morally obligated to prefer cash payments to farmers to my investing in some other enterprise that would otherwise advance my own purposes. A decision that generates a socially optimal outcome treats the social decision as if it were an individual decision to produce an efficient allocation of that individual's resources, but, as Rawls argued, this decision fails to acknowledge the separateness of persons. Where individual actions that are morally permissible contribute in some way to external effects that are undesirable, this result is not unjust, and injustice rears its head when we enter into conflict with one another over the appropriate response, which is highly likely since no one has done anything that is morally blameworthy.[69] Anyone can reasonably reject such a decision.

While Hayek is not a theorist of rights, his distinctions are useful in thinking about how rights differ from some other kinds of rules. In particular, the rights I have in mind here are rights that antecede any kind of political organization and are rights that persons have by virtue of being persons. Because, as I am arguing here, such rights are not derived from their contribution to aggregate utility or a Pareto-optimal social outcome, they are not to be weighed against such patterns of social outcome and are not overridden by such considerations.

2.2.3. Egalitarianism

Suppose that persons agree upon terms of their cooperation, interact repeatedly to establish a system of social and economic cooperation, and subsequently discover that some prosper more than others under this arrangement. Those who benefit less might assert that they are due compensation for their observance of the terms of cooperation, and they might reject these terms if they are not compensated. Where none of these persons can reasonably reject the terms of their cooperation, those who benefit more could reasonably reject the claim that they must compensate the others. After all, this is thus far a voluntary arrangement. But suppose further that the persons interact as part of a larger social and economic system established and perpetuated by rules enforced with coercive sanctions and that they have not actually consented to this arrangement. Now all are alike subject to a social and economic system to which they have not actually consented. Does this strengthen the hand of those who could reasonably reject these terms without compensation?

---

[69] Tibor Machan, *Individuals and Their Rights* (La Salle, IL: Open Court, 1989), 144–46; Hans-Hermann Hoppe, *A Theory of Socialism and Capitalism*, 2nd ed. (Auburn, AL: Ludwig von Mises Institute, 2016) 162–63.

Thomas Nagel argues that it does.[70] He offers a contractualist argument employing the reasonable rejection standard[71] that given the historical states we have, which are based upon coercion and not voluntary choice, we should treat these states as an exogenous factor in settling upon principles of justice. Some people will prosper more than others in a given system, for a whole variety of reasons, many of which are beyond their power to control. Nagel argues that in these circumstances, those who prosper more should have some of their wealth redistributed to those who have less in order to promote material equality among all the people subject to this state. Part of the rationale for this is that those who prosper more benefit more from this arrangement than those who prosper less and that those who prosper less could reasonably reject this arrangement given that they prosper less. Nagel glosses over the fact that neither those who prosper more nor those who prosper less have necessarily chosen this arrangement. Generally, this kind of arrangement has been imposed upon all of them by some third party, by the force of history, or generally by the force of something external to them. It is not chosen by them, and it is not necessarily supported by them. And those who prosper more can reasonably reject a principle that requires the redistribution of their wealth by this third party who has erected or perpetuated that system to those who have prospered less. They are all equally subject through the coercion of this third party or by the historical circumstance that has imposed this system on all of them. So we cannot examine it just from the standpoint of those who prosper less but also from that of those who prosper more, and the latter can reasonably reject a principle that requires them, because of their being subject to this system, to have their wealth redistributed to others.

Nagel's argument about redistribution would be stronger if the principle were reached in a freely negotiated bargain among the people, so let us say the parties themselves agree that they will enter into a certain kind of social and economic arrangement with each other knowing that some might prosper more than others. They might agree that it would be a mutually beneficial bargain if they agreed to redistribute wealth among themselves

---

[70] Thomas Nagel, *Equality and Partiality* (Oxford: Oxford University Press, 1991).

[71] While Nagel endorses Scanlon's contractualism, he arguably "treats Scanlon's general claim (an act is wrong iff some *principle* forbidding it is *un*rejectable) as equivalent to the claim that an act is wrong iff every principle *permitting* it is rejectable." Hanoch Sheinman, "Act and Principle Contractualism," *Utilitas* 23, no. 3 (September 2011): 289. See also Shelly Kagan, "The Unanimity Standard," *Journal of Social Philosophy* 24, no. 2 (Fall 1993): 149.

from the more prosperous to the less prosperous parties. But in the absence of such a bargain, anyone could reasonably reject a principle that required them to compensate others for their less prosperous position. Nothing in the circumstances of justice—that is, limited benevolence—mandates such a principle.

3. Articulating Rights: Abstract and Specified Rights

Rights to liberty are general principles derived via contractualist reasoning that require further specification to form part of working systems of rules to facilitate cooperation among persons under the circumstances of justice among separate, free, and equal persons. This section includes two parts. In the first part, I explain how the separateness of persons under the circumstances of justice and contractualist moral reasoning enables us to derive abstract rights to liberty. In the second part, I explain the problematic nature of abstract rights for a workable system of rules, and I show how contractualist reasoning not only establishes abstract rights but supports more fully specified rights as well.

3.1. Deriving Abstract Rights to Liberty

In sections 1 and 2, I showed how some principles are ruled out by the contractualist method of ethical reasoning in light of the separateness of persons considering principles to govern their social interaction under the circumstances of justice. I began in section 1 with the familiar objections of Nozick, Rawls, and Williams that utilitarianism fails to consider the separateness of persons because it treats a social decision as if it were a decision of a single person. Utilitarianism fails to respect the separateness of persons because it treats individuals and their preferences as fungible parts of an aggregate decision and morally compels individuals to prefer the socially preferred choice over their own, even at the cost of the integrity of their own goals, plans, and projects.[72] From there, I considered persons examining principles to govern their social interaction under the circumstances of justice, which are limited benevolence, limited scarcity, and a rough equality of persons. Under these circumstances, separate individuals, who are not morally required to give greater weight to the ends of others than their own, are likewise not morally required to give greater weight to a social preference

---

[72] Loren Lomasky calls them "projects," or ends chosen by persons, because they take on a motivating and guiding role in their lives. See *Persons, Rights, and the Moral Community*, 52–55.

ordering than to their own preference ordering. Under the circumstances of justice, persons are free and equal, and any person may reasonably reject a proposed principle that fails to acknowledge them as a separate, valuing individual who is not morally required to abandon their goals, plans, or projects for the sake of the goals, plans, or projects of other persons. Since utilitarianism demands that they do this, any person can reasonably reject a utilitarian moral principle as the basis for governing social interaction among persons under the circumstances of justice. In this way, contractualist moral reasoning enables persons considering principles to govern their social conduct under the circumstances of justice to rule out principles that anyone can reasonably reject.

In section 2, I employed the foregoing approach to rule out some alternative principles. Paternalist consequentialism fails to respect the separateness of persons because it compels or prohibits certain choices to generate "better" choices, where "better" is defined in terms of want satisfaction or well-being. Paternalist policies breach the separateness of persons because they compel or prohibit choices and actions by everyone in order to advance the want satisfaction or well-being of persons who would make "worse" choices. As I argued in section 2, there are legitimate, value-related reasons why people may want the freedom to make mistakes, even if this results in some "worse" choices, because these develop their capacity for choice, and some persons may simply have an individual preference ordering that reflects different values or discounts the future differently than many other people do. Not only these persons, but anyone, may reasonably reject paternalism for these reasons. Welfare economics supports policies that breach the separateness of persons though regulation, taxes, subsidies, and the like. These breach the separateness of persons because they compel or prohibit individuals to pay, act, or refrain from acting as they otherwise would in order to promote an outcome deemed socially superior in terms of preference satisfaction. Everyone is morally required to subordinate their goals, plans, and projects to the social goal of efficiency as understood by welfare economics. Anyone can reasonably reject such policies because they fail to respect the separateness of persons, subordinating them to an overarching social goal. Finally, egalitarianism and its associated policies of redistribution and prohibitions on acts that would upset an egalitarian distribution also fail to respect the separateness of persons. Egalitarianism does this because it harnesses individuals with their separate goals, plans, and projects to the social goal of material equality. Anyone can reasonably reject this principle, as well as paternalism and egalitarianism, because in breaching the separateness of persons, these principles and their policies fail to give due regard to the generic interests that persons share under the circumstances of justice.

The foregoing set forth the structure to derive rights to liberty from the background conditions of justice and associated separateness of persons conjoined with contractualist moral reasoning to show why there are abstract rights to life and liberty as traditionally understood in classical liberal and libertarian thought. The arguments presented in sections 1 and 2 can be used to derive and defend rights to liberty in the following way. The circumstances of justice underscore the separateness of individuals. These circumstances—limited benevolence, limited scarcity, and rough equality of persons—mean that persons can be expected to be partial to their own ends and that the ends of individuals may conflict. The function of principles of justice, including rights, is to mediate such conflicts. Separate persons have their own ends and commitments and a sense of their own good, and rights to liberty enable them to pursue and promote those. To reasonably reject a principle, a person must refer to the circumstances of justice, the separateness of persons, the free and equal nature of moral agents, and the generic interests of such agents to show that someone or anyone could reasonably reject a proposed principle. In considering such principles, each must consider the claims of others in order to find principles that no one can reasonably reject, since reasonableness includes the quality of taking into account the generic interests of other persons. Darwall nicely characterizes these kinds of interests as those we have in "living self-directed lives on terms of mutual respect with others."[73] Principles that no one can reasonably reject will be reversible in the sense that each person cannot reasonably reject having that principle applied to themselves as well as to other persons.

I showed in sections 1 and 2 how claims people may make on each other in several approaches to moral and political philosophy may be reasonably rejected by persons in light of the separateness of persons and the "neo-Kantian" contractualist procedure for considering claims. Negative rights to liberty, as principles of justice, are subject to the same scrutiny and will withstand that scrutiny. Negative rights to liberty, as traditionally formulated, will survive such scrutiny because they take into account the separateness of persons who are partial to their own ends and commitments and have a sense of their own good. Free and equal moral agents have the generic interests encapsulated in Darwall's idea of self-directed lives on terms of mutual respect. Negative rights to liberty protect those generic interests by permitting persons to pursue their own ends and commitments as defined and chosen by them subject to the reversible and thus equal nature of negative rights to liberty as principles of justice. This means that such rights

---

[73] Darwall, *Second-Person Standpoint*, 308.

are not absolute and that they must be defined in such a way that persons may exercise their rights equally as negative rights to liberty.

The contractualist procedure for identifying such principles embodies the concept of reasonableness in that (a) a principle surviving examination would be one that will enable people observing it to justify their conduct consistent with that principle to others, so that others cannot reasonably reject the principle permitting or proscribing the conduct, (b) insofar as proposed principles include factual claims, these claims have not been proven false, and (c) insofar as the arguments over the principle and conduct rely on proffered ends, each person must accept that each person may pursue their own ends. Condition (c) does not require that each person give equal weight to the ends of other persons in considering principles to govern their social interaction. That condition does not require that any person disregard the greater weight they bestow upon their own ends. Instead, it requires that as a condition of practical reason, each person must recognize that others have ends and reasons of their own that perform the same function for those other persons as his ends and reasons do for him. He cannot reasonably disregard this characteristic of other persons in promoting his claims and considering theirs. Each person must be able to justify his conduct to others in terms of consistency with a principle that all others must concede is a legitimate rule to govern their social conduct because none can reasonably reject that principle.

Persons considering principles of just conduct could not reasonably reject the basic rights to liberty that are generally recognized among liberal societies that protect freedom of thought, expression, conscience, and action and that correspond in a rough and general way to the classical liberal rights to "Life, Liberty and the pursuit of Happiness."[74] Rather than identifying a collection of such rights, I employ some of them as examples here to show how to offer a contractualist defense of such abstract rights, which I follow in the next section with a contractualist method for specifying them. These abstract rights are prima facie rights in that they must be given more specific form as rules that function as part of a system of rules to govern interpersonal conduct.

Rights are grounded in the separateness of persons because each person may reasonably reject any principle that would subordinate their ends to any purported social objective or to any end but the protection of the like liberty of other persons. Anyone can reasonably reject forcible prohibitions on freedom of thought, expression, and association. The basis for

---

[74] Declaration of Independence, ¶ 2 (1776).

considering such norms is to establish morally acceptable conditions under which persons may choose and pursue ends that are valued by them. It is inherent in the idea that an end is valued by a person and promoted by that person regardless of the end's object—that is, to promote the well-being of others.

Persons considering rights cannot reasonably reject principles protecting the rights of themselves and others to pursue their self-chosen ends. All persons advancing a contention that they should be permitted to pursue their own ends must agree that others should have the liberty to do the same. Thus, for example, rights protecting freedom of conscience protect the rights of persons to worship, or not to worship, as they choose. The same is true of rights to freedom of expression, travel, and choice of an occupation or subject of study.

Anyone could reject a principle that granted persons unequal rights to liberty of action. Where one person contends for the freedom to pursue his or her own ends, that person must concede a like freedom to others as well. Rights to freedom of action extend to a freedom to engage in categories of action, and such rights are compossible. That is, everyone can exercise those rights, where the object of the rights is to engage in categories of acts in pursuit of one's self-chosen ends.[75] In this sense, rights establish "moral territories"[76] in which individuals can choose and act, and it is the compossibility of those territories that is the subject matter of the justice of rights. It is for this reason that persons considering such rights should not prevail with the contention that their freedom to act is nullified by the acts of others that are mutually exclusive with their own, such as winning a foot race. If the ends of agents are mutually exclusive, an actor may defend the position that their successful acts that entail the failure of another's are reasonable, provided each agent retained freedom to act in promoting their own ends.

Universal moral rights as I conceive them here are abstract principles and do not of themselves comprise a full-blown legal regime of rights. Such principles must be interpreted to be applied to particular cases or to be formulated into more specific legal rules for governing interpersonal conduct, but abstract principles help to narrow the bounds of collective decision by ruling out some alternatives that would clearly violate these general

---

[75] Cf. Hillel Steiner, "The Structure of a Set of Compossible Rights," *Journal of Philosophy* 74 (1977), 767–75.

[76] Douglas B. Rasmussen and Douglas J. Den Uyl, *Liberty and Nature: An Aristotelian Defense of Liberal Order* (La Salle, IL: Open Court, 1991).

principles.[77] This is not an embarrassment to a philosophical theory of rights. In Locke's formulation of natural rights, he notes that "the law of nature being unwritten, and so nowhere to be found, but in the minds of men," it is subject to erroneous interpretation by them "through passion or interest."[78] Generally, "there wants an established, settled, known law, received and allowed by common consent to be the standard of right and wrong, and the common measure to decide all controversies between them: for though the law of nature be plain and intelligible to all rational creatures; yet men being biassed by their interest, as well as ignorant for want of study of it, are not apt to allow of it as a law binding to them in the application of it to their particular cases."[79]

Lockean natural rights are general moral principles that are more specifically defined in legislation, but these function as limits on the content of legislation: "The obligations of the law of nature cease not in society, but only in many cases are drawn closer, and have by human laws known penalties annexed to them to enforce their observation. Thus the law of nature stands as an eternal rule to all men, legislators as well as others. The rules that they make for other men's actions, must, as well as their own and other men's actions, be conformable to the law of nature."[80] The function of universal moral rights, in Locke's system, is a negative one: rights prohibit some interpretations of these principles but do not constitute a set of fully specified rules that must be applied uniformly throughout all human societies.

3.2. Specifying Rights

The rights I have described in the preceding section are abstract rights. That is, they are general principles that do not of themselves fully specify the actions permitted or prohibited thereunder. Abstract rights are indeterminate in that there may be more than one morally acceptable means of implementing them. In this section, I consider the function that such rights perform in a system of rules governing individual conduct. My chief conclusion is that abstract rights go a long way toward eliminating a broad range of alternatives because of their negative nature and function and are therefore critically important to any set of rule-making institutions or processes. Further, I argue that the contractualist method of practical reason

---

[77] Cf. Gaus, *Order of Public Reason*, 335.
[78] John Locke, *Second Treatise of Government*, sec 136.
[79] Ibid., sec. 124:
[80] Ibid., sec. 135.

in ethics can be employed to specify rights in particular contexts or systems of rules.

It is a mistake to assume that universal, abstract rights must translate into a fully specified legal system. Such rights are blunt instruments that impose prohibitions on individual and collective behavior. They are blunt in that they are sufficiently open textured[81] that there is room for reasonable disagreements about their application in readily imaginable cases. Because universal, abstract rights are justified from a decontextualized, abstract moral point of view, the process of justification yields abstract principles that do not of themselves contain the keys to their application to particular contexts. This should not be a great surprise. Such principles as "Congress shall make no law… abridging the freedom of speech" do not of themselves explain how to interpret and apply them to specific instances. The problem is how to apply abstract principles, formulated in a decontextualized milieu, to concrete cultural and historical situations while not violating the abstract principle.

How far can the "neo-Kantian" contractualist method I have defended here be used to specify the content of rights to liberty? It can go quite a long way, though it does not of itself fully specify the content of these rights and leaves multiple options for implementing them; hence their partial indeterminacy. Kurt Baier distinguished "true moralities" and "absolute morality" as follows. True moralities are those of particular groups. These may differ from the true moralities of other groups, but what makes each of them a true morality is that they can all "pass the test which moralities must pass in order to be called true."[82] Absolute morality consists of the shared features of the "true" moralities: "Every true morality must contain as its core the convictions belonging to absolute morality, but it may also contain a lot more that could not be contained in every other true morality."[83] I suggest that this distinction is useful for the partially indeterminate contractualist method I have defended here. The contractualist method of practical reasoning and the general principles that can be derived from it from the background of the circumstances of justice and separateness of persons are shared by all morally defensible systems of rules. These systems may have content that differs from others' and yet remain defensible from this contractualist perspective.

Gaus, for example, who argues that more-specific rules applying abstract rights require public justification, recognizes that public justification

---

[81] Hart, *Concept of Law*, 120–32.
[82] Baier, *Moral Point of View*, 181.
[83] Ibid., 183.

yields a "socially eligible set" of interpretations of an abstract right but not a unique agreed-upon interpretation.[84] The specification of abstract rights is thus limited in scope yet partially indeterminate. If there are two interpretations of an abstract right, and no one can reasonably reject either interpretation, both interpretations are morally permitted. If no one can reasonably reject a right, for example, against unprovoked violence, and if there are two interpretations of (a) what constitutes adequate provocation and (b) whether provocation is a complete defense against prosecution or only a partial defense that reduces the severity of a charge for violence, none of which can be reasonably rejected, then all of them are morally permitted. All of them are morally acceptable, and this is a reason for the indeterminacy of abstract rights, indeterminate in the sense that to the extent they can be interpreted in more than one reasonable way they may have more than one application that could be used in different places at different times. In fact, both across time and across jurisdictions, provocation as a defense against prosecution for violent actions has been treated differently, both as to what constitutes adequate provocation and as to whether it is a partial or (in a minority of jurisdictions) a complete defense against prosecution for some violent acts.[85] Unless someone can offer a reasonable rejection of some of these alternate interpretations of this aspect of the right against violent assaults, there is therefore a "blameless liberty" of choice among them. That is, all of them are morally acceptable and none are morally proscribed, and yet the right against unprovoked violence remains justified as an abstract right.

Even when formulated into constitutional rules, rights protecting liberty will take the form of abstract principles, such as "Congress shall make no law... abridging the freedom of speech."[86] Reasonable interpretations of this general principle may incorporate limitations on the exercise of this right that are defensible in terms of the agency claims that a right of free speech protects. Thus, for example, one could reasonably defend a limitation denying legal protection to speech that was intended to incite persons to immediate violence and was likely to be successful in doing so under the circumstances.[87] One could defend this interpretation of the First Amendment's Speech Clause in terms of the agency interest it protects in

---

[84] Gaus, *Order of Public Reason*, 369–70.

[85] See, e.g., Mitchell N. Berman and Ian Farrell, "Provocation Manslaughter as a Partial Justification and Partial Excuse," *William & Mary Law Review* 52 (March 2011), 1027–1107.

[86] U.S. Const. amend. I.

[87] *Brandenburg v. Ohio*, 395 U.S. 444 (1969).

preventing violent injury. There could easily be other formulations of this limitation on speech that could be defended in the same way, such as a denial of protection to speech that posed a "clear and present danger"[88] of bringing about some harm to the physical safety or agency claims of other persons. In this example, the "clear and present danger" rule authorizes a narrower scope to freedom of speech because it does not require that the speaker intends to incite others to bring about harm to anyone. Either of these formulations could be defended in terms of the agency claims that support a right of freedom of speech, and as a result both might populate the "socially eligible set" of interpretations, to borrow Gaus's term. The question presented here is not the particular limitation on speech but rather the scope of the right of freedom of speech. The set of rules that delimit that right are those that no one can reasonably reject, in terms of the agency claims on which the universal and abstract right of liberty is defensible in the first instance, as an alternative to having no rule to protect freedom of speech at all.

What would it take for an application of this rule to become one that anyone could reasonably reject on the grounds that it breaches the separateness of persons to promote an end that is not their own? One historical interpretation of this rule was the "bad tendency" test, which required no evidence that the speech would result in violations of the law. Thus, for example, a group of left-wing activists were prosecuted for publishing their objections to President Woodrow Wilson's decision to send US forces to Russia to intervene in the fighting among Bolshevik and other forces at the end of the First World War and for calling for a general strike by American workers to signal their opposition to this military action. The Supreme Court affirmed their convictions for violating the federal Espionage Act on the ground that, had American workers heeded the call for a general strike, this could have obstructed the US military effort.[89] There was no evidence that there was a danger of this happening. The "bad tendency" test is one that anyone could reasonably reject as an interpretation of a right of freedom of speech because, inter alia, it prohibits pure speech that is not likely to result in a violation of any other person's rights to liberty or personal safety. It is not simply that there is another, better test available, but that anyone can reasonably reject this rule on its own merits. In this case, the test prohibited speech criticizing a public policy on the ground that it might successfully convince people to oppose the policy, and anyone could reasonably reject a rule prohibiting such criticism because this is precisely the agency interest that separate, free, and equal persons have against a purported

---

[88] *Schenck v. United States*, 249 U.S. 47 (1919).
[89] *Abrams v. United States*, 250 U.S. 616 (1920).

Deriving Rights to Liberty

overarching social goal such as continuing a war effort unhindered by the expression of dissenting views.

For example, consider four attributes that might constitute the requisite act for a specific rights violation: intent, recklessness, negligence, and strict liability. These options are drawn from American law.[90] *Intent* means that the actor intended the consequences of their actions. *Recklessness* means that the actor consciously disregarded a substantial and unjustifiable risk of harm to others and caused the consequences of his or her actions. *Negligence* means that the actor should have been aware of the risk of harm to others posed by his or her actions but was not and caused the consequences of those actions. *Strict liability* means that the actor caused the consequences of their actions. A group of persons is to consider whether an act that causes a physical injury to another person constitutes a violation of the latter's rights. It seems unlikely that anyone could justify to others a rule that permitted intentional, reckless, or negligent acts that cause physical harm to others and refused to regard such acts as violations of their recipient's rights to physical integrity.[91] Likewise, it seems unlikely that one could justify to others a rule that would hold a true, faultless accident as a violation of another person's rights. The reasons that support a universally held right must themselves be universal. Any person could reasonably object to a rule that permitted intentional, reckless, or negligent acts causing physical harm to others. The reasons that defeat a universally held right must also be universal reasons. In this case, the universally held right to autonomous choice refutes the claim in favor of a rule that would punish or otherwise hold liable a person's choice that plays a causal role in a true, faultless accident.

This conclusion has important implications for the function that rights perform: rights to liberty impose conditions on rule-making processes and eliminate some rules from consideration. A rule-making process that articulates a rule prohibiting intentional, reckless, and negligent acts that cause physical harm to others is a justifiable protection against violations of rights. On the other hand, it seems that a rule that prohibits acts that result in true, faultless accidents is not justifiable because reasonable persons could interpose defensible objections to such a rule. These objections could themselves readily be grounded in rights to liberty on the basis that a person has the right to do that which does not violate the rights of others, and acts

---

[90] See, e.g., *Prosser and Keeton on the Law of Torts*, 5th ed. (St. Paul, MN: West, 1984).

[91] Consent can, of course, be a moral (and generally a legal) defense to such activities as surgery and boxing.

that play a causal role in true, faultless accidents do not violate the rights of others and hence are permissible acts.

Note that in the foregoing example we are still in the realm of abstract rights. Thus, it will not do to say that there might be some persons who would punish others or hold them financially liable for true, faultless accidents, because they would be unable universally to justify such a rule. Hence, such a rule is excluded from consideration. It is not difficult, though, to find issues for which more than one rule might be an acceptable means of giving expression to a general right, and this illustrates why these general principles are indeterminate.

The standard of reasonable rejection would tend to render rights to liberty negative rather than positive, or at least would seem to rule out some kinds of positive rights. The distinction between negative and positive rights is a familiar one, and I will not outline the distinction here.[92] I have shown that people cannot reasonably reject abstract rights to personal or civil liberties, but I have not addressed whether people can reasonably reject proposed rights to some kinds of positive rights, such as rights to due process. Note that I am not making the stronger claim that it would rule out all positive rights. Instead, I am claiming that we can see how this approach would rule out some kinds of positive rights.

Recall the discussion earlier about how some moral theories, such as utilitarianism, violate the separateness of persons by placing some persons at the service of others' ends, depending on where they come out in the social calculation of utility over choices of principles, rules, or policies. It seems clear that positive rights of some sorts would have a similar effect. For example, a policy designed to give effect to a "patterned" principle of distributive justice, to borrow Nozick's term, would have the effect of denying persons the liberty to enter into mutually agreeable transactions or to require confiscation of property for redistribution. Under the circumstances of justice, the conditions of limited benevolence and limited scarcity would permit persons to reasonably reject claims that they were obligated to advance a patterned principle of distribution that would restrict their liberty in these ways.

---

[92] See Isaiah Berlin, "Two Concepts of Liberty," in *Four Essays on Liberty* (New York: Oxford University Press, 1969), 118–72.

4. Conclusion

There are solid moral foundations for the rights to liberty championed by classical liberal and libertarian theorists. These foundations, I have argued, rest initially on the idea that the separateness of persons is embedded in the circumstances of life that make justice a meaningful concept. We can discover the duties justice imposes on us through a procedure for identifying principles of justice based on the concept of reasonableness, which supports a testing procedure for proposed principles for human interaction. A contractualist ethics vindicates principles that establish duties to others that also constitute rights to liberty, which are principally negative in character and rule out many forms of social decision rules and intrusions upon individual liberty that anyone could reasonably reject. The indeterminacy of these prima facie, abstract rights is not an embarrassment to them. The same standard of reasonable rejection can be used to specify such rights into applicable rules, including qualifications and variations of their application across time and place.

THE USE OF TORRENTS IN SOCIETY

RADU USZKAI[*]

1. Introduction

Within the general libertarian framework, recent scholarly work on intellectual property (IP) is quite rare. For example, in analyzing the foundations of libertarianism and its positions on a wide array of topics, from the nature of liberty to civil rights, Brennan (2012) discusses, at length, why libertarians think property rights are important, yet disregards issues involving IP with the sole exception of a paragraph discussing how patents might inhibit innovation. The same is true when we take a close look at the *Routledge Handbook of Libertarianism* (Brennan, van der Fossen, and Schmidtz 2018), where there is no discussion of IP in the chapter dedicated to property rights (Stilz 2018), save for a short examination of patents in Flanigan's effort at developing a libertarian approach to medicine (2018).

In the absence of such a unified stance on IP (Long 1995; Bell 2014, 6; Uszkai 2015, 188–94), we can identify a wide array of libertarian positions on copyrights and patents. One of the first libertarian defenses of IP from a natural rights perspective comes from Lysander Spooner (1855). Robert

---

[*]Radu Uszkai teaches in the Department of Philosophy and Social Sciences, Bucharest University of Economic Studies. An earlier version of this paper was presented at the PPE Society Meeting in New Orleans in 2017. I would like to thank Anda Zahiu, Emi Socaciu, Mihail-Valentin Cernea, Cristina Voinea, Scott Scheall, and Constantin Vică for their valuable comments and suggestions. I would also like to thank the two anonymous reviewers and the journal editor for their valuable feedback and recommendations.

CITATION INFORMATION FOR THIS ARTICLE:
Radu Uszkai. 2018. "The Use of Torrents in Society." *Libertarian Papers*. 10 (2): 343-372. ONLINE AT: libertarianpapers.org. THIS ARTICLE IS subject to a Creative Commons Attribution 3.0 License (creativecommons.org/licenses).

Nozick also famously argues, within a Lockean framework, that inventors are entitled to patents in a minimal state but the duration of the legal protection should be drastically shortened (1974, 141, 181–82). Previously, Ayn Rand posited that an individual has the "right to the product of his mind" (1967, 130), while criticizing the idea of perpetual IP protection. Other libertarian-leaning scholars such as Bryan Cwik have highlighted that labor, understood in a neo-Lockean way, should be the basis of IP (2014). Outside of the natural rights framework, some economists have pointed out that copyrights and patents should be understood as incentive mechanisms for creators, thus providing a utilitarian case for copyright and patents (Landes and Posner 2003).

Other libertarian philosophers and economists have mounted a robust critique of the moral acceptability of granting property rights to ideas (and their expression), either in the form of artistic creations or inventions and technological innovations. In three seminal papers, Tom G. Palmer (1989; 1990) and Stephan Kinsella (2001) attack the normative foundations of the natural rights, utilitarian, and personhood-based accounts in favor of IP. Samuel Edward Konkin III argues that copyrights are not a creation of the market, criticizing both utilitarian and natural rights accounts (1986). More recently, Michele Boldrin and David K. Levine (2008) try to show that, on utilitarian (or broadly consequentialist) terms, copyrights and patents actually hinder innovation and competition by promoting toxic monopolies.[1] Last but not least, Wendy McElroy reiterates the argument that only scarce goods can be the object of property rights and sees a dangerous implication of the protection of copyrights: authors could claim ownership to what is in the minds of their readers (2011, 10).

With this general map of libertarian positions on copyright in mind, the current paper aims at exploring whether the anti-IP case could be strengthened by appealing to a surprising figure: F.A. Hayek. At first glance, this choice might seem bizarre, as his remarks and ruminations on copyright (and other IP rights) and copyright infringement are rather brief and sketchy, and are scattered through various works (seemingly) without any conceptual unity. Without rejecting previous work done by libertarians on the question of whether copyright is morally legitimate (quite the contrary), this paper will firstly strive to establish a Hayekian research agenda on copyright by providing a unified reading of Hayek's remarks in the bigger picture of the contemporary philosophy, politics, and economics of IP. Secondly, exploring

---

[1] When it comes to policy recommendations, some positions are a bit more nuanced. For more details, see Bell (2014).

peer-to-peer (P2P) file sharing and copyright infringement through a Hayekian lens suggests what might be a useful analogy between the ability of torrent downloads and prices to convey information. Last but not least, the paper will end on a skeptical note concerning the moral and economic foundations of copyright by presenting what I consider a more Hayekian alternative: crowdfunding platforms.

Taking into account the fact that Hayek is recognized for the study of knowledge, complex social phenomena, and spontaneous orders, establishing such a research agenda not only would strengthen the libertarian case against IP, but it could also be of great interest for Hayekian scholars interested in the many ramifications of his work. There are similar examples in current classical liberal/libertarian debates, with the libertarian case in favor of a universal basic income being at the forefront. While Hayek does not explicitly discuss a universal basic income, he is referenced by some scholars who try to establish such a case (Munger 2011; Zwolinski 2011) and features in Zwolinski's philosophical reconstruction of why he would support such a policy (2013). We could think about my exploration here in a similar way.

2. The Philosophy, Politics, and Economics of Copyright

In 2014 Swedish police raided the headquarters of The Pirate Bay, seizing its servers and computers and shutting down what used to be "the galaxy's *most resilient* BitTorrent site" (Beyer and McKelvey 2015, 899). The Pirate Bay's founders had already been treated similarly in 2006, when their headquarters were raided by Stockholm police for the same reason. The four founders of the website were found guilty by a Swedish court in 2009 for assisting in violations of copyright law and were each sentenced to prison time and charged a hefty fine for the damages The Pirate Bay (allegedly) caused (Larsson 2013, 354).

Neither of these was, however, the first major case involving copyright infringement in the internet era. That honor is reserved for the American rock band Metallica and its infamous 2000 suit against Napster, the first major P2P file-sharing system (Merriden 2001). While it might be successfully argued that the digital revolution and the emergence of online P2P file sharing have increased the scope of media piracy,[2] cases like Metallica's are not unique to the contemporary landscape; copyright infringement and IP wars have existed ever since Gutenberg's invention (Johns 2009; Baldwin 2014).

Neither Napster nor The Pirate Bay enjoys a good reputation among most moral philosophers and economists. They hold this position because they see copyright the way they see any other property right, as grounded either in Lockean natural rights (Tavani 2005; Spinello 2011), neo-Lockean labor considerations (Cwik 2014), neo-Kantian and neo-Hegelian personhood arguments (Schroeder 2006), or even (albeit very rarely) Rawls's theory of justice (Merges 2011).

While not directly denying the value of this principled approach to copyright, a distinct cohort of mostly economists and legal scholars tend to focus on the consequences of copyright, thereby formulating a utilitarian case for a property right in expressing ideas. Perhaps one of the best examples of this approach can be found in the works of Landes and Posner, who write within the general American approach to IP. The crux of the problem for the utilitarian rests on the incentives available for the creative individual: would an artist write, paint, or compose without the power to exclude others from copying her work? Landes and Posner (2003) believe that few would and that that is why we need to grant property rights in the expression of ideas. In this way society will benefit from the existence of books, music, and art. Moreover, even if protecting copyrights is expensive,[3] the trade-off between free access and incentives is worth making. Because of copyright, copies of books, movies, and video games are artificially scarce and, as the laws of supply and demand predict, more expensive for consumers. However, because (to take only one example) copies of video games are more expensive, more and more game developers are incentivized to produce new and better gaming experiences through their work.

---

[2] It can be argued that the usage of the term "piracy" is dishonest since the term is tantamount to saying that copying or downloading is theft. While I do not agree that it is theft, I will still use in some instances the term "piracy" as it is entrenched in the scholarly debate. In most instances I will, however, opt for a more neutral label such as "copyright infringement."

[3] Copyright enforcement has become even more expansive in the wake of the digital revolution, following the wide availability of computers with internet connections, which slashed the costs of producing copies.

3. The Fatal Conceit of Copyright

Hayek is largely an unknown figure within the scholarly debate surrounding copyright.[4] The reason for his absence is warranted because he barely mentions the issue and only in some of his works. Regardless, the particular way he does it is quite insightful, and that is why he deserves a place in the ring, especially in the anti-utilitarian corner.

In the second chapter of *The Fatal Conceit*, Hayek aims at answering a couple of questions regarding the nature and purpose of property rights, such as "Where do they come from?" and "Where are they going?" While the answer to the former is simple (they originated in customs and then were shaped by common law and legislation), the answer to the latter involves invoking the names of Arnold Plant, Ronald Coase, Armen Alchian, and Harold Demsetz and their promising proposals for improving our current legal framework.

It is at this point that Hayek feels the need to distinguish between material and immaterial objects and talk about one particular form of property, namely IP:

> Just to illustrate how great our ignorance of the optimum forms of delimitation of various rights remains... a few remarks about one particular form of property may be made. Those very intellectuals who are generally inclined to question those forms of material property which are indispensable for the efficient organisation of the material means of production have become the most enthusiastic supporters of certain immaterial property rights invented only relatively recently, having to do, for example, with literary productions and technological inventions (i.e., copyrights and patents). (1988, 36)

Why does Hayek find it strange that some intellectuals[5] who are skeptical about the value of private property rights in material objects tend to

---

[4] Hayek's name can, however, be found mentioned in Kinsella (2001) and Bell (2014).

[5] It is interesting that in his "The Intellectuals and Socialism" Hayek sees a strong correlation between the growth of the intellectual class and copyrights, as their development can be seen as a result of the IP system. As they have a vested interest to maintain the status quo, we can tentatively explain why most people tend to generally accept copyrights by taking into account the role that intellectuals have in setting trends in the realm of ideas. Whether an honest debate surrounding copyright is possible in this context is, according to Hayek, highly problematic: "One of the important points that would have to be examined in such a discussion would be how far the growth of this class

embrace private property rights in immaterial objects such as ideas? His answer is of great importance for the copyright debate:

> The difference between these and other kinds of property rights is this: while ownership of material goods guides the use of scarce means to their most important uses, in the case of immaterial goods such as literary productions and technological inventions the ability to produce them is also limited, yet once they have come into existence, they can be indefinitely multiplied and can be made scarce only by law in order to create an inducement to produce such ideas. (1988, 36)

This has to do, first of all, with the fundamental ontological distinction between these two types of goods. When defining a copyright (or any other intellectual property right, such as a patent or a trademark), scholars find it useful to distinguish between ideal objects and their material substrata. As Palmer puts it, "Intellectual property rights are rights in ideal objects, which are distinguished from the material substrata in which they are instantiated" (1990, 818). An alternative way of conveying a similar idea is by applying the classical distinction from metaphysics and the philosophy of language between *types* and *tokens* to IP. What is the object of IP law, then?

> The objects of intellectual property are types and not tokens... The tokens are distinct, physical things, but they are instantiations of the same abstract type. Types are multiply realizable; thus they may be instantiated in more than one place at any time. Tokens, on the other hand, are unique occurrences. (Biron 2010, 382–84)[6]

Secondly, Hayek's answer dwells on the purpose of ownership. We need property rights because they are the best tool we have (one we stumbled upon) to rationally and efficiently allocate scarce resources and reduce the incidence of conflict over material goods (Kinsella 2001). This idea is of great importance because, in contrast to material objects such as laptops or plots of land, ideal types, once produced, can have an indefinite number of tokens. For example, the number of copies produced of George R.R. Martin's closing

---

has been artificially stimulated by the law of copyright... It would be interesting to discover how far a seriously critical view of the benefits to society of the law of copyright or the expression of doubts about the public interest in the existence of a class which makes its living from the writing of books would have a chance of being publicly stated in a society in which the channels of expression are so largely controlled by people who have a vested interest in the existing situation" (1949, 420). I would like to thank one of the anonymous reviewers for directing me to this passage.

[6] Long (1995) has a similar idea, asserting that IP protects property rights in "universals." Schulman's "logorights" (1990) also come close to this.

novel in the *A Song of Ice and Fire* saga will depend solely on the projected sales. There is no reason not to multiply the *type* into an infinite number of *tokens* except for market concerns.

Utilitarians who are in favor of copyright argue that forced scarcity for literary works has a positive effect, as it incentivizes authors such as Martin and his publishing house to be more creative and productive and take more risks when promoting and investing in authors. Indeed, the fundamental idea Landes and Posner had was exactly this: the purpose of copyrights is exactly this forced scarcity. For Hayek though this idea is fuzzy at best:

> Yet it is not obvious that such forced scarcity is the most effective way to stimulate the human creative process. I doubt whether there exists a single great work of literature which we would not possess had the author been unable to obtain an exclusive copyright for it. (1988, 36)

Hayek's skepticism regarding the core of the utilitarian case for copyright is at least partly warranted. Firstly, we should note that some of the greatest literary works that might be found on our bookshelves or in high school and college syllabi, from Homer's *The Iliad* and *The Odyssey* through Ovid's poems and finishing with Shakespearean plays, were created before anything even closely resembling our current copyright legislation was in place. While it is true that authors did have some financial incentives to write, they did so within a different framework, one involving literary and artistic patronage (Lytle and Orgel 1981; Gold 1982). Forced scarcity is not the only or necessarily even the best way to produce great literary works.[7] Even some legal scholars and practitioners of IP law such as William F. Strong ungrudgingly accept this idea. Strong asserts that the problem of what incentives and disincentives authors have is such a complex one that it is difficult to provide a simple, definitive answer. While not a critic of the copyright system for literary works (quite the contrary), he feels that most scholars tend to uncritically accept the idea that copyright automatically fosters innovation and creativity:

> Nearly all great English poetry and drama (not to mention Latin, Greek, and French), and nearly all great music, painting, and sculpture that existed in 1787 had been created in the absence of copyright. The English copyright law, which had been on the books

---

[7] In fact, following Demsetz, it can be argued that IP scholars who believe copyright automatically plays this role commit something close to the "nirvana fallacy." An interesting argument exploring the nirvana approach to IP can be found in Vică and Socaciu (2017).

less than a century, had been enacted more as a narrow-gauge protection to printers and booksellers (who were the publishers of those days) than out of compassion for authors, or as a stimulus to intellectual innovation. And while that testing period of the English law was a period of great intellectual output, you would be hard pressed to say that this was a result of the copyright law. (1986, 33–34)[8]

The same Hayekian skepticism[9] can be useful in evaluating the impact copyright had on classical-music output. Using data from Frederic M. Scherer's research, Boldrin and Levine (2008, 187–89) propose a method to test the potential benefits of forced scarcity by taking a closer look at the consequences of the introduction of copyright protection in Europe for such musical productions. Copyright protection was introduced in the last decades of the eighteenth century and spread to the whole continent by the mid-nineteenth century. With the UK being the first and the strongest supporter of IP and one of the wealthiest countries of its day, the introduction of copyright for printed music in 1777 should have had a positive effect. Yet it appears that the number of composers per million declined almost everywhere, from Germany and Austria to Italy, but especially in the UK, where the numbers dropped especially quickly. With the sole exception of France, the introduction of copyright for printed music did not serve the intended purpose utilitarians think it should have served.

---

[8] There might be some situations in which we can say, beyond any reasonable doubt, that the forced scarcity imposed by copyright directly hinders creativity and innovation: in the scientific output of researchers from the developing world. The high costs that researchers from those countries have to endure to access cutting-edge academic papers or books means that they will either produce (i) fewer research papers and books or (ii) outdated research outputs (Uszkai 2016a). For a more comprehensive analysis of IP and copyright as incentive mechanisms, see McNally (2012) and Johnson (2012). Some advocates of IP in the libertarian camp such as William Shughart admit that a lower level of dissemination of ideas is one of the intended purposes of these rights, especially in the case of the pharmaceutical industry. For an in-depth analysis of their proposals, see Kinsella (2016).

[9] One of the specific features of Hayek's approach to the social sciences is his skepticism toward forms of nonspontaneous orders generated through a top-down approach, something he inherited from figures of the Scottish Enlightenment such as Adam Smith and David Hume. It is in this sense that I find his skepticism of great value in the debate surrounding copyrights. I would like to thank one of the anonymous reviewers for pointing out the necessity of highlighting this methodological feature of Hayekian thought.

Before moving on, an additional note on incentives, copyright, and music is in order. Pro-IP utilitarians argue that the absence of copyright protection might be not only a disincentive for artists, novelists, or musicians, but also an incentive for digital piracy (Aversa, Hervas-Drane, and Evenou 2019). Because of digital piracy, both companies and artists lose money; as a consequence, fewer invest their time, effort, or money in bringing new products to the market. This idea was also central for the US District Court for the Northern District of California in the legal battle between A&M Records and Napster in 2000: "The court finds that Napster use is likely to reduce CD purchases by college students, whom defendant admits constitute a key demographic."[10] In analyzing the impact P2P file sharing has had on media output, sales, and revenue, Oberholzer-Gee and Strumpf dispense a healthy dose of skepticism toward this well-entrenched narrative.

First of all, if the sales of an artist are on a downward slope, blaming BitTorrent, The Pirate Bay, and copyright infringement might be a knee-jerk reaction. The equivalence of illegal album downloads and potentially legally acquired albums is a stretch. If someone does not have the resources to buy an album from one of her favorite artists and decides to download it from The Pirate Bay, this does not mean that in the absence of this alternative, she would either go to the record store, order it online, or pay for a subscription to Spotify. It means rather that she would either abstain from listening to it or search for other cheap or free alternatives such as listening on YouTube.

Secondly, because artist revenue nowadays is not solely based on album sales (in turn because of the growing role of live shows and merchandise), an argument could be made that, in fact, copyright infringement in the digital age has increased the exposure of artists and their chances of receiving higher concert fees.[11] Starting in 2000 (after the Napster revolution in the P2P distribution of music and the increasing availability of internet connections worldwide), Oberholzer-Gee and Strumpf point out, the music industry underwent a significant boom, with the annual release of albums more than doubling. The trend was similar in other areas as well. The rate of publication of new books increased by 66 percent from 2002 to 2007. From 2003 to 2010 the rate of film production also increased worldwide—by more than 30 percent (2010, 20)—coupled with a staggering increase in film budgets (especially in Hollywood) even though more and more big productions are proving to be box office disappointments (McMahon 2018).

---

[10] A&M Records, Inc. v. Napster, Inc., 114 F. Supp. 2d 896 (N.D. Cal. 2000).

[11] More on BitTorrent and digital piracy as a discovery mechanism can be found later in the paper.

Despite the ubiquity of digital copyright infringement, it is very difficult for artists to actually make a living from their talents. With over 50,000 albums released annually and only 950 of them selling over twenty-five thousand copies in 2007 (Oberholzer-Gee and Strumpf 2010, 47), the explanation of what incentivizes an artist to be creative, to compose, and to sing should be sought elsewhere. Maybe a more promising way to answer the question is to return to the so-called "theory of superstars" (Rosen 1981). The idea that copyright plays the essential role of an incentive may well just be a fallacy (Johnson 2012).

While Hayek is skeptical that forced scarcity is effective in stimulating creativity, he is certain of the economic consequences of copyrights: monopolies and a decrease in competitiveness. Applying something like the concept of property, which, Hayek says, developed for material objects, to immaterial objects such as ideas has led to

> the growth of monopoly… drastic reforms may be required if competition is to be made to work. In the field of industrial patents in particular we shall have seriously to examine whether the award of a monopoly privilege is really the most appropriate and effective form of reward for the kind of risk-bearing which investment in scientific research involves. (1948, 114)

Intellectual monopoly is of great importance for Hayek because it has an impact on what he labels as "the fund of experience" (1978, 43). Restricting the spread of ideas and knowledge by making them artificially scarce through copyrights and patents limits progress because it limits the ability of the market to provide the "free gift of the knowledge" that would allow all individuals and nations who are worse off "to reach the same level at a much smaller cost" (1978, 47).

4. Copyright: The Result of Human Action and of Human Design

Hayek's discontent with Cartesian rationalism and his methodological "love affair" with the Scottish Enlightenment's anti-rationalism and its proponents (Bernard Mandeville, David Hume, Adam Ferguson, and Adam Smith) is well known (1967, 96–105). Some commentators on Hayek even consider this his "most striking feature" (Barry 1986, 74). Gerald Gaus expands on this point, arguing that the Hayekian approach to understanding complex phenomena such as human interaction is based on two main concepts: cultural evolution and spontaneous order (2006, 233).

Echoing Adam Ferguson's famous analysis of human institutions,[12] Hayek believes that to understand our civilization,

> one must appreciate that the extended order resulted not from human design or intention but spontaneously: it arose from unintentionally conforming to certain traditional and largely moral practices, many of which men tend to dislike, whose significance they usually fail to understand, whose validity they cannot prove, and which have nonetheless fairly rapidly spread by means of an evolutionary selection—the comparative increase of population and wealth—of those groups that happened to follow them. (1988, 6)

Drawing upon an earlier distinction that Hayek makes between two types of order, *cosmos* and *taxis* (1968; 1982, 35–55), and his preference for the former (spontaneous orders), it is easy to see why he preferred evolved institutions and *nomos* to *thesis*.[13] How well does copyright fare in the Hayekian *cosmos* of spontaneous orders and evolved institutions? Was copyright a product of human action without human design, or was it *rationally* designed?

The first thing we have to ask ourselves is when human beings began to think that, just like apple trees, tools, and plots of land, ideas could be thought of as something to be owned. Some historians argue that ever since antiquity we something similar to this idea has existed, with early craftsmen and traders using something close to trademarks to protect their reputations (May and Sell 2006, 44–45). While some Greek poets and painters did sign their works with their names, it was the Romans—and in a similar fashion, the Islamic scribes—who came closer to assigning what we might currently

---

[12] "Nations stumble upon establishments, which are indeed the result of human action, but not the execution of any human design" ([1767] 1995, 119).

[13] Some, like Shearmur, tend to be skeptical of this general reading of Hayek: "It is such considerations that, presumably, underlie Hayek's enthusiasm for evolved institutions in his *Law, Legislation and Liberty* and *The Fatal Conceit*. Indeed, this enthusiasm at times seems to verge on a Panglossian conservatism to the effect that, whatever is, is good—provided it was not designed. But this is clearly not an attitude that Hayek sustains. For *Law, Legislation and Liberty* starts from the problem that older institutions which divided and limited constitutional powers have broken down—something which, in Hayek's view, was clearly neither designed nor desirable. And, as we have seen, throughout his work Hayek exhibits a concern for the improvement of inherited institutions" (1996, 108). Whether or not Shearmur is right, what matters is that Hayek did have an overwhelming bias against designed rules and in favor of evolved norms and institutions.

label as "authorship" (45–49; Hesse 2002, 28). However, it was not until the European Enlightenment that IP in the modern sense arose:

> The concept of intellectual property—the idea that an idea can be owned—is a child of the European Enlightenment. It was only when people began to believe that knowledge came from the human mind working upon the senses—rather than through divine revelation, assisted by the study of ancient texts—that it became possible to imagine humans as creators, and hence owners, of new ideas rather than as mere transmitters of eternal verities. (2002, 26)

The reason the Enlightenment (and the early modern precursor period) is such a decisive moment in the history of IP has to do with several interconnected elements: (i) Gutenberg's technological revolution; (ii) the ongoing social, cultural, and economic transition toward capitalism, (iii) the emergence of the modern notion of authorship (Uszkai 2015, 184–85), and (iv) increasing state centralization and the resulting growth of state power, two essential elements IP relies on because of their specific status (as opposed to other natural rights such as the right to self-ownership and the right to tangible property).[14]

The impact of Gutenberg's 1439 invention of the printing press on the very notion of copyright is difficult to underestimate (Atkinson and Fitzgerald 2014, 15). The reason this invention is one of the keys to understanding how copyright appeared has to do with some practical consequences of the invention and spread of the printing press in medieval Western Europe. First, up to the middle of the fifteenth century, books were one of the most expensive consumer goods available for purchase because of their scarcity. This had much to do with the fact that the process of copying them was resource consuming. Gutenberg's printing press slashed those costs to an unimaginably low level and thus increased the availability of books. Second, books were becoming more available to an ever-increasing middle class of the emerging and soon-to-be very important bourgeois class that invested more in the education of their offspring. Soon enough, some of them began writing and publishing books, thus drastically increasing the total pool of available creative works. If you add to the mix growing rates of literacy, an interesting picture emerges:

> In the 1700s, cultural life in Europe underwent a dramatic transformation. A shift from intensive to extensive reading and the

---

[14] I would like to thank one of the reviewers of this paper for pointing out this essential fourth element, which helps paint a more accurate picture of the "primordial historical soup" that IP and copyright emerged from.

rise of a middle-class reading public led to an explosion of print commerce in the eighteenth century. In England, it is estimated that annual book production increased fourfold over the course of the eighteenth century. France, too, saw a marked increase in the literacy rate and a dramatic increase in the demand for modern secular literature. (Hesse 2002, 31)

Until the Enlightenment, there was little recognition of authors qua authors. Ancient Greek poets or philosophers (with the exception of the highly criticized sophists) were said to be inspired by muses in their creative endeavors. Likewise, Chinese authors had no property right to their published books. Moreover, a medieval European scholar "might lay claim to the manuscript he created, and the printer to the book he printed, but neither could claim to possess the contents that lay within it. The Renaissance elevated the poet, the inventor, and the artist to unprecedented social heights, but their 'genius' was still understood to be divinely inspired rather than a mere product of their mental skills or worldly labors" (Hesse 2002, 28).[15]

Unlike Greco-Roman antiquity or Christian Europe, the Enlightenment provided fertile land for the emergence of the modern conceptions of "author" and "authorship" made possible by the contributions of John Locke, Edward Young, Gotthold Lessing, and Diderot (Hesse 2002, 33–36). Following this epistemic revolution of the Enlightenment, people began to recognize that particular individuals, be they poets, philosophers, or novelists, were the true source of human knowledge and creativity. They should not thank external sources such as the muses or God.

While these (mostly cultural and economic) transformations were the result of spontaneous and contingent forces, we cannot say the same thing when it comes to the institutional aspects. Some historians argue that IP was born in the fifteenth century, during the so-called "Venetian moment" (May and Sell 2006, 58). Pressure to enact the laws did not come from authors (or inventors), but from powerful lobbying groups—the Venetian guilds—which

---

[15] There are some dissenting views claiming that in the Byzantine world there was something similar to authorship and copyright in the arts: "The *Institutes* of Justinian (AD 533) distinguished between corporeal and incorporeal property and they also interpreted the doctrine of *accessio* or merger to favour, in some circumstances, ownership by the artist of objects embodying art. Whether the artist owned the object seemed to depend on the quality of the art" (Atkinson and Fitzgerald 2014, 10). Regardless, the general picture shaped by Carla Hesse remains largely correct and authorship became really important only during the Enlightenment.

wanted to block competitors from copying their techniques. Labeled *privilegi*, the Venetian IP statutes were similar to the later English monopolies.

Just like in the Venetian Republic, the creation of the UK's copyright-and-patent system was not the result of spontaneous order and an invisible-hand process. In fact, it was almost the complete opposite of this desirable Hayekian filtering process; the system was a direct result of the visible hand of monarchs distributing favors. The background of the story is the ideological and political fight between Catholics and Protestants, which made controlling book publishers and printers a useful way of ensuring the success of one's faction. In Continental Europe, something similar happened a century earlier, with the backlash of tech-savvy Lutherans who extensively used the printing press against Catholics, who had established a licensing system for the printing of new books (Atkinson and Fitzgerald 2014, 16–17). In England, the act creating copyrights was signed by the Catholic queen Mary in 1557, who bestowed on the Stationer's Company the exclusive right to publish and sell books. Starting in 1558, the Protestant queen Elizabeth I was also known for her activist approach to offering patents as court favors. The passing of the Statute of Monopolies in 1623 by Parliament excluded the English monarchs from the patent game, and, by 1710, with the Stationer's Company's monopoly rescinded, the English copyright-and-IP system reached adulthood[16] (Johnson 2012, 635–40). Copyright was not the result of an "uprising of authors," but "an outgrowth of the privatization of government censorship in sixteenth-century England" (Fogel 2005, 2).

What does this short historical foray tell us, from a Hayekian standpoint? Firstly, some cultural and epistemic norms did evolve, in the face of technological, economic, or social factors. "Authorship" may very well be a result of a spontaneous, unplanned order. When it comes to copyright, the narrative is, alas, different:[17]

> If you travel back in time attempting to trace the origins of intellectual property law, you will find that in the vicinity of the 17th century, the ideas of "patents" and "copyrights" become snarled and intertwined not only with one another but also with "monopolies." All of these legal concepts represented variations on a theme: a monarchy's efforts at maintaining control and doling out favors in an era of increasing threats to royal power. Thus, the origins of modern IP law are not found in a scholarly disputation of

---

[16] Interestingly enough, according to the *Oxford English Dictionary* the phrase "intellectual property" first appeared only in 1845 (Hesse 2002, 39).

[17] As Johnson so eloquently puts it, "with intellectual property, the *d'être* preceded the *raison*" (2012, 635).

economics, but rather in the vast political struggle between the monarchy and the various power bases in mid-millennium society. (Johnson 2012, 635)

5. The Use of Torrents in Society

Game of Thrones is, undoubtedly, one of the most important and culturally significant TV shows of the second decade of the third millennium, with millions of viewers per episode. Unsurprisingly, the fantasy drama based on George R.R. Martin's saga is one of the most pirated TV shows in history. How pirated? According to the available data, it holds the honor of being the most torrented TV show for six years in a row, starting from 2012 (Van der Sar 2017).

If the utilitarian case for copyright were correct, we should expect the producers and other important stakeholders of the show (directors, actors, etc.) to have railed against this injustice. If anything, this clear encroachment on their property rights is nothing short of theft, as the punishment for The Pirate Bay's founders has shown.[18] Jeff Bewkes, the CEO of Time Warner (the parent company of HBO, the network on which *Game of Thrones* aired), begs to differ. In a piece in *Forbes*, he compares having the most pirated show in the world with receiving an Emmy award:

Basically, we've been dealing with this issue for years with HBO, literally 20, 30 years, where people have always been running wires

---

[18] An interesting rejoinder on utilitarianism, incentives, copyright, and piracy could be made if we took a look at the fashion industry. As Raustiala and Springman have shown, it might be the case that in some industries, piracy actually has had a straightforwardly positive impact: "We have argued that the lack of IP rights for fashion design has not quashed innovation, as the orthodox account would predict, and this has in turn reduced the incentive for designers to seek legal protection for their creations. Not only has the lack of copyright protection for fashion designs not destroyed the incentive to innovate in apparel, it may have actually promoted it. This claim—that piracy is paradoxically beneficial for fashion designers—rests on attributes specific to fashion, in particular the status-conferring, or positional, nature of clothing. We do not claim that fashion designers chose this low-IP system in any conscious or deliberate way. But we do claim that the highly unusual political equilibrium in fashion is explicable once we recognize its dynamic effects: that fashion's cyclical nature is furthered and accelerated by a regime of open appropriation. It may even be, as one colleague suggested to us, that to stop copying altogether would be to kill fashion" (2006, 1775–76). Johanna Blakley concurs, arguing "that one reason that fashion design has been elevated to an art form is precisely because of the *lack* of copyright protection" (2010).

down on the back of apartment buildings and sharing with their neighbors... Our experience is, it all leads to more penetration, more paying subs, more health for HBO, less reliance on having to do paid advertising... If you go around the world, I think you're right, Game of Thrones is the most pirated show in the world. Well, you know, that's better than an Emmy. (Tassi 2014)[19]

This assessment of copyright infringement, which happens (almost exclusively) in P2P file-sharing architectures facilitated by BitTorrent, sounds paradoxical both on theoretical and empirical grounds, as big-media corporate conglomerates have had the tradition of lobbying for extensions of copyright protection (Boldrin and Levine, 97–120) and pushing for the legal shutdown of those who facilitate the infringement of copyrighted materials. There is, however, a sense in which Jeff Bewkes is right, and there is also a (Hayekian) case in favor of more leniency for copyright infringement, as it might actually have a positive long-term financial impact within certain parameters.

A recent study commissioned by Ofcom UK,[20] prepared by Kantar Media with the financial support of the UK Intellectual Property Office, might shed some preliminary light on this issue. The purpose of the *OCI Tracker Benchmark Study* was to provide key insights and data regarding media consumption in the UK during 2011 detailing the extent of copyright infringement and behaviors and attitudes among people older than twelve.

One of the elements the study addressed was the likelihood of consumers paying for certain goods (music, movies, books, video games) after taking into account two variables. The first one was price sensitivity: how likely they were to buy something as the price of that good increased. The second divided the consumers into three main categories based on their consumption habits: (i) 100 percent legal consumers; (ii) consumers with a mix of legal and illegal activities; and (iii) 100 percent illegal customers. Their findings concerning music and movies vindicated Jeff Bewkes's take on copyright infringement.

When it comes to music, individuals who follow a combined legal-and-illegal consumption pattern were willing to pay the highest mean price for

---

[19] As one anonymous reviewer pointed out, it is not clear whether in a no-copyright world movie producers would adopt such a position. However, the point I am trying to make is smaller, namely, that copyright infringement in the digital age is not necessarily harmful to owners of IP and that it actually might have some positive spillovers.

[20] The Office of Communication is a UK statutory corporation tasked with regulating British broadcasting and telecommunications.

both a single track (seventy-two pence/track) and a subscription service (£4.69/month), with the 100 percent legal consumers lagging behind at forty-two pence/track and £2.59/month. Using the same scale of willingness to pay in the case of movies, the author of the study notices a similar distribution within the examined groups. The mix of legal and illegal was willing to pay both the highest absolute and the highest mean price for downloading a film (£4.92) and also for movie subscriptions, with the 100 percent legal crowd lagging behind (Kay 2012, 31, 41–42).

The findings of this 2012 study are complementary to some previous research done on the positive economic impact of piracy. For example, Khouja and Park have argued that "from an economic viewpoint, tolerating some piracy has been shown to have some positive aspects in that piracy makes a product available to those who cannot afford it, increases the consumer base for a product, and creates positive network externalities" (2007, 110).

The positive externalities are derived products like spin-off books, t-shirts, or other forms of merchandise that can appeal to the fan base of a musician, a movie, or the like. More recently, Kim, Lahiri, and Dey embarked on a similar task with an empirical twist. Their conclusion?

> Piracy reacts with double marginalization in a rather interesting manner that could lead to higher profits for both the manufacturer and retailer as well as a higher surplus for consumers, resulting in a surprising win-win-win situation. To the best of our knowledge, no other work has viewed piracy in this light and, as a result, all have overlooked this beneficial aspect that ought to make businesses, consumers, and governments rethink the value of anti-piracy enforcement. (2018, 40)

We could shed some light on the (seemingly) bizarre value of media piracy by turning to a Hayekian analogy. Knowledge, as many Austrian economists and Hayek scholars[21] are surely aware, is one of the central conceptual tenets of Hayek's economics and social philosophy (Scheall 2016, 205) because it is closely tied to the idea of a rational economic order:

> The peculiar character of the problem of a rational economic order is determined precisely by the fact that the knowledge of the circumstances of which we must make use never exists in concentrated or integrated form but solely as the dispersed bits of incomplete and frequently contradictory knowledge which all the

---

[21] Some even consider it to be "his most distinctive contribution both to economics and to social science" (Gamble 2006, 111).

separate individuals possess. The economic problem of society is thus not merely a problem of how to allocate "given" resources—if "given" is taken to mean given to a single mind which deliberately solves the problem set by these "data." It is rather a problem of how to secure the best use of resources known to any of the members of society, for ends whose relative importance only these individuals know. Or, to put it briefly, it is a problem of the utilization of knowledge which is not given to anyone in its totality. (Hayek 1945, 519)

Firstly, a conceptual caveat is in order: knowledge should not be understood in the epistemological sense of a "justified true belief," but as any belief or "subjective data" that play a role in our decisions and actions (Scheall 2016, 207–8). Secondly, taking into account the fact that knowledge is dispersed among many people, it is crucial to identify a mechanism that could coordinate our actions toward an efficient result. Hayek's contention is that this is precisely what the function of prices is. Namely, prices convey essential signals to both entrepreneurs and consumers, and, based on that knowledge and their preferences, they manage to optimally allocate their resources (Hayek 1945, 526–30).

Returning to the matter of the positive value of copyright infringement, my hypothesis is that because of the artificial scarcity induced by copyrights, music and movies are more expensive in comparison to what they would be absent such protection. Furthermore, just as in the case of price ceilings enacted by the state, one of the foreseeable consequences of copyright protection is the emergence of something similar (in functionality) to a black market, namely P2P file sharing through the BitTorrent protocol. Using this protocol, individuals have found a way of acquiring and transmitting local, decentralized knowledge, which is beneficial to all the parties involved, be they consumers, artists, or producers. To see how this happens, a short digression regarding how the BitTorrent protocol works is in order.

Launched in 2001, BitTorrent soon became, alongside related P2P file-sharing protocols, responsible for a significant chunk of internet usage worldwide, with some studies suggesting that, in 2006, P2P file sharing was responsible for 71 percent of internet traffic (Van der Sar 2006). The number of BitTorrent users grew exponentially in the next few years, reaching 150 million a month in 2011 (Van der Sar 2012).[22]

---

[22] In more recent years, the "internet share" of BitTorrent (and P2P file sharing in general) has been decreasing (Lareida and Stiller 2018) in part because of movie- and music-subscription platforms such as Netflix and Spotify.

One of the reasons why BitTorrent emerged as the favorite protocol of digital copyright infringement has to do with the architecture of the system, as it manages to incentivize cooperation and achieve coordination between a group of users called a *swarm* (Hales and Patarin 2005). Assume someone wants to see her favorite episode of *Game of Thrones*. She might go online and download, via The Pirate Bay or a similar website, a torrent file that doesn't contain the episode, but only the metadata of that file. In downloading that file, she enters into the swarm interested in that specific media file; the swarm contains *leechers* (people interested in downloading the episode) and *seeders* (users who have the episode stored on their hard drive and who allow people access to bits and pieces of it via the torrent file, which plays the role of a road map). The process is mediated by the BitTorrent protocol, which has the purpose of recomposing, on the user's computer, the desired file from the pieces obtained from seeders.

The BitTorrent ecosystem is a market of its own that managed to solve through both technical and moral/institutional tools the problem of coordination and cooperation;[23] Hayek would have undoubtedly taken a keen interest in this development. For present purposes, I will, however, focus on a different aspect. Just as prices are the best tools available to allocate resources, torrent files constitute, to the user and consumer, a mechanism by which she can test the desirability of investing in a particular good but also the desirability of those goods in general, as the dynamic between seeders and leechers shows.

From a strictly technical perspective, a rational consumer of music is an individual who manages to obtain the best return on investment of her scarce resources (mostly time and money). The problem of knowledge lingers: the consumer is not acquainted, ex ante, with intellectual goods, which are more expensive because of the artificial scarcity induced by the existence of copyrights and the increased opportunity cost of each acquisition. That is why being part of BitTorrent swarms can be understood as a discovery mechanism for rational consumers of music, movies, or video games. In other words, to take a simple example, before deciding whether paying a

---

[23] The emergence and evolution of the so-called "copynorms" (Schultz 2006; Svensson and Larsson 2012) would have definitely been a topic of interest for Hayek (Andreozzi 2005).

hypothetical hundred-dollar fee for a summer music festival is worth it, individuals download and listen to the bands that will play gigs there.[24]

Furthermore, an analogy can be made between prices, on the one hand, and the number of seeders and leechers a file has, on the other. Just as the increasing price of craft beers signals that people are more interested in consuming them, incentivizing established producers to produce more or aspiring entrepreneurs to enter the market, the more leechers and seeders a torrent file for a movie has, the more valuable it is in market terms. This is why the comparison with the Emmys makes sense and also how the positive externalities of copyright infringement kick in: producers are aware that, for a certain premium reward, users will spend money on those goods with additional value in the form of memorabilia or another type of merchandise because they now know and love the product.[25]

---

[24] This is especially true if we talk about rational consumers from the developing world who would be more inclined to pay for a premium service (e.g. a live gig from a rock band) than for an MP3 or a physical copy of an album.

[25] Someone might argue that while my take on the use of torrents is correct for the beginning of the second decade of the 2000s, it is not correct today, as internet users have started to abandon BitTorrent and P2P file sharing for other, legal alternatives such as Netflix, Hulu, and Spotify. While this seems correct, we may ask ourselves what triggered the migration to subscription-based services. Moreover, a similar explanation might be needed for the ever-increasing use of 3D technology in Hollywood movies and for the increasing number of gamers who exclusively use platforms such as Steam. My hypothesis is that this is another case of "the use of torrents in society." Keeping it Austrian, it seems that our consumption pattern has shifted this way because of something close to a Schumpeterian creative destruction initiated by the torrent and digital revolution. For example, in the case of movies, producers are incentivized to offer a premium to their future viewers who always have the alternative of watching the latest Hollywood production at home, on their laptops, or on their desktop PCs. This premium comes in the form of 3D experiences. Likewise, with instant gratification a part of our day-to-day online lives and with broadband and 4G internet connections the norm in infrastructure, Netflix and Spotify deliver, at a fraction of the cost of physical copies and also instantly (as opposed to a download with the BitTorrent protocol) the song we are in the mood for or the latest episode from our favorite fantasy drama. In the absence of torrents, P2P file sharing, and piracy, it seems reasonable to think that these entrepreneurial and technological developments would have at least taken significantly more time to emerge.

6. Conclusion: Crowdfunding, Online Patrons, and a Renaissance of the Renaissance Spirit

To sum up, a Hayekian research agenda on copyright and piracy through P2P file sharing should start with a healthy dose of skepticism regarding foundational questions (is the utilitarian argument in favor of copyright correct?) and empirical issues (is copyright infringement harmful?). To paraphrase Hayek, it is still far from obvious that the most effective solution we have at our disposal is the artificial scarcity produced by copyrights or that media downloads through P2P file-sharing protocols such as BitTorrent should be treated as anything other than a victimless crime (Uszkai 2016b).

Is there room for a positive Hayekian research agenda in proposing an alternative way of stimulating the human creative process? My educated guess is that, yes, we might already have at our disposal the prerequisites of such a proposal, and the name of this alternative is online[26] crowdfunding.

While platforms such as IndieGoGo, Kickstarter, and GoFundMe are relatively new, the way they function is not: the French philosopher Auguste Comte used a scheme similar to modern-day crowdfunding to support his work as a philosopher during the middle of the eighteenth century (Gupta 2018). The internet changed crowdfunding's magnitude and expanded its possibilities, with total funding generated in 2014 being estimated at around $16.2 billion worldwide (Belleflamme, Omrani, and Peitz 2015, 12). In 2012, for example, underground artist Amanda Palmer managed to raise $1,192,793 for the release of a record, an art book, and a US tour (McIntyre 2015). Furthermore, the growing popularity of Patreon means that the hundred thousand content creators registered on the platform are expected to receive, in 2019, $500 million from the three million patrons that have constantly contributed to a wide array of creative and scientific endeavors by funding, for example, musicians and podcast creators such as Mike Duncan with his popular *The History of Rome* and *Revolutions* shows (Roettgers 2019).

The basic idea behind crowdfunding schemes on online platforms is pretty simple:

> Crowdfunding involves an open call, mostly through the Internet, for the provision of financial resources either in form of donation or

---

[26] Writing more than a decade ago, Fogel believed that the "arrival of the Internet, with its instantaneous, costless sharing, has made that business model obsolete" (2005, 2). While the model is not yet obsolete, there are clear developments that could bring about such an outcome in the foreseeable future.

in exchange for the future product or some form of reward to support initiatives for specific purposes. (Belleflamme, Lambert, and Schwienbacher 2011, 8)

Imagine you are a talented musician in need of funds to launch a new album. To raise those funds you promote your project with a trailer of your future production, which is then uploaded on a platform such as Kickstarter and promoted using social media platforms such as Facebook, Twitter, and Instagram. Afterward, at each threshold a support pledge from the users of the platform comes with a premium reward: while generally for a pledge like $10 people receive a digital copy of the album or a signed physical copy, with each increase in the pledge the premium becomes more enticing. For example, the individuals with the highest pledge could also have their names on your album or be invited to an exclusive behind-the-scenes event. Both "personal networks and underlying project quality are associated with the success of crowdfunding effort" (Mollick 2013, 1).

While it is true that crowdfunded projects are still (at least most of the time) protected by IP, this need not be the case in the future. Some argue that the advent of an online solution for artistic production can render current copyright policies obsolete as creators are starting to "forgo monopoly returns, instead marketing their works widely and cheaply" (Bell 2014, 163) through the internet with the aid of crowdfunding platforms. Moreover, as Bell observes, a future with consumer specialization, better use of technology (to reduce the costs of both production and distribution of artistic works), and common law rights could actually be better at fostering innovation and creativity in expressive works (2014, 165–66).

Leaving the issue of the future of copyright aside for a moment, what is interesting, from a Hayekian standpoint, is that crowdfunding manages to bring closer the artist, her project, and a real market. In the absence of large media corporations, the only actor who decides the value of a particular project is the actor who should have that prerogative to begin with: the potential consumer. Moreover, the logic of supply and demand works better when artistic entrepreneurs and consumers are closer. Last but not least, future consumers are the ones who are able to decide how much they want to pay in order to have access to a product.

In Karen Vaughn's reading, Hayek's implicit economics implies that

> entrepreneurship can only be exercised if the entrepreneur already knows a great deal about the circumstances surrounding the opportunity he believes he has identified. That is, an entrepreneur can exploit profit opportunities only insofar as he knows how to buy in one market and sell in another with all the rich detail that those activities encompass. This knowledge of "how to" is knowledge of

at least the relevant parts of the institutional structure that makes up a market economy. While such knowledge does not guarantee entrepreneurial success, it does load the dice, so to speak, in the entrepreneur's favor. (1999, 142)

Crowdfunding platforms can be viewed, then, as knowledge-enhancing mechanisms for creative entrepreneurs, as they manage to connect the artists directly to their markets. Moreover, Kickstarter and Patreon do this by significantly reducing transaction costs. While up until recently musicians almost exclusively used record labels to acquire capital and promote their work, with the advent of the internet and digitization crowdfunding platforms increasingly play that role at only a fraction of the previous cost (Galuszka and Bystrov 2013).[27]

Virtually all historians consider the Renaissance as characterized by a return to Greco-Roman values in art and philosophy and as an emancipation from the more rigid norms and institutions of the Middle Ages. If Michael Munger (2018) is right in predicting that Tomorrow 3.0 will be achieved by a reduction in transaction costs (associated with triangulation, trust, and transfer), then we might soon witness a renaissance of the Renaissance spirit, with the role that the state, wealthy aristocratic families such as the House of Medici, or the Catholic Church played as patrons taken over directly by consumers. Will the sharing economy of the future still need the rigid norms of copyright? I am sure that Hayek's answer would be no.

References

A&M Records, Inc. v. Napster, Inc., 114 F. Supp. 2d 896 (N.D. Cal. 2000). Available at: https://law.justia.com/cases/federal/district-courts/FSupp2/114/896/2343353/.

Andreozzi, Luciano. 2005. "Hayek Reads the Literature on the Emergence of Norms." *Constitutional Political Economy*, 16(3): 227–47.

Atkinson, Benedict, and Brian Fitzgerald. 2014. *A Short History of Copyright: The Genie of Information*. Dordrecht: Springer.

---

[27] While they are right in saying that crowdfunding platforms are not better at reducing the transaction costs associated with the distribution of a musician's album, when we take into account the recent shift toward digital-music consumption (via subscription platforms such as iTunes and Spotify) their assessment might not be so problematic after all.

Aversa, Paolo, Andres Hervas-Drane, and Morgane Evenou. 2019. "Business Model Responses to Digital Piracy." *California Management Review*. https://doi.org/10.1177/0008125618818841.

Baldwin, Peter. 2014. *The Copyright Wars: Three Centuries of Trans-Atlantic Battle*. Princeton: Princeton University Press.

Barry, Norman. 1986. *On Classical Liberalism and Libertarianism*. London: Macmillan.

Bell, Tom W. 2014. *Intellectual Privilege: Copyright, Common Law and the Common Good*, Arlington, VA: Mercatus Center.

Belleflamme, Paul, Thomas Lambert, and Armin Schwienbacher. 2011. International Conference of the French Finance Association (AFFI) 2011, May 11–13. Available at: http://ssrn.com/abstract=1836873.

Belleflamme, Paul, Nessrine Omrani, and Martin Peitz. 2015. "The Economics of Crowdfunding platforms." *Information Economics and Policy*, 33: 11–28.

Beyer, Jessica L., and Fenwick McKelvey. 2015. "You Are Not Welcome among Us: Pirates and the State." *International Journal of Communication*, 9: 890–908.

Biron, Laura. 2010. "Two Challenges to the Idea of Intellectual Property." The *Monist*, 93(3): 382–94.

Boldrin, Michele, and David K. Levine. 2008. *Against Intellectual Monopoly*. New York: Cambridge University Press.

Blakley, Johanna. 2010. "The Costs of Ownership: Why Copyright Protection Will Hurt the Fashion Industry." *Design Observer*. Available at: https://designobserver.com/feature/the- costs-of-ownership-why-copyright-protection-will-hurt-the-fashion-industry/15078.

Brennan, Jason. 2012. *Libertarianism: What Everyone Needs to Know*. Oxford: Oxford University Press.

Brennan, Jason, Bas van der Fossen, and David Schmidtz. 2018. *Routledge Handbook of Libertarianism*. New York: Routledge.

Cwik, Bryan. 2014. "Labor as the Basis for Intellectual Property Rights." *Ethical Theory and Moral Practice*, 17 (4): 681–95.

Flanigan, Jessica. 2018. "A Libertarian Approach to Medicine." *Routledge Handbook of Libertarianism*, edited by Jason Brennan, Bas van der Fossen, and David Schmidtz, 405–417. New York: Routledge.

Ferguson, Adam. (1767) 1995. *An Essay on the History of Civil Society*. Cambridge: Cambridge University Press.

Fogel, Karl. 2005. *The Surprising History of Copyright and the Promise of a Post-Copyright World*. Available at: https://questioncopyright.org/promise.

Galuszka, Patryk, and Victor Bystrov. 2013. "Development of Crowdfunding in Poland from the Perspectives of Law and Economics." *Polish Yearbook of Law and Economics*, vol. 3, edited by Jaroslaw Beldowski, Katarzyna Metelska-Szaniawska, and Louis Visscher, 14-66. Warsaw: C.H. Beck Publishing.

Gamble, Andrew. 2006. "Hayek on Knowledge, Economics, and Society." *The Cambridge Companion to Hayek*, edited by Edward Feser, 111–32. Cambridge: Cambridge University Press.

Gaus, Gerald F. 2006. "Hayek on the Evolution of Mind and Society." *The Cambridge Companion to Hayek*, edited by Edward Feser, 232–59. Cambridge: Cambridge University Press.

Gold, Barbara K. 1982. *Literary and Artistic Patronage in Ancient Rome*. Austin: University of Texas Press.

Gupta, Rohit. 2018. *Reward and Donation Crowdfunding: A Complete Guide for Emerging Startups*. Chennai: Notion Press.

Hales, David, and Simon Patarin. 2005. "How to Cheat BitTorrent and Why Nobody Does." *Technical Report UBLCS-2005–12*. Available at: http://citeseerx.ist.psu.edu/viewdoc/download?doi=10.1.1.61.9337&rep=rep1&type=pdf.

Hayek, Friedrich A. 1945. "The Use of Knowledge in Society." *American Economic Review*, 35(4): 519–30.

Hayek, Friedrich A. 1948. *Individualism and Economic Order*. Chicago: The University of Chicago Press.

Hayek, Friedrich A. 1949. "The Intellectuals and Socialism." *University of Chicago Law Review*, 16(3): 417–33.

Hayek, Friedrich A. 1967. *Studies in Philosophy, Politics and Economics*. Chicago: University of Chicago Press.

Hayek, Friedrich A. 1968. *The Confusion of Language in Political Thought*. London: Institute of Economic Affairs.

Hayek, Friedrich A. 1978. *The Constitution of Liberty*. Chicago: University of Chicago Press.

Hayek, Friedrich A. 1982. *Law, Legislation and Liberty*. London: Routledge.

Hayek, Friedrich A. 1988. *The Fatal Conceit: The Errors of Socialism*. London: Routledge.

Hesse, Carla. 2002. "The Rise of Intellectual Property, 700 B.C.–A.D. 2000: An Idea in the balance." *Daedalus*, 131(2): 26–45.

Johns, Adrian. 2009. *Piracy: The Intellectual Property Wars from Gutenberg to Gates*. Chicago: Chicago University Press.

Johnson, Eric E. 2012. "Intellectual Property and the Incentive Fallacy." *Florida State University Law Review*, 39: 623–79.

Kay, Danny. 2012. *OCI Tracker Benchmark Study Q3 2012. Prepared for Ofcom*. Available at: https://www.ofcom.org.uk/research-and-data/internet-and-on-demand-research/online- copyright-infringement/copyright-infringement-tracker.

Khouja, Moutaz, and Sungjune Park. 2007. "Optimal Pricing of Digital Experience Goods under Piracy." *Journal of Management Information Systems*, 24(3):109–41.

Kim, Antino, Antanu Lahiri, and Debabrata Dey. 2018. "The 'Invisible Hand' of Piracy: An Economic Analysis of the Information-Goods Supply Chain." *MIS Quarterly*. Available at: https://ssrn.com/abstract=2426577.

Kinsella, Stephan. 2001. "Against Intellectual Property." *Journal of Libertarian Studies*, 15 (2): 1- 53.

Kinsellla, Stephan. 2016. "Independent Institute on the 'Benefits' of Intellectual Property Protection." Available at: http://c4sif.org/2016/02/independent-institute-on-the-benefits-of-intellectual-property-protection/.

Konkin, Samuel Edward, III. 1986. "Copywrongs." *Voluntaryist*, 20: 4–5.

Landes, Willliam M., and Richard A. Posner. 2003. *The Economic Structure of Intellectual Property Law*. Cambridge, MA: Harvard University Press.

Lareida, Andri, and Burkhard Stiller. 2018. "Big Torrent Measurement: A Country-, Network-, and Content-centric Analysis of Video Sharing in BitTorrent." NOMS 2018 - 2018 IEEE/IFIP Network Operations and Management Symposium. Taipei: IEE, DOI: 10.1109/NOMS.2018.8406243.

Larsson, Stefan. 2013. "Metaphors, Law and Digital Phenomena: The Swedish Pirate Bay Court Case." *International Journal of Law and Information Technology*, 21(4): 354–79.

Long, Roderick T. 1995. "The Libertarian Case against Intellectual Property Rights." *Formulations*. Available at: http://freenation.org/a/f31l1.html.

Lytle, Guy Fitch, and Stephen Orgel (eds.). 1981. *Patronage in the Renaissance*. Princeton, NJ: Princeton University Press.

May, Cristopher, and Susan K. Sell. 2006. *Intellectual Property Rights: A Critical History*. London: Lynne Rienner Publisher.

McElroy, Wendy. 2011. "Contra Copyright, Again." *Libertarian Papers*, 3(12): 1–10.

Merges, Robert. 2011. *Justifying Intellectual Property*. Cambridge, MA: Harvard University Press.

Merriden, Trevor. 2001. *Irresistible Forces. The Business Legacy of Napster & the Growth of the Underground Internet*. Oxford: Capstone.

McIntyre, Hugh. 2015. "These Are the Top 5 Most-Funded Music Kickstarter Campaigns." *Forbes*. Available at: https://www.forbes.com/sites/hughmcintyre/2015/04/13/these-are-the- top-5-most-funded-music-kickstarter-campaigns/#2bf663285d7e.

McMahon, James. 2018. "Is Hollywood a Risky Business? A Political Economic Analysis of Risk and Creativity." *New Political Economy*, DOI: 10.1080/13563467.2018.1460338.

McNally, Michael B. 2012. "Intellectual Property and Its Alternatives: Incentives, Innovation and Ideology." *Electronic Thesis and Dissertation Repository*. 458. Available online: https://ir.lib.uwo.ca/etd/458.

Mollik, Ethan. 2013. "The Dynamics of Crowdfunding: An Exploratory Study." *Journal of Business Venturing*, 29(1): 1–16.

Munger, Michael. 2011. "Basic Income Is Not an Obligation, but It Might Be a Legitimate Choice." *Basic Income Studies*, 6(2): 1–13.

Munger, Michael. 2018. *Tomorrow 3.0: Transaction Costs and the Sharing Economy*. Cambridge: Cambridge University Press.

Nozick, Robert. 1974. *Anarchy, State and Utopia*, New York: Basic Books.

Oberholzer-Gee, Felix, and Koleman Strumpf. 2010. "File-Sharing and Copyright." *Innovation Policy and the Economy*, vol. 10, edited by Josh Lerner and Scott Stern. Chicago: University of Chicago Press.

Palmer, Tom. G. 1989. "Intellectual Property: A Non-Posnerian Law and Economics Approach." *Hamline Law Review*, 12 (2): 261–304.

Palmer, Tom. G. 1990. "Are Patents and Copyrights Morally Justified? The Philosophy of Property Rights and Ideal Objects." *Harvard Journal of Law & Public Policy*, 13 (3): 817–65.

Rand, Ayn. 1967. *Capitalism: The Unknown Ideal*. New York: New American Library.

Raustiala, Kal, and Cristopher Springman. 2006. "The Piracy Paradox: Innovation and Intellectual Property in Fashion Design." *Virginia Law Review*, 92(8): 1687–77.

Roettgers, Janko. 2019. "Patreon Now Has over 3 Million Patrons, Expects to Pay $500M to Creators in 2019." *Variety*. Available at: https://variety.com/2019/digital/news/patreon-3- million-patrons-500-million-dollar-payout-1203114979/.

Rosen, Sherwin. 1981. "The Economics of Superstars." *American Economic Review*, 71(5): 845–58.

Scheall, Scott. 2016. "A Brief Note Concerning Hayek's Non-standard Conception of Knowledge." *Review of Austrian Economics*, 29(2): 205–10.

Schroeder, Jeanne L. 2006. "Unnatural Rights: Hegel and Intellectual Property." *University of Miami Law Review*, 60: 453–503.

Schulman, J. Neil. 1990. "Informational Property: Logorights." *Journal of Social and Biological Structures*, 13(2): 93–117.

Schultz Mark F. 2007. "Copynorms: Copyright and Social Norms." In *Intellectual Property and Information Wealth: Issues and Practices in the Digital Age*, edited by P.K. Yu, Greenwood: Praeger Publishers, 651–728.

Shearmur, Jeremy. 1996. *Hayek and After: Hayekian liberalism as a Research Programme*, London: Routledge.

Spooner, Lysander. 1855. *The Law of Intellectual Property: or an Essay on the Right of Authors and Inventors to a Perpetual Property in Their Ideas*. Boston: Bela Marsh.

Spinello, Richard A. 2011. "A Case for Intellectual Property Rights." *Ethics and Information Technology*, 13(3): 277–81.

Stilz, Anna. 2018. "Property Rights: Natural or Conventional." *Routledge Handbook of Libertarianism*, edited by Jason Brennan, Bas van der Fossen, and David Schmidtz, 244-59. New York: Routledge.

Strong, William F. 1986. "Notes from the Carrot Patch: Copyright Incentives and Disincentives for Intellectual Innovation." *Book Research Quarterly*, 2(2): 33–42.

Svensson, Måns, and Stefan Larsson. 2012. "Intellectual Property Law Compliance in Europe: Illegal File Sharing and the Role of Social Norms." *New Media Society*, 14(7): 1147–63.

Tavani, Herman T. 2005. "Locke, Intellectual Property Rights and the Information Commons." *Ethics and Information Technology*, 7(2): 87–97.

Tassi, Paul. 2014. "'Game of Thrones' Sets Piracy World Record, but Does HBO Care?" *Forbes*. Available at: https://www.forbes.com/sites/insertcoin/2014/04/15/game-of-thrones-sets- piracy-world-record-but-does-hbo-care/#4346762d4196.

Uszkai, Radu. 2015. "A Critique of Intellectual Property Globalization: Libertarian and Rawlsian Arguments." *Re-thinking the Political in Contemporary Society: Globalization, Consumerism, Economic Efficiency*, edited by Viorel Vizureanu, 183–203. Bucharest: Pro Universitaria Press.

Uszkai, Radu. 2016a. "Global Justice and Research Ethics: Linguistic Justice and Intellectual Property." *Public Reason*, 7 (1–2): 13–28.

Uszkai, Radu. 2016b. "Is Online Piracy a Victimless Crime?" *Revista de Filosofie*, 63(5): 597–610.

Van der Sarr, Ernesto. 2006. "BitTorrent: The 'One Third of All Internet Traffic' Myth." *TorrentFreak*. Available at: https://torrentfreak.com/bittorrent-the-one-third-of-all- internet-traffic-myth/.

Van der Sarr, Ernesto. 2012. "uTorrent & BitTorrent Surge to 150 Million Monthly Users." *TorrentFreak*. Available at: https://torrentfreak.com/bittorrent-surges-to-150- million- monthly-users-120109/.

Van der Sar, Ernesto. 2017. "'Game of Thrones' Most Torrented TV-Show of 2017." *TorrentFreak*. Available at: https://torrentfreak.com/game-of-thrones-most-torrented-tv-show-of- 2017–171226/.

Vaughn, Karen I. 1999. "Hayek's Implicit Economics: Rules and the Problem of Order." *Review of Austrian Economics*, 11: 129–44.

Vică, Constantin, and Emanuel-Mihail Socaciu. 2017. "Mind the Gap! How the Digital Turn Upsets Intellectual Property." *Science and Engineering Ethics*. https://doi.org/10.1007/s11948-017- 9996-x.

Zwolinski, Matt. 2011. "Classical Liberalism and the Basic Income." *Basic Income Studies*, 6(2): 1- 14.

Zwolinski, Matt. 2013. "Why Did Hayek Support a Basic Income?" *Libertarianism.org*. Available at: www.libertarianism.org/columns/why-did-hayek-support-basic-income.

The Anatomy of Nationalism: A Fresh Appraisal Based on Recent Case Studies

Jamin Andreas Hübner[*]

1. Introduction

NATIONALISM IS ONE of the most pervasive forces of human culture and society. In all of nationalism's forms, from socialist statism to the "God and country" mantra of the Americanized West, the consciousness of the individual is eclipsed in the triumphant ethos, mythos, and authority of the societal group. This atmosphere is notoriously foggy, so it is often difficult for the average citizen to both see and identify the properties of nationalism at any given time.

An insightful way of cutting through the fog, however, is contemporary description. This is perhaps what made Rothbard's essay "The Anatomy of the State" so persuasive to his readers.[1] In no uncertain terms, Rothbard courageously sidestepped political debates and public opinion (viz., "We all know what the government is"), and simply described the state's nature and functions. The result was a remarkably short and disturbing diagnosis of countless societal evils.

---

[*]Jamin Andreas Hübner (ThD University of South Africa) is a scholar, musician, and entrepreneur from South Dakota. He is a former instructor of economics, Associate Professor of Christian Studies, and Dean of John Witherspoon College, the General Editor of the *Christian Libertarian Review*, and chief architect of Creative Common Law.

CITATION INFORMATION FOR THIS ARTICLE:
Jamin Andreas Hübner. 2018. "The Anatomy of Nationalism: A Fresh Appraisal Based on Recent Case Studies." *Libertarian Papers*. 10 (2): 373-413. THIS ARTICLE IS subject to a Creative Commons Attribution 3.0 License (creativecommons.org/licenses).

[1] Murray Rothbard, *Egalitarianism as a Revolt against Nature and Other Essays* (Auburn: Mises Institute, [1974] 2000), 55–88.

In this article, I want to offer a similar appraisal of nationalism—specifically, contemporary American nationalism. The primary sources for this brief analysis will consist (firstly) of three recent editions of Hillsdale College's *Imprimis*, and (secondly) of the inaugural speeches of Presidents Obama and Trump.

Regarding the first, *Imprimis* is a mass-mailing publication that reaches over 3.7 million (primarily neoconservative) readers per month.[2] There are many other contemporary venues one might turn to in locating the vibrant spirit of the nation. But, for reasons that cannot all be explained here, this particular publication largely represents the current on-the-ground spirit of American nationalism as good as (or better than) any other. The authors are either popular pundits or qualified professors, and the essays themselves are often transcripts of speeches given at political events across the country. Expositing the content of *Imprimis*, which may often be described as political propaganda, reveals the inner mechanics, rhetorical strategies, and mythologies of one of the most integrated, dogmatic, and influential social fabrics of contemporary society. My selection includes "The Problem of Identity Politics and Its Solution" by Matthew Continetti (editor of *Washington Free Beacon* and political commentator), "Immigration in the National Interest" by Tom Cotton (senator from Arkansas, JD graduate of Harvard, and first lieutenant of the US Army), and "How to Meet the Strategic Challenge Posed by China" by David Goldman (columnist for *Asia Times*, journalist, and former consultant for the Department of Defense).[3] Thus, within a half-year period, this single publication features a spectrum of dimensions and perspectives, such as the political, cultural, and economic.

The second source of analysis is the inaugural speeches of presidents Barack Obama and Donald Trump, which I tabulate according to topic and then compare and contrast. The point of this exercise is to show (a) that nationalism is used to justify the work of the state, and (b) the rhetorical strategies of this enterprise are fundamentally the same for the political "left" as they are for the political "right."

Before beginning this project, it should be mentioned that the rise of the Trump administration spurred a massive resurgence of American nationalism. Slogans such as "America First" and "Make America Great Again" continue to saturate the ears of millions, and legislation on immigration, global trade, and foreign policy regularly make headlines. It is

---

[2] This statistic is featured on the cover of *Imprimis*.

[3] These essays were published in the October, November, and March editions of *Imprimis*, respectively. Full citations are given below.

therefore an ideal time to appraise the inner workings of this social phenomenon, and to do so in detail and without party loyalties.[4] The general outline for this article is to discuss some introductory issues such as the definition of terms, then to engage in the two case studies described above before concluding.

2. Defining Terms

To begin, how is "nationalism" typically defined?

This is not an easy question to answer. As one peruses reference works, such as the *Oxford Reader* on the subject, it becomes apparent that "nationalism" conceptually overlaps with such terms as "patriotism" and "statism," and evades uniform definition.[5] In fact, sociologists and political theorists are far from agreeing on what any of these terms mean, mainly because their immediate referents (e.g., "nation," "state," and "patriot") are sometimes diachronically unstable. The etymology of "nation," for example, shows a gradual shift from a racial and familial sense to a more political one.[6] Lord Acton (1834–1902), for example, remarked that "nationality is 'our connection with the race' that is 'merely natural or physical,' while patriotism is the awareness of our moral duties to the political community" (Acton

---

[4] As a libertarian anarchist (anarcho-capitalist), my biases are directed at politics in general and not any political party. (I do, however, acknowledge some degree of use for organizations such as the Libertarian Party, but more as a platform for disseminating ideas and less as a means of controlling political machinery.)

[5] John Hutchinson and Anthony Smith (eds.), *Nationalism* (New York: Oxford University Press, 1994).

[6] The *Online Etymology Dictionary* entry for "nation" contains:

"c. 1300, from Old French *nacion* 'birth, rank; descendants, relatives; country, homeland' (12c.) and directly from Latin *nationem* (nominative *natio*) 'birth, origin; breed, stock, kind, species; race of people, tribe,' literally 'that which has been born,' from *natus*, past participle of *nasci* 'be born' (Old Latin *gnasci*), from PIE root *gene-'give birth, beget,' with derivatives referring to procreation and familial and tribal groups. Political sense has gradually predominated, but earliest English examples inclined toward the racial meaning 'large group of people with common ancestry.' Older sense preserved in application to North American Indian peoples (1640s). *Nation-building* first attested 1907 (implied in *nation-builder*)." Available at: https://www.etymonline.com/word/nation (accessed August 8, 2018).

Note also that ἔθνος ("nation," or "people"), from which we get "ethnic" and "ethnicity," exhibits a distinctive us-vs.-them idea in its second-temple Jewish rendering of the word "gentiles" in the Greco-Roman era.

1972, 163).[7] This differentiation was not uncommon before the twentieth century. As our analysis will suggest, however, "patriotism" and "nationalism" today appear to have swapped emphases.

2.1 "Nations" and "Nationalism"

Walker Conner argues that nations should be sharply distinguished from states (territorial and political authorities), and that perceived national identities (and national borders) do not always correspond to actual nations:

> My definition describes the nation as the largest group that shares a belief in common ancestry and it is the largest group that can be influenced or incited by appeals to common kinship. Is there a Welsh or Flemish, or Basque nation? Yes. Is there a British, Belgian, or Spanish nation? No. Nor is there an American, Argentinean, Filipino, Indian or Indonesian nation. A nation, then, is neither a state, nor the population of a state without regard to its ethnic composition. Nationalism is identity with and loyalty to the nation, not to and with the state.[8]

In this particular interpretation, nations are more or less "big families that go way back."[9] They need not have a political apparatus, or at least one distinctive enough to be easily confused with a state. They also need not have "national borders" (which can therefore occasionally be an oxymoron). Nevertheless, because of its generally collective orientation, and because of the collectivist orientations of states, nations can easily be confused with states, or, indeed, ultimately evolve into states (hence "nation-state"). There often is, after all, some kind of formal organization of nations. Furthermore, when distinctive genetics, language, and cultural customs are not so easily identified, demarcating the boundaries of "in" and "out" for a nation becomes particularly difficult, and since the nation is inherently an identity marker, whatever nation that did exist can no longer be called a nation. Both in principle and in history, nations come and go with the ebb and flow of time.

---

[7] Nenad Miscevic, "Nationalism," cited in *The Stanford Encyclopedia of Philosophy*, edited by Edward Zalta (Stanford: The Metaphysics Research Lab, 2018). Available at: https://plato.stanford.edu/entries/nationalism/.

[8] Walker Conner, "The Dawning of Nations," in *When Is the Nation? Towards an Understanding of Theories of Nationalism*, edited by Atsuko Ichijo and Gordana Uzelac (New York: Routledge, 2005), 40.

[9] Consider the Han dynasty, the world's largest ethnic group ("nation"), which makes up 92 percent of mainland Chinese and almost a fifth of the world population.

Consider the Sioux nation or Lakota tribe in (and yet distinguished from) the state of South Dakota. The complex dynamics of the situation are revealed when observing interracial adoption. If two foster parents of a Native American child are white, they cannot adopt the child, regardless of their location (unless given special exemption by a tribal court).[10] This is because the Indian Child Welfare Act, a federal law enforced by the American nation-state, seeks to "promote stability and security of Indian tribes and families."[11] That is, the purpose of the law is to preserve (another's) national (group) identity.[12] In this somewhat awkward organization and mixture of property rights, the tribe or nation has distinct jurisdiction (e.g., over reservations, its own courts) and yet does not have clearly defined borders (e.g., interracial adoption within US borders is forbidden). The nation also functions with legal and coercive authority.[13]

Like any nation, with enough time, cultural convergence, and "dilution," the Sioux and Lakota tribes might no longer self-identify as a nation. This has already happened to countless nations throughout history. It is witnessed most vividly in contemporary multiethnic and multicultural cities, where it is not uncommon for younger generations to be ignorant of their ancestry entirely. Many adopted persons, furthermore, never discover

---

[10] See Native American Rights Fund, *A Practical Guide to the Indian Child Welfare Act*, 9.17. Available at: https://narf.org/nill/documents/icwa/faq/recognition.html#Q17.

[11] See the National Indian Child Welfare Act (1978), at https://www.nicwa.org.

[12] The political philosophy of nationalism significantly overlaps social-identity theory in psychology, which addresses intergroup behavior and discrimination: "Tajfel et al (1971) attempted to identify the minimal conditions that would lead members of one group to discriminate in favor of the ingroup to which they belonged and against another outgroup." University of Twente, "Social Identity Theory." Available at: https://www.utwente.nl/en/bms/communication-theories/sorted-by-cluster/Interpersonal%20Communication%20and%20Relations/Social_Identity_Theory.

[13] Note that in this paragraph I am not making any judgments about the legitimacy or morality of tribes or tribal-governance structures in general, nor am I making judgment about the concept of cultural and national preservation. My own view is that peoples, nations, and families have every right to preserve whatever cultural identity they wish, so long as it does not involve coercion (whether directly through physical violence, or indirectly through political means). I would therefore take issue with laws that (for example) force a child or group to "assimilate," as well as laws that force a child or group to depart from their family (whether biological or nonbiological). For a modified Rothbardian-anarchist solution to the relationship between child and parent/guardian (and their respective rights), see the relevant portions of Creative Common Law (creativecommonlaw.com).

their "race" or lineage at all. The concern of many is straightforward: Is all of this a travesty, or a blessing? And does it warrant legislation? Answering questions like these (especially the first) extend beyond the scope of this paper.[14] But they highlight the sensitive ideological, cultural, and social nature of this subject.

Whatever the case, it is increasingly difficult today to directly associate "race" with the nation.[15] This is particularly true in the United States and other multicultural and multiethnic communities, where dozens of different peoples are native-born citizens and yet (allegedly) live "*the* American dream." As one walks the streets of New York City or San Jose, it is common to see a variety of skin colors and forms of cultural expression, and hear a variety of languages spoken.[16] Constructing a single socio-political category from this mixture is next to impossible.[17] It is almost as if *diversity itself*, and not any particular combination of characteristics, is what constitutes the "American." In countries where the native populations are a minority, associating any common characteristics beyond current geographical location easily becomes somewhat arbitrary.[18] To an American citizen's neighbors who are Dutch, Asian, and African American, none of whose ancestors lived on the continent four centuries ago (much less had the same experience living in America

---

[14] For starters, the answer may depend on who is answering it, and on, among other things, the kind of values and culture one's ancestors promulgated in the past. (Or it may not.)

[15] Note that "ethnicity" is increasingly used to refer to one's biological family ("race") instead of one's national association. It is now common in literature and popular communication to see "nationality" being distinguished from "ethnicity" (despite their tight historical connection), with "race" falling out of use altogether (it is not inaccurate to say that "race" has become an almost racist term). I here use "race" merely to draw attention to this delineation, not because I uphold all the connotations associated with it.

[16] Consider also the development and significance of mixed ethnic categories (e.g., *mestizo*), though this anthropological phenomenon is as old as humanity itself (consider, for example, the various ethnic debates in the first century regarding Samaritans, the Arab-Jewish Herodian dynasty, etc.).

[17] Clifford Geertz in *Nationalism*, 32–33, identifies six common variables in this discussion: "assumed blood ties," "race" ("common decent as such"), "language," "region," "religion," and "custom."

[18] Cf. Walker Connor, "A Nation Is…," cited in *Nationalism*, 36: "Defining and conceptualizing the nation is much more difficult [than defining a state] because the essence of a nation is intangible."

when first moving there), the fact of all now being "American" simply cannot bear the weight of a truly unified identity.[19]

If people cannot be grouped, one can either (a) abandon the collectivist attitude and group identity in the first place and search for more meaningful (and naturally emergent) categories, and stop trying when categories do not emerge, or (b) double down, and fabricate a narrative of shared experience, language, heritage, values, and so on to create an artificial "sense of homogeneity,"[20] even if the evidence points in the opposite direction. This second option, as will become evident below, is a primary feature of American nationalist propaganda.

"Nationalism," then, may more generally refer to celebration of the national entity and its values, narratives, institutions, and cultural markers, whether defined by borders or not and whether there is coercive power or not. Those who perform such celebrations are nationalists. In the words of some scholars, nationalism's overarching features are said to be "autonomy, unity, and identity."[21] Or, as Joseph Stalin put it, the nation can be defined as "a historically constituted, stable community of people, formed on the basis

---

[19] The same may also apply to "the West." Eric Hendley summarizes Samuel Huntington's views on this matter in reviewing a critique of Huntington's thesis:

"Huntington famously argued that all inhabitants of Western civilization share a common heritage. Features of this heritage include Christian religious traditions and an emphasis on human rights and the rule of law. In Todorov's view, this is an oversimplification. Even within supposed 'civilizations,' there are often clear differences of cultural traditions and political values. The individual is born into a particular culture, and exposed to its various traditions, but this individual can make independent judgments in the case of moral or political ideals. For this reason, though democracy may have matured during the Western Enlightenment, it is not, Todorov thinks, exclusive to Western civilization." ("Freedom Fear," *Harvard Political Review* [December 6, 2010])

This topic is fiercely debated today, as witnessed (for example) in the "defense of the West" work of popular social-media personalities and intellectuals such as Jordan Peterson, Laura Southern, and others. Because "civilization" is so remarkably broad, it is debatable to what extent "the West" is or is not a meaningful category. Nevertheless, one can read standard works on the subject, such as Jackson Spielvogel, *Western Civilization*, 10th edition (Boston: Cengage Learning, 2017), and judge for themselves whether a single grand story can be coherently told.

[20] Ibid., *Nationalism*, 36.

[21] Hutchinson and Smith, *Nationalism*, 5. "These three," the authors contend, "have been pursued by nationalists everywhere since Rousseau, Herder, Fichte, Korais, and Mazzini popularized them in Western and Central Europe."

of a common language, territory, economic life, and psychological make-up manifested in a common culture."[22] To the extent that this popular definition is true or meaningful, nation is a relative concept and exists on a spectrum. One nation can be more "national" or "nationalist" than another based on how well it exists as a "stable community" and shares the "common" traits.

But, as nations and peoples have scattered and become more closely associated with states, "nation" and "nationalism" have come to concern (*political* not ancestral) identity. This is for many reasons, some intentional (e.g., increasing political power over a people or peoples through unification) and others unintentional (e.g., the cumulative effect of immigrations, intermarriages, conquests, etc., over time within a certain political domain). Against Conner's distinctions, "nation" and "nationalism" now *do* generally refer to Americans, Canadians, Indonesians, and so on, whether we like this or not. A nation without national borders is difficult to imagine, as is a large city without a good "Mexican" restaurant.[23] As nations and peoples have lost their distinctive group identities, so has the older meaning of "nation."

2.2 "Statism" and "Patriotism"

This political form of "nationalism" is almost synonymous with "statism," and also exists on a spectrum. Some nationalisms are more statist than others. Statism glorifies the political apparatus. Military parades are one vivid example of this glorification. Men and women, of various ethnicities and histories, are dramatically displayed marching in step in the same uniform holding the same guns defending the same country. There is therefore less focus on statism than nationalism when it comes to cultural heritage. But, despite this distinction, the two concepts have often gone together, as witnessed in the near obsession with genealogies, ancestry, and ethnic identity in the statist regimes of Hitler, Stalin, Kim Jong Il, and others.

---

[22] Joseph Stalin, "The Nation," in *Marxism and the Natural Question,* from *The Essential Stalin: Major Theoretical Writings 1905-1952,* edited by Bruce Franklin (Croom Helm: London, 1973), 57–61.

[23] The limits of contemporary imagination on this issue are being challenged by projects such as Bitnation (bitnation.co), Ulex (tomwbell.com), the Creative Common Law Project (creativecommonlaw.com), the Seasteading Institute (seasteading.org), and others, all of which propose borderless governance.

"The state," we should be reminded, typically refers to political authority in general, and it is always associated with territory and violence.[24] It involves "the right to coerce and the duty to obey" (to borrow from Huemer),[25] presumed upon ownership or regulation of specific property. It is typical to attribute these features to only the modern nation-state. But the political apparatus exhibits these same basic features whether in the form of an ancient pharaoh, king, feudal lord, democracy, republic, etc.[26] This oppressing class, often labeled by sociologists as "the political means" (Oppenheimer), or "the state" for short, is "the only organization in society that obtains its revenue not by voluntary contribution or payment for services rendered but by coercion."[27] It is a territorial monopoly on physical violence.

The "nation-state" solidified boundaries of jurisdiction and the wielding of power, and operated according to contemporary models of political rule (e.g., democracy). Other sociologists, such as Anthony Giddens, therefore make definitions such as the following: "The nation-state... is a set of institutional forms of governance maintaining an administrative monopoly over a territory with demarcated boundaries (borders), its rule being

---

[24] This delineation is noted by a number of authors in Hutchinson and Smith, *Nationalism*. Few, however, give it the significance Oppenheimer and Giddens do.

[25] Michael Huemer, *The Problem of Political Authority: An Examination of the Right to Coerce and the Duty to Obey* (New York: Palgrave Macmillian, 2012).

[26] For instance, Thomas Woods (*The Church and the Market* [Lanham: Lexington Books, 2005], 202) argues that "sovereignty [with reference to the modern nation-state and its self-defining powers] is a thoroughly modern notion." If I understand Woods correctly, I disagree. The nation-state is distinctive but not with respect to the kind of sovereignty addressed here. It can easily be argued that the pharaohs of Egypt and Caesar Augustus in the Roman Empire exhibited as much, or even more, of a sense of sovereignty and power as the modern nation-state.

[27] Rothbard, *Egalitarianism*, 57. Cf. Franz Oppenheimer, *The State*, translated by John Gitterman (Black Rose Books, 2007, 15; Bruce Benson, *The Enterprise of Law* (San Francisco: Pacific Research Institute for Public Policy, 1990), 43; Max Weber, "Politik als Beruf," in *Gesammelte Politische Schriften* (Muenchen, 1921), 396–450; David Friedman, *The Machinery of Freedom*, 3rd edition (Createspace, 2014), 108; Robert Higgs, *Delusions of Power: New Explorations of the State, War, and Economy* (Oakland: Independent Institute, 2012), 12; Anthony Giddens, *Contemporary Critique of Historical Materialism* (Cambridge: Polity Press, 1985), 2:121; Rose Wilder Lane, *The Discovery of Freedom* (New York: John Day Company, 1943), 139; Isabel Paterson, *The God of the Machine* (New Brunswick: Transaction Publishers, [1943] 1993), 88.

sanctioned by law and direct control of the means of internal and external violence."[28]

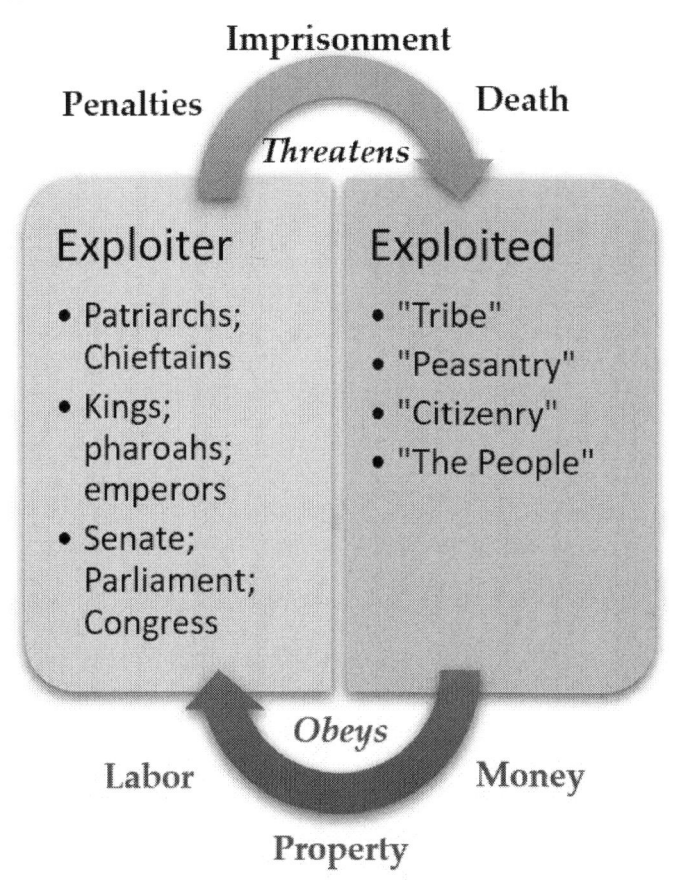

Imprisonment

Penalties — *Threatens* — **Death**

Exploiter
- Patriarchs; Chieftains
- Kings; pharoahs; emperors
- Senate; Parliament; Congress

Exploited
- "Tribe"
- "Peasantry"
- "Citizenry"
- "The People"

Labor — *Obeys* — **Money**

Property

In any case, all political authorities—whether they are called "nations," "states," "nation-states," or otherwise—operate on a "proprietary theory whereby ruling elites claim a material share of all things: land, production, traded goods, and labor."[29] There is a ruling, taxing, and parasitic class, and a ruled, taxed, and productive class.[30] There are those with a monopoly on

---

[28] Giddens, *Contemporary Critique*, 2:121.

[29] Warren Carter, "Taxation," in *The New Interpreter's Dictionary of the Bible* (Nashville: Abingdon, 2006), 4:478.

[30] It is noteworthy that the phenomenon of taxation is transcultural and transhistorical. It can be found in almost every civilization in almost every period of human history and in almost every form of government, from Ancient Near Eastern

force (who exercise *involuntary* exchange) and those that without it (who exercise *voluntary* exchange). Concrete proof of this arrangement is found not only in the regular threats for noncompliance (e.g., for owning a "dangerous" plant, for failing to obtain a dog license, etc.) and double standards of ethics,[31] but in the existence of borders (typically walls and fences).

"Patriotism" used to be more "civic" (politically oriented).[32] Currently, however, it denotes more focus on love for the homeland, family, and (often nonpoliticized) cultural traditions than on the political apparatus. *Merriam-Webster's Online Dictionary* defines it simply as "love for or devotion to one's country."[33] It is therefore not uncommon to hear some libertarians make such comments as "I'm patriotic but not nationalist." Although this may not make much sense historically, the purpose of such comments is clear: to pay due loyalty to family and property (even as they exist within the national borders), but without giving credit to the state (i.e., politicians).

Thus it appears "nationalism" and "patriotism" have essentially swapped meanings in the last century; nationalism is what patriotism used to be, and vice versa. Nationalism today, then, can be provisionally thought of as a subset of a political authority's stories, values, and symbols that are embodied within a particular nation-state and within the lives of its enclosed inhabitants.[34]

If one were to attempt to crassly summarize the conceptual relationship between patriotism, nationalism, and statism as they are frequently and

---

tribal societies, to Middle Eastern Greek city-states, to medieval European monarchies, to twenty-first-century nation-states.

[31] Huemer, *The Problem of Political Authority*, 332–33: "Acts that would be considered unjust or morally unacceptable when performed by nongovernmental agents will often be considered perfectly all right, even praiseworthy, when performed by government agents… Why do we accord this special moral status to government and are we justified in so doing? This is the problem of political authority."

[32] Refer to the quote of Acton above, and also the remarks of Conner, "The Dawning of Nations," 40.

[33] "Patriotism." *Merriam-Webster's Online Dictionary* (2018). Available at: https://www.merriam-webster.com/dictionary/patriotism (accessed August 9, 2018).

[34] This mixture of meanings is adequately captured in the current Wikipedia definition of "nationalism": "Nationalism is a political, social and economic system characterized by the promotion of the interests of a particular nation, especially with the aim of gaining and maintaining sovereignty (self-governance) over the homeland." Available at: https://en.wikipedia.org/wiki/Nationalism (accessed September 17, 2018).

popular understood (not how they are technically or historically situated), one might arrive at a loose relationship such as the following:

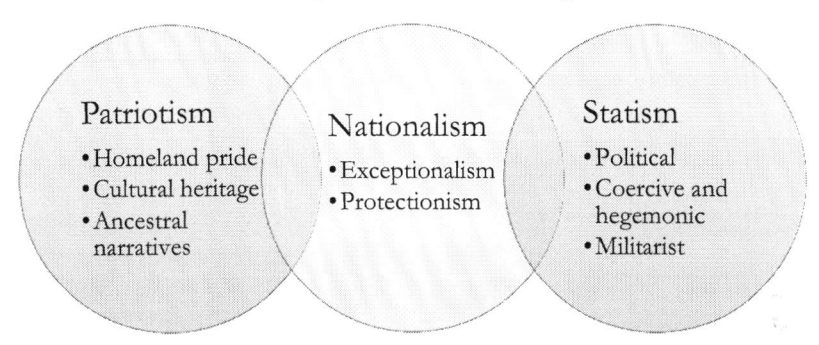

Patriotism
- Homeland pride
- Cultural heritage
- Ancestral narratives

Nationalism
- Exceptionalism
- Protectionism

Statism
- Political
- Coercive and hegemonic
- Militarist

Again, this is a crass and contemporary illustration that only serves as a provisional construct. But it adequately gives justice to (a) the kind of contemporary discourse we encounter on this subject (more on this below), (b) the ways in which nationalism contains elements of both patriotism and statism, and (c) the ways in which nationalism can exist on a spectrum, with some nationalisms being more patriotic or more statist than others.

2.3 Nationalism and Religion

Another pertinent issue surrounding nationalism is its connection with religion. It is necessary to address this controversial subject in any discussion of nationalism because (a) nationalism so plainly and often resembles formal religion,[35] and (b) nationalism and religion almost always, historically and especially in a contemporary American context, hijack each other in a variety of ways.

Regarding (a), nationalism on full display is highly religious. It exhibits symbols (e.g., flags, icons, emblems, tattoos), rituals (e.g., removing headwear at recitations, physical gestures, pledges, festive calendars), sacred documents (e.g., keeping constitutions, decrees, and letters of correspondence behind glass), histories and narratives (e.g., the founding of the nation inaugurated a "turning point" in world history,[36] prophecies, miraculous interventions),[37]

---

[35] Contrary to some scholars, I am assuming there is such thing as "religion" that, while not always clearly definable, and not necessarily bound to modern categorical distinctions, is, at the very least, a legitimate and observable anthropological phenomenon (just like music, sexuality, communication, etc.).

[36] Elie Kedourie, cited in *Nationalism*, 51, remarks that "nationalists make use of the past in order to subvert the present." Later in the volume (221), Mary Matossian describes

institutions (e.g., departments, agencies, associations, training organizations), authoritarian and charismatic figures (e.g., presidents, senators), buildings and memorials (e.g., the Lincoln Memorial, Pentagon, Washington Monument), heroes (e.g., legendary military leaders), artifacts (e.g., weapons, manuscripts), and veneration (praise-and-worship response with national hymns at services). Similar arguments have been made regarding other quasi-religions such as Marxism, humanism, and consumerism, thus raising questions about the modern category of religion.[38] Regardless, one is left asking: how and why is nationalism so religious?

Many explanations have been offered, but René Girard's anthropological account of violence and religion is particularly noteworthy. Girard argued that all people have psychological "mimetic" desires that ultimately terminate in envy and rivalry between individuals. These accumulate, infect society, and threaten to break down the social order. The escalation of this conflict then becomes focused on a single individual or group chosen by the social whole, who becomes a scapegoat for discharging the conflict. Hostile desires of "all against all" become "all against one."[39] The victim of this sacrifice becomes sacred (even divine) because crises give way to peace, and because the victim is essential for regularly keeping violence in check. Fundamental aspects of religion emerge from this whole repetitive process, such as prohibition (things not to be done), myth (narratives and stories), and ritual (procedures of how to bring restoration).

Two major implications of this theory should be noted. First, because of the basic restraining function of religion, a society that rejects all religion puts itself at risk for increased violence. As one scholar put it, "While the injustice of scapegoating the innocent has certainly become evident to

---

a similar feature: the "attempt to resurrect a supposed 'golden age'—which is known as 'archaism.'"

[37] E.g., the "Valley Forge Prayer."

[38] "Once colonies were established…Western scholars and bureaucrats began to fit indigenous cultural systems into taxonomies of 'world religions.' Confucianists and Hindus protested that Confucianism and Hinduism were not religions. The religious/secular dichotomy was nonetheless imposed on non-Western cultures; as in Europe, the distinction encoded acts of power." William Cavanaugh, "Girard and the Myth of Religious Violence," in *Does Religion Cause Violence? Multidisciplinary Perspectives on Violence and Religion in the Modern World*, edited by Scott Cowdell, Chris Fleming, Joel Hodge, and Carly Osborn (New York: Bloomsbury, 2018), 13.

[39] René Girard, *Violence and the Sacred,* translated by Patrick Gregory (New York: W. W. Norton & Co., 1979).

modernity, this moral advance comes at the expense of weakened cultural protections. It leads to the possibility of unrestrained, 'apocalyptic' violence, according to Girard."[40]

It seems Girard may have been right. While the generic idea that more religion equals less violence is overly simplistic, impossible to verify, and in desperate need of qualification, the statist, postreligious twentieth century is the most violent century on record, not to mention the way it has given birth to new waves of religious fanaticism, Islamic terrorism, and the like. "Both Hitler and Stalin were hostile to religion," Girard reminds readers, "and they killed more people than all past religious wars combined."[41] Philosopher David Bentley Hart makes this point more eloquently:

> We live now in the wake of the most monstrously violent century in human history, during which the secular order (on both the political right and the political left), freed from the authority of religion, showed itself willing to kill on an unprecedented scale and with an ease of conscience worse than merely depraved. If ever an age deserved to be thought an age of darkness, it is surely ours. One might almost be tempted to conclude that secular government is the one form of government that has shown itself too violent, capricious, and unprincipled to be trusted.[42]

The modern "myth of religious violence"[43] is therefore turned on its head. For Girard, it is the loss of the sacrificial mechanism, "the only system able to contain violence,"[44] that poses a new threat to the modern world.

Girard, of course, was not arguing for the reinstitution of animal or human sacrifice, but (along with Jean-Pierre Dupuy) simply that political substitutes are not adequate:

---

[40] Joel Hodge, "Why Is God Part of Human Violence? The Idolatrous Nature of Modern Religious Extremism," in *Does Religion Cause Violence?*, 42.

[41] Cited in *Does Religion Cause Violence?*, 18.

[42] David Bentley Hart, *Atheist Delusions: The Christian Revolution and Its Fashionable Enemies* (New Haven: Yale University Press, 2009), 105–6.

[43] I.e., (a) there is a transcultural and transhistorical essence to religion that separates it from politics and economics and (b) this core religion "has more of a tendency to promote violence than secular phenomena have." For an explanation and refutation of this popular perspective, see Cavanaugh, "Girard and the Myth of Religious Violence," in *Does Religion Cause Violence?*, 8, as well as his monograph, *The Myth of Religious Violence: Secular Ideology and the Roots of Modern Conflict* (New York: Oxford University Press, 2007).

[44] Ibid., Cavanaugh, "Girard and the Myth," 18.

> Dupuy argues, then, that although sacred terror evokes (we might say) sacral resonances, it fails either to transcend or contain its own violence. It is thus a sham form of the sacred, a simulacrum—that is, an image without the substance of the original. This violence no longer functions to bring even a provisional peace, and thus reveals the collapse of the power of the sacred even as it clads itself in religious garb.[45]

This point relates to a second and more pertinent implication: "The functional equivalent of archaic religion is still operative in many societies."[46] This is seen in the judicial system, which shares the same function of sacrifice (i.e., to put a final end to the conflict). It is also seen in the modern nation-state:

> The state in this context is inevitably a latecomer, an upstart that wants to take away from religion some part of the management of violence, until with the modern state it finally claims the monopoly on the use of legitimate violence, that is, the sole authority to distinguish between good and bad violence. From the beginning, religions and politics (or the state) have been in competition for the management of violence and their relationships have rarely been peaceful.[47]

In other words, the nation-state has functionally replaced (or attempted to replace) the traditional role of ancient religion—namely, systematically managing violence.[48] Nuclear bombs, for example, now play the role of the sacred: "We must not be too close to the sacred, because it would release the violence that it keeps in check, like a Pandora's box; we must not be too far from the sacred, because it protects us from our own violence."[49] The bomb is our own "violence exteriorized in the form of a nonhuman entity," which threatens our own survival.[50] Modern nation-states cannot live with nukes, but cannot live without them either.

---

[45] Ibid., Sarah Batchelard, "Forms of the Sacred and the Texture of Hope," 108.
[46] Ibid., Cavanaugh, "Girard and the Myth," 16.
[47] Ibid., Paul Damouchel, "Violence, Religion, and the Sacred," 171.
[48] Cf. Hodge, "Why Is God Part of Human Violence?", 44. "Girard's position is not that religion motivates violence… but that violence gives rise to and is remedied by the cultural functioning of religion. The original function of religion according to Girard was to mitigate and minimize violence in order to prevent social collapse and to stabilize human societies."
[49] Jean Pierre Dupuy, "The Sacred Is Back—but as Simulacrum," 103.
[50] Ibid.

The merits of this perspective can be debated on their own terms. However valid or invalid Girard's perspective is though, it does offer a sophisticated explanation regarding why nationalism so naturally resembles ancient religion: it performs many of the same functions, including the management of aggression.[51]

Regarding point (b) above, nationalism and religion often appear to hijack each other. This becomes evident as one reads important volumes such as *Violence and the World's Religious Traditions* by Juergensmeyer, Kitts, and Jerryson. I have elsewhere pointed out that this relationship is actually the dominating theme of the entire subject:

> There is, in fact, a semantic thread that binds all the contributions together, namely, the inescapable relationship of the political apparatus (the state) with religious violence... It becomes clear that religious adherents do not always cause government machinery to wield influence (though this certainly happens), but rather the reverse often occurs: the government wields religion to serve its political ends... The so-called "religion of the state" (or "statism") is practically a thematic subtext underlying the book, as the authors frequently and explicitly lament the marriage of religion and state. This emerging triangle (religion, state, violence) did not merit a chapter in this volume, but it will hopefully get attention elsewhere.[52]

Indeed, because of the raw power of religion—its grand narratives, symbolic systems, ethical imperatives, and so on—those operating the political machinery have a ready-made tool to seize control.

It should finally be noted that American nationalism emerges from a unique religious context that utilizes a select strand of Christianity—namely, conservative evangelicalism. For however substantial the association is

---

[51] It is noteworthy that Christianity, in Girard's account, is not like ancient religion in this respect, but actually challenges this dominating framework. Hodge, "Why Is God Part of Human Violence?", 43, summarizes: "In contrast to the mythic gods, the recognition of Jesus' divinity is because of his *nonviolence*, that is, his ability to live outside the cycles of mimetic violence even in this death as *crucified and risen victim*. The gospels' recognition of the injustice and self-sacrifice of Jesus' death saw them relocate the experience of the transcendence in the nonviolent love of Jesus, rather than in the violence of the mob."

[52] Jamin Hübner, review of *Violence in the World's Religious Traditions*, edited by Mark Juergensmeyer, Margo Kitts, and Michael Jerryson, in *Reading Religion* (November 8, 2017). Available at: http://readingreligion.org/books/violence-and-worlds-religious-traditions (accessed September 19th, 2018).

between white evangelicals (80 percent of whom voted for Trump in the last presidential election)[53] and American nationalism, the connection is evident. Numerous scholars have demonstrated that the association is so tight that being "Christian" (read: a contemporary American evangelical) and being "American" (read: pro-US nation-state) are almost indistinguishable.[54]

The theological argument behind this relationship is essentially the following: if "God" (whatever this might mean)[55] is active and living in the world, then this activity and divine purpose can be known. And if they can be known, they can be wielded for political purposes. The problem with this argument (especially the second premise) has been pointed out by both those who advocate the standard myth of religious violence and those who do not, and need not be elaborated here.[56] The main problem is not "What is real?" or even "What is right?" but "What can be known?" and "How certainly can we know it?" Standing behind the American nationalist's "will to power," then, is the ability and *will to know* (to borrow from Nietzsche and Foucault).

---

[53] Sarah McCammon, "After Alignment with Trump, Some Evangelicals Are Questioning Movement's Leaders," on *All Things Considered*, NPR Radio (March 14, 2018). Cf. Janelle Wong, "This Is Why White Evangelicals Still Support Donald Trump. (It's Not Economic Anxiety.)" *Washington Post* (June 19, 2018).

[54] See George Marsden, *Religion and American Culture* (Grand Rapids: Eerdmans, 2018); Kenneth D. Wald and Allison Calhoun-Brown, *Religion and Politics in the United States*, 8th edition (Lanham: Rowman and Littlefield Publishers, 2018); John Fea, *Believe Me: The Evangelical Road to Donald Trump* (Grand Rapids: Eerdmans, 2018); Daniel Williams, *God's Own Party: The Making of the Christian Right* (New York: Oxford University Press, 2012); Matthew Sutton, *American Apocalypse: A History of Modern Evangelicalism* (Cambridge: Harvard University Press, 2012); Frances FitzGerald, *The Evangelicals: The Struggle to Shape America* (New York: Simon and Schuster, 2017); Mark Noll and Luke Harlow (eds.), *Religion and American Politics: From the Colonial Period to the Present* (New York: Oxford University Press, 2007); Brian Stanley, *The Global Diffusion of Evangelicalism: The Age of Billy Graham and John Stott* (Downers Groves: InterVarsity Academic, 2013); George Marsden, *Fundamentalism and American Culture* (New York: Oxford University Press, 2006); Harriet Harris, *Fundamentalism and Evangelicals* (New York: Oxford University Press, 2008).

[55] For a critical discussion of this topic, see Gordon Kaufman, *In Face of Mystery* (Cambridge: Harvard University Press, 1993). For a more traditional perspective, see Thomas Oden, *Classic Christianity* (New York: HarperOne, 2009).

[56] See, for example, Kaufman, *In Face of Mystery*; Juergensmeyer, et. al., *Violence and the World's Religious Traditions*; Cowdell, et. al., *Does Religion Cause Violence?*; Sathianathan Clarke, *Competing Fundamentalisms: Violent Extremism in Christianity, Islam, and Hinduism* (Louisville: Westminster John Knox, 2017). See also the various articles published in the *Christian Libertarian Review*.

This concludes our introductory remarks to our study of contemporary nationalism. Much has been unraveled and hopefully clarified. But the best way to understand nationalism is not hammering out nuanced definitions as much as giving the microphone to a person (or group) unconditionally committed to "their" country. Definitions can be refined from there.

3. *Imprimis* Articles

3.1 "Immigration in the National Interest" (Cotton)

Senator Cotton begins his essay on immigration with a hearty lament. Many Americans have "lost faith in both the competence and the intentions of our governing class—of both parties!"[57] From the start, the aforementioned dichotomy between the regulating, taxing, political class (the "governing class," in his words) and the regulated, taxed, productive class is both explicit and central to what follows. How consistently this distinction is maintained throughout the essay is arguable. At any rate, the author then unfolds a story of the victorious emergence of President Trump and a brief history of the immigration controversy. Immigration is a key topic for nationalists because the acceptance of different peoples has the potential to threaten homogeneity (real or imagined) of the extant group. Cotton is well aware of this "problem," as noted below.

The use of first-person plural becomes immediately evident as one reads on (e.g., "*we* killed it," in reference to an immigration bill; "*our* country," contrasted with the country as it would have been under Clinton's policies), as well as a mentality of domestic warfare between the plans of an ambiguous "cosmopolitan elite" and "the people's legitimate concerns."[58] The competitive "our side"/"their side" framework stands in plain view. The basic problem, we read, is that the elite has "put its own interests above the national interest." Immigration is attached to this national interest, as it "touches upon fundamental questions of citizenship, community, and identity."[59] Allowing anyone to become a citizen therefore trivializes the nationalist triad of "autonomy, unity, and identity."[60]

---

[57] Tom Cotton, "Immigration in the National Interest," in *Imprimis* 46:10 (October 2017), 1.
[58] Ibid., 2.
[59] Ibid.
[60] Hutchinson and Smith, *Nationalism*, 5.

This problem is said to have begun with former president Obama (often framed as the polar opposite of President Trump), who at least once referred to himself as a "citizen of the world." This phrase, in Cotton's view, "revealed a deep misunderstanding of citizenship" and a "globalist mindset" that renders "real citizenship… meaningless."[61] It should be noted, however, that this is a rather odd objection because the concept of non-national citizenship and a united humanity finds its location in a variety of cultural and literary contexts. In fact, the idea of the "citizen of the world" can be traced to at least the Renaissance humanist scholar Desiderius Erasmus,[62] is transformed in a Roman context in Paul's first-century letter to the Christians in Philippi (a Roman colony),[63] and has a variety of contemporary manifestations, such as in the writings of Gandhi.[64] The choice of Obama therefore appears more of a convenient one designed to erect a political contrast—and perhaps invoke negative political memories for the audience—than a matter of principle. Ultimately, this creates the impression that the ideal political party is nationalist and the problematic political party anti-nationalist.

Cotton goes on to construct a case for citizenship, which "by definition means that you belong to a particular political community."[65] By "political community," Cotton apparently assumes that this term does not have any

---

[61] Cotton, "Immigration," 2.

[62] Desiderius Erasmus, *The Correspondence of Erasmus*, vol. 9 (Toronto: Toronto University Press, 1989), 185: "My own wish is to be a citizen of the world, to be a fellow-citizen of all men—a pilgrim, better still." Cf. Leon Halkin, *Erasmus: A Critical Biography*, translated by John Tonkin (New York: Blackwell, 1993); Desiderius Erasmus, *The Essential Erasmus*, edited by John Dolan (New York: Meridian, 1983), 174–204.

[63] See Philippians 3:20 (ἡμῶν γὰρ τὸ πολίτευμα ἐν οὐρανοῖς ὑπάρχει; "for our citizenship exists in heaven") and the discussion in Todd Still and Bruce Longenecker, *Thinking through Paul* (Grand Rapids: Zondervan, 2014), 193–209; 336–45; N. T. Wright, *Paul and the Faithfulness of God* (Minneapolis: Fortress Press, 2015), 1.1.5, 2.4.12; James Dunn, *The Theology of the Apostle Paul* (Grand Rapids: Eerdmans, 1997), 506–37.

[64] Mahatma Gandhi, *The Essential Gandhi* (New York: Vintage, 2002), 308: "Whatever the legal pundits may say, they cannot dominate the mind of man. Who can prevent the friend from declaring himself as a citizen of the world even though legally he is not, as though he may be, as he will be, prevented from entering many States under their laws? Legal status should not worry a man who has not reduced himself to the state of a machine as many of us have." It is no coincidence that all three of these citizen-of-the-world figures were profoundly antinationalist, and harshly criticized (even killed) for being such.

[65] Cotton, "Immigration," 2.

alignment with a political party, but is rather a feature of being under the authority of a political entity. In prooftext fashion, we read that "America is a real, particular place with real borders and real, flesh-and-blood people. And the Declaration [of Independence] tells us it was so from the very beginning."[66] In other words, the concept of the nation is not currently arbitrary. Why not? Because the Founders meant to create "one people," using "the words 'we' and 'us' throughout the Declaration."[67] And what is this one people? In Cotton's view, the united people can be seen in the process of "naturalization," where foreigners "can cast off… race, class, ethnicity—and take on, by reflection and choice, a new title: American. This is a wonderful and beautiful thing."[68] How exactly one casts off "race" is not explained. (Might one cast off their sex, height, and religion as well—to become "American"?) The category error is obvious, but the implication is more pertinent to underscore: for all practical purposes, the concept of "the American" is totalizing. Modern citizenship consumes all fundamental aspects of human existence and creates an entirely new human identity, nullifying any previous identifiers.

Naturally, this new human has new rights. It is wrong to suggest that "because anyone can become an American, we're morally obligated to treat everyone like an American," for everyone who wants to be associated with the nation must "play by our rules."[69] "In our unique brand of nationalism," the author goes on, "among our highest obligations is to ensure that every working American can lead a dignified life."[70] This means that (referencing James Madison in 1790) we must "increase the wealth and strength of the community," which is to say that "our immigration system… ought to benefit working Americans and serve the national interest."[71]

At this point, the argument for "America first" has come full circle. The thrust of the argument is this: the nation's responsibility (*qua* nation) is first and foremost to benefit itself; the main responsibility of Americans (*qua* Americans) is to benefit Americans. What is puzzling about this reasoning is that it explicitly requires the "working American" to sacrifice a substantial degree of freedom from the start. In a strange and ironic twist, Cotton claims it is *against* the national interest to "allow American businesses to import as

---

[66] Ibid., 2–3.
[67] Ibid., 3.
[68] Ibid., 3.
[69] Ibid., 3.
[70] Ibid., 3–4.
[71] Ibid., 4.

much cheap labor as they want."[72] This leaves readers asking: What is "the national interest" if it is not located in the entrepreneurial pursuits of "hard-working" Americans? How then can the "national interest" even be known? In Cotton's argument, the national interest can (evidently) be completely cut off from the desires of "hard-working Americans." This trivializes the entire concept and immediately implies that the true source of identifying the "national interest" is from outside or above—that is, from federal interest and decree (or, perhaps even more ironically, from the mysterious "cosmopolitan elite"). Whatever the case, it is clear that the sacrifice of individual and corporate freedom is absolutely essential for achieving the (apparently higher) goal of "the national interest," which is not actually expressed by the people as much as it is expressed by the "political community."

The grotesqueries of past American immigration policy—"the Chinese Exclusion Act, the national-origins quota system imposed by the 1924 Act, the indifference to the Jews in the 1930s"[73]—are then given quick acknowledgement followed by a rediagnosis and defensive galvanization: the political class simply should have "heeded the concerns of the working Americans," and people should not have been "ignoring those concerns and slandering the people as bigots."[74] That is, the reason Chinese people and Jews were treated inhumanely by past immigration policies was not really because the laws were a poor idea and stemmed from a problematic anthropology, but because anti-immigration advocates were not given due political attention.

Turning to the economic argument, Cotton argues that "there's no denying that a steady supply of cheap unskilled labor [in addition to automation and globalized trade] has hurt working-class wages."[75] "There is *no job* Americans won't do... Americans will do any job."[76] This is a popular phrase in contemporary nationalist discourse and, for many readers, appears to make sense. (After all, if Americans do not work hard at so many jobs, why is national GDP so high?) But it is actually a bold claim that implies at least five major concerns worth iterating.

First, it is unclear what "American" means in this context and how it is meaningful, since, as noted in the introduction of this essay, it might easily

---

[72] Ibid., 3.
[73] Ibid., 4.
[74] Ibid., 4–5.
[75] Ibid., 5.
[76] Ibid., 5.

include a variety of persons from a variety of countries, languages, and ethnicities. (And must one really believe illegal immigrants do not do "any job"?) Second, even if this is not true, can it really be suggested that Australians and Canadians (or any other group) fall outside the proposition that "if the wage is decent and the employer obeys the law,"[77] they will do any job? There are serious questions as to whether one nationality is really more willing to be employed than another, even if one could make such a generalized observation in the first place.[78] Third, the argument is further problematized by the common nationalist claim that people are immigrating to America precisely because the quality of the work is better than in other countries. If many Americans are living in America because they would rather work there than elsewhere, does not that suggest Americans *do* have a strong preference over the kinds of work they will accept and reject? Fourth, does not a large quantity of unemployed, work-searching American citizens combined with a supply of vacant American jobs suggest that Americans are *not* really willing to perform any kind of work? In other words, if one is economically consistent with the claim that Americans will do any job, jobs should be instantly filled by the unemployed to the extent that it is possible. But we do not witness this kind of economic phenomenon. Especially given the welfare state, there is no question that many native-born citizens of the United States would prefer to be unemployed until next week rather than flip burgers today. If this was not the case, unemployment numbers would be different.

After proposing immigration reform, the essay ends with a reminder about national blessing: "Citizenship is the most cherished thing our nation can bestow."[79] National identity—not legal systems, economic resources, or even national security—is considered the greatest gift of political lordship.

3.2 *"How to Meet the Strategic Challenge Posed by China"* (Goldman)

Global trade reveals nationalist agendas about as much as immigration does. China's remarkable growth as an economic superpower has become the center of much discussion, especially for American citizens, many of whose

---

[77] Ibid., 5.

[78] The cultural indicators regarding this fierce debate are visible almost anywhere. For example, I recently saw a meme of a Hispanic man leaning against a fence wearing a t-shirt that reads, "Roses are red, tacos are enjoyable, don't blame a Mexican just because you're unemployable."

[79] Ibid., 7.

possessions are produced in China.[80] As we turn to the second essay, we once again notice the peculiar framework that motivates the discussion: "China poses a formidable strategic challenge to America."[81]

This statement assumes, of course, the legitimacy of competition among nation-states. This is problematic. Even if it was not, countless other peoples and countries have benefited from American production and economic activity, so it seems worth asking why another country's economic success should be immediately perceived as a challenge instead of a blessing.

Indeed, Goldman tries to direct his (apparently) alarmist audience toward more national concerns: "The greatest danger to America is not a lack of strength, but complacency."[82] Again, one wonders what exactly the danger is (and why it is great). Readers are not told. Readers also are not given any clue as to why such danger is associated with "strength." The rhetorical approach from the beginning seems to emerge from a covert xenophobia (i.e., "Get ready, the Chinese are coming for you"), Western masculine values (i.e., "We have to be strong, not sissies"), and a wartime mentality, even if the two countries are at peace.

On all these counts, one might easily argue the contrary, and many have since the violent twentieth century came to a close. Indeed, the greatest danger to any nation or people is not interdependence, but the intentional, isolating centralization of power and monopolization of economic production (which is the most straightforward explanation for over 120 million deaths due to murder and forced famine). It would therefore seem that the quicker the American empire can dissolve into powerlessness (and even irrelevancy), the safer and more empowered individuals around the world might become. Especially given the sober insights in such works as *The Black Book of Communism*[83] (by Courtois and coauthors) and Higgs's *Delusions of Power*,[84] one would think the most pressing concern of American citizens today would be disarming the government, its war-making machine, and the

---

[80] A recent (and insightful) work on this subject is Bradley Gardner, *China's Great Migration: How the Poor Built a Prosperous Nation* (Oakland: Independent Institute, 2017).

[81] Goldman, "How to Meet," 1.

[82] Ibid.

[83] Stéphane Courtois, Nicolas Werth, Jean-Louis Panné, Andrzej Paczkowski, Karel Bartošek, and Jean-Louis Margolin, *The Black Book of Communism: Crimes, Terror, Repression*, translated by Jonathan Murphy and Mark Kramer (Cambridge: Harvard University Press, 1999). Although critiques of this work exist, its total numerical estimates for democide have proven somewhat conservative.

[84] Higgs, *Delusions*.

power of politicians. For "with regard to large-scale death and destruction, no person, group, or private organization can even begin to compare to the state, which is easily the greatest instrument of destruction known to man."[85] Instead, from a nationalist perspective, the entire framework for discussing global economics and non-American nations—nations that are now (ironically) imitating a number of "American principles" in a significant manner—is presented in terms of alarm and conflict. This is all the stranger when one considers the indisputable economic facts: millions of Chinese are no longer starving, and millions of Americans are now wealthy from Chinese products. This state of affairs is worth pondering, yes, but is it really cause for alarm?

For Goldman, the American way and the Chinese way are diametrically opposed. They have to be because there is only one America. Just how are they opposed? According to Goldman, China "is an empire based on the coercion of unwilling people. Whereas the United States became a great nation populated by people who chose to be part of it, China conquered peoples of different ethnicities and with different languages and has kept them together by force."[86] One wonders how Native Americans and African Americans would respond to these remarkable claims. In any case, Goldman once again refuses to acknowledge the violent nature of the political apparatus itself, regardless of geographical location, structure, political affiliation, or otherwise. "Here in the West," he elaborates, "we have a concept of rights and privileges that traces back to the Roman Republic—we serve in the army, we pay taxes, and the state has certain obligations in return. There is no such concept in China. Beijing rules by whim."[87] These types of statements border on the absurd. In this scenario, it is as if American citizens can simply demand that the federal government do A, B, or C and the government will automatically obey—and as if entire agencies (run by unelected officials) in Washington, DC, never "rule by whim."[88] This is not to suggest there are no differences of governance between the two nations. But, just as the media plays up differences between the political left and right,

---

[85] Ibid., 36.

[86] Goldman, "How to Meet," 2.

[87] Ibid., 4.

[88] It hardly needs to be stated, but the power of the US federal government is, by definition, superior to the individual and is demonstrated by regular demands that are explicitly followed by threats of physical punishment. Whatever rights the individual does have in text, theory, or elsewhere, they are contingent on the federal government's own interpretation and enforcement of them, again pointing to the final power and authority of the state.

so it seems the nationalist must manufacture an epic battle between two sides to vindicate the values and disposition of one's own team.

In more insulting images, Goldman depicts the lack of unity in China in various ways: "In Hong Kong, you'll see two Chinese screaming at each other in broken English because one speaks Mandarin and the other speaks Cantonese and they don't have a word in common,"[89] and "If you go to a Chinese wedding or a restaurant where families gather, the same people are loud and bumptious."[90] Readers are given the impression that it is not really desirable to be Chinese, at least, not when compared to being American. Again, all of this is presented in the overarching context of American concern (i.e., what American wants to be like the Chinese?).

Goldman then digs into economic statistics about Chinese and American production. The us-vs.-them mentality saturates charts and tables. "The Chinese have pushed us out," we read at one point.[91] Talk about the benefits of economic competition is absent—which is all the more significant coming from a perspective that would traditionally uphold such free market values. The various economic imbalances and distortions are argued to be non-trivial. The lopsided importing of technology is particularly alarming: "America can't build a military aircraft without Chinese chips. That's a national security issue."[92] As with any facts, however, there are many possible interpretations. One might look at the same situation and *celebrate*: "The two biggest national superpowers depend too much on each other to go to war. Hooray! Peace and prosperity for everyone!" But that is not the attitude taken. Mutual, voluntary exchange, free markets, and economic interdependence are considered problems, not blessings. "I'm a free trader," Goldman conclude, "but national security sometimes supersedes the free market."[93]

The same goes for economic success. China has grown substantially, and Goldman spends some time surveying China's economic successes in

---

[89] Goldman, "How to Meet," 2.

[90] Ibid., 3.

[91] Ibid., 5.

[92] Ibid., 5.

[93] Ibid., 5. This statement is reminiscent of George Bush's remarks during the Great Recession: "I've abandoned free-market principles to save the free-market system." Cf. "Bush Says Sacrificed Free-Market Principles to Save Economy," *The Economic Times* (December 7, 2008). Available at: http://economictimes.indiatimes.com/articleshow/3848694.cms?utm_source=contentofinterest&utm_medium=text&utm_campaign=cppst (accessed September 19, 2018).

various sectors—transportation, telecommunications, finances, innovation and invention, education, and so on. Readers of this portion will be tempted to rejoice about all that is happening around the globe—until finding themselves smitten with nationalist envy, because little of this is happening in America. When the question comes, "So what do we do about China?", the answer is not "Nothing; let's keep calm and carry on," and certainly not "Let's stop privileging certain war factories in the name of nationalist interest." Instead, the answer is, "If we're going to compete with China, we've got to do it the American way... innovation."[94] And what does innovation mean in this nationalist context? Private innovation? Serving each other in peaceful, productive ways across languages, borders, and cultural traditions? No. It means funding the Pentagon and various government agencies. In fact, readers are told that "we get the best kind of innovation" from developing weapons.[95]

Thus, the real answer to the China "problem" is not to establish free trade agreements, thus making mass death a lesser possibility and increased freedom and prosperity a greater possibility. Rather, the answer is to gear up, hold high the stars and stripes, and consciously spoon-feed the most notorious military machine in history.[96]

---

[94] Ibid., 5.

[95] Ibid., 5. One cannot help but read this section with a bit of déjà vu from the national events of the early twentieth century and Cold War period. The national government of the United States showed signs of envy of Soviet Russia's communism. At one point, it was proposed to essentially socialize huge portions of the entire American economy (e.g., the Swope Plan). Later on, it was argued that the United States should imitate the economy of its greatest enemies. In a similar way, Goldman suggests imitating China as much as distinguishing it from the United States, such as by initiating greater federal subsidies.

[96] This conclusion highlights an inherent contradiction in neoconservative political thought: big government is bad, but nationalism requires an ever-expanding government to compete with other large governments. A diminished government, one that is severely "limited," can never serve the "national interest." Of course, this conclusion could be empirically demonstrated by comparing the size of government (e.g., budget, employee count) under Republican and Democratic administrations throughout history; the difference between political administrations is usually nonexistent, despite frequent rhetoric to the contrary.

3.3 "The Problem of Identity Politics and Its Solution" (Continetti)

As observed above, diversity is a problem for the nationalist. If there is no common humanity under a banner or flag, then the legitimacy of the nation-state itself is thrown into question—and with it, one's political team. As a modern phenomenon, today's nationalism abolishes human difference in its effort to create a transcendent anthropological category.

It is unsurprising, then, that in a late/postmodern culture sensitive to and celebratory of difference and diversity,[97] the nationalist instinctively responds to discourse about diversity with ridicule and scorn, even as general subject matter. Furthermore, with increasing attention given to minorities, those in majority categories within the borders (e.g., white American males such as Continetti) feel increasingly threatened.[98] This is the essence of Continetti's essay on identity politics.

After a one-page summary of how the education system is failing, Continetti sounds the sirens: "The Soviet Union had collapsed in a heap of warring nationalities… America [could] be next."[99] Citing Samuel Huntington (whose work is now thoroughly discredited),[100] Continetti repeats some of Cotton's sentiments, but adds more flesh to the bones: "America, Huntington said, has both a creed and a culture… The culture derives from the Anglo-Protestant settlers."[101] Immigration threatens this ancestry with

---

[97] On these broader subjects, see Anthony Giddens, *The Consequences of Modernity* (Stanford: Stanford University Press, 1990); Joseph Natoli and Linda Hutcheon (eds.), *A Postmodern Reader* (Albany: State of University New York Press, 1993); Stanley Grenz, *A Primer on Postmodernism* (Grand Rapids: Eerdmans, 1996).

[98] For the privileged majority, moves toward justice and equality can feel like injustice and oppression.

[99] Continetti, "The Problem," 2–3.

[100] See, for example, Chiara Bottici and Benoit Challand, "Rethinking Political Myth: The Clash of Civilizations as a Self-Fulfilling Prophecy," *European Journal of Social Theory* 9:3 (2006):315–36; Fouad Ajami, "The Summoning," *Foreign Affairs* (September/October 1993); Bruce Russett, John Oneal, and Michaelene Cox, "Clash of Civilizations, or Realism and Liberalism Déjà vu? Some Evidence," *Journal of Peace Research* 37:5 (2000): 583–608; Errol Henderson and Richard Tucker, "Clear and Present Strangers: The Clash of Civilizations and International Conflict," *International Studies Quarterly* 45:2 (2002): 317–38; Jonathan Fox, "Clash of Civilizations or Clash of Religions: Which Is a More Important Determinant of Ethnic Conflict?" *Ethnicities* 1:3 (2001): 295-320; Tzvetan Todorov, *The Fear of Barbarians: A European's Take on Islam in Western Democracies* (Chicago: University of Chicago Press, 2010).

[101] Ibid., 3.

mixed blood: "Intermarriage and assimilation will affect immigrants from these groups just as they have affected other immigrant group[s]."[102] Furthermore, giving attention to people based on their ethnicity proved a failure for Democratic politics during Obama's presidency and for Hillary Clinton. "Identity politics" therefore does not work.

Continetti does not really define "identity politics" in his essay, though he seems to mean giving attention to various characteristics of a person, and to certain events and properties associated with those characteristics, in public discourse. Presumably, a detailed conversation about American slavery, one of the few versions of slavery in human history that specifically targeted a racial group, would be stigmatized, for in that case one would be having a conversation about identity politics. The same goes for any other popular issue associated with the "progressive left."[103]

The major concern, however, is summarized by the author in pseudo-Marxist terms. After discussing examples of politically charged legislative issues (e.g., transgendered students and bathrooms, obligatory support for contraception, prosecuting cake bakers for not serving gays, etc.), we read the following:

> These stories… are more than [the culture war]: they are examples of a coastal, metropolitan, highly schooled upper-class warring against the traditions and freedoms of a middle American, exurban and rural, lower-middle and working class with some or no college education. In short, examples of a privileged few attempting to impose their will on a recalcitrant majority… The result of this class conflict is an America in danger of coming apart.[104]

The extent to which this summary is in any way accurate is beside the point. What concerns us is the conclusion drawn from it: that America is "in danger of coming apart." This assumes that America was (at some point in

---

[102] Ibid., 4.

[103] The inability to publicly address sensitive topics such as these (e.g., racism, sexism, prejudice, discrimination) in the context of a "regressive left" culture has been the subject of constant discussion by highly popular alternative-media (i.e., YouTube) personalities and post-progressives such as Joe Rogan (host of *The Joe Rogan Experience*) and Dave Rubin (host of *The Rubin Report*). Sam Harris (host of the *Waking Up* podcast) has highlighted this problem as well with regard to racial and religious statistical analysis. What is ironic, of course, is that both the neoconservative "right" and "progressive left" suffer from the same inability to discuss such topics without reacting in an allergic and demonizing fashion.

[104] Ibid., 6.

the near or distant past?) "together." It is not clear what this means or why it is desirable (e.g., does anyone really know what America's founders would have said about transgender persons and dimorphic bathrooms?). It is especially odd since America is often held up as an example by its supporters because of its tolerance to diversity of opinion, religion, ethnicity, and the like, which is evidenced by its fierce divisions through time. In other words, a nation that is truly tolerant and free should be more concerned about enforced public uniformity, not the lack of it. Continetti has confused the conditions necessary for long-term social stability.

What is it, then, that holds Americans "together"? The answer given is:

> We are united by our creed of freedom and equality, and also by our habits, our manners, our national language, our territorial integrity, our national symbols—such as the National Anthem, the Flag, and the Pledge of Allegiance—our civic traditions, and our national story. We should tell that story forthrightly and proudly; we should continue our traditions of local government and patriotic displays; we should guard the symbols of our heritage against attack; and we should recognize that the needs of our citizens take priority. We should also remember the words of a great American nationalist, Abraham Lincoln… "Though passion may have strained it must not break our bonds of affection. The mystic chords of memory, stretching from every battlefield and patriot grave to every living heart and hearthstone all over this broad land, will yet swell the chorus of the Union, when again touched, as surely they will be, by the better angels of our nature."[105]

Thus ends Continetti's essay.

There is much packed into this closing paragraph that concisely confirms previous observations and deserves further comment. The major problem is that almost every assertion within the definition of unity is potentially incoherent when specifically applied to American history. For instance, what was "our creed of freedom and equality" in a country that recognized slave ownership and did not recognize women's property as property? What might this mean today, when some US citizens are forbidden from collecting rainwater off their own roofs and others are not, when it is illegal for anyone within the national borders to use gold as currency, when the United States consistently fails to rank among the top-ten countries in the

---

[105] Ibid., 7.

world in terms of freedom, even in studies produced by Americans?[106] The American experiment certainly and explicitly made room for more freedoms than other political experiments of the era.[107] But it is highly questionable whether this amounts to license for creating and enforcing (effectively) a national religion—or legitimizing the formation of a timeless "creed"— especially when the very foundation of the republic, its Constitution, assumes the state's higher claim on the bodies and properties of citizens than the citizens have over themselves.[108]

The same concern applies to "our habits, our manners, our national language." What exactly are the timeless American "habits" and "manners," and how can they be known? If they exist, are they really desirable? (The US government arguably has a "habit" of invading countries, legitimizing torture, and more recently, drone-bombing innocent women and children.) And is the English language really American, since it has far deeper roots in European and British literature, law, and practice than the United States? In Continetti's conclusion, one should also observe the capitalization of national symbols, such as the "Flag," and, of course, the ultimate prioritization of the citizen.

If this portion of Continetti's essay were taken as seriously as it could be, the American nation should be considered immortal and immutable. It is an eternal empire that does not evolve and change through time, nor should it.[109] It is the responsibility of all citizens to prevent any such change from

---

[106] See Ian Vásquez and Tanja Porcnik, *The Human Freedom Index* (Washington, DC: Cato Institute, 2017) and Terry Miller, Anthony Kim, and James Roberts, *2018 Index of Economic Freedom* (Washington, DC: Heritage Foundation, 2018).

[107] See Murray Rothbard, *Conceived in Liberty* (Auburn: Ludwig Von Mises Institute, [1979] 2011).

[108] As a libertarian, I would suggest that those who protected their property from foreign aggression in the American Revolution are to be respected and remembered (especially by their own familial descendants, or whoever thereafter owns the property) precisely for that reason—not because of any secondary political loyalties, political actions, elections, or other reasons. Continetti may be right: symbols, stories, traditions, and the like should both be perpetuated and protected, but it can be argued that the referent to all of these things must be the people, families, and property themselves, perpetuated as they freely choose to in their own lives. In short, to the extent that the revolution was an expression of voluntary defense of private property and the freedom of the human spirit, it can and should be celebrated, but to the extent that it was a project of aggression and political interests, it should not.

[109] Hence the name of the nationalist tune "Stars and Stripes Forever" (1987), the official "national march" of the United States.

occurring, no matter what new challenges get in the way. Again, all of this shows the all-encompassing, hegemonic nature of contemporary nationalism.

4. The Inaugural Speeches of Presidents Obama and Trump

Dominant political discourse suggests that the political left and right exhibit fundamentally opposing perspectives with little common ground. Yet as we see all too often, just the opposite is the case. A number of basic aspects unite the "one party" in Washington—such as support for drug wars, the police state, the surveillance state, taxation and regulation, crony capitalism and political favoritism, and more. Above all, however, is the uniting force of nationalism.

This is vividly demonstrated in presidential inaugural speeches. The table below compares Obama's and Trump's inaugural speeches according to topic and rhetorical strategy. Key agreements are marked in bold text.[110]

Subject matter	Obama	Trump
Historical significance of this present moment	"**At these moments**, America has carried on not simply because of the skill or vision of those in high office… **On this day, we gather** because we have chosen hope over fear, unity of purpose over conflict and discord."	"You came by the tens of millions to become part of a historic movement the likes of which **the world has never seen before**." "**We stand at the birth of a new millennium**, ready to unlock the mysteries of space, to free the Earth from the miseries of disease, and to harness the energies, industries and technologies of tomorrow."
Perpetual problems demanding an immediate political solution	"Our nation is at war against a far-reaching network of violence and hatred. Our economy is badly weakened, a consequence of greed and irresponsibility on the part of some, but also our collective	"Mothers and children trapped in poverty in our inner cities; rusted-out factories scattered like tombstones across the landscape of our nation; an education system, flush with

---

[110] The text of the speeches comes from WhiteHouse.gov. Bold text indicates thematic nationalist agreement.

	failure to make hard choices and prepare the nation for a new age. Homes have been lost, jobs shed, businesses shuttered. Our health care is too costly, our schools fail too many—and each day brings further evidence that the ways we use energy strengthen our adversaries and threaten our planet… **These challenges… will be met.**"	cash, but which leaves our young and beautiful students deprived of knowledge; and the crime and gangs and drugs that have stolen too many lives and robbed our country of so much unrealized potential. **This American carnage stops right here and stops right now.**"
The call to action and loyalty to the state	"And those of us who manage the public's dollars **will be held to account**, to spend wisely, reform bad habits, and do our business in the light of day, because only then can **we restore the vital trust between a people and their government.**"	"At the bedrock of our politics will be a **total allegiance** to the United States of America… **"We will no longer accept politicians who are all talk and no action**—constantly complaining but never doing anything about it. The time for empty talk is over. **Now arrives the hour of action.**"
Divine favor and authorization	"This is the source of our confidence—the knowledge that **God calls on us** to shape an uncertain destiny." "With eyes fixed on the horizon and **God's grace upon us**, we carried forth that great gift of freedom and delivered it safely to future generations."	"**The Bible tells us**, 'how good and pleasant it is when God's people live together in unity.'" "We **are protected by God.**"
The historical myth	"Our Founding Fathers faced with perils that we can scarcely imagine, drafted a charter to assure the rule of law and the rights of man—a charter expanded by the blood of generations. Those ideals still light the world, and we will not give them up for expedience sake."	N/A

Continuing the myth	"Time and again these men and women struggled and sacrificed and worked till their hands were raw so that we might live a better life. They saw America as bigger than the sum of our individual ambitions, greater than all the differences of birth or wealth or faction. "This is the journey we continue today."	N/A
National superiority ("exceptionalism")	"**We remain the most prosperous, powerful nation on Earth**. Our workers are no less productive than when this crisis began. Our minds are no less inventive, our goods and services no less needed than they were last week, or last month, or last year. Our capacity remains undiminished."	"Do not let anyone tell you it cannot be done. **No challenge can match the heart and fight and spirit of America**. We will not fail. Our country will thrive and prosper again."
Homage paid to those sacrificed	"As we consider the role that unfolds before us, we remember with humble gratitude those brave Americans who at this very hour patrol far-off deserts and distant mountains. They have something to tell us, just as **the fallen heroes who lie in Arlington whisper through the ages. We honor them.**"	"We will be protected by **the great men and women of our military and law enforcement** and, most importantly, we are protected by God."
Political authority and the people	That "**we are** in the midst of crisis is now well understood. **Our nation** is at war.... **America**: In the face of our common dangers..."	"And **this, the United States of America, is your country**. What truly matters is not which party controls our government, but whether our government is controlled by the people... "At the center of this movement is a crucial conviction: that **a nation exists to serve its citizens**."

The end of diversity and united people	"On this day, we gather because we have chosen hope over fear, unity of purpose over conflict and discord. On this day, we come to proclaim an end to the petty grievances and false promises, the recriminations and worn-out dogmas that for far too long have strangled our politics… **The time has come to reaffirm our enduring spirit; to choose our better history; to carry forward that precious gift,** that noble idea passed on from generation to generation: the God-given promise that all **are equal, all are free, and all deserve a chance** to pursue their full measure of happiness."	"And this, the United States of America, is your country. "What truly matters is not which party controls our government, but whether our government is controlled by the people… **"We are one nation—and their pain is our pain. Their dreams are our dreams; and their success will be our success. We share one heart, one home, and one glorious destiny."** "The oath of office I take today is an oath of allegiance to all Americans."
The new humanity and nationalism's power to cure	"For we know that our patchwork heritage is a strength, not a weakness. We are a nation of Christians and Muslims, Jews and Hindus, and non-believers. **We are shaped by every language and culture,** drawn from every end of this Earth; and because we have tasted the bitter swill of civil war and segregation, and emerged from that dark chapter stronger and more united, we cannot help but believe that **the old hatreds shall someday pass;** that **the lines of tribe shall soon dissolve; that as the world grows smaller, our common humanity shall reveal itself; and that America must play its role in ushering in a new era of peace."**	**"A new national pride will stir our souls, lift our sights, and heal our divisions.** "It is time to remember that old wisdom our soldiers will never forget: **that whether we are black or brown or white, we all bleed the same red blood of patriots, we all enjoy the same glorious freedoms, and we all salute the same great American Flag.** "And whether a child is born in the urban sprawl of Detroit or the windswept plains of Nebraska, they look up at the same night sky, they fill their heart with the same dreams, and **they are infused with the breath of life** by the same almighty Creator."

Ultimate meaning found in service to the state	"We honor [dead soldiers] not only because they are the guardians of our liberty, but because they embody the spirit of service—a willingness to **find meaning in something greater than themselves.**"	"**Through our loyalty to our country, we will rediscover our loyalty to each other.**"
Self-serving citizenship and protectionism	"Starting today, **we must pick ourselves up**, dust ourselves off, and begin again the work of remaking America. "For everywhere we look, there is work to be done. The state of **our economy calls for action, bold and swift. And we will act**, not only to create new jobs, but to lay a new foundation for growth. We will build the roads and bridges, the electric grids and digital lines that feed our commerce and bind us together. We'll restore science to its rightful place, and wield technology's wonders to raise health care's quality and lower its cost."	"At the center of this movement is a crucial conviction: that **a nation exists to serve its citizens.** Americans want great schools for their children, safe neighborhoods for their families, and good jobs for themselves… For many decades, we've enriched foreign industry at the expense of American industry… We've made other countries rich while the wealth, strength, and confidence of our country has disappeared over the horizon… One by one, the factories shuttered and left our shores, with not even a thought about the millions upon millions of **American workers left behind**. "**Every decision on trade, on taxes, on immigration, on foreign affairs, will be made to benefit American workers and American families.** We must protect our borders from the ravages of other countries making our products, stealing our companies, and destroying our jobs. Protection will lead to great prosperity and strength."

"Distinctive" values of the nation defined	"Values upon which our success depends—honesty and hard work, courage and fair play, tolerance and curiosity, loyalty and patriotism—these things are old."	"We must speak our minds openly, debate our disagreements honestly, but always pursue solidarity... There should be no fear."
Threats of punishment	"And for those who seek to advance their aims by inducing terror and slaughtering innocents, we say to you now that our spirit is stronger and cannot be broken—you cannot outlast us, **and we will defeat you.**"	"We will reinforce old alliances and form new ones and unite the civilized world against Radical Islamic Terrorism, which **we will eradicate completely from the face of the Earth.**"
Hopeful eschatology	"With hope and virtue, let us brave once more the icy currents, and endure what storms may come. Let it be said by our children's children that when we were tested we refused to let this journey end, that we did not turn back nor did we falter; and with eyes fixed on the horizon and God's grace upon us, we carried forth that great gift of freedom and delivered it safely to future generations."	"We Will Make America Wealthy Again. "We Will Make America Proud Again. "We Will Make America Safe Again. "And, Yes, Together, We Will Make America Great Again."

Most of the content of each speech is substantially the same. This is true across a wide variety of subjects, the vast majority of which function to bolster key elements of nationalism (e.g., autonomy, identity, superiority).

This is also true for specific topics. For example, each president believes that God's blessing is specifically upon him, and that the state is both able and willing to "defeat" (Obama) and "eradicate completely from the face of the Earth" (Trump) evil-doers. More disturbingly, involvement in the nation-state is shamelessly portrayed as a bridge to the meaning of life itself. For Obama, the service of the state's primary protectors (soldiers) is to "find meaning in something greater than themselves," and, for Trump, "through our loyalty to our country, we will rediscover our loyalty to each other." Nationalism offers a remedy for existential angst.

There are differences, of course, but they pale in comparison to the similarities. Both presidents are right about one thing: national identity absorbs and nullifies all other identities, including political polarities between red and blue. In that sense, the sovereignty of the state comes into its own.

5. Critically Defining Contemporary Nationalism

Having reviewed three essays propounding nationalism and comparing two presidential speeches, what now can we say about nationalism's meaning and function, at least within the context of present-day America?

First, *nationalism is inherently collectivist*. Individual freedoms, desires, and characteristics are always subordinate to the larger, social goals of "the people." The extent to which the individual must be sacrificed is never explicitly mentioned (for obvious reasons), but it remains an ever-present subtext in the discussion.

Second, *the state's existence and function is never clearly acknowledged, but rather intentionally confused*. The people who are contained within the national walls are regularly and necessarily confounded with the ones responsible for establishing borders in the first place. Entire linguistic categories enter into the fray to make this confusion possible. Most immediately, what central banks and crony capitalists want, as expressed through congressional legislation, is labeled the "the national interest."[111] This "national interest" is then identified through propaganda with the desire of "the people." As Frédéric Bastiat (1801–50) so eloquently put it, "Government is the great fiction, through which everybody endeavors to live at the expense of everybody else."[112] For the nationalist, however, government is the great *truth* through which knowledge is dispensed, decrees are made, and a transcendent category of the human is brought into existence by fiat.

---

[111] E.g., "Let's keep the local tire factory open," or "We have a war to fight; these bad guys hate America." Cf. Higgs, *Delusions of Power*, 64–65: "The aircraft companies that suddenly profited so greatly during WWII, for example, became permanent, highly successful feeders at the government's trough, where some of them are feasting lavishly even now, the post-2001 military buildup having proved a godsend and boon to their stockholders... The last thing these vultures want, of course, is an abatement of the perceived terrorist threat, and we can count on them to hype any signs of an increase in such threats and, of course, to crowd the trough, happily slurping the taxpayer's money."

[112] Frédéric Bastiat, *The Law*, translated by Dean Russell, forward by Walter E. Williams, introduction by Richard Ebeling, afterward by Sheldon Richman (Irvington-on-Hudson, NY: Foundation for Economic Education, 1998).

Rothbard made a similar point with regard to national conflict:

> With the land area of the globe now parceled out among particular States, one of the basic doctrines and tactics of the rulers of each State has been to identify *itself* with the territory it governs. Since most men tend to love their homeland, the identification of that land and its population with the State is a means of making natural patriotism work to the State's advantage. If, then, "Ruritania" is attacked by "Walldavia," the first task of the Ruritanian State and its intellectuals is to convince the people of Ruritania that the attack is really upon *them*, and not simply upon their ruling class. In this way, a war between *rulers* is converted into a war between *peoples*, with each people rushing to the defense of their rulers in the mistaken belief that the rulers are busily defending *them*. This device of nationalism has been particularly successful in recent centuries; it was not very long ago, at least in Western Europe, when the mass of subjects regarded wars as irrelevant battles between various sets of nobles and their retinues.[113]

Third, *nationalism is fundamentally incompatible with the diversity of human nature as it exists*. Rothbard argued that egalitarianism (of a certain kind) is a "revolt against nature": to try to make one out of the many does violence to individuals because it is their peculiarities that distinguish them from others.[114] The same is true for nationalism. The (imaginary) American, with (imaginary) uniform properties, "manners," and "habits," can nullify one's race (and cultural background, sex, religion, etc.) simply by obtaining citizenship. This "naturalization" is said to be "beautiful." Here, the religious overtones are unmistakable. Like Jesus in the Christian Gospels, all the marginalized, foreigners, and hopeless are now given dignity. Or to use the apostle Paul's words from a different context (cf. Gal 3:28): "There is neither

---

[113] Rothbard, *Anatomy of the State*, 71.

[114] Rothbard, *Egalitarianism as a Revolt against Nature,* xvii: "A fundamental reason and grounding for liberty are the ineluctable facts of human biology; in particular, the fact that each individual is a unique person, in many ways different from all others. If individual diversity were not the universal rule, then the argument for liberty would be weak indeed. For if individuals were as interchangeable as ants, why should anyone worry about maximizing the opportunity for every person to develop his mind and his faculties and his personality to the fullest extent possible?" Cf. Nietzsche on the totalizing function of abstracting universal principles. Grenz, *A Primer on Postmodernism,* 89, summarizes his view as follows: "Although all leaves may share certain characteristics, each leaf differs from every other leaf. We can form the concept of 'leaf' only by overlooking these differences. Nietzsche held that the concept 'leaf' is thus a falsification of the reality of leaves… It… robs reality of those qualities that differentiate individual leaves from one another."

Jew nor Greek, neither slave nor free, nor is there male and female, for you are all one in" the United States of America.[115]

Fourth, *the tone of nationalism is regularly alarmist and apocalyptic.* Discourse is framed in such a way that it either assumes or invokes the audience's worry. Danger is simultaneously attributed to the present moment. The most pivotal moment in the national story is always right now. And without action, something terrible will happen. Keeping the peace is never the solution. The socio-economic problem is complacency, lack of strength, lack of gall. In short, nationalism regularly thrives on scare tactics.

Fifth, *nationalism is incompatible with the laws of economics and, as such, cannot reap the benefits of free enterprise.* Instead of a market in which buyers and sellers meet to make voluntary exchanges, the state must control prices against private supply and demand out of the "national interest." Like all price controls—whether price floors or price ceilings for wages, grain, interest rates, imports, or anything else—the result is either a shortage or an oversupply (and therefore waste and excess inventory). Tariffs, limits on imports, and laws forbidding international trade and labor are the most popular form of economic controls implemented by nationalists. The purpose is to force certain jobs to exist within the borders by artificially creating an isolated economic environment in which those jobs can continue, thereby forbidding real economic competition on a global level. Since all voluntary exchange is beneficial to both parties, laws prohibiting such exchange also hurt both parties. In the case of trade laws, select American jobs are temporarily propped up at the expense of everyone else, who must now pay higher consumer costs for certain products than they otherwise would have (e.g., a law forbidding steel imports to "save American jobs" will force Americans to pay more for steel). As the saying goes, "Nobody wins a trade war."[116] But, as is made explicit, free market principles and the laws of economics must be suspended in the name of national security, national interest, or whatever other reason a political power provides.

Sixth, *because nationalism is collectivist and ignorant of basic economic laws, the freedoms of individuals must be regularly violated, which works against nationalism's own goals.* Continuing to engage in voluntary exchange with business partners and

---

[115] I bring this up not to criticize religion or to impugn nationalism by its mere association with religion, but to demonstrate that nationalism regularly oversteps all sorts of cultural, linguistic, and intellectual boundaries; in other words, the spirit of the collective state is highly infectious.

[116] An excellent resource on this is Pierre Lemieux, *A Primer on Free Trade: Answering Common Objections,* Mercatus Center (Arlington, VA: George Mason University, 2017).

friends must result in fines or imprisonment. This violation of freedom leaves "working Americans" with less productive income and, if imprisoned, pulls a productive American entirely out of the workforce. Since all people want to profit and few want to be under constant threat, this creates an underground economy from which the state cannot benefit anyway, alienating the entrepreneurs from any sense of loyalty they once had to their country. When conditions are critical enough, American businesspeople leave "the homeland" for another country to do business. After an entrepreneur is threatened with punishment for moving,[117] what strategy is left for the politician? Little but sanctions and war, two more policies that fuel nationalism's insatiable lust for uniformity.

Dutch prime minister Abraham Kuyper lamented this unfortunate state of affairs in a speech delivered in 1869. It touches upon most of the pertinent concerns regarding nationalism:

> For once the peoples have been robbed of their characteristic genius and rendered homogenous, the triumph of imperial unity is assured. Hence the slogan of false unity today has become: through uniformity to unification, by centralization toward Caesarism. Should that effort succeed, the victory of that false unity will be celebrated on the ruins of what land and folk, race and nation, had that was peculiarly their own... The cries for brotherhood and love of fellow-man are but a slogan. Not fraternity but a false uniformity is the goal toward which its glittering images drive us... If multiformity is the undeniable mark of fresh and vigorous life, our age seeks to realize its curse in its quest for uniformity.[118]

Seventh, *nationalism always presumes some form of comparative superiority*. All governments and nations believe they are superior to others in one way or another. This exceptionalism has its own apologetic, narrative, and process of legitimation to show why America (to use one example) is better than all other nations. This self-aggrandization is necessary to keep the taxpayers from leaving the field and producing a harvest for other national farmers. In extreme conditions, such as those in North Korea, citizens are not even free to cross the border into another country.

Finally, *nationalism is bipartisan*. In an American context (and elsewhere), nationalism cannot be exclusively associated with one political party or

---

[117] See, for example, Damian Paletta, "Trump Working on Bill to Punish Firms for Sending Jobs Overseas," *Washington Post* (October 10, 2017).

[118] Abraham Kuyper, "Uniformity: The Curse of Modern Life," in *Abraham Kuyper: A Centennial Reader* (Grand Rapids: Eerdmans, 1998), 23–25.

another. A vivid example of this was witnessed in comparing the inaugural speeches from Obama and Trump, which also serve as excellent illustrations of nationalism in general. This comparison is not intended to trivialize real differences between political parties (or of their representatives). But from a big-picture perspective, the differences are superficial and marginal at best. All political parties serve the same masters (e.g., crony capitalists). This is especially clear when it comes to allegiance to political identity, as any presidential-inauguration speech will testify.

6. Conclusion

If what I have observed above is generally true, then nationalism is (at the very least) an extremely powerful, entrenched, and toxic ideology. This article has not even addressed historical cases of nationalism, which demonstrate the huge costs involved when benefiting the collective becomes more important than the humanity of individuals. Indeed, nationalism is not a concern for libertarians alone, but for anyone who values individuality, freedom, independent thinking, new social possibilities, innovation, and the faithful preservation of human life.

Committed nationalists ought to consider long and hard the (ir)rationality of their hegemonic ideology, especially one that dictates an existential narrative on behalf of others instead of respecting individuals' right to forge their own life stories with their neighbors (including their "illegal" and "foreigner" neighbors). True, there are many variables in life that are not chosen: the century, place, and context in which one is born, for instance. But these are not factors typically determined by politicians, nor should they be. No political entity can (or should) trivialize one's ancestry, skin color, sex, gender, religion, or other attributes (especially coercively) in the name of *any* cause, for this would mean the abolition of human nature and individuality from the outset. The image of the superior, ideal Aryan human being was thankfully abandoned after the Holocaust. It is high time that the image of the superior, ideal American human being likewise be abandoned.

To conclude with some words from Rose Wilder Lane:

> The Nation is nothing at all but simple force. Not in a single Nation are the people of one race, one history, one culture, nor the same political opinion or religious faith. They are simply human beings of all kinds, penned inside frontiers which mean nothing whatever but military force.[119]

---

[119] Lane, *The Discovery of Freedom*, 139.

Review Essay: *Selfish Libertarians and Socialist Conservatives? The Foundations of the Libertarian-Conservative Debate*

Aleksandar Novaković

Nathan W. Schlueter and Nikolai G. Wenzel: *Selfish Libertarians and Socialist Conservatives? The Foundations of the Libertarian-Conservative Debate*. Stanford, CA: Stanford University Press, 2016, pp. 215; xii. ISBN: 9780804792912.

THIS BOOK MAKES INTERESTING READING not only because of the subject but also because of the authors' approach to it. It is, in fact, an energetic and thought-provoking dialogue between a libertarian political economist, Nikolai G. Wenzel, and a conservative political philosopher, Nathan W. Schlueter. By setting aside the journalistic urge for simplifications and catering to the biases of partisans—a stance summed up in the title of the book—the authors are laying the groundwork for intellectually honest investigation of the key principles of conservatism and libertarianism and the main arguments that stem from them.

The aim of the book is not to propose a reconciliatory theory, as was attempted long ago, unsuccessfully, by Frank Mayer (1996). Today it is only

---

*Aleksandar Novaković is a research associate at the Institute for Political Studies, Belgrade.

CITATION INFORMATION FOR THIS ARTICLE:

Aleksandar Novaković. 2018. "Review Essay: *Selfish Libertarians and Socialist Conservatives? The Foundations of the Libertarian-Conservative Debate*. *Libertarian Papers*. 10 (2): 415-425. ONLINE AT: libertarianpapers.org. THIS ARTICLE IS subject to a Creative Commons Attribution 3.0 License (creativecommons.org/licenses/).

too obvious that differences are overcoming similarities, sometimes grossly, preventing any feasible unification. Instead, the authors want to show the fundamental problems in the structure of the opposing theory. Given this goal, an optimistic reader should be aware not to expect a happy ending.

Still, there are important similarities between the two philosophies that inspired the original debate some 60 years ago (Nash 2017). Libertarianism and conservatism might share common traits in which Wenzel and Schlueter find their own points of concurrence: the rejection of modern liberalism (progressivism), the importance of economic freedom and virtue, the moral and political priority of persons, and contempt for the modern, over-bureaucratized state (5-8). All this led Ronald Reagan to remark that "the very heart and soul of conservatism is libertarianism" (Klausner 1995).

*

The discussion begins with particular interpretations of what the authors believe are the ideal types of conservatism and libertarianism within predominantly American political experience.

Schlueter's proposal (Ch. I) is as neat and attractive as it can be. It combines the historical experience of what he calls the American Founding (the American constitutional revolution and its sacred scrolls) and natural law theory conceived from an evolutionist's perspective. Schlueter argues that the most preferable state only emerges under certain fortunate circumstances. Schlueter calls this situation the "equilibrium of liberty" and the circumstances it describes consist of liberty, tradition, and reason. The equilibrium is not invented but discovered in the process of the birth of a political culture where "opinions, sentiment, and habits favorable to liberty" (17) exist. This much echoes the Burkean narrative. Furthermore, "The equilibrium of liberty is a rare and always fragile achievement that must be won anew in every generation" (19), a venerable Hayekian insight that Schlueter acknowledges. The American Founding is the expression of classical liberalism or what Schlueter calls natural law liberalism, and here he substantially draws on philosopher John Finnis.

The equilibrium is established on the back of natural law, a moral framework for a free society. Schlueter rejects a fixed understanding of the natural law; every historical period needs a new interpretation and rediscovery of its core principles, and natural rights are derived from such conceptions of natural law (31). With the last point, a barrier is lifted to the (progressive) concept of a free-floating essence of rights.

For Schlueter, natural law is not an abstraction. It secures the "means of human flourishing," that is, the framework for the development of intrinsic goods such as all the things human beings naturally aspire to (knowledge, friendship, religion) (p. 28). This framework consists of instrumental goods (such as freedom from coercion and social life) that are to be secured by government. And because a vast range of human action is left to the free and spontaneous arrangements of various actors in a society, only limited government can be justified. However, sometimes a government cannot be completely neutral as to "competing conceptions of good." Sometimes it has to secure intrinsic goods too. And against the background of eudemonistic ethics and an organicist understanding of political community, Schlueter argues for "soft-perfectionism" in contrast to the antiperfectionism of libertarians and the full perfectionism of totalitarian conceptions of society (28).

Consequentially, the "state," "government," or political authority, is not necessarily some alienated bureaucratic monster that preys on human wellbeing. In a society with a developed culture of liberty and fruitful traditions (understood in Hayekian terms) there exists a special relationship between the authority and members of society, and here rests a justification of political authority as such, similar to a justification of parental authority within a family. Only within such a moral and political framework can there emerge a "citizenship" that too is not some abstract entity, a social security number, a passport, or a right to vote, but shared feeling of common heritage, values, traditions, and religion, the "we-membership" of the sort Roger Scruton writes about (38).

*

Nothing of this can be found in Wenzel's "ideal-type" libertarianism (Ch. II), although it is a well-constructed and attractive proposal, at least for libertarian souls. The main idea is that libertarian natural law (and rights) theory should be accepted only as a regulative ideal, and the political economy of public choice as an appropriate instrument for reaching the ideal. Wenzel is concerned with the epistemological foundations of natural rights (47), and although he accepts the theory,[1] as an economist he can speak only the language that he is most familiar with in making his own case for libertarianism (47). He thus prefers the "simpler approach of robust political economy" (47), that is, the public choice theory of James Buchanan and Gordon Tullock (1999) with its characteristically grim account of human nature.

---

[1] Wenzel enthusiastically mentions John Hasnas' concept of "empirical natural rights" (2005) as an "approximation of Lockean natural rights" (53-4).

Readers upset with the constant enlargement of the modern state in the last hundred years or so might find this reliance on public choice a sensible and useful proposal. If they are worried that the expansion of the state will eventually annihilate individual freedom, they should reject sterile and abstract theorizing with its oversimplified romantic vision of the common good (56) and look instead at the way people really behave in the world of politics. Non-libertarians especially should be warned that calling on the government to "fix market failures" leads to a dangerous Nirvana fallacy (53) of comparing imperfect with perfect, and in fact, impossible states:

> Far too often, the market is seen to yield an imperfect outcome, so the government is called in to regulate without anybody asking the question whether the government will do a better job (53).

Thus, if freedom is to be preserved, institutions of a robust character must be introduced and bridles put on the political animal: "the political problem comes down to adopting institutions that will constrain bad behavior and provide incentives for good behavior" (56).

Wenzel also observes that humans are "nonomniscient" (57), and here he rejects neoclassical economics as a child of the 20th century's trend toward mathematization and positivism that encouraged the implementation of models from natural science in the sphere of social phenomena. But the trend was widespread, and its effects more visible in those societies where it was more completely adopted. Thus, Wenzel quotes Mises that communism was "the reductio of absurdum of central planning" (57) assuming that the idea of central planning naturally follows from positivistic impulses of social scientists who, in Hayek's opinion, want to "engineer society as if it were mere clay in an omniscient potter's hand's" (57). Against this trend, and the introduction of new economic methodology, stood the works of Mises who demonstrated (1920) why economic calculation is impossible under socialism and Hayek, who introduced the knowledge problem (1948), which is principally unsolvable under socialism. As nonomniscient agents, humans need economic institutions that can acknowledge these Hayekian and Misesian insights and prevent any kind of social engineering. Thus, Wenzel proposes an institutional framework with only a few governmental prerogatives and with strict constitutional restrictions on governmental power, "lest the state become an instrument to impose coercively the will and knowledge of some on others" (63).

All these lead to the concept of minarchist libertarianism, where the state has only one function—to protect individual rights. All other functions of the productive state (the classical liberal state of Adam Smith that corrects market failures and allows for a mild version of interventionism[2]) and redistributive (welfare) state are left to the spontaneous actions of individuals. By adhering to the non-aggression axiom[3] Wenzel is at pains to reject anarcho-capitalism in favor of the ultra-minimal state. He is aware that the consistent implementation of non-aggression axiom disallows any kind of state,[4] even the most minimal one. Yet, as we have seen, he rejects rights-based justifications of libertarianism, and in the last instance evokes (72) Buchanan's admonition: "The libertarian anarchist who dream of markets without states are romantic fools who have read neither Hobbes nor history" (1964).

Wenzel is well aware that the same problems that exist for a productive state exist for every other state (justification of taxation and political authority, defense spending) (72), and concludes again that the best hope in this imperfect world is to "provide the most robust institutions possible to cope with those facts" (73).

*

What are the merits of these two philosophies? Both Wenzel and Schlueter elaborate on many of their arguments (Ch. III & IV), which can be summarized in one main critique addressed to the rival side.

(A) For Wenzel, conservatism *lacks firm principles* (86), and because of that, cannot constitute either a consistent theory or, consequently, a preferable model of social organization. Too often in human history, natural law has been used as a legitimization framework for invasion of individual freedom,

> from slavery to the execution of those who did not attend weekly church services in colonial times, and from denial of a basic rights to women or racial minorities, to arbitrary deprivation of property or life by an absolute monarch (82).

---

[2] Wenzel thinks Friedrich Hayek was also a classical liberal of this sort, given his sympathetic attitude to policies like a guaranteed minimal income and correction of market failures (66). But he shows certain understanding for this mild interventionism of the great liberal, because "Hayek does not offer free rein to state intervention but provides careful conditions, arguing that redistribution must occur according to the principles of rule of law and generality (that is, there must be no favored groups) (66).

[3] In what other way could Wenzel's "protection of individual rights" be understood if one has in mind a libertarian perspective?

[4] A position staunchly defended and most thoroughly elaborated by Rothbard (1998).

The upshot is that the objective moral order cannot be deduced from natural law even if the latter objectively exists. There is an unbridgeable gap between a general understanding of natural law and specific ethical concepts. Consequently, every historical instantiation of natural law served only as a justification for state-sponsored coercion that infringed on individual rights. Yet natural law cannot be used as justification for coercion (83) since it too cannot be justified.

Does this then open the door to moral relativism? Wenzel thinks not, since moral attitudes concern, in the first place, individuals, not communities. Conservatives believe in moral norms favored by certain communities and traditions. But, Wenzel asks, "what… constitutes community?" (87), and who can determine what is or should be a social or moral norm for a community? Thus, "conservatism… is arbitrary in its claims because it seeks justification for the public imposition of private preferences" (87). And from here Wenzel goes even further, claiming that there cannot be any non-coercive state imposition of virtue (87), but without going into the discussion of why conservatives are not so squeamish about the idea that sometimes state has to impose moral values. When such action is required, society needs a morally committed government. But it is naïve to believe in the possibility of good and wise government caring for the moral wellbeing of society, and conservatism rests on a naïve understanding of human nature. That this is not just a theoretical conclusion, but also historical fact, Wenzel illustrates with the case of the "American Founding," which in his opinion was merely a "big grab for central power" (95) conveniently presented as a struggle for higher causes.

Finally, Wenzel delivers a death sentence to conservatism:

> [it is] internally inconsistent, it is arbitrary in its preferences, it involves an imposition of private preferences through public means, and it is ultimately inimical to liberty and human flourishing (90)

(B) For Schlueter, libertarianism adheres to *the reductionist understanding of human nature* and is incapable, therefore, of understanding the nature of political association. It reduces the political animal to a homo economicus (98), the "utility-maximizer" equipped only with (enlightened) self-interest, and otherwise completely inept at grasping an idea of the common good, let alone the need to sacrifice for a higher cause. But politics is much more than a struggle for limited resources: it is, above all, cooperative action (100).

This truncated understanding of human nature is mirrored in the "dilemma of public choice"—and here Schlueter strikes hard at Wenzel's libertarianism. Public choice is either descriptive, but then untrue (e.g. people sometimes die for a higher cause), or prescriptive, and true, in which case it makes political life meaningless (99). If everybody would agree that the public choice approach is true (and would thus yell, "the emperor has no clothes!") there would be no need for politics. Yet this is quite an unimaginable. So, there is a need, after all, for romantics, since:

> [people do] honor the important political figures and events of their history; they respect their flag; they learn their national anthem; they take time to vote even when they know their individual vote has only an infinitesimal chance of affecting the outcome of the election, and often against what libertarians regard as their own individual interests; and, in exceptional cases, they are willing to expend their "last full measure of devotion" in service to their country (101).

For these observations, Schlueter finds confirmation from no less than Buchanan himself, who acknowledged the importance of political myths and public-interest-oriented behavior (103). Schlueter concludes that "leading public choice theorists do not support Wenzel libertarianism" (104). Neither does Hayek's classical liberalism. Schlueter's critique of Hayek rests on the same challenges posed long ago by Michael Oakeshott (1962). Namely, Hayek's theory assumes the very Cartesian rationalism it wants to renounce: "How can principles that are derived from the evolutionary process guide the evolutionary process? Indeed, what does "improvement" in terms of evolution even mean?" (109).

Even more, Hayek's idea of the Open Society introduced in *Law, Legislation and Liberty* (1976) is projected through severely reduced political choice: either tribal society on the one hand, or a society where no concept of common good exists (antiperfectionist society, or the Open Society), on the other (110). As a consequence, the only feasible, proper, and historically verified choice, one in which individual freedom coexists with the common good in a productive symbiosis, is not listed on the menu.

Schlueter distinguishes moral judgments, like in the sentence "rape is wrong," from our subjective preferences, such as "I don't like bananas" (111). The vision of homo economicus, embodied in a libertarian picture of the world, reduces moral judgments to subjective preferences. Yet moral neutrality is "principally impossible" (115). Libertarianism tacitly fosters a specific morality that enables various sorts of nonphysical harm—e.g. harm to reputation (defamatory speech, libel, and slander), or harms to social order (open borders) (112). Furthermore, how flawed and unrealistic the libertarian understanding of human nature can be is evident in Robert Nozick's interpretation of a self-ownership principle that cannot justify parental authority, all the more so state authority, since "it makes all forms of rule without consent equivalent to slavery" (119). Schlueter concludes with strong words:

> [Libertarians] do not understand the nature of the political association; insofar as they undermine the self-understanding and norms that underlie citizenship, libertarians inadvertently assist in the growth of the managerial administrative state. If there is hope for the restoration of a decent political order, it rests in those who understand the nature of politics, the specific good of politics and the limits of politics, better than modern liberals or libertarians. That hope rests in conservatism (120).

*

When it comes to the case studies of immigration, education, and marriage (Ch. V, VI), the ferocious rhetoric of ideal-type ideological narrative gives way to more sober and reconciliatory language.

This is especially noticeable in the case of immigration, where Wenzel advocates classical libertarian support for open borders without governmental benefits for immigrants and, on the other side, Schlueter espouses the argument (147), similar to the one made by Hans-Hermann Hoppe (2014), that crossing the border should be treated as entering into a zone of private property. Schlueter recognizes the complexity of the issue and the need for a more balanced approach. He admits that there are two types of immigration, both legitimate under certain conditions (that is, immigration cannot be a threat to security and immigrants must not have access to governmental benefits): citizenship-seeking immigration, and work-seeking immigration. In the latter case it is up to markets to decide on numbers—thus, Schlueter extends an olive branch to Wenzel.

Concerning education, Wenzel's argument is that the market will provide all necessary education without coercion (135). To think otherwise—that the coercive governmental apparatus would provide better education—means repeating the Nirvana fallacy. On the other side, Schlueter opts for a change of the principles on which education stands and asks for a retreat to more traditional forms where parents, families, and communities are the backbone of the educational system. This presupposes rejecting both the progressive idea of a nanny state overseeing the educational process and the libertarian solution, which can have negative consequences for children. Schlueter targets here mainly a left-libertarian vision of education, not Wenzel's libertarianism. A government should have some role, and Schlueter advocates the introduction of voucher schemes, a solution supported by many libertarians today.

In the would-be society ordered completely in libertarian fashion, the institution of marriage becomes an ordinary legal contract between consenting individuals, and it is up to spontaneous arrangements within society (churches, local communities, associations) to regulate it. Here

Wenzel suggests that classical marriage "can even be strengthened if state enforced 'one size fits all' marriage" has been removed (142). This is reminiscent of Rothbard's vision of a stateless society as a predominantly conservative one (Rothbard 1998) with strict hierarchical orders and binding moral codes (except for small, ousted groups of "free-spirits" living on the fringes). Schlueter retorts that marriage as a state-enforced contract paves the way for a never-ending enlargement of the state and the demise of limited government, thus making, indirectly, a libertarian point also.

*

In his final reply (Ch. VII), Schlueter stresses that Wenzel's rejection of natural rights presupposes a version of natural rights, since there is an evident (objective) moral ground from which Wenzel assessed the development of natural rights throughout history (see p.5). In reply, Wenzel reiterates (Ch. VIII) his previously-given arguments. What we know as achieved moral order is as a rule usurpation of "a majority, or a vocal majority that has captured the political process," usually for the sake of some "abstract" community (170).

In reply to Schlueter's objection that obligation to moral neutrality (e.g. "government ought to be neutral") does not follow automatically from moral skepticism, Wenzel stresses the epistemological humbleness of libertarianism. Libertarians can only "persuade" but not compel anyone to accept a particular set of moral principles. So when Schlueter remarks that libertarian antiperfectionism still invokes some concept of the common good, Wenzel agrees, but warns that libertarian "common good" is an outcome of the voluntary actions of individuals, and not imposed by the state. In contrast to a conservative vision of society, this libertarian view still allows for communist communities to exist (173).

*

This book is a good read, both for "beginners" and "experts." It offers an introduction to the subject matter, a clear explanation of the nature of the debate, a handful of citations to relevant literature, and a survey of the final theoretical reach of both political philosophies. In the end, it further strengthens the idea that there are sharp and mutual differences between conservatism and libertarianism. Yet there are also some shortcomings to the book. The arguments and counterarguments could have been presented in a more systematic, stringent, and even itemized manner so that the reader could follow the main argumentative trajectory more easily. This might have prevented unnecessary repetitions, elaborations, and summaries. But for the reader passionate for debate, this is a minor shortfall.

Still, the book suffers from one serious deficiency, although it introduces an interesting possibility at the very end. The urge to present an ideal-type, "true face" account of conservatism and libertarianism leads the authors to sidestep an analysis of the prevailing understandings of both doctrines. Today's libertarianism is reduced not only to the opinion-moldering of the extravagant and uninfluential group that Russel Kirk called "chirping sectaries" (1981), but to a movement on the rise that elevates lifestyle liberties to the forefront of political struggle, thereby undermining the fundamental liberal concern for economic freedom. This trend challenges Hayek's prediction, his triangular political compass (1960), that only conservatives—because of their lack of principle—will, willingly or unwillingly, adopt a progressive agenda. Today libertarians adopt the agenda too, more willingly than unwillingly, when standing alongside leftists in promoting "antidiscrimination policies" (Hoppe 2014). This trend was foreseen by Murray Rothbard, who sketched a psychological profile of the "modal libertarian" (1990), and Lew Rockwell, who underlined the important distinction between the doctrine and its practitioners (1990, 35).

Wenzel indeed, dismisses libertinism entirely, but today, when the "Woodstockian flavor of the movement" (Rockwell 1990, 6) is strongly present, it seems insufficient to discard it solely on the grounds that true-type libertarianism is not entirely opposed to the idea of rules and authority (74). At least some explanation for the resilient tendency should have been given since it too might say something about the nature of libertarianism. On the other hand, because of the same ideal-type fixation, Schlueter fails to address the measure in which the conservative movement still cherishes individual liberties and economic freedoms. The deterioration of American Founding values has been a strong tendency for many decades, and seems today to be accelerating. More generally, the book could have elaborated in greater detail the relationships these political philosophies have with other ideologies, especially socialism.

An interesting possibility emerges with the conclusion of the book. Imagine that both critiques (A and B) are true. Imagine then that there is someone who, in spite of acknowledging these critiques, still highly values shared elements of both political philosophies and rejects socialism. What would this mean for our understanding of these ideologies and of ideal-type theory modeling? Would we not find ourselves at the beginning again? Should not we seek some kind of fusion after all?

References

Buchanan, James, and Gordon Tullock. 1999 [1962] *The Calculus of Consent*. Indianapolis: Liberty Fund.

Buchanan, James. 1964. What Should Economists Do? *The Southern Economic Journal*, XXX (January): 3.

Hasnas, John. 2005. Towards a Theory of Empirical Natural Rights. *Social Philosophy and Policy*, 22(I), 111-147.

Hayek, F.A. 1948. The Use of Knowledge in Society, in *Individualism and Economic Order*. Chicago: University of Chicago Press.

Hayek, F.A. 1976. *Law, Legislation and Liberty*, Vol. 2. Chicago: University of Chicago Press.

Hayek, F.A. 2011 [1960]. *The Constitution of Liberty: The Definitive Edition*. Edited by Ronald Hamowy. Chicago: University of Chicago Press.

Hoppe, Hans-Hermann. 2014. A Realistic Libertarianism. Available at: https://mises-media.s3.amazonaws.com/A%20Realistic%20Libertarianism.pdf.

Kirk, Russel. 1981. Libertarians: the Chirping Sectaries. *Modern Age*, Vol. 25, No. 4 (Fall 1981): 345–351.

Klausner, Manuel. 1995 [1975]. Inside Ronald Reagan: a Reason Interview. *Reason* (July). Available at: www.reason.com/archives/1975/07/01/inside-ronald-reagan.

Meyer, Frank S. 1996. Freedom, Tradition, Conservatism (1960) in *Defense of Freedom and Related Essays*. Edited by William C. Dennis. Indianapolis: Liberty Fund.

Mises, Ludwig von. 2012 [1920]. Economic Calculation in the Socialist Commonwealth. Auburn: Ludwig von Mises Institute.

Nash, George. 2017 [1976]. *The Conservative Intellectual Movement in America since 1945*. Wilmington: Intercollegiate Studies Institute.

Oakeshott, Michael. 2010 [1962]. *Rationalism in Politics and other essays*. (New, Expanded edition). Indianapolis: Liberty Fund.

Rockwell, Llewelyn. 1990. The Case for Paleo-libertarianism. *Liberty*, (January): 34–38.

Rothbard, Murray. 1990. Why Paleo? *Rothbard-Rockwell Report*, (May): 1–5.

Rothbard, Murray. 1998 [1982]. *The Ethics of Liberty*. New York University Press.

Ten Years of Libertarian Scholarship

Stephan Kinsella[*]

In 1977, the preeminent libertarian scholar Murray Rothbard founded the *Journal of Libertarian Studies*. It was later to be published by the Mises Institute, which was itself co-founded by Rothbard in 1982. Upon Rothbard's death in 1995, the *JLS* was edited for a decade by his colleague and protégé Hans-Hermann Hoppe. I was personally a devoted reader of the journal for many years and later, during Hoppe's tenure as Editor, I served as book review editor. For several decades the journal was the key outlet for important interdisciplinary scholarship in the radical libertarian tradition. But by the late 2000s, the Internet was in full flower and the *JLS* was in decline.

One night in early January 2009, while texting about these matters with Jeff Tucker, then at the Mises Institute, I had the idea to form a new journal for libertarian scholarship, which would help fill the gap left by the declining *JLS*, and also take advantage of new publishing possibilities: entirely online and free, and with no artificial space constraints, but still of high-quality and peer-reviewed. Tucker was enthusiastic and brainstormed about the project with me. Within just a few days, we had established the website and the basic design, assembled an impressive editorial board, and collected and edited an initial set of articles, which were published later that month, starting on January 18, 2009. That year *Libertarian Papers* published 44 peer-reviewed articles, from new work by libertarian luminaries such as Robert Higgs, Jan Narveson, Pascal Salin, and Frank van Dun, to previously-unpublished pieces

---

[*]Stephan Kinsella is a patent attorney in Houston, Executive Editor of *Libertarian Papers*, and Director of the Center for the Study of Innovative Freedom.

Citation Information for this Article:
Stephan Kinsella. 2019. "Ten Years of Libertarian Scholarship." *Libertarian Papers*. 10 (2): 427-428. Online at: libertarianpapers.org. This article is subject to a Creative Commons Attribution 3.0 License (creativecommons.org/licenses).

by Murray Rothbard and Ludwig von Mises and translations or previously-obscure articles by Adolf Reinach and Bruno Leoni.

In the first few years I was doing most of the work myself, as a labor of love, with the assistance of a variety of volunteers. I was then was fortunate enough to recruit Matt McCaffrey as Editor. A brilliant young Austrian economist and learned scholar in the Rothbardian libertarian tradition, Matt stepped into the mostly thankless role of editor and spent countless hours fielding submissions, having them peer reviewed and edited, expanding the editorial board, and improving the website.

Matt and I shared the same vision for *Libertarian Papers*. One of my goals was to publish the journal for at least ten years, i.e., through 2018. We achieved that goal last year, to our relief, and then learned, fortuitously, earlier this year, that the *JLS* is going to be revived in 2019. Since *LP* has met its goal of publishing for a decade, and since one of its original motivations was to fill the *JLS* lacuna, we have decided to cease publication of *Libertarian Papers*, and are excited about the revival of the *JLS*. The *LP* archives will remain online indefinitely.

I would like to express my gratitude to innumerable supporters—to the contributors, the Editorial Board, to many volunteer peer-reviewers and referees, to the volunteers who contributed audio recordings for some of the early articles, to various donors and other supporters over the years, and also to PJ Doland, of dancingmammoth.com, for web hosting services. I would also like to personally thank Matt McCaffrey for his many hours of work and collaboration on this project over the past seven years. It is now his project as much as mine, and would not have been possible without his efforts, integrity, and impressive scholarly and intellectual skills. Neither of us did any of this for pecuniary reward; we both did this out of devotion to the ideas of liberty.

Stephan Kinsella

July 2019

Reflections on Ten Years of *Libertarian Papers*

Matthew McCaffrey[*]

ALL GOOD THINGS must come to an end, and after ten years, the end has come for *Libertarian Papers*.

Libertarian Papers was an experiment in publishing, and one I believe was ultimately successful. Those who contributed—as editors, reviewers, or authors—can be justly proud of their achievements, and I would like to take this opportunity to thank and congratulate them for their service to the journal. Through their efforts *Libertarian Papers* became a respectable outlet for a wide range of scholarship on many topics and from many disciplines, and it is with a spirit of gratitude that I will use this editorial to reflect on some of their (and the journal's) accomplishments.

Journals are judged by the material they publish, so I will begin by mentioning some of the high points of our history. No journal can succeed without attracting outstanding authors, and we are proud to have published works by leading libertarian thinkers as well as promising young researchers. Contributors have included scholars from Colombia University, the London School of Economics, Bocconi University, the University of Manchester, University College Dublin, and Boston University. Among the older generation of researchers, we were fortunate to work with many distinguished scholars, including some who have since passed away, especially the late Tibor Machan, who was quite active with the journal and frequently submitted his work. We have also been eager to support outstanding younger

---

[*]Matthew McCaffrey is assistant professor of enterprise at the University of Manchester, and was editor of *Libertarian Papers* from 2012-2019.

CITATION INFORMATION FOR THIS ARTICLE:

Matthew McCaffrey. 2019. "Reflections on Ten Years of *Libertarian Papers*." *Libertarian Papers*. 10 (2): 429-432. ONLINE AT: libertarianpapers.org. THIS ARTICLE IS subject to a Creative Commons Attribution 3.0 License (creativecommons.org/licenses).

academics at the start of their careers; for instance, authors who published with us as graduate students have gone on to work at universities as diverse as King's College London, the University of Southampton, Texas Tech, and Oklahoma State.

On the administrative and business side of the journal, only a few years after its launch *Libertarian Papers* was already listed in a wide range of databases and journal indexes, in some cases receiving high rankings. Our acceptance rate dropped dramatically over the life of the journal, while at the same time we consistently received a larger number of high-quality submissions. These outcomes are difficult to achieve in the best of circumstances, but especially for a journal starting essentially from scratch. *Libertarian Papers* was ahead of most academic publishers in other respects as well, including our use of social media, experimentation with podcasting articles, reduction of publication times, and above all, with our commitment to making all content available free of charge.

Yet it is our hope that the most important contributions made by the journal are to our understanding of liberty in its varied forms and throughout many areas of human inquiry. Although we leave it posterity to judge the value of individual articles, we are confident that on the whole they have enriched our knowledge, and that some will be read for many years to come. This is why we were devoted from the beginning to making the journal available to as wide an audience as possible, and also why we will continue to make the print and online editions available in the future.

Editors face a paradox: on the one hand, it has never been easier to start an academic journal. On the other hand, the proliferation of new journals means it is harder than ever to craft a distinct publication with a genuinely valuable mission—one that succeeds in publishing high-quality research while also finding an audience for it. However, this was a challenge *Libertarian Papers* met and overcame. Understanding this only requires looking at the numerous other journals in the libertarian, classical liberal, and free-market orbit that were founded at about the same time as *Libertarian Papers*, or during its run. I believe it is fair to say that, by all conventional metrics, *Libertarian Papers* outpaced these competitors and was more successful at increasing its audience while also refining the quality of its published research. Nevertheless, despite its achievements, we are bringing the journal to a close. There are a number of reasons for this decision.

First, the original mission of the journal has now been completed. *Libertarian Papers* was intended as a more versatile replacement for the *Journal of Libertarian Studies*, which ceased publication in 2009. Now that the *Journal of*

Libertarian Studies is returning to print, however, the original gap filled by *Libertarian Papers* has ceased to exist, and we can safely say its watch is ended.

A second reason is that *Libertarian Papers* no longer fills the technological gap in publishing it once did. Although academic publishing is still a cartelized, out-of-touch industry in many respects, it has changed dramatically since the journal was founded, sometimes for better, sometimes for worse. For example, journals in many disciplines have drastically shortened review and publication times, and a few prestigious outlets are even distributing content free of charge. Online repositories are also thriving, providing additional ways to access research that would otherwise be unavailable. Together, these developments reduce the need for a journal like *Libertarian Papers*.

Third, specialized outlets like *Libertarian Papers* are not as necessary as they once were because for many years there have been an increasing number of alternatives. For example, publishing in mainstream philosophy, politics, and economics journals is common, and there is thus less need for a central libertarian journal, even a wide-ranging, multidisciplinary one like *Libertarian Papers*. Moving away from specialized outlets is also practical: if libertarians are concerned with a search for truth, it is reasonable that if they find it they should want to spread it far and wide. Yet publishing within the libertarian community can actually be a barrier to this goal, as it risks preaching to a particularly uncritical choir. Of course, it can be useful to have outlets for research on topics of interest only to libertarians. However, there is a real danger that these outlets will become insular, self-absorbed, and disengaged from the wider world of scholarship. This is an especially important issue for early-career scholars trying to build their research profiles. While I do not think it applies to *Libertarian Papers*, the passing of time makes mission drift almost inevitable, and is one more reason why the moment is right to bring the journal to a close. After helping to encourage a decade's worth of young scholars, there is now a chance for them to find or create their own places in the literature.

I would like to conclude on a personal note. Editing *Libertarian Papers* has been an extraordinary experience, equal parts educational and humbling, and one I will look back on fondly. In particular, I will always be grateful to Stephan Kinsella for placing his trust in me by appointing me Editor, and for his tireless support of the journal ever since. At the time I became Editor I was inexperienced and Stephan must have had little reason to think I would survive in the role. As a way of repaying his kindness I have always tried in my turn to encourage the work of young scholars in similar positions to my own. One way in which I attempted this was by maintaining an ecumenical editorial policy that strove to place the quality of research above considerations of loyalty to individuals or schools of thought. It is my firm opinion that this is the only viable way to encourage outstanding research, which is usually frustrated by a dogged devotion to orthodoxy. And while I cannot speak for the other Editors, my experience was that this policy was both correct and successful.

Matthew McCaffrey

University of Manchester

August, 2019

Printed in Great Britain
by Amazon